MW00700778

HEALING THE FISHER KING

"How at the Castle of Corbin a Maiden Bare in the Sangreal and Foretold the Achievements of Galahad"
by Arthur Rackham (1867–1939)

Illustration, 1917

Parsifal in Quest of the Holy Grail by Franz Stassen (1869–1949)

Illustration, 1903

HEALING THE FISHER KING

SPIRITUAL LESSONS WITH PARZIVAL, GUMP, THE GRAIL, TAO, AND STAR WARS

BY SHELLY DURRELL

To Ken —
For the Adventures
of your life!
Shelly 5/1/08

Art Tao Press

Miami, Florida

HEALING THE FISHER KING

SPIRITUAL LESSONS WITH PARZIVAL, GUMP, THE GRAIL, TAO, AND STAR WARS

06 05 04 03 02 10 9 8 7 6 5 4 3 2 1

Copyright acknowledgments are listed after the Table of Contents.

Publisher's Cataloging-in-Publication
(Provided by Quality Books, Inc.)

Durrell, Shelly.
Healing the Fisher King : spiritual lessons with Parzival, Gump, the Grail, Tao, and Star wars / by Shelly Durrell. -- 1st ed.
p. cm.
Includes bibliographical references and index.
ISBN 0-9710768-0-4

1. Self-realization. 2. New Age movement. 3. Perceval (Legendary character)--Romances--History and criticism. 4. Grail--Romances--History and criticism. 5. Star Wars films--History and criticism. 6. Forrest Gump (Motion picture) 7. Tao. I. Title.

BJ1470.D87 2002 291.4'2
QBI33-9

ISBN 0-9710768-0-4
Library of Congress Control Number 2001119703

Art Tao Press, Miami, Florida

www.arttaopress.com

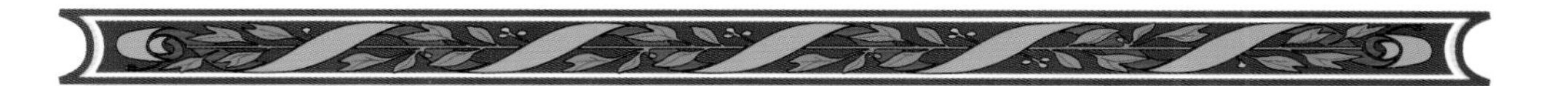

To Wei Lun

Parsifal in Quest of the Holy Grail
by Ferdinand Leeke (1859–1925)

ca. 19th century

Contents

First Billing - Acknowledgments XI

Part I - The Call 15

A Tap on the Shoulder 17

Unlikely Inspiration

Crash Course 21

Parzival ◦ The Fisher King ◦ Forrest Gump ◦ Good Will Hunting ◦ Star Wars ◦ The Natural ◦ Heart of Darkness and Apocalypse Now ◦ Siddhartha

The Structure and Elements of the Book 26

Part II - Cast of Characters 29

Chapter 1 - The Maimed Fisher King and the Wasteland 30

What Caused the Wasteland? ◦ Exile ◦ Asking the Right Question ◦ Reeling It In ◦ Throwing in a Monkey Wrench

Chapter 2 - The Great Fool Rides the Red Horse of Tao 42

Foolish Images ◦ Riding the Red Horse of Tao ◦ The Tao of Gump ◦ The Yin/Yang of Parzival

Chapter 3 - The Goddess of Sovereignty and the Grail 52

The Geography of the Soul ◦ The Gifts of Sovereignty ◦ The Forms of the Grail ◦ Balance of the Grail ◦ What Makes the Grail Holy? ◦ It's Not Just For Olden Times

Part III - The Adventure 65

Path 1 - The Age of Innocence and Its Perils 66

Chapter 1 - The Mysterious Birth 68

Birth and Youth of Parzival ৩ Standing on the Shoulders of Our Ancestors ৩ The KKK and the Knights Templar ৩ The Natural ৩ Magic Shoes ৩ Heart and Soul (and Birds)

Chapter 2 - An Encounter with Angels 80

Knights on the Road ৩ Synchronicity ৩ The Abduction ৩ The Beautiful Fountain ৩ Hidden Disease ৩ With Friends Like These - Who Needs Enemies ৩ Manners 101 ৩ Heritage ৩ Death of Mother

Chapter 3 - Stumbling into the OtherWorld 96

Lady of the Tent ৩ The OtherWorld ৩ A Pocketful of Posies ৩ Meeting Sovereignty ৩ Impoverishing Sovereignty ৩ The Karmic Dilemma

Chapter 4 - The King's Road 106

Road to Arthur's Court ৩ My Name is Gump, Forrest Gump ৩ The Maimed Queen ৩ Judging Experience ৩ The Taker ৩ Challenger to Sovereignty

Chapter 5 - Clowns in the Court 116

Arthur's Court ৩ Recognizing Hope ৩ Hollow Words ৩ The Rash Boon ৩ The Trickster ৩ Greed Gets Us Going ৩ Prophetic Laugh

Chapter 6 - I Was Thinking of Something in Red 128

Defeat of the Red Knight ৩ Too Easy Victory ৩ David and Goliath ৩ Improper Response ৩ Second Noble Truth - Craving ৩ Old Clothes ৩ Roses Are Red ৩ Grief for the Red Knight ৩ A Touched Heart

Chapter 7 - Rules of the Road 142

Gurnemanz ☙ Climbing on the Red Horse ☙ New Rules for the Road ☙ Gurnemanz' Instructions ☙ Warrior Princess ☙ The Wrong Face ☙ Yes Syndrome ☙ Worthy of Love

Chapter 8 - True Love 156

Condwiramors ☙ The Tao of Love ☙ Kundalini and the Rightful Queen ☙ Foreshadowing ☙ The First Perfection ☙ Waiting For Love ☙ The Modern Woman - Circa 1200 ☙ Message to Arthur ☙ Thoughts of His Mother ☙ Absence Makes the Heart Grow Fonder

Path II - The Shadow of the Grail 166

Chapter 9 - Discovering the Grail Castle 168

Grail Castle ☙ By Invitation Only ☙ Merlin, Anakin, Free Will, and The Force ☙ The Eyes of Argus ☙ Axis Mundi - The Mount of Salvation ☙ The Bleeding Lance ☙ The Unobtrusive Grail ☙ Sustenance of the Grail ☙ Three Strikes and You're Out ☙ Trying It On For Size ☙ Gift of the Sword ☙ Stay Awake!

Chapter 10 - You're Not Good Enough For This Party 184

Parzival Rebuked ☙ Suffering Begins ☙ Grail Castle Shuts You Out ☙ The Cost of Grief ☙ Sacred Trees ☙ The Breaking Sword ☙ Slap in the Face

Chapter 11 - Doing the Right Thing 192

Orilus and Jeschute ☙ Righting the Wrongs ☙ The Spear and the Relics ☙ Great Love ☙ Positive Fallout

Chapter 12 - Trance-lvania 200

Trance of Parzival ☙ The King Looks for the Red Knight ☙ Trances and Concentration ☙ The Challenge ☙ How to Meditate (One Way) ☙ The Balanced Trinity ☙ Return to Transylvania ☙ Vengeance ☙ Mirror Spirit ☙ Completion of Tasks ☙ Broken Spear ☙ Kisses of the Queens ☙ Miracles and Adventures

Path III - The Grueling Road 216

Chapter 13 - Loathly Lady Pays a Visit 218

Cundrie the Sorceress ☙ The Truth Hurts ☙ The Mirror Has Two Faces ☙ The Dark Brother ☙ Determination ☙ "Alas, What Is God?" ☙ Castle of Wonders ☙ The Individual's Path ☙ Gawan's Preparation

Chapter 14 - Cloning 230

Gawan's Adventures ☙ Service to Others ☙ More Magic Animals ☙ Early Flight ☙ Sovereignty Speaks ☙ The House of the Mind ☙ Fight of the Mirror Brothers ☙ The Virgin ☙ The Land of Ascalun ☙ Birds of Prey ☙ The Mother ☙ The Chessboard ☙ Honor of Word and Honor of Hospitality

Chapter 15 - Direct Experience 252

Trevrizent ☙ Direct Experience ☙ Need for Spiritual Guidance ☙ Obstacles ☙ Return to the Right Path ☙ Noble Company ☙ The Chymical Grail ☙ If It Was God's Right to Judge ☙ The Right Question ☙ Hubris ☙ Less Is More ☙ Atonement and Redemption ☙ Titurel ☙ Ritual of Spirit

Chapter 16 - Castle of Wonders 270

Orgeluse ☙ Sword Necessary for the Grail ☙ Tests of Love ☙ Creatures of the Boar ☙ Doubtful Justice ☙ The Ferryman ☙ The Wonder Bed ☙ Almost Death ☙ Beyond Brotherly Love ☙ Pillar of the Soul ☙ Leaving the Castle ☙ The Tree Branch ☙ Sins of the Father ☙ Sending the Message

Chapter 17 - Reconciliations 292

Gawan and the Courts ☙ King of the Realm of the Individual ☙ Path to Peace ☙ The Guardian of the Tree of Life ☙ Surrendering ☙ Spiritual Knight and Physical King

Chapter 18 - Are You Twins? 302

Feirefiz ☙ Forces of the Spirit Meet ☙ Win with the Name of Love ☙ Finding Joy in Sorrow ☙ Secundille - Shekina - Shakti - Sophia ☙ The Last Battles

Path IV - The Healing 310

Chapter 19 - Second Chance 312

The Healing ∞ Another Try ∞ The Question Asked ∞ The New Grail Family ∞ The Death of Sigune ∞ Sacred Landscapes

Chapter 20 - A New Grail Procession 324

New Grail Kingdom ∞ The Grail Procession ∞ The Invisible Grail ∞ Amnesty International, Medieval Style ∞ Lohengrin ∞ Prester John ∞ The Death of Secundille

Chapter 21 - The Healthy King 334

Where Do We Come From? ∞ What Are We? ∞ Where Are We Going? ∞ How Do We Rule as a Healthy King?

Chapter 22 - Brighter Son 340

Teach Your Children Well ∞ Being Your Own Mentor ∞ Final Thoughts

Backstory - Appendix 346

Bibliography ∞ Synopses - Filmography ∞ Index ∞ List of Meditations / Journal Reflections

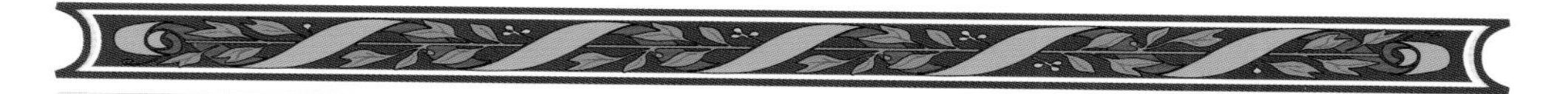

First Billing - Acknowledgments

This is a book of art, as well as text, inspired by my visits to art museums around the world. One of the games I play when visiting a museum is "Find the Self-Portraits," where without looking at the information plaques, I guess which paintings are the masters of themselves. I'm usually right. The secret is in the eyes. Regular portraits look *at* you, while self-portraits look *into* you and allow you to look into them, revealing a sense of their history. This book will make you look into yourself, at the same time revealing a sense of my own history. And thankfully, the good parts of me have much to do with the people I acknowledge here.

For help in bringing this book into your hands, I must give Gretchen Schmidt the greatest recognition for patient editing and criticism. She is a great writer who unselfishly gave her expertise and time correcting and streamlining the manuscript. I could not have chosen a better person to help me, and I am fortunate that she is also such a wonderful friend.

Speaking of friends—I have been blessed with friends that no matter where we've lived, and no matter how long it has been since we've last spoken, they can be counted on for support and needed help when necessary. Besides Gretchen, I have three other friends I have weathered the ups-and-downs of life with. My thanks for such good friendships goes to Ann Schmidt, Sherry Watanabe Hinman, and Maggie Sotolongo Marsh.

My next level of friendships is so vast, I do not have the space to recognize each one individually, but thanks goes to my Kung Fu, Tai Chi, and martial art friends, students, brothers and sisters, and especially my *sifus,* Master Chan Pui and Master Huang Wei Lun. My martial arts training has been one of the most significant influences in my adult life, teaching me discipline, courage, body and mind control, and giving me a chance to explore friendships with people of differing cultures and backgrounds. All of these attributes and experiences carry over to the writing and development of this book.

It has been most comforting to have a family that gave unconditional love, even when their daughter/sister/aunt did not always follow that wide, smooth, safe, well-worn path. My love goes to my mom and dad, Mary and Rudy Belobraydich, my brothers and sister, Don, Mike, Corky, and Sue, and their spouses and children. My love also goes to my husband's family, Chao Zhang Huang, Nie Lie, Sui Fen, Sui Fang, and Wei Cong, as well as their spouses and children. And a special memory and love goes to our mother, Jin Ai.

Most of all, my love and thanks goes to my husband, Wei Lun. You have been a hero to me, and I thank you for your trust, caring, and love. More people would find their Grails if they had partners like you.

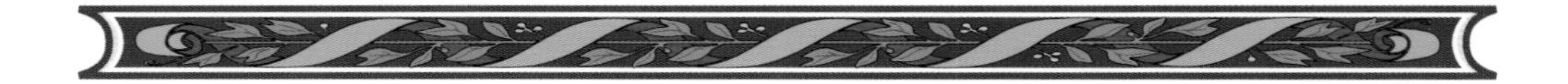

Copyright and Providers Acknowledgments

I wish to thank the artists, authors, image banks, licensing organizations, and publishers who kindly gave permission to reproduce the works in this book. If there has been any omissions or errors, please notify the publisher and future editions will be corrected.

Text

Forrest Gump by Winston Groom. Copyright ©1986 by Perch Creek Realty and Investments Corp. Published by Bantam Doubleday Dell Publishing Group. Reprinted by permission from the publisher.

"Girl From Ipanema" English lyrics by Norman Gimbel. Copyright ©1963 by New Thunder Music, Inc., All rights reserved. Used by permission.

The Gospel of Sri Ramakrishna as translated into English by Swami Nikhilananda and published by the Ramakrishna-Vivekananda Center of New York. Copyright ©1942 by Swami Nikhilananda. Reprinted by permission from the publisher.

The Gunslinger: The Dark Tower I by Stephen King. Copyright ©1982 by Stephen King. Published by the Penguin Group. Reprinted by permission from the publisher.

Heart of Darkness by Joseph Conrad. First Published 1902.

The High Book of the Grail: A translation of the thirteenth-century romance of Perlesvaus trans. Nigel Bryant. Copyright ©1978 by Nigel Bryant. Published by D. S. Brewer. Reprinted by permission from the publisher.

"The Hollow Men" by T.S. Eliot. Copyright ©1925 by T.S. Eliot.

The Innocents Abroad by Mark Twain. First published 1869

"I Have Had to Learn to Live with My Face" from *The Motorcycle Betrayal Poems* by Diane Wakoski. Copyright ©1971 by Diane Wakoski. Published by Simon and Schuster. Reprinted by permission of the author.

The Koran, translated by N. J. Dawood. Copyright © N. J. Dawood, 1956, 1959, 1966, 1968, 1974, 1990, 1993, 1997. All rights reserved. Published by Penguin Books Ltd., England, 1997. Quote from page 378. Reproduced by permission of Penguin Books Ltd.

"La Belle Dame Sans Merci" by John Keats. Written 1884.

"Me and Bobby McGee" Words and Music by Kris Kristofferson and Fred Foster. Copyright ©1969 (Renewed 1997) TEMI COMBINE INC. All rights Controlled by COMBINE MUSINE CORP. and Administered by EMI BLACKWOOD MUSIC INC. All rights reserved. International Copyright Secured. Used by permission.

The Mists of Avalon by Marion Zimmer Bradley. Copyright ©1982 Marion Zimmer Bradley. Published by Ballantine Books.

The Natural by Bernard Malamud. Copyright ©1952, renewed by Bernard Malamud. Reprinted by permission of Farrar, Straus and Giroux, LLC. In U.K. and British Commonwealth, reprinted by permission of Russell & Volkening as agents for the author.

On the Road by Jack Kerouac. Copyright ©1955, 1957 by Jack Kerouac; renewed ©1983 by Stella Kerouac, renewed ©1985 by Stella Kerouac and Jan Kerouac. Used by permission of Viking Penguin, a division of Penguin Putnam Inc.

"Second Hand Rose" by Grant Clarke. Copyright ©1921 by Grant Clarke.

Seven Arrows by Hyemeyohsts Storm. Copyright ©1972 by Hyemeyohsts Storm. Published by HarperCollins Publishers, Inc. Reprinted by permission of HarperCollins Publishers, Inc.

Siddhartha by Herman Hesse. Copyright ©1951 by New Directions Publishing Corp. Reprinted by permission of New Directions Publishing Corp. In U.K. and British Commonwealth, reprinted by permission of Laurence Pollinger Limited, as agents for the author.

"Synchronicity" Written and Composed by Sting. Copyright ©1983 G. M. SUMNER. Published by MAGNETIC PUBLISHING LTD. and Administered by EMI BLACKWOOD MUSIC INC. in the USA and Canada. All rights reserved. International Copyright Secured. Used by permission.
Tao Te Ching by Lao Tsu, translated Gia-Fu Feng and Jane English. Copyright ©1972 by Gia-Fu Feng and Jane English. Reprinted by permission of Alfred A. Knopf, a Division of Random House, Inc.
The Tarjumán Al-Ashwáq by Muhyi'ddín Ibn al-'Arabí, trans. Reynold A. Nicholson. Copyright ©1911 by Royal Asiatic Society.
Traditional Navajo Prayer in *Spider Woman: A Story of Navajo Weavers and Chanters,* translated by Gladys A. Reichard. Copyright ©1934 by Gladys A. Reichard. Originally published Macmillan, New York. Second printing, University of New Mexico Press.
"The Waste Land" by T.S. Eliot. Copyright ©1922 by T.S. Eliot.
"The White Goddess" by Robert Graves. Copyright © Robert Graves. Published by Carcanet Press, London. Used by permission of publisher.

Art

Information and credits on artwork obtained from artists, museums, and their representatives are listed with the illustrations. Credits for photos, film stills, and images obtained from photo and image banks are credited below with page numbers. Images not noted are from private sources or are public domain images from various sources.

Film Stills

Apocalypse Now. ©1979 Omni Zoetrope. Everett Collection: pg. 24, 278. Photofest: pg. 30.
The Fisher King. ©1991 ORIX Film Enterprises Number 4. Studio: TriStar Pictures.
Everett Collection: pg. 52 (2 images). Photofest: pgs. 22, 133, 194.
Forrest Gump. ©1994 Paramount Pictures Corp.
Everett Collection: pg. 52. Photofest: pgs. 22, 30, 302.
Good Will Hunting. ©1997 Miramax Film Corp. Photofest: pgs. 23, 30, 52, 162, 329.
The Natural. ©1984 TriStar Pictures.
Everett Collection: pg. 24, 130. Photofest: pgs. 30, 52, 284.
Star Wars. ©1977 Twentieth Century-Fox Film Corp. Studio: Lucasfilm Ltd.
Corbis: ©Bettmann/Corbis pg. 23. Photofest: pgs. 84, 145, 230.
Star Wars: Episode V - The Empire Strikes Back. ©1980 Lucasfilm Ltd. Photofest: pg. 252.
Star Wars: Episode VI - Return of the Jedi. ©1983 Lucasfilm Ltd. Photofest: pgs. 30, 52.
Star Wars: Episode I - The Phantom Menace. ©1999 Lucasfilm Ltd. Photofest: pgs. 92, 100, 207.

Photos and Artwork

Art Today. ©2000–2002 www.arttoday.com. Clip Art and Photos.
pgs. 42, 62, 116, 172, 216, 220, 228, 287, 288, 315.
Corel Professional Photos. Images and Photos. pgs. 25, 91, 94, 96, 104, 152, 188.
Ragnarok Press. Heading Fonts and Images. pgs. 15, 65, 250, 299, 300.

Illustration (1921) by N. C. Wyeth (1882– 1945)

Part I – The Call

Parsifal by Jean Delville (1867–1953)

Private Collection
Oil on Canvas, 1890. 25¼ x 21¼ in.

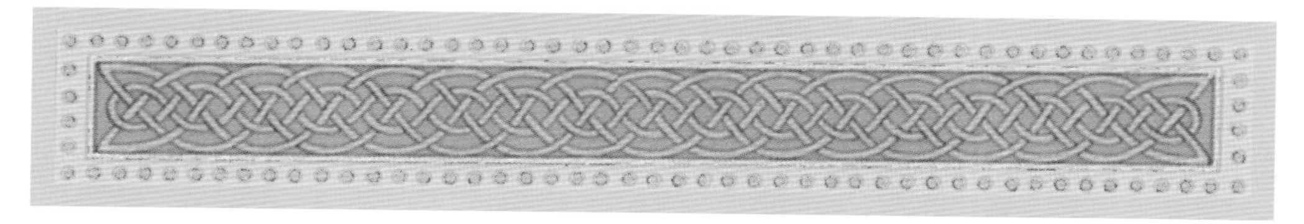

A Tap on the Shoulder

Who is the Fisher King?

Once upon a time, there was a King who suffered from a wound. He searched for relief by fishing on a magical lake, but the suffering was so great, it affected all of his kingdom. In spite of the wealth of his castle and lands, the people suffered, the cows suffered, the trees suffered, the worms suffered. The kingdom was a Wasteland. There was a solution, as all problems have a solution, that depended on a Good Knight doing the Right Thing. Then the Fisher King would be healed and so would the land.

Once upon a time there was a movie called *The Fisher King* which is based on this story and went on to win Academy Awards. Ditto for the movie *Forrest Gump.* And *Apocalypse Now, Good Will Hunting, Star Wars,* and *The Natural.* Some of these films came from novels by the same names. There were also other books called *Heart of Darkness* and *Siddhartha.* There was even a poem called *The Waste Land.* By the way, some of the authors won Pulitzer and Nobel Prizes. All from this simple story. (Among a few other works of literature.)

So—Who is this Fisher King? Who is this Knight who must heal him? What does he have to do to heal him? And why would I care?

You are the Fisher King and you are the Knight and this is a book about your Destiny.

This book covers the journey of Parzival—the journey of every person who searches to find what he or she was truly meant to be and accomplish. It is a story of personal development and spiritual maturity, and of our relation to the world around us and the responsibilities that requires. It is not a book of haphazard adventures with battle trophies, but an exploration of the geography of the soul. Intuition becomes as important as discipline. Inspiration from love is more important than the inspiration of a king. We learn that the need of the individual does not conflict with the need of the community, as long as the individual approaches with good intent. Though the initial lessons are tempestuous, the healthy balance between men and women is essential to the kingdom and the individual. We learn the importance of being guided by values instead of pulled by a nose ring of rules. If we build a world that can respond with compassion, then we can build a world that flourishes and endures.

Parzival is a mighty book filled with mighty lessons. This book has been written to share this remarkable story in the framework of the modern world, and to interpret the lessons for the adventures we will chase in this new millennium.

Unlikely Inspiration

Joseph Campbell writes eloquently in *The Hero with a Thousand Faces* of the "Call to Adventure" for a prospective hero. The Call is directly tied to the destiny of your life, though it may not be apparent at first. It may be delivered by an ugly or dangerous person. It may be a reaction to a supposed chance mistake, or it may be a distraction that pulls you from your normal routine. Think of it as the man behind you on the bus who taps your shoulder to speak with you, and changes your life forever. Often the Call is ignored, but eventually it must be answered. You may respond to that stranger on the bus with a courteous yet disinterested reply, but he will again tap your shoulder until you say "Yes, I'll do it."

The distraction that planted the seed for the writing of this book occurred in 1994. I sat in a movie theater being charmed by an innocent named Forrest Gump. His mother was forthright and caring, his girlfriend tragic, and his son a parent's dream. We loved Gump enough to bulge the theaters and video stores and the Academy Awards lined mantels with golden Oscars. At least most of us loved Gump. Some of us couldn't stand him. He was too stupid. And way too lucky. But I loved the story, for here was one of my favorite myths played out in an arena for people who do not typically read medieval German literature exposing them to the spiritual lessons of *Parzival.* "Spiritual lessons?" you ask. "Medieval literature? I just liked the movie. But literature? I don't think so. It's Entertainment."

Like many of you, I grew up with television. Despite the evils that are intoned on that box of plastic and electronics, I am forever grateful for it, because I have been introduced to literature, history, and art that I would not have been aware of. No one ever introduced me to *Cyrano de Bergerac* by Edmond Rostand, but one afternoon, I came home from grade school, turned on the television, and watched Jose Ferrer die among autumn leaves at the foot of Cyrano's Roxanne. I then read the book. In our study, we are embarking on a tale that is intertwined with the "Matters of Britain," more commonly known as the Arthurian tales—the stories of King Arthur and his Knights of the Round Table. My initial involvement in these stories did not originate in a classroom, but in popular culture. I was invited into this realm listening to Lerner and Loewe's "If Ever I Would Leave You" sung to Vanessa Redgrave portraying Guenevere. This exposure to the movie *Camelot* led me to search out T.H. White's *The Once and Future King,* my first reading of Arthurian stories.

It is too easy for those who pride themselves as intellectuals to discount movies and television as fluff. It is too easy for those growing up in the techno age to regard books of the past as being dead men's words, irrelevant to these times. We must finally realize that all is interconnected. What is important is that the dusty books and the DVDs are still trying to teach us lessons, and our personal responsibility to ourselves is to discover those lessons.

This book explores the character of Parzival, known as a Great Fool, and what his quest means to us today. A more familiar name may be Perceval, the French and English name of the same character, but I will focus on the structure of the story in the German poem by Wolfram von Eschenbach. Parzival was also known as Peredur in the Welsh legends, and Perlesvaus in other French stories. I will include vignettes from these works, in addition to modern novels and movies following the story line of *Parzival.* In these stories his name is Forrest Gump, Will Hunting, Luke Skywalker, Roy Hobbs in *The Natural,* Charlie Marlow in *Heart of Darkness,* and Benjamin Willard in *Apocalypse Now.* He is Siddhartha.

Do not think that because I have chosen popular movies to help illustrate profound learnings, this is a light-hearted romp with ten easy quick fix steps to redeem your life while you watch Tom Hanks and Robert Redford. To do so would cheat you of real learning, real in depth experience. Our Road Trip, Down the River dramas have reflected the linear path of our thinking of life. However, in the age of the Internet, webs of information crisscross from many sources without regard to any hierarchy, except for what we individually impose on it. Likewise, this book freely brings in literature, art, movies, music, history, psychology, myth, and philosophy which beams us across centuries to help us on our individual paths. This book is my own foray into personal myth, and you should bring it into your life at the level it speaks to you. It may speak to your inner life, or your social life, or the life of your community. How it speaks to you today may be interpreted differently five years down the line, and that is the beauty of this story—it has been refreshing us for a thousand years.

Most people only know of Arthurian literature as a story of King Arthur whose kingdom fell apart when his wife Gwenevere messed around with a knight named Lancelot. Very fin-de-siècle. The story is more than brave knights and beautiful damsels, for we will examine the story as it centers around the Grail and the significance of the people we meet along the way.

The story is within us all. We have been the Great Fool, the Goddess of Sovereignty, the Wounded Fisher King, the Initiator, the Grail Maiden. Maybe nobody gave us those names directly, but we've lived those roles and continue to do so in both our physical and spiritual lives. Though I will present the mythical characters in their literary gender, these people have no gender and no age. When I write of the Mother Who Binds Her Son, I write of any mother, father, teacher, boss, husband, wife, sister, brother, friend, and enemy who managed to hold you back. Often, it is someone who resides in your mind. When I write of the Goddess of Sovereignty, a representative of the psychic, spiritual right to rule the land, I am connecting to the moral spirit you must appease to rule your own self.

This book has been my own personal exercise in an alchemy mixing many interests of my life. It reflects my own personal observations built on the reading of scholars, creative thinkers, psychologists, and philosophers. My interest with Oriental philosophy ties in with my life as a martial artist for the past twenty-five years. As a *sifu* (teacher—think of it as a Ph.D. in Chinese martial arts), I found it important to study the philosophical roots as well as the physical training of martial arts. I have visited many revered sites of Confucianism, Buddhism, and Taoism in China, Hong Kong, and Malaysia, and personally witnessed the enduring presence of these ancient ways of thought surviving tumultuous histories. The Arthurian literature side comes from my lifelong passion for mythology. Often when I was small, I wished that the stories of the myths were true. I wanted Venus, Zeus, Thor, and Merlin to be real. It wasn't until I was in my thirties that I realized they were. Contrary to what some people think, Myth is Truth. The Myth I speak of is the study of folklore, legend, religion, and storytelling. The characters may be fictional but the lessons hold true today as thousands of years ago. My more serious inquiries into the Grail legends led me to become a member of the International Arthurian Society, which brings together scholars and dilettantes to explore the history, myth, and meaning of these legends. Like many of you, my interest in movies started when I rushed home from grade school every day to watch the 4:00 P.M. movie on my family's TV. Art was one of my first truly religious experiences and continues to be so. When I was twelve years old and first went to the Art Institute of Chicago to experience the works of the masters, I felt my heart quiver and drop to my feet several times. I have visited numerous art museums in Europe, Asia, and America, and have had the good fortune to enjoy in person many of the paintings you see in this book.

As you read this book, I want you to be an active participant. Rent the movies, read the books, and use my approach to enlarge your own personal understanding. Trust your own intelligence. Never hamper yourself with excuses of lack of formal education, or defeat yourself by not reading difficult passages. As we will discuss later, Direct Experience is one of the most important keys to unlocking your own genius. I believe people are smarter than they allow themselves to be. I am telling you up front that I am only an Initiator with this book: the Herald who announces the Adventure. I am Tapping you on the Shoulder. It is up to you to make it your own personal experience.

With that in mind, enjoy and learn with the romp. Listen to the Call.

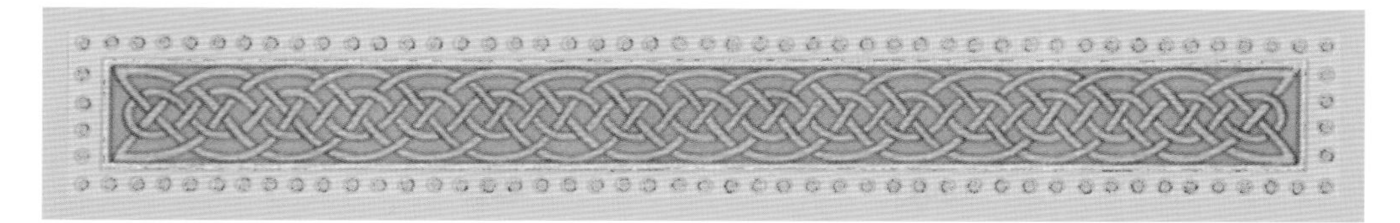

Crash Course

Before we begin our in depth discovery, we should have an overview of Parzival and how this story compares with the plots of the modern novels and movies. Think of it as a AAA Road Atlas that will give you the direction you are going. Plot Synopses and Filmographies are provided in the *Backstory - Appendix* of this book, so you can review the stories you are familiar with or get an idea of a storyline. Still, the best experience is the Direct Experience, so I hope that as we go along, you will read the books and watch the films.

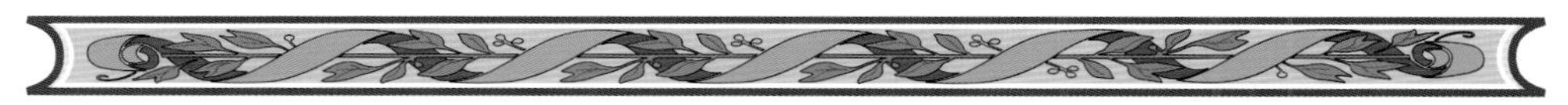

Parzival

Parzival is a young man who has been separated from society by his mother, growing up unaware that he has special abilities that could make him a great knight. He finally ventures into the real world, which is ruled by King Arthur. Alas, this real world is beset by problems. It is a Wasteland brought about by the wounding of the Grail King, Anfortas, who is the Fisher King. His kingdom is called the Land of Salvation, and the Grail is kept at his castle. Parzival blunders through his inital knighthood adventures, but is able to take on more significant challenges as he matures, including saving the kingdom of the woman who will be his wife, Condwiramors. Finally, he meets the Grail King, and is given a chance to heal him. Parzival fails to heal the king, because Parzival is still living in ignorance as to how to react with compassion instead of rules. He continues with his knightly adventures, but always has Condwiramors on his mind. He becomes more conscious of his responsibilities, and even thinks he's doing a rather fine job. While celebrating his successes, Cundrie the Sorceress shows up telling him he is a disgrace, and if he wants to be truly great, he has to Heal the Fisher King. She also challenges the other knights of Arthur's court to search for adventures, instead of languishing in the castle. Gawan, nephew of Arthur, is also challenged at the same time from an outsider. There is a series of adventures involving both Parzival and Gawan, until finally Parzival is able to go back to the Grail King and heal him. Parzival and Condwiramors reunite, with Parzival meeting his twin sons for the first time. The kingdom rejoices for the Healing of Anfortas and Parzival becomes the new Grail King.

Not a bad summary for a 25,000 line poem. Now for the modern renditions.

The Fisher King

Jeff Bridges as Jack Lucas

Henry Sagan, who goes by the name Parry, is the true Wounded Fisher King, though the "Grail" is found in the "castle" of Lanny Carmichael. Parry has lost his mind when his wife was shot by a crazed man, partially instigated by the prodding of Jack Lucas, a radio shock jock. Though Henry carries the Parzival name (Parry) and tries to be the hero, he is only a shadow of the knight he needs, and it is Jack who is the real Parzival character. Parry lives this fantasy as he was once a professor who had written a dissertation on "The Fisher King," and knew deep inside himself what was necessary for his own healing. We see in this film a trade-off of the Parzival and Fisher King characters between the two men as they attempt to retrieve the "Grail." Anne Napolitano is Jack's love and initiating sorceress combined, while Lydia Sinclair is Parry's *amour.* Parry is well aware that he has to earn the love of Lydia, following the tradition of knightly virtues set in *Parzival.* Hollywood does give us the happy *Parzival* ending when Jack saves Carmichael and Parry. Jack can return to Anne as a more mature, wiser man, deserving of her love.

Forrest Gump

Tom Hanks as Forrest Gump

Forrest Gump is Parzival, and he is more the fool than Parzival ever was. His natural abilities will lead him to football and later to war. This is consistent with the natural warrior abilities that Parzival possessed. The wounded Grail King in this story is Lt. Dan, and Parzival's true love is Jenny. She is rarely with Gump during his adventures, but is always his inspiration, just like Parzival and Condwiramors. Gump's series of adventures will include building a shrimping business inspired by his war buddy, Bubba. Eventually, Dan will be healed, and Gump will get with Jenny, though the ending of this story is more bittersweet than its inspiration. Jenny will die, but will bring Forrest's son to him.

Good Will Hunting

Matt Damon as Will Hunting

Will Hunting is a mathematical genius who insists on living in his own fool's environment, when he has all the abilities to work and thrive at the highest echelons of modern society. He prefers hanging out with his best friend, Chuckie, who plays the Gawan role. Will encounters a mathematics professor, Gerald Lambeau, with his dreams of mathematical greatness dimming. He is like King Arthur when his court no longer lives up to its former days of glory. Gerald hopes to help Will, partially so Will can shore up Gerald's reputation. Gerald sends Will to a psychiatrist friend, Sean Maguire, in an effort to get Will pointed in the right direction. Sean is the Fisher King, as he has been wounded by the loss of his wife. Will also will have his love interest in the form of Skylar, who inspires him to seek love and fortune. It will be through the interactions of Sean and Will that both men can find wholeness in themselves and a promise of the future.

Star Wars

Mark Hamill as Luke Skywalker

The main story line for Parzival is found in the initial *Star Wars* Classic Trilogy—*Star Wars, The Empire Strikes Back,* and *Return of the Jedi,* which are Episodes 4, 5, and 6. Luke Skywalker's Grail always seems to be "Saving the Universe." The Universe is littered with various Wastelands, perpetuated by the anger and evil of the Maimed Fisher King in the form of Darth Vader. Though Luke's love inspiration turns out to be his sister, Princess Leia, it is still a compelling force that keeps him focused on his path. Han Solo is Gawan, and we will come to know Obi-Wan "Ben" Kenobi and Yoda as Parzival's uncles and mentors. The Parzival legend requires compassion to heal the Fisher King, and so it will be at the end of the *Star Wars* Trilogy, when Luke can heal Darth Vader by demonstrating love and not giving in to anger.

In *Episode 1, The Phantom Menace,* we see the themes of Parzival also played out, with a few twists of Arthur's story. The lessons are the same, and are emphasized in scenarios which are setups for issues to be examined in future films. Anakin Skywalker will have to leave his mother to have an adventure with a Goddess of Sovereignty. This is the beginning stage of Parzival leaving his mother to find his Destiny.

The Natural

Robert Redford as Roy Hobbs

Roy Hobbs is baseball's best pitcher and hitter rolled into one. Just as Roy was to enter the professional baseball arena, he was brought down by the modern equivalent of Cundrie the Sorceress, Harriet Bird, when she shoots him. Roy will have to endure years of healing and semi-pro baseball before he will have the chance to help Pop Fisher (notice the name) win the elusive pennant. By the way, the team he plays for is the Knights. His separated love is Iris (Gaines in the film, Lemon in the novel), which is an appropriate name as the Goddess of Sovereignty is also the Flower Bride, who rules in the OtherWorld where flowers abound. Roy is always getting into trouble because of his pride, a fault that is pointed out as a serious character flaw in *Parzival.* In the movie, all ends well, including the hero meeting his son. The book, however, shows the darker side, one that happens when the attempted healing doesn't come from an innocent place.

Heart of Darkness and Apocalypse Now

Martin Sheen as Benjamin Willard

Marlow is a master seaman, hired by the Company to go into the Congo. This is the same as Arthur's court sending Parzival to the OtherWorld for adventures. Marlow doesn't realize initially that he has been sent to find Kurtz, a remarkable man who ran the business in the interior, but seems to have fallen ill. Kurtz is our Maimed Fisher King. Marlow sees the enslavement of the natives, evidence of the Wasteland, and learns more of Kurtz as he ventures down the river. Kurtz' fiancée will be Marlow's muse, whom he will go to when he returns from the Congo. There will be a scene in *Parzival* where Parzival is entranced by a vision of Condwiramors. By the same token, Marlow is enchanted with a painting of Kurtz' fiancée. Kurtz is not physically healed in this story, but there is a sense of spiritual truth. The death of Kurtz actually follows some of the other Grail legends where the old king dies so the young king may rightfully take his place. Though the book is dark, it is a tribute to finding Truth and bringing it back to the world at large. Francis Ford Coppola placed *Heart of Darkness* into the Vietnam War to create *Apocalypse Now.* Willard is Marlow/Parzival who has been sent to bring out the mad Colonel Kurtz. As in *Parzival,* Willard starts with foolish ignorance, and by the time he returns, he is aware, wise, and enlightened. Like *Heart of Darkness,* the healing comes from a full smashing in the face of dark truth.

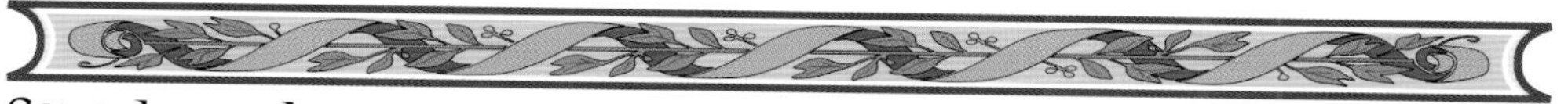

Siddhartha

Siddhartha opens his eyes one day, and sees the suffering of people in the Wasteland about him. He leaves his rich home and sets himself on the road with his friend Govinda. They respectively represent the Parzival and Gawan characters. They go to Gotama, the Buddha, who offers a plan to ease suffering, but Siddhartha sees flaws in Gotama's arguments. Gotama is the Fisher King, still searching for the truth which would ease the suffering of people. Siddhartha leaves Govinda, who stays with Gotama, and has his own adventures, just as Parzival leaves the Fisher King's castle. Along his path, Siddhartha will be the student lover of Kamala, the wealthy courtesan. She will give him a son, and as Jenny in *Forrest Gump* passes away, so does Kamala. By the end of the book, Govinda and Siddhartha meet. Siddhartha has now recognized the Buddha within himself, a definite true healing.

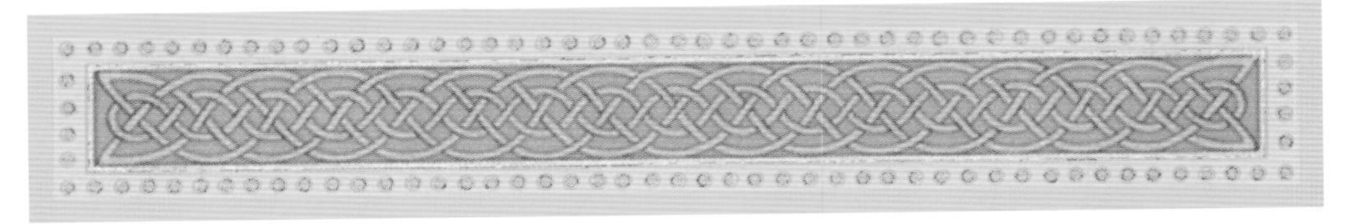

The Progress of the Soul
Movement 1: The Entrance
by Phoebe Traquair (1852–1936)

National Gallery of Scotland
Silk & Gold Thread on Linen, 1893–1902
71 ⅛ x 28 in.

The Structure and Elements of the Book

Before we jump into the plot of *Parzival,* I want to introduce you to some of the most important figures of the story in the section titled "Cast of Characters." Since we must Heal the Fisher King, we will first explore who the Maimed Fisher King is and get a feeling for his Wasteland Kingdom. Parzival is the Great Fool, representing ourselves at our most innocent, unknowing level, full of potential, but nowhere to put it to good use. I also want you to meet the Goddess of Sovereignty and the Loathly Lady, women who are the beating hearts of Arthurian literature. The Grail itself is an icon magnified in many uses from literature to commercials, but few people are exposed to its many aspects.

The heart of our journey is found in the section called "The Adventure," which is split into four major areas. These are the major divisions of our own spiritual path. We first are in "The Age of Innocence and Its Perils," which explores how we get off of our own personal Grail path very early on in life. Then we are given a glimpse of what the Grail is in "The Shadow of the Grail." When we become aware of what the Grail is, everything in our life changes. When we are not in its presence, we suffer, and many of the heartaches in our life come from trying to get back to it. Next, we learn the difficulty of rediscovering the Grail in "The Grueling Road." Finally, we begin to become enlightened and can perform "The Healing." Within each of these four areas are chapters which summarize the *Parzival* legend, then go on to explore the significance of the chapter's lessons.

I want this book to be a multi-sensory experience, and I want you to think beyond whatever is presented in the main text. In addition to the prose, I have included art, quotes, *I Ching* Hexagrams, and boxes containing reflections and working suggestions to bring the ideas of the book into your real life. Some of you may wish to create a journal to work through these suggestions and record your impressions.

Art is an integral part of this book. It is Myth displayed with unspoken truth. Sometimes I comment on a piece of art, more often, I do not. It is your duty to note the title, study the painting, and come to an understanding of what the artist is presenting to you and why I may have chosen a particular piece. Meditate on the art work, and note how it relates to you personally. These thoughts can make up part of your journal work.

One of the tools of Taoist study is the *I Ching.* As a divination tool, it relies on the chance throwing of coins or the dividing of yarrow stalks to obtain a hexagram. Interpreters would look up one of the sixty four hexagrams to give advice as to how to proceed on a course of action. Rather than a fortune teller's device, I view it as a philosopher's tool which can give you a different view of a situation. It would be similar to the image of standing on a Native American Medicine Wheel. If you stand on the North End of the Medicine Wheel, things look different than if you stand on the South End. Throughout the book, all sixty-four hexagrams are presented as sidebars to the events in the chapters and sections. The oracle of three thousand years ago, the story of a thousand years ago, and our own lives share truths that will endure for eons to come. As you read, consider how the Hexagram may apply to recent and past situations in your own life.

Journal Reflections and Suggestions are presented in aqua colored boxes. These make you look into the present state of your own life and give you exercises to implement in your daily life. These exercises and discoveries are well worth the time and energy. If you record these reflections and the response to your work, you will be left a diary of Spiritual introspection and individual progress.

The Progress of the Soul
Movement 2: The Stress
by Phoebe Traquair (1852–1936)
National Gallery of Scotland
Silk & Gold Thread on Linen, 1893–1902
71 1/8 x 28 in.

Let us now meet some of the remarkable personalities who are going to teach us of ourselves in "Cast of Characters."

The Progress of the Soul
Movement 3: Despair
by Phoebe Traquair (1852–1936)

National Gallery of Scotland
Silk & Gold Thread on Linen, 1893–1902
72 3/4 x 29 1/2 in.

The Progress of the Soul
Movement 4: The Victory
by Phoebe Traquair (1852–1936)

National Gallery of Scotland
Silk & Gold Thread on Linen, 1893–1902
74 1/8 x 29 1/4 in.

Finding of Moses by
Lawrence Alma-Tadema (1836–1912)

Private Collection
Oil on Canvas, 1904. 54 ⅛ x 84 in.

Part II – Cast of Characters

Marlon Brando as Col. Walter E. Kurtz
in *Apocalypse Now*

Wilford Brimley as Pop Fisher
in *The Natural*

Faces of the Fisher King

Robin Williams as Sean Maguire
in *Good Will Hunting*

Gary Sinise as Lt. Dan Taylor
in *Forrest Gump*

David Prowse as Darth Vader
in *Star Wars* Trilogy

Chapter 1 – The Maimed Fisher King and the Wasteland

Here is no water but only rock
Rock and no water and the sandy road
The road winding above among the mountains
Which are mountains of rock without the water
— *The Waste Land* by T.S. Eliot

You live, yet are dead to your bliss.
— Sigune in *Parzival*, Book v, ¶ 255

Removing his cap, Pop rubbed his bald head with his bandaged fingers. "It's been a blasted dry season. No rains at all. The grass is worn scabby in the outfield and the infield is cracking. My heart feels as dry as dirt for the little I have to show for all my years in the game."
— Pop Fisher in *The Natural* by Bernard Malamud

This is the end, beautiful friend
This is the end, my only friend, the end...
Lost in a Roman wilderness of pain
And all the children are insane
— from the song "The End" by The Doors
(opening music for *Apocalypse Now*)

Our journey begins in a dreadful place. It is a land where nothing grows, beasts prowl the edges of the towns, women are barren, and neighbors betray neighbors. We see it in the flicker of the TV screen as Forrest Gump rollicks through his life. That blue-white flicker revealing napalm in Vietnam, assassinated political leaders, a president resigning in disgrace. Homeless people eat moldy pies from a dumpster in *The Fisher King*. Pop Fisher can not win a baseball pennant. Poverty lurks in Boston slums where Will Hunting calls home. R2-D2 and C-3PO comb shifting desert sands. Willard rides Valkyrie copters as they bomb Vietnamese villages so the beach can be claimed for surfing. Buddhists tell us that this is the first of the Four Noble Truths—that of *dukkha,* life is hard. It is the realm of the Wasteland.

Though Parzival will not encounter the Fisher King until a little down the road, I choose to start our exploration here, so that you can grasp early on the concept of the

Maimed Fisher King and the Wasteland. Here we are, innocent babes thrown into a world of tragedy and hardship. The first time I sat down to write this, I glanced at my email and the news of the day. The president of the United States had admitted to unbecoming personal behavior in the White House. While on vacation, he had ordered missile attacks on two suspected terrorist camps in the Middle East in retaliation for the bombings of U.S. embassies in Africa. The Russian and Asian economies were faltering and pulling the U.S. stock market down. The Yangtze River in China and the Rio Grande in Texas were flooding, and Hurricane Bonnie was making its way toward the Southeastern United States. Another typical week of violence and catastrophe in the world. The last time I sat down for final editing of this book, the week was not so typical—the World Trade Centers were brought down by terrorists crashing hijacked planes into the buildings. The Pentagon was also attacked, and a fourth hijacked plane crashed in a farm field due to the courage of passengers refusing to allow the terrorists to reach their destination. Over five thousand lives were lost. The Wasteland became more monstrous than we had even known or imagined.

No wonder we have such a difficult time in life. Some days the cards are stacked against us before we even begin. It's enough to make you want to give up. Every day, we see and hear of people who have done just that. You and I shall do something different. We will walk that dusty road. We will learn why it is dusty and barren. We will discover what will change the Wasteland and make it live.

What Caused the Wasteland?

The Dolorous Blow.

Dolores who?

dolorous (dō′ lər əs, dol′ ər-), adj. full of or causing pain or sorrow.

Wastelands don't just happen. Something happens to the King of Paradise and the whole place goes awry. It is the Dolorous Blow, the straw that breaks the camel's back and there is no going back.

In *Parzival,* the Dolorous Blow is dealt when the Fisher King, Anfortas, is wounded by a poisoned spear. In his younger days, he ignored his duty to the Grail Castle and pursued the attentions of Queen Orgeluse. He is challenged and during the battle is struck in the thigh, which in the polite society of medieval literature is a metaphor for a wounding of the genitals. The king is rendered infertile and his land will reflect this.

In Christian and Jewish legend, Eve eats that apple, gets Adam involved, and their residence gets changed. In fact, a theme running through the Grail legends is one of looking for the New Adam, the one who will make everything right again. He is often referred to as The Good Knight, as Will is known as Good Will Hunting.

The Elucidation is a thirteenth century prologue to Chrétien de Troyes' "The Story of the Grail." In this writing the Maidens of the Fountain, who nourish travelers with the fountain's magical waters, are raped by King Amangons and his men. In Malory's *Le Morte D'Arthur,* a knight of Arthur's court throws a spear into the Grail King, and then murders his own brother with the Dolorous Sword.

Lt. Dan in *Forrest Gump* gets his Dolorous Blow when his legs are blown up in a war which went on to wound the United States. Gump, noting the shootings of John Kennedy, Bobby Kennedy, George Wallace, Gerald Ford, John Lennon, and Ronald Reagan, realizes that being a king is a hard life. Pop Fisher's legs will fail him when he is running to base in the World Series and he can not find professional success from that moment on. The strife in *Heart of Darkness* comes with the beating of an old, black native chief. The natives of the Congo could no longer trust the foreigners working their jungles and waterways. A restaurant of yuppie diners is strafed with bullets from the weapon of a disillusioned soul living out his own Wasteland in *The Fisher King.* Parry's Dolorous Blow happens when his wife is killed in that rampage, but it is his physical wounding that finally brings Jack to help him. Darth Vader has lost his sword hand.

For these times, the September 11th attack was a Dolorous Blow affecting many nations and lives.

When I was young and would be injured, I generally trusted the body to heal itself. A few days after a fall or twist of the ankle, I would be off running again, confident that I was healed. Now that I am much older and still actively work out, I have learned that everything did not heal. I still suffer from those past injuries with reinjuries and flexibility loss. I have since learned of healing methods, such as *chi kung*, which now help me, but it took me many years to realize that I must take an active approach to healing. Pills and doctors may be necessary, but I am the one who can not be passive about healing.

So it is with the Wounding of the Fisher King and the Wasteland. The Fisher King lies in pain for years, affecting all around him. It is such a painful blow, it is so devastating, that it can not just heal itself. It takes a conscious act, hard work, and a spiritual awareness to mend the King. In *The Fisher King,* Parry tells Jack directly that he is unable to get the Grail. He needs Jack to do it for him.

Bryce Canyon

Exile

It's fun to visit the dream world and the world of story to examine the symbolic. But we must always remember to root ourselves in reality and ask, "What does this really mean to me?"

It means that we are talking about suffering, and if we want to know how to have a healthy spirit, we must examine suffering. All major religious, philosophical, or psychological movements seriously examine the pain in people's lives. That is because the creators and leaders of these movements know they will be the ones people turn to when personal agony drives them to search for peace.

Buddha sat under a Bodhi tree for nine years to achieve enlightenment. His initial impetus was "What is suffering?" Jesus did not say "Let the children come to me," but "Suffer the little children to come unto me." The Koran tells us "of them is he who makes his soul suffer a loss."

The suffering that must be explored goes beyond what the physical and material world heaps on us. Obviously, if our home has burned down, or we are starving from malnutrition, or we are racked with pain from a crippling disease, we are anguished. However, there are times when we have more than adequate material resources in our lives, yet inside us are maelstroms of near clinical depression. Other times we watch the debt pile up, deprive our bodies of needed sleep, yet experience moments of pure joy. True suffering goes beyond just the physical. And sometimes, what we don't have in our physical world is many times related to the suffering of our inner spirit.

The Fisher King is also the Grail King. This means that he has been entrusted to safekeep the Grail at his castle. We will look at the Grail in more depth in a few chapters, but I want you to know what the Grail represents to me and this book's study.

THE GRAIL IS OUR INNERMOST HEART'S DESIRE AND NEED.

Did I confuse you? Surprise you? Did you expect me to say the cup of Christ that the Crusaders went after? In fact, the Grail represents many things, but at the heart of it is the idea that we feel lost, frightened, empty, powerless, and despondent unless our personal Grail is in our lives. When we are apart from the Grail, when we exile ourselves from the deepest desires of our hearts, we suffer. This is our private Wasteland.

The Grail may represent your religion, and your loss of a relationship to your higher spirit. It may also be your art, your loved ones, your nature, your deep calling in life. You may be a writer trapped at the accountant's green glass lampshade. You may be a woman, deserving gentle love, who is cornered in an abusive relationship. You may be a man who achieves much financially, but has given up the deep joy of nurturing your children because of long hours and exhausting emotional demands of the business world. Your nature may demand that you live among mountains and streams, but you exist in a concrete condo, barely surviving on a small paycheck. In the film *Heart of Darkness*, Kurtz grills Marlow to examine not what he respects, but what he loves with all of his soul. Kurtz knows that the power of the Grail is that innermost heart's desire.

The Grail has the great power to keep you alive, but it will also allow your suffering. The Fisher King has suffered from his Dolorous Blow, but he cannot die because he is in the presence of the Grail. Your hopes and dreams will keep you alive, but if you do not actively pursue them, you condemn yourself to pain. You will suffer until you know the Grail that lies in your soul, and you heal the blow that prevented you from living in its majesty.

Ivan Albright, in his chilling painting *That Which I Should Have Done I Did Not Do (The Door)*, speaks directly to the heart of all of the "I should haves" we carry around with us. We cry over the children we could have helped, the scoundrels we should have pushed away, the risks we did not take. Lamenting is one of the deepest wounds which continues to bleed in so many of us. When you stand in front of the painting, you have an immediate sense of melancholy. It is almost as large as a real door, and you sense that perhaps if that cautious hand had only pushed the door open earlier in her life, she would have found treasure instead of death. Now, once fragrant flowers hang decayed and lifeless, evidence of a life wasted.

That Which I Should Have Done
I Did Not Do (The Door)
by Ivan Albright (1897–1973)

The Art Institute of Chicago,
Mary and Leigh Block Charitable Fund. (1955.645)
Oil on Canvas, 1931–41. 97 x 36 in.

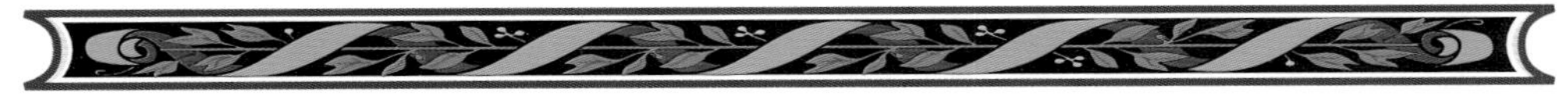

Asking the Right Question

The evolution of all learning and discovery orbits around asking the proper questions. The dialogues of Plato consist of conversation built on questions. Scientific process and psychological analysis center on the proper question. Zen monks use *koans,* spiritual questions which aim for instantaneous insight. I have witnessed an exercise in the tutelage of Buddhist monks demonstrated by the Drepung Gomang Monks of Tibet. The master monk, moving his whole body about the stage, fires off questions to the student monk. The student must respond at the same speed, setting up a singsong debate.

Integral to the healing of the Fisher King is asking the right question at the right time. It is a very simple question, one founded on spontaneous compassion. The healing happens when Parzival asks "What ails thee?" As simple as it is, it takes a lot of trouble and work to get to that point.

The Grail and the Dolorous Blow

Look at your own life and answer a few questions to begin our path of healing and insight.

1. What Ails Thee?

What in your life gives you the most unhappiness? Our bodies do not lie, and when you think on the various problems in your life, the worst ones will give you a physical clue. Broken hearts don't lie. What gives you a sense of dread and powerlessness?

2. What is your Grail?

What do you long for that would give you peace and happiness? The answer to this is related to the pains that "ails thee." If your children are your Grail, your ailing may be related to a feeling of not being able to give them what you want. If art is your Grail and you are in a "traditional" line of work, you will feel a dissatisfaction and yearning, no matter what financial successes are heaped on you. Until you can name your Grail, you will not find it, and you will continue to suffer.

3. What was your Dolorous Blow?

What denied you the nourishment of your Grail and created your own personal Wasteland? Was it choosing engineering over medicine in college? Was it marrying the guy with the bank account whom your parents liked instead of the poor, but kind man who could only give you grocery store daisies? The sorrows and the mistakes of the past offer insight to habits and patterns which may still be preventing you from getting back to your Grail.

This exercise is only a starting point, but it is an eye opening one. Even at this stage, you possess more wisdom about yourself than you realize, and the answers here will be reflected in much of your work down the line.

Reeling It In

That's a fish reel, not a movie reel.

Right after the movie *The Fisher King* came out, I quizzed people about who the Fisher King was. Some recalled the scene in the middle of the movie where a nude Parry tells the story of the Fisher King healed through the compassion of a fool. I then asked what that had to do with fishing. The answer? 100% blank stares. Don't feel bad if you don't know the answer. This is one of the motifs that scholars have debated for many years.

When Parzival first meets the Wounded King, the king is out in a boat fishing. Parzival is told that the king can only feel comfortable when he is taken by Lake Brumbane. In fact, people assume he is fishing, but he doesn't catch anything. It seems to be such a trivial activity, so why mention it at all? Why is this Wounded King known as the Rich Fisher King?

There have been several theories why a fishing king is so important. Several tie into Christian thought. Jesus has been associated with fish through several stories and meanings. One is that the Greek word for fish, *ichthys,* was also an acronym for "Jesus Christ, Son of God." With this explanation, the Fisher King is trawling for faith. In another story, Christ calls Peter and Andrew to be his disciples saying "Follow me, and I will make you fishers of men." The two drop their fishing nets by the sea of Galilee and follow. In this sense, the Fisher King is the man who fishes for good men who can heal him and the land. The Pope's ring is known as the Fisherman's Ring.

Another story reflects one of the attributes of the Grail as a source of replenishing sustenance. It is the tale of Christ blessing two fishes and five loaves of bread, and miraculously feeding a multitude. This story is repeated in several Grail legends—one of the original Grail keepers also feeds his family and followers with one fish. One of these tales is in the French Vulgate Cycle, a group of Arthurian tales written in the vulgar. Vulgar here does not mean bad taste, but a term indicating ordinary language. *The History of the Holy Grail* is part of the Vulgate Cycle, in which we find a story of Joseph of Arimathea. He has a relative, Bron, who has a son, Alan. Their tribe, traveling with the Grail, comes to a land which is a Wasteland. Though the spiritually pure are sustained by the Grail, the sinners have no food. Alan is sent to the lake to fish. He only catches one fish, but in the presence of the Grail, it is able to feed everyone. Alan is then called the Rich Fisherman and becomes the Grail Guardian. In some legends, Alan's father, Bron, is called the Fisher King.

The Celts, too, have legends of fish and heroes. Bron is sometimes considered as the giant god Bran, also known as the son of the sea god, Lyr (Lir). In other legends, a humanized Bran is on a sea voyage and is treated to prophecies by another sea god, Manannan (Manawydan). (Please note that when I refer to Celts in this work, I am loosely referring to all groups of people who lived in the British Isles, including Ireland, Scotland, Wales, and Britain.)

Another Celtic legend is about Finn MacCumhail. He wandered to the shores of the Boyne, where Finn the Seer had been fishing seven years for the Salmon of Wisdom. The Seer finally caught the fish and told Finn MacCumhail to watch over the roasting of the fish, but not to eat it. MacCumhail accidentally burned his thumb on the hot fish, and when he licked his thumb, obtained all knowledge. The Seer realized the fish was meant for the young Finn and gave it to him to eat. Thereafter Finn only had to suck his thumb to obtain wisdom. (No wonder babies are always sucking their thumbs.) This could almost fit in with our Parzival story where the King is always out fishing, but doesn't catch anything. That's because the real power is waiting for the Chosen One.

Feminine myth has strong association with fish lore and would possibly have been a forerunner to the Christian meanings. The Greek word *delphos* had two meanings—fish and womb. The Grail has been associated with womb/cauldron motifs. The Boyne river, where Finn caught his salmon of knowledge, was created by the goddess Boann, as waters from a sacred well overflowed in her presence. The quest for feminine knowledge is a theme of Grail myths, and the fishing for the goddess' knowledge and wisdom is a viable interpretation.

The Chinese have a type of Fisher King who also retreated for his health. In the painting, *Catching Fish*, we see P'ang Te-kung living the life of a hermit farmer. He has been offered a government position several times, but has refused all of them. He views the court's corruption as the worse type of Wasteland inflicted on his country and he refuses to be part of it. He chooses to live a healthy life away from politics. His choice of healing is to seclude himself and not be part of the problem. P'ang actually inspires the governor of his district to do the same.

Catching Fish by Ni Tuan
(15th century A.C.E.)

National Palace Museum, Taipei
Ink and Color on Silk. 46 3/8 x 16 5/8 in.

The first *Avatar* (incarnation) of Vishnu was of Matsya, the Fish. The earth was flooded, so Vishnu ordered Satyavrata to go to a boat with the seven great sages and specimens from all animals and plants. In the form of a giant, gold fish, Vishnu pulled the boat until the waters subsided. This is very similar to the story of Noah and the Ark.

Jungians view the fishing in the lake as delving deep into the unconscious to reveal what lives buried in our psyches. Once we catch something, we can begin the healing process. It is appropriate that Parzival's Fisher King doesn't catch anything because he cannot heal himself. It will take a better fisherman than himself.

Perhaps a fisherman like Forrest Gump, who creates Bubba Gump Shrimping Company. It takes his boat to help the maimed Lt. Dan get on his course to healing. I bet you thought that fishing motif was just a clever device of the author. Now you know that there was some real conscious (or unconscious) work put into the story. Marlow and Willard must search their course on the water. Will Hunting and Jack Lucas are on the shores of the Atlantic, while Roy Hobbs slams homers next to Lake Michigan. Jenny lives on Creek More Avenue with her grandmother and unites with Forrest at the reflecting pond in Washington D.C.'s Mall. Plenty of fishing to be done.

Throwing in a Monkey Wrench

You now have an idea that there is a king, he is wounded, he must be healed, and then the world will be fine. Now, I'm going to throw in a monkey wrench and splinter the problem. *Parzival* doesn't deal with just one wounded king, but three. All three kingdoms suffer and all three must be healed. I knew Wolfram was a smart man and woudn't just repeat himself. Each King must represent something. After careful reading, thought, and analysis, I saw a pattern emerge that made not only common sense, but spiritual sense. Each king will be highlighted as we go through the story, but you should have an idea about what each one represents.

The three kings are Anfortas, Clinschor, and Arthur.

Anfortas is the King of Munsalvaesche, the Mountain of Salvation, the Grail Castle. He is the one known as the Fisher King. His kingdom is the Kingdom of the Spirit. That is why the focus is on him as the primary wounded king. He has been speared in the thigh, a metaphor for the wounding of the genitals, or fertility—the fertility of the Spirit. If the Spirit is failing, nothing else matters. The healing of this wound is predicated upon compassion.

Clinschor is the wounded Mage King of the Land of Wonders, also known as the Land of Maidens. He once was the lover of a queen, but as soon as their affair was discovered, he was castrated by the queen's husband. Talk about wounded genitals! Clinschor has cursed the lands and it will take tests of bravery to remove the dark magic. His realm is the Kingdom of the Individual.

Arthur is the King of Britain. His loss of fertility is demonstrated when his only son is killed in battle. His kingdom has become weak, and he, with most of his knights, has become a coward. His kingdom is the Kingdom of the Community. Action will heal this realm.

This is the triad of kingdoms which must be healed for all to be healed and this is the trinity of our own lives. All three kingdoms are tied together and if one is out of kilter, than the other two will follow suit.

Though bound together, there is a hierarchy. Foremost, our own Spirit must be healthy. If our hearts cannot sing, if our eyes cannot recognize the wonders around us, if we cannot touch in love, we become automatons that are dead to our bliss.

We must also take care of our Individual lives through the development of skills to achieve what we want, and to balance our relationships with our family and friends. We learn that the Spirit and the physical world of the Individual go hand in hand. We can extend our own healing to those in our business, family, and school, and what we do there feeds back to our spiritual life. In fact, if we do not make deliberate efforts to make our lives right with others, we can never achieve the final healing of the Spirit.

Once our Spiritual and Individual lives have met their tests, then the Community can heal. We can rush about negotiating here, and throwing money there, but without strong, compassionate individuals, the results will be temporary and weak.

Every year I create my own Holiday cards to celebrate Christmas, Hanukkah, Kwanzaa, Winter Solstice, Ramadan, et al. Several years ago, I reflected this connection principle of the Spirit through the Individual to the Community with these words:

When the heart is at peace,
The family is at peace.
When the family is at peace,
The town is at peace.
When the town is at peace,
The nation is at peace.
When the nation is at peace,
The world is at peace.

We wish you peace in your hearts.

For us to Heal the Fisher King and the Wasteland, we start with ourselves and make ourselves happy, well, and whole. We then direct our energies to our immediate families and friends, and this goodness will spill over to the community. Oftentimes, people start working on the outside problems, ignoring themselves, but this leads to a breakdown in health and builds resentment. For lasting results, we need to work from the Inner to the Outer, from the Spirit to the World.

The Kingdoms of Your Life

Some of you may think the only way to achieve your Grail is to give up on everything else in your life and concentrate on just one thing. You may end up happier in that one aspect of life, but you will not find total satisfaction and peace unless your life is in balance. Let's explore the Kingdoms of your Life.

1. The Kingdom of the Spirit

This Kingdom is where the Grail is kept. Now look deeper and make the connection of your Spiritual Life to your Grail. Describe the uplifting feelings that you would experience if you were in the presence of your Grail. Then feel these sensations. Even if we are not directly involved with our Grail, we can begin to experience its goodness. Note how your life would feel in the presence of your Grail.

2. Kingdom of the Individual

The Kingdom of the Individual is important because that is where we spend most of our time. It involves our personal life, from our loved ones and our profession to our health and our living environment. It involves the most immediate concerns of our life. Jot down what you would like to improve in these areas. Imagine that you have found a certain peace and wholeness from having found your path to your Grail, and see how this would benefit these other important realms of your life.

3. Kingdom of the Community

Now expand your thinking to see how your work on your Spirit and your Individual life could benefit the Community. Sometimes, people think that the Community can only be helped with large amounts of cash and time. Without that, they give up thinking that they are a force in the Community. What is most important is realizing that when we do goodness in our life, it extends and ripples through the Universe. Note how achieving your own personal Grail passes from you to your Immediate Life and out to the World at large.

We've so far examined the Wasteland and the Maimed King, and brushed up against the Grail. However, the Maimed King is incapable of healing himself, so we must meet the Good Knight who will.

Illustration by Gustave Doré (1832–1883)

Chapter 2 - The Great Fool Rides the Red Horse of Tao

I was the first of the fools
(So I dreamed)
And all the fools of the world
were put into me and I was
the biggest fool of all.
— from the poem "Dreaming Fool" by Carl Sandburg

I been a idiot since I was born.
— Forrest Gump in *Forrest Gump* by Winston Groom

We are all the Fool. Not exactly like Forrest Gump, with his IQ of 75, but a fool nonetheless. Skylar tells Will Hunting he's an idiot, while Marlow in the film *Heart of Darkness* asks the Doctor if he thinks Marlow is a fool. Thankfully, there are two types of fools. One is the common, ordinary, stumbling-through-life fool. The other is what the Celts called the *Amadan Mor,* the Great Fool.

The first type is the one we are when we are completely ignorant and innocent about the world around us. How many times were you absolutely sure about the reality of a situation, but after more information or introspection, discover that the truth may even be the complete opposite? Our lives are filled with distractions, agendas, and disasters that appear out of nowhere. We lament with "If I had only known."

Sometimes innocence can be alluring. But it also causes problems. Ordinary fools are not aware of the consequences of their actions. This is part of their quest: to discover how they fit into the great cosmos, and realize—sometimes with celebration, sometimes with despair—that they have directly affected the lives of others.

Parzival will appear in Arthur's court dressed as a fool. His initial adventures will reflect his lack of concern for others and poor judgment of situations. He will go through many trials to break the chrysalis of the Fool, eventually emerging as the Grail King.

Being a fool has nothing to do with intelligence. Will Hunting is a mathematical genius, but he is a fool because he cannot relate to the world which is ready and willing to reward him with fame, finance, and love. Jack, the radio shock jock, easily manipulates the people around him as he believes he is above everyone else. His foolishness rebounds on him with a fury when his words inflame a young man to kill diners in a restaurant. Willard in *Apocalypse Now* thinks he knows it all with his knowledge of covert actions, but is stunned to be pulled in by a man with an unusual conscience in the midst of mayhem. Siddhartha has been sheltered from the world at large and cloistered in a cage of comfort. Being the fool has nothing to do with intelligence and everything to do with keeping our eyes, ears, and souls closed.

The Great Fool is the master unconcerned with the distractions of the "normal" world. The Buddhist monk who seals his senses to the earthly world is one. The Druid priest, sprawled in his cold stone *cochclan,* dark to the lush Celtic nature, silently concentrating on the essential, is another. This is the nature of the Great Fool. He may not answer to questions of others' physics or grammars, but he is patient in his own development. Once he knows his true course, he is unfailing in his pursuit of it.

To move from being an ordinary fool to the Great Fool is to move from blindness and ignorance to a life of potential, hope, and righteousness. Do not worry that it has taken you awhile to do so; as Wolfram writes of Parzival, he was *"A courageous man slowly becoming wise—"*

Foolish Images

Rider-Waite Deck

The Tarot deck contains a card called The Fool, which is the Joker in the modern deck of playing cards. When we look at the card, we see the attributes of what it is to be a fool. Our fool wears a cap of leaves and a feather, showing he is of the natural world. This is our natural state, foolish and ignorant, and we must be kind to ourselves as no one is exempt from this state. That cap looks very similar to the one Jack Lucas wears as he enters the fortress that houses the "Grail." The fool's clothes on the Tarot card are spotted with the Wheels of Fortune, indicating that we have many opportunities. How to fully utilize those opportunities becomes a lifelong challenge. The fool gazes upwards, unaware that he is about to walk off a cliff. He is saved by the yapping dog at his heels. That dog is one of those caring creatures that comes from the OtherWorld. For some, it may be the Angel over your shoulder or a friendly spirit guide. More importantly, it is our Intuition. As we go through the story, we will see that it is just as important to rely on an Inner Mirror, our own sense of judgment, as well as the learned dictates of society. Doing the Right Thing may come from a source within, rather than without. We must always keep our intuitive friend close by, as the outer world may distract us.

More so, across the fool's shoulders is a staff with a satchel, which just happens to have an Eye. It is the All-Seeing Eye, which looks out from Buddhist stupas and from the pyramid on the lowly U.S. one dollar bill. It is the Third Eye that illuminates Inner Truth and Wisdom. It is the eye of the One-Eyed Herdsman who guards entrances to the OtherWorld. Inside the bag are the mysteries of the elements found in the Tarot; our fool has all the secrets, but he just keeps them crushed in a heap, like our own mysteries and natural talents. They're there, waiting to be used, but we merrily swing along, ignorant of what we have. The fool carries a rose in his left hand; perhaps he just innocently picked it as he climbed the mountain. That is no ordinary rose. It is the Alchemical Rose, the Mystical Rose, and we have seen it in its splendor as sunlight streaming through the Rose stained glass window in Chartres.

The Orient's idea of the Great Fool exists as one of the Eight Immortals, Li Tieh-kuai. Li was a mystic, whose mortal form was accidentally destroyed while he was out soul surfing, and he had to take on the body of a beggar. Coincidentally, the Fool in Western myth also comes back to life in a Mummers' play where a Rose Elixir is used to revive a slain Fool. We can see in the illustrations that there are many similarities of our Western and Eastern Fools. Both carry a staff and bag of magic, both are poised on a precipice and both have a magical plant. Our Western Fool has the Rose that Transforms, and our Eastern Fool has a Gourd which Heals and Restores Life. Transformation, Healing, and Restoration are all attributes of the Grail.

The Taoist Immortal, Li Tieh-kuai
by Yen Hui (14th century A.C.E.)
Kyoto National Museum, Japan
Ink and Color on Silk. 31 ⅞ x 63 ¾ in.

The court jester was more than just a stand-up comic; he was certainly a Great Fool. He could satirize the political situation of the court, revealing truths that would cause others to lose their heads. In Native American culture, there is the *heyoka.* He is the person who heard the voices on the wind, and bathed in sand, and was a living *koan* for others to check the sanity and value of their own lives.

We only have to look at our own Charlie Chaplin in his hobo caricature to see the same innocent, silly, woeful figure. Notice the word "silly?" The original meaning of silly was "blessed" and "happy" which went through various evolutions including "pious, innocent, harmless, feeble" and finally "foolish." The roots of our foolishness is our blessedness, and that is something that we should not forget. Whatever errors and faux pas we may create in our foolish lives, we are at the very base, Blessed.

Pablo Picasso painted a family of circus performers, titled *Family of Saltimbanques.* It is a family of fools, entertainers who lamentably wait for their next performance in life. They wear the expression of the fool who did not know he was blessed, who did not know he was great. Rainer Maria Rilke, the German poet, lived with this painting and was inspired to write of it in his *Duino Elegies.*

But tell me, who are they, these acrobats, even a little
more fleeting than we ourselves—so urgently, ever since childhood,
wrung by an (oh, for the sake of whom?)
never-contented will? That keeps on wringing them,
bending them, slinging them, swinging them,
throwing them and catching them back; as though from an oily
smoother air, they come down on the threadbare
carpet, thinned by their everlasting
upspringing, this carpet forlornly
lost in the cosmos.
— from "Fifth Elegy" by Rainer Maria Rilke

Family of Saltimbanques by Pablo Picasso (1881–1973)
National Gallery of Art, Chester Dale Collection
Oil on Canvas, 1905. 83 ¾ x 90 ⅜ in.
©2000 Board of Trustees, National Gallery of Art, Washington D.C.

We are all fools, but we have a choice in life to open the magical bag that we carry. We have a chance to transform ourselves and we can be reborn many times. We have a sturdy staff to carry us over the hills, we must only open our eyes to the land we walk in and not be "lost in the cosmos." We must not ignore our intuition as we embark on our adventures, taking us through many landscapes fraught with hidden dangers. We then can move from the common fool to the Great Fool; a Fool of Destiny, Promise, and Intuition.

Playing the Fool

It can be a joyful discovery to admit our own foolishness, especially if we remember that "foolish" once meant "blessed." Do these exercises with an attitude of forgiveness for yourself.

1. Pause to think of the good and the bad that has resulted from the innocence and the ignorance of your life's actions. Reflect on the wisdom this has given you.

2. Reacquaint yourself with how your Intuition helped you (or could have helped) when the Outer World gave no clues. Remind yourself to consult with your Inner Knowing as well as your outer senses.

Riding the Red Horse of Tao

Under heaven all can see beauty as beauty only because there is ugliness.
All can know good as good only because there is evil.

— *Tao Te Ching* by Lao Tzu

His horse had certain qualities—hard work was nothing, if it was hot or cold, if it journeyed over stones and tree trucks, it would not sweat. If Parzival rode for two days, he did not have to adjust the saddle strap by even one notch. Fully armed, the simple lad rode in one day what a wiser man, without armor, would ride in two.

— from *Parzival,* Book III, ¶ 161

Parzival is one of the most Taoist books I have ever read. There are three main themes underlying Taoism—one is the Duality of Life, one is the Interdependence of Life, the other is following the Flow of Life.

The Duality of Life is represented with the Yin/Yang symbol, shown as the page marker in this chapter. Yin (the dark color) is the feminine, Yang (light color) is the masculine. Together, they make a whole while a little bit of each drips into the other's center and their tails swirl into each other's head like mixing cake batter. We know this innately. Male and Female balance. Light and Dark. Rain and Sunshine. Mountains and Valleys. Good and Bad. *ad infinitum*

The Interdependence of Life says that everyone, everything, and every action are connected. A band of butterflies beats its wings in Africa, causing that last drift of wind to start rain, which tracks across the Atlantic over an orange grove in Central Florida, giving life to oranges that are squeezed by migrants from Cuba, and the juice is packed in a cardboard container to be consumed by an Eskimo in Alaska. On top of that are the meteorologists who tracked the rain, the harvester of the trees who made the cardboard boxes, the train engineers who delivered the juice, the store that carried the juice, and so on. We know this, but we rarely live our lives realizing this. We are myopic in our choices in life, when we should be using our All-Seeing Eye.

Will Hunting declines a job at the NSA by demonstrating how code breaking could affect everything from the fish in the ocean to a man losing his job in his neighborhood. One of the simplest connections we have with all of humanity was one shown in *Forrest Gump* when Jenny and Forrest both stare at the moon, though they are thousands of miles apart. It is the same moon you and I look at. It is the same one our ancestors pondered for millenniums before us.

The Flow of Life is to follow nature. At the most basic level, this would be to live with the seasons and in harmony with the world. At the highest level, it is subtly realizing your unique place in the world and effortlessly following along the path that was meant for you. This is your Destiny.

Some readers may find it difficult that I am applying an Oriental term to German literature written in the late twelfth/early thirteenth century, but Wolfram von Eschenbach lived in Germany during exciting times. During that time, the Templars, or The Order of the Poor Knights of Christ and the Temple of Solomon, were on the march, and bringing back treasures from the Orient; not only silks and metal filigrees, but legends, writings, and mystical practices from nomadic tribes, elite warriors, and tradespeople traversing the continents. The Cathars were defying the Roman Church with their concept of the Prince of Light and the Prince of Darkness, with the church advancing its own dualism of God and Satan. Wolfram recognized a wisdom that embraces a vision of a total world, comprising of varying degrees of opposites, and contemplated on what it is for a hero to live in such a world.

The Tao of Gump

The movie *Forrest Gump* opens with a single, silken, floating, white feather. It must be the feather that was in our Tarot Fool's cap as he stood at the mountain cliff. It drifts towards earth, snatched up by invisible gusts of wind, whirled by passing cars, finally landing at the feet of Forrest Gump. A striking composition of opposites with that simple, white feather lying on his dirty running shoes. He is sensitive to the little feather and he picks it up to be preserved in his favorite book, *Curious George.* Others had the opportunity to glimpse the feather through their windshield, and it almost landed on one man's shoulder, but it is Gump who takes it and makes it his own and incorporates it into his own life. That feather is Destiny.

Parzival also opens with a Taoist vision. Wolfram's metaphor is the magpie, the bird that is both black and white. Throughout the book, we see the clash of opposites, with Wolfram choosing the way that melts and blends the two together. Even Parzival's name is interpreted to be *perce à val,* "pierce the valley," or "right through the middle."

Forcing the Buffalo by Fan Niu
Private Collection, Ink and Color on Paper, 1987. 27 ¾ x 14 ⅝ in.

The first line in *Parzival* says that if the heart wavers, the soul will be unhappy. Gump epitomizes this statement. He does not have to choose between his white friend Lt. Dan, nor his black friend, Bubba, because his heart does not waver; it has the peace of following the middle valley where love for both reside. When he is given a command, his heart tells him what is right. When he is told to put his rifle together quickly, his heart knows it's okay to do so, and does it. When Lt. Dan tells him not to go back in the jungle to look for the wounded Bubba, Gump's heart chooses the right course. When Jenny drifts in and out of his life, a situation that would make most men write her off, Gump still does not waver.

Anyone who comes along, anything that comes along, is fine with Forrest. He rides with the opportunities of life. Parzival rides a magic red horse that he cannot control. Gawan, who is an alter ego of Parzival, rides a horse with red ears. These are horses of the OtherWorld, more specifically, of the Grail Castle. Once Parzival says giddyap, the horse takes him where he is suppose to go and does not stop until they get to their Destination. Poor Parzival doesn't even know what the destination is when he first mounts the horse.

Zen mystics use an Ox to represent our relationship to our True Nature. The parable tells of a young boy who has lost his ox, and must leave his home to search for it. He finds clues along the way, which he follows until he sees the ox. The boy approaches the ox, but the creature balks and runs away. The boy again catches up with the ox, and the two struggle. Only when the boy stops struggling can they work together peaceably. The ox now allows the boy to ride him and both are joyful. The boy can now achieve spiritual enlightenment, and later return to the world.

The path of the Grail is the same. We lose our own True Nature and must go search for it. We see clues along the way and even come into the presence of the Grail, but we don't know how to achieve the Quest of the Grail. There is much struggling along this path, but when we can finally accept who we are, we are able to achieve the Grail. Riding a Zen Ox or a Red Horse gifted from the OtherWorld will take us there, but we must stop struggling within ourselves.

Roy Hobbs rides a train taking him to the tryouts for the Chicago Cubs. Will Hunting rides Boston's trains between South Boston and Harvard. Luke Skywalker and Han Solo cruise the universe in the *Millennium Falcon.* Willard takes a boat through the dangers of Vietnam towards Cambodia. Marlow must dig his boat out of the muck to make his trek into the Heart of the Congo. Destiny does take effort. The Tao always presents our Destiny to us in some way, but it is the Duality of Tao that makes it so difficult to know which train or boat to get on. Few of us have Red Fairy Horses outside our doors snorting with all of the answers. There are always choices in front of us, but finding the one that we were meant to follow can be agonizing, though eventually, rewarding.

The Yin/Yang of Parzival

> *A green hunting cap squeezed the top of the fleshy balloon of a head. The green earflaps, full of large ears and uncut hair and the fine bristles that grew in the ears themselves, stuck out on either side like turn signals indicating two directions at once.*
>
> — from *A Confederacy of Dunces* by John Kennedy Toole

A Confederacy of Dunces is a Pulitzer Prize-winning novel whose main character, Ignatius Reilly, seems to be the antithesis of Parzival. But he is Parzival through and through. Ignatius is literate, but still the fool when it comes to life. Instead of being handsome like Parzival, he is overweight and rather disgusting, in a friendly sort of way. The above quote opens the novel, bringing us back to the struggle of Yin/Yang. We can see our own automobiles with a stuck turn signal pointing both ways. It is the Scarecrow giving Dorothy directions and pointing North and South.

The duality battles of Parzival are the ones we encounter everyday. Do we create our life or are we at the whim of forces beyond us? Do we follow a list of learned rules or do we count on an inner wisdom? Do we forgive ignorance or do we take responsibility? Do we alter the river or ride its flow? Do we tolerate a Wasteland or do we build a Paradise? The Freelance Photographer (Dennis Hopper) in *Apocalypse Now* reminds us that everything is simple Dialectics.

Wolfram will take on the relationships of Men and Women, Blacks and Whites, Christians and Infidels, the Real World and the OtherWorld. In spite of all of these, everything comes down to the actions of an Individual.

It is both powerful and poetic that we as individuals count. That is Tao. In the first stanza of the *Tao Te Ching,* we learn that named existence is the "mother of ten thousand things." "Ten thousand things" represents an infinity of objects, but Taoist philosophy recognizes that each individual is important. Rather than throwing everybody into an unrecognizable mass, we are enumerated and brought to a graspable concept that while there are many of us, each of us counts.

Once you know what your Grail is, you must always be prepared and look for the opportunities that can take you to it. Understand the patterns in your life that haven't allowed you to ride along the path you were meant for. In the meantime, keep a saddle ready.

Riding That Red Horse

Think of the times that you have approached your own Grail, especially the first time you were introduced to it. Was it an easy or difficult ride to get there? Did you allow it to happen, or did you fight it along the way?

Now think of the opportunities that you allowed to pass by. Why didn't you allow yourself to get on that Horse of Destiny? What part of your True "Oxen" Nature did you struggle with that stopped you from enjoying the presence of your Grail?

Even heroes with a destiny need help, inspiration, and goading to achieve their goals, so now we will meet the Women of the Grail.

Mercedes Ruehl as Anne Napolitano
in *The Fisher King*

Minnie Driver as Skylar
in *Good Will Hunting*

Robin Wright as Jenny Curran
in *Forrest Gump*

Faces of the Goddess of Sovereignty

Amanda Plummer as Lydia Sinclair
in *The Fisher King*

Carrie Fisher as Princess Leia Organa
in *Return of the Jedi*

Glenn Close as Iris Gaines
in *The Natural*

Chapter 3 - The Goddess of Sovereignty and the Grail

I met a lady in the meads,
Full beautiful—a faery's child
Her hair was long, her foot was light
And her eyes were wild.

— from the poem "La Belle Dame Sans Merci" by John Keats

It was a virtue not to stay,
To go our headstrong and heroic way
Seeking her out at the volcano's head.

— from the poem "The White Goddess" by Robert Graves

Tall and tan and young and lovely,
The Girl From Ipanema goes walking,
and when she passes,
each one she passes,
goes "a-a-h!"

— from the song "Girl from Ipanema" English lyrics by Norman Gimbel

We have held the image of the Goddess of Sovereignty in our psyches longer than any other vision. There were eons when we refused to acknowledge her, but patient Mother that she is, she waited until we decided to drop her a postcard. She has appeared in so many guises that it would take a volume just to list her many names. Sometimes she comes to us with wild eyes or hair of snakes. Sometimes she is a withered, aging woman who invites young, strapping men to her bed for a "kiss." She sleeps in hundred year slumbers until a prince slashes through bramble thorns to awaken her and her sleeping kingdom. She is the beauty of spring days, and she is the chilling death that pulls sailors to the bottom of the sea. She is the mother of heroes and gods. In fact, she is the Mother of us all. She is the Great Earth Mother.

In the *Parzival* legend, almost all of the women represent some aspect of the Goddess of Sovereignty. Ultimately, a hero must honor and fulfill his duties to this Queen of the Land for him to become King. She in turn, will give him the power, the right, the gifts, and the inspiration to make it all possible. It is the same in our personal spiritual lives. If we honor and strive to do what is right in our spiritual practice, we will be rewarded with the energy and source to enhance our own world.

There is a Yin/Yang aspect to the Goddess of Sovereignty. She may beautiful and desirable as Gwenevere or she may be ugly and demanding as the Sorceress Cundrie. As the beautiful Flower Maiden, she inspires and motivates us to strive for what is best. Sometimes we get sidetracked, so Cundrie comes riding in on her mule as the Loathly Lady and berates us to get going again. At the heart of it all, is the necessity to make a whole, healthy kingdom.

In all of the movies and books, the dual status of the Goddess of Sovereignty appears. In *The Fisher King,* Lydia inspires Parry, who fully realizes that love must be courted and earned. Jack needs a little kick in the rump from Anne, the sexy, Italian Loathly Lady. Forrest Gump's love, Jenny, shows both sides of the Goddess: deep down goodness and beauty, and drug addiction and fickle ways. Loving her is truly a test worthy of some of the *Parzival* women we will meet. Princess Leia is the Muse for Luke Skywalker and the Initiator for Han Solo in the *Star Wars* Classic Trilogy. Skylar fills both roles for Will Hunting, though we are most touched by the love of Sean Maguire for his dead wife. Iris represents what is good and best for Roy Hobbs, while he is sorely tested with a gunshot from Harriet Bird and the treachery of Memo Paris. Queen Amidala forces Anakin to action and she will become his love interest.

The Geography of the Soul

> *I began crying and swearing and socking myself on the head for being such a damn fool.... "What the hell am I doing up here?" I cursed, I cried for Chicago. "Even now they're all having a big time, they're doing this, I'm not there, when will I get there!"—and so on.... It was my dream that screwed up, the stupid hearthside idea that it would be wonderful to follow one great red line across America instead of trying various roads and routes.*
>
> — from *On the Road* by Jack Kerouac

Kerouac's lament has been the lament of many. We see other people having a wonderful life, being exactly where they want to be, accomplishing their goals, while we head off in the wrong direction. Jack was right about that initial dream. He thought the simple straight line would get him where he wanted to go, but there are so many places one has to go to really arrive.

Why do we love Road Trip stories so much?

Because at the deepest level, we know it is not the scenery that surrounds us that is so important, but the road that curves the Geography of the Soul that will make us live. In this story, we will visit forests and streams and fountains and valleys and castles and bridges. Don't think for a moment that these are accidental meeting places. They chart experience, and magic, and illumination. We know of the Wasteland which hovers over all of the lands of the soul, but to heal, we must enter the Realm of the Goddess.

Where does one find this Goddess of Sovereignty? Usually, she will send henchmen and fairy women to do her work in the real world. Occasionally, she will venture out herself if the work demands it. Most of the time, you will find her in the OtherWorld, reigning over sacred wells and groves, in a land where time is immeasurable.

The OtherWorld is a parallel universe existing in the same space as our own. Time has its own rules here. Buildings turn on their own, and mazes wind beneath ancient castles. Many times the OtherWorld is a place of testing. Streams and fountains are defended by giant knights in black armor. One-eyed herdsmen jealousy guard magic flocks. To enter the OtherWorld, one must know the mystical phrases or know the right turn in the bend of the road. More often, the OtherWorld waits for you and opens its magic portals with you unaware. A Ferryman may exact a toll for crossing her rivers and entering her enchanted territories. If you are deserving, she will give you one of her tireless Red Horses.

Typically, people have the idea that knights just ran around rescuing helpless damsels in distress, but actually these rescues were tests to determine the worthiness of a potential suitor. If you want the love of a Goddess, you better deserve her. In most fairy tales, it is the princess who rules her kingdom and needs a suitable husband to help her. Who better to help than someone who can fight dragons, lead war bands, and destroy her enemies? Even when we find women in the legends who have lost their names and are only referred to as "maidens," their presence as Initiators are still the test of worthiness. Robert Graves is not exaggerating in his poem "The White Goddess" when he says the goddess can be met at the mouth of the volcano, and it takes heroism to search her out.

The OtherWorld is, of course, the Spiritual World. If we learn to reconcile our physical world with the OtherWorld, then we have no problem knowing the magic phrases or the right turn on the road. Learning all of this is the greatest lesson we all can learn. Parzival early on has a glimpse of the OtherWorld, but he is totally unaware. We, too, get chances in life to receive the grace of this world, but we often mangle our opportunities.

When we go on our own road trips, we are searching the OtherWorld, that place of adventure which we return from with stories and insight. Luke Skywalker uses the cosmos as his OtherWorld, while Marlow enters Leopold's Congo and Willard trolls the rivers of Vietnam. Willard loses all sense of time and location in Saigon when he is readied for his quest to go after Kurtz. Both his body and his soul have grown soft and need to enter a different realm for his next stage of learning. No matter where you enter the OtherWorld, you will come back wiser and changed, whether you physically travel to it, or you spiritually enter and are refreshed by it. The most important tests of your life occur here and success here expands to all parts of your life.

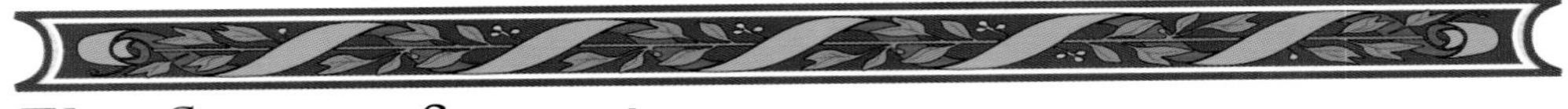

The Gifts of Sovereignty

> *Upon green achmardi (silk) she bore the pureness of Paradise, which was both root and blossoming, the thing called the Grail, more magnificent than the splendor of the earthly world.... Whatsoever man stretches his hand to receive, he finds it readied for him in front of the Grail.*
>
> — from *Parzival,* Book v, ¶ 235, 238

In Arthurian tales, the queens and maidens—the disguised goddess we just met—tend to hand out and present gifts to potential heroes to help them in their tasks. Fairy Godmothers are always conjuring up special gifts to help their chosen prodigies. It can be a ring, or cloak, or sword that has magical powers. The Grail is the most significant of these and we only see it held and protected by the Grail Maiden. She is the one who presents it in the Grail Ceremony, and allows all who are worthy to be in its presence to receive the abundance it promises.

One of the first questions I am asked when friends discover that I study the Grail and Arthurian legends is "What is the Grail?"

Anyone who has studied the legends can only smile because they know that it encompasses such a wide variety of interpretations, that it becomes a daunting task to explain briefly. It seems a simple question, but scholars still debate what the Grail is, what it signifies, and where it came from. Is it Celtic, Christian, Scythian, Chymical, Transformative, French, Irish, Pagan, a Cup, a Stone, a Cauldron, a Platter, a Body, Magical, Occidental, or Feminine? My answer to this is: all of the above and much more. Each legend around the Grail has derived its own vital mythology and there are noted writings on all of the above meanings. I am going to concentrate on what I consider to be the most important concept—that the Grail represents what lies truly and deeply in your heart. It is what you are in exile from and you will never be satisfied until you achieve it.

For each of us, what lies deepest in our hearts is unique, and the depth of our suffering from not having our heart's need can be silent and constricted, or barbaric and uncontrollable. This Grail promises joy if only you find it.

Gifts of Your Life

Think of the Gifts that others have given you that have empowered and enlarged your life. These may not be material items, but teachings and skills that have served you. How you can pass these Gifts onto others?

The Riders of the Sidhe by John McKirdy Duncan (1866–1945)

Dundee Art Galleries. Tempera, 1911. 45 x 69 in.

The Forms of the Grail

The Grail is one of many Hallows, or Holy objects, found in various mythologies. Celtic myth provides one of the most accessible categorizing of the Hallows as it presents The Four Hallows. They are the Cup/Chalice, the Disc (Plate or Orb), the Sword, and the Spear. Though the Chalice as Grail gets the most press, the other Hallows are important, because they provide balance and strength. John Duncan beautifully illustrates fairy women known as *Sidhe* (pronounced shee), carrying the Four Hallows in his painting *The Riders of the Sidhe.* By the way, *Sidhe* is also from the same universal root found in the name Siddhartha. The Sanskrit word *siddhi* means "achievement, success, fulfillment." Siddhartha's name has been translated to mean "rich in magic."

Besides those, there is another significant representation of the Grail as Stone, which is the Grail of the *Parzival* story. This could be considered a form of the Disc, though some people consider it a fifth transmutation.

One of the earliest forms of the Grail is the Cauldron. It is no accident that this early form is the shape of the womb, harkening to a time when the Earth Mother was held in supreme awe. It is her Spirit that shapes the legends. Just as the family cauldron could cook the foods and formulate the medicines to sustain life, the cauldron of legends gave food, life, and poetry.

The Magic Circle
by John William Waterhouse (1849–1917)
Tate Callery, London. Oil on Canvas, 1886. 72 x 50 in.
Photo: Tate Gallery, London / Art Resource, N.Y.

In the Welsh version of *Parzival,* "Peredur Son of Evrawg," which is found in *The Mabinogion,* women nightly bathe the dead sons of the King of Suffering in a tub, which brings the men back to life. Also in *The Mabinogion* is the story of "Branwen Daughter of Llyr," where heroes are also brought to life, but cannot speak. In these examples, we see the Cauldron of Rebirth and Regeneration.

In Welsh legend, Gwion tastes the magic potion of wisdom that the goddess Cerridwen has boiled up in her Cauldron for her son, Morfrans. Angry that Gwion has stolen the potion, she chases him, both changing shapes throughout the pursuit, until she eats Gwion as a wheat grain while she is a chicken. Nine months later, she gives birth to the poet/bard Taliesin, who is considered an historical figure. The Grail here is shown as a source of Wisdom and Poetry.

In *The Welsh Triads,* Merlin is entrusted with the care of the Thirteen Treasures of Britain, including the Cauldron of Dyrnwch. This Cauldron has an unusual attribute: it does not boil meat for a coward, and boils meat quickly for a brave man, thus separating the two. Certainly bravery is a trait to keep in mind when searching for what lies in our hearts. Or is it that our heart's desire will give us bravery?

In many of the Grail legends, including *Parzival,* the Grail supplies an abundance of food, of the type each individual yearns for. It is the same legend as the Horn of Amalthea, who was the she-goat goddess who fed Zeus. Her horn flowed with food and flowers, and was the forerunner of our Cornucopia, the Horn of Plenty. If we look to the source of our heart's nourishment, it will always be filled.

Throughout stories, we see women who "boil, boil, toil and trouble" over a cauldron of magic. They are but offshoots of the Threefold Goddess, whether they are

Shakespeare's witches, the Norns at the Well of Destiny, or a Disney sorceress conjuring visions and potions. Modern versions of these all-knowing women make them wicked, but that is just the flip side of the Grail. One must be worthy to receive the goodness of the Grail. The unworthy may find themselves blinded, as Lancelot was in Malory's version.

The Mystical Knight by Odilon Redon (1840–1916)

Bordeaux Musées des Beaux-Arts
Charcoal and Pastel on Beige Paper, 1869. 39 3/8 x 32 in.
© Cliché du M.B.A. de Bordeaux / photographe Lysiane Gauthier

The Grail may take the form of a platter, also part of the Disc Hallow. Besides having a motif of serving foods at a feast, the Disc Hallow also has other connotations. Some legends view it as the paten, which carries the host of the Eucharist, the sacrament of Holy Communion. For Peredur, a more sinister item is presented on the platter—the head of a man. When Willard is tied up, Kurtz delivers Chef's head on Willard's lap. Shocking as this may seem, the Cult of the Head has flourished through many mythologies. The Jews tell the story of Judith with the head of Holofernes. Christians give us John the Baptist beheaded at the request of Salome. The Norse have the head of Mimir, which dispenses wisdom at the root of the World Tree, Yggdrasil. The Head of Bran figures prominently in Celtic legend. It instructed followers in esoteric knowledge through the Mysteries, and kept the enemies of Britain at bay when buried in the ground looking out over the sea where foes would attack. Pict warriors (a tribe of Scotland) preserved the heads of fierce opponents as trophies. One of our beginning examples, that of the Eucharist, represents the blood and body of Christ, reduced to an earthly symbol.

Odilon Redon frequently depicted the Cult of the Head in his drawings and pastel renderings. One of my favorites is *The Mystical Knight,* where a knight encounters a Sphinx. I surmise that the head he carries will give the correct answer to the Sphinx's question, allowing the knight to continue his spiritual journey.

Though we feel a little squeamish discussing dismembered bodies and heads, we are never far removed from the spiritual dismemberment many people feel. Somewhere, a part of us that was cut off a long time ago holds the wisdom that gives us direction and strength. Rather than viewing this as simply a macabre relic, we can envision it as a source of Wisdom.

The cauldron shrank in size to a manageable cup or chalice. The Welsh legends do talk of cauldrons strapped to the backs of the caretakers for moving, but if we are going to have elegant Grail processions, we must have exquisite cups. Whichever came first, the cauldron or the cup, is left to debate, but the cup is one of the most important forms of the Grail, because it is the one that most people envision.

Most commonly, people think of the cup that Christ drank from at the Last Supper. This image helped fuel the Crusades, or perhaps more correctly, helped manipulate the politics of the Crusades. The introduction of Christ's cup as the Grail was in Robert de Boron's poem "Joseph d'Arimathie" (1200 A.C.E.). In this story, Pilate gives Joseph the cup from the Last Supper and Joseph uses it to catch Jesus' blood at the cross. Joseph is imprisoned when Christ's tomb is found opened, but he is nourished by the Grail. Jesus comes to him, saying Joseph will be the Guardian of the Grail. After Joseph's release, he takes the Grail to Britain with his band of followers and settles at Glastonbury. The Grail in this case takes on the visage as a Cup of Redemption. To drink from it would be to drink from God's grace.

Besides being a Cup of Redemption, it is also the Cup of Kingship, which the Goddess of Sovereignty offers. This motif plays an important part to Parzival's introduction to Arthur's court, as Ginover's (Gwenevere's) cup is stolen as an insult to the kingdom. The Peredur legend contains Three Cups of Sovereignty which are given to Peredur by the Empress of Constantinople, which he then passes to the Miller's Wife.

The cup is important to us in modern times as Restorative and Honoring. We greet guests with liquid refreshments, and we honor people with toasts of fine wines. These customs follow tradition over many years in many lands. As generous as we are to others, we must also offer this cup to ourselves.

The Disc can enlarge and become a Table. You guessed it, a Round Table. Many interpret the Round Table as a politically equalizing tool, but that is only an afterthought. The Round Table was a wedding gift from Gwenevere to Arthur, a continuing of the Goddess of Sovereignty giving her gift to her consort of the Sacred Marriage. The Kingdom becomes spiritually whole when the Goddess of Sovereignty marries the King of the Land. In some legends, Merlin creates the Round Table. In the Vulgate Cycle, Merlin orders the making of the Round Table for Uther (Arthur's father), following the Trinity. He says the first table was the one of the Last Supper. Then, when Joseph took the Cup of Christ, a second table was built to be The Grail Table. The Round Table was then to be the final object of the Sacred Trinity of Tables. Gnostic thought recognized the trinity as being comprised of the Father-Son-Mother, with the Mother being represented by the Dove. In Christian theology, she was replaced as the Holy Spirit.

Whether a gift of the goddess, or a table of the Holy Spirit, the legends meant the Round Table to be more than just a table where quarreling men would feel equal.

> *"Grandfather," the Youngman said, "I hear that somewhere there Exists a Singing Stone, and that when it is Found, it will Hold great medicine for its Finder. Is this True?"*
>
> — from *Seven Arrows* by Hyemeyosts Storm

The Native Americans had a healing stone and in the *Parzival* saga, the Grail is a stone. Muslims have a sacred stone of forgiveness called the Ka'bba. It is the black stone in the Great Mosque in Mecca, and is considered a gift to Adam after his expulsion from Eden.

The Grail in *Parzival* serves a function similar to the platter, but with special legends attached to it. It was called *lapsit exillis.* There is no direct Latin translation, which could have been due to Wolfram's misunderstanding of a phrase, or a copying problem of manuscripts. The closest translations make it *lapis ex caelis,* "stone from the heavens;" *lapsit ex caelis,* "it fell from the heavens;" *lapis elixir,* "Philosopher's Stone;" and *lapis lapsus ex caelis,* "a stone fallen from heaven." When I look closely at the differing characteristics and the story, I imagine that Wolfram purposely made up his own "Latin" because he wanted us to view all of the meanings.

The Philosopher's Stone fits in the Parzival legend. Long before Harry Potter searched for his Philosopher's/Sorcerer's Stone, medieval Alchemists were pursuing theirs. These Alchemists were the forerunners of our modern chemists, but their ostensibly quaint formulas contained more than ill directed chances for creating gold from base materials. While these early scientists were experimenting in the physical world, they were also working side by side with a philosophical base. Perhaps they weren't able to create gold from tin, but this is certainly a gemstone of philosophical thought. The Alchemists sought the Philosopher's Stone, which would create a perfect substance, such as gold, from the ordinary. Even with such a Stone, it took refinement, refinement, refinement. This is an invaluable lesson for us. We can take what is ordinary (ourselves) and work our refinement until we reach perfection. What is interesting is that this Philosopher's Stone was known as the Universal Medicine. What ever came in contact with it would be healed. Certainly a faithful motif for our story.

The legend of the Grail as stone fits in with the other translations. Parzival learns during his journey that the Grail resided in Heaven until God and Lucifer had their falling out. Some angels took God's side, some took Lucifer's side, but the Neutral Angels were the ones who came to earth with the Grail to give to humankind. I absolutely adore this image. It fits a Taoist image of living between ultimate opposites, as all humans do, but it is comforting to know we have our own band of angels working on our side.

Balance of the Grail

Illustration by Louis Rhead (1857–1926)

The Grail is one of several holy objects known as Hallows. The feminine Yin side is represented with the forms we just discussed. The round, nurturing forms of the Disc and Cup/Cauldron, give us Spiritual sustenance. However, we cannot always drift in good feeling utopias where Mom is always feeding us delicious morsels. Sometimes, we must be out in that real world, developing skills and earning the right to be in the presence of the Grail. The Balance of the Disc and Cup is achieved with the presence of the Sword and Spear. They are considered the masculine Yang element.

The Sword is found as a power element throughout the Arthurian legends. The most famous is Excaliber, given to Arthur by the Lady of the Lake. When Parzival first comes to the Grail castle, he is given a wondrous sword with a ruby hilt, which is the sign he should ask the healing question. In *Parzival,* Gawan will also be enlisted to search for the Grail, but in the *Perlesvaus,* he must search for the Sword that beheaded John the Baptist (back to that Cult of the Head). Peredur is given a sword which breaks and must be mended. In Malory's version, the Sword of David is placed in a ship ordered built by Solomon's wife to be carried upon the seas for years until claimed by the Grail winners. The important one-on-one battles in the *Star Wars* series are fought with swords and staffs—weapons directly wielded by individual skill. No matter what, one must have The Sword to find The Grail. We must have worldly skills to survive at the physical level while we seek the spiritual.

The Spear is the weapon which Wounds and Heals, because it is Truth. The Fisher King will be wounded with a spear in the thigh. Parzival will kill the Red Knight with his javelin, a light spear. A bleeding spear marks the Grail Procession. In a few legends, the bleeding spear is Longinus' spear, the one that pierced Christ's side. Just as Cauldrons and Cups interchange, we have Clubs and Staffs that can replace the spear. Joseph of Arimathea walks to Britain aided by a staff, which sprouts into a thorn bush at Glastonbury when planted in the ground. The Welsh legends have giants who overlook portals to the OtherWorld, one-eyed and brandishing great clubs. In a few cases, we have one-horned stags, sometimes referred to as unicorns.

As a Healing implement, Anfortas will find temporary relief from sticking the Spear in his wound. The Spear coagulates the poison in Anfortas' blood, so some of the pain is reduced when this poison is removed. In Malory's story, Galahad heals the Maimed

King by touching the wound with blood from the spear tip. Medieval writings note that the rust from spears was sometimes used as a type of homeopathic medicine to heal wounds. We make a full circle with the spear as Truth can Harm, but eventually Truth can be used for Lasting Healing.

What Makes the Grail Holy?

As you may notice, I use the term Grail, not Holy Grail. In most of the legends, the vessel, no matter what form, is called the Grail, not the Holy Grail. Some people considered it holy when Robert de Boron made it the cup of Christ in his story. Some legends made the Grail procession and eating from the Grail a ritual of the Eucharist, again a holy act.

There was an interesting theory that there may have been several linguistic misunderstandings which allowed new interpretations of the Grail legend. One possible misinterpretation was from the word *cors benoit,* which meant Blessed Horn, as in the Horn of Plenty. However, the word *cors* can also mean body, so one could translate the passage to mean, Blessed Body, referring to the body of Christ. Another linguistic note involves the use of *San Graal* or Holy Grail being read as *SangRaal,* which is Holy Blood, another Eucharist motif. Though there are scholars who disagree with this theory, I still like the idea of viewing the symbols of the Grail legend from several vantage points. Layperson etymology alone cannot be used as the definitive source for scholarly mythological examination, but it certainly can be used creatively, giving us fresh insights. We will use this type of creative scrutinizing several times in this book. It's just like Luke Skywalker figuring out Old Ben was Obi-Wan Ben.

For me, ultimately the term *Holy* has to refer to the original root of the word—to make Whole. The ultimate power of the Grail is its ability to transform and make a person whole as he pursues his life's destiny. In this sense, it becomes the most Holy of objects.

"And Down the Long Beam Stole the Holy Grail"
by M. L. (Maria Louise) Kirk (*1860–1930*)
Illustration, 1912

It's Not Just For Olden Times

You may think that all of these symbols just exist in stories that are a thousand years old, but I assure you that they exist in a very tangible form today. Queen Elizabeth II was surrounded by the Four Hallows at her coronation. In her right hand she held the Orb, symbol of the world, reminiscent of the Disc. In her left hand was the scepter, which could be construed to be the Sword. In her crown is a point, symbol of the Spear Tip. Below her is the Lia Fail Stone, better known as the Stone of Destiny.

The Lia Fail Stone was the Coronation Stone of the Scots, and for the last thousand years of British Kings and Queens. Legend places it back even further to the Milesian Kings of Ireland, coronated on the sacred hill of Tara. The most ancient story is that it is the stone that Jacob slept on, hence it is called Jacob's Pillar-Stone.

The attributes fit the concept of the Grail, in that only the worthy may sit above it. It will emit a bone chilling scream when a rightful monarch comes to it, certainly the shriek of the fairy women, the *Bean Sidhe,* from where we get our word *banshee.* An unworthy person could be destroyed. This story becomes the Siege Perilous, the Perilous Seat, which in Arthurian legends was an empty seat placed at the Round Table. It would only be filled by the person destined to be the Grail winner. In the *Didot-Perceval,* Perceval rashly sits in the Siege Perilous when warned not to. The Stone beneath the chair splits and the ground opens up with an "agonizing sound." A voice booms that the promise to keep it empty until the greatest knight came had been broken. Had it not been for his heritage, Perceval would have been swallowed up. The voice tells of the Grail and how the Fisher King must be healed with the right question from the best knight. Then the stone will be reunited. At that point, Perceval doesn't know that the voice speaks of him. In *The Fisher King,* when Jack is first rescued by Parry and his band of fellow bums, one of them screams loudly, and Parry joins in. Little did Jack know that the scream was the banshee scream denoting that he was the Grail hero.

We have several interesting notions here. One of the interpretations is that Perceval himself caused the wounding of the Fisher King through his brash actions. We see this image again that the wounder and the healer are the same. It hints to a responsibility that we must take as wounders. We are the ones that must make things right.

We also have the scream of the Stone, indicating a proper monarch, but the monarch isn't properly prepared, isn't worthy yet, so it almost destroys him. This reminds us that we have the right to the Grail, but we must come prepared and worthy of it. Learning how to do that is the focus of the book.

I haven't heard reports that the Lia Fail Stone screamed when Queen Elizabeth II took the throne, but we do know it didn't swallow her up either, and she has had one of the longest reigns of modern British monarchs.

You now have an overview of the most important people
we will meet on our journey. Now we will begin The Adventure.

Illustration (1902) by Ivan Bilibin (1876–1942)

Part III – The Adventure

The Girl I Left Behind Me by Eastman Johnson (1824–1906)

Smithsonian Institution National Museum of American Art
Oil on Canvas, 1870–75. 42 x 34 7/8 in.
Photo: National Museum of American Art, Washington D.C. / Art Resource, N.Y.

Path I – The Age of Innocence and Its Perils

One gets large impressions in boyhood, sometimes, which he has to fight against all his life.

— from *The Innocents Abroad* by Mark Twain

In Taoism, there is a concept called *Wu Chi* which represents the ultimate potential of energy before there is movement. It is a living nothingness before existence. If you were observing a Tai Chi Master who was beginning a form, he might appear to be standing still, where in reality, he is collecting his energy, which will be expressed in the movement. How well he does this will speak in the quality of the movement.

We are all born with the potential to create wondrous movements in our lives. We contain enormous learning capabilities which often get squandered during our youth on false or irrelevant teachings. We have to learn to counter these forces so we may again gather our unique energies to express quality in our lives.

In this section, we will examine what events occur in our lives that may force us away from the Grail.

It is the *Age of Innocence* and it is fraught with *Perils.*

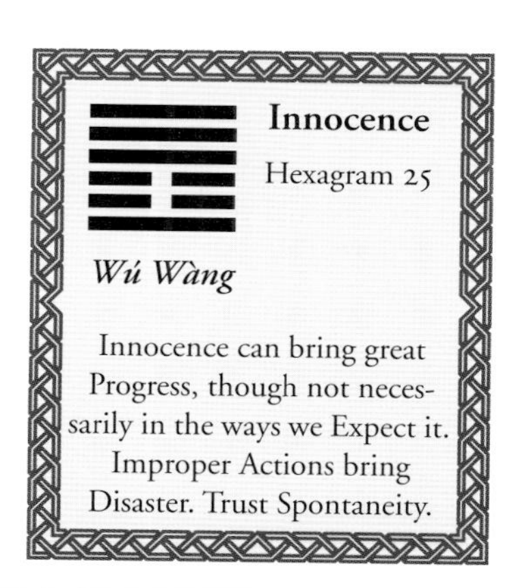

Chapter 1 - The Mysterious Birth

"What's vacation mean?"

Forrest Gump asks this question of his mother as he only knows that his father is always "on vacation." It is the question that many heroes before him have asked: Moses, Oedipus, Merlin, Arthur, Luke Skywalker. They used different words, but it is the same search. Tell me of my Mysterious Birth. Tell me who I am.

Mrs. Gump does not give a straight answer to Forrest. She simply defines "vacation" as a place you go to and never come back. Ironically, she is reading *Curious George* to Forrest. He accepts the rudimentary answer, and does not pursue the real question. He is less curious than George, who happens to be a monkey.

Heroes of legends are not born to regular moms and dads and grow up in the warm bosom of a two-parent family with caring siblings. Sometimes a hero knows his mother, but he rarely knows his father, and hardly ever has brothers and sisters. No matter what other actions the hero is involved with, the question of his father is the starting point of the real adventures. Arthur has no idea he is to be King until he knows Uther Pendragon is his father. Merlin is brought to notice when Vortigern needs a "fatherless" child to be a sacrifice to his tower. In the stories we are examining, almost all of the heroes have lost a parent. Will Hunting and Luke Skywalker are orphans. Roy Hobbs, Skylar and Jenny have each lost a parent. Parry has no family whatsoever.

When the father is not known, this means the hero must truly discover who he is through his own actions. This carries great responsibility, as the hero cannot say—"I am lazy because of my father. I deserve this because of my father. You cannot do this to me because of my father." The hero is rewarded or punished because of who he is.

Birth and Youth of Parzival

Parzival was born to Queen Herzeloyde and Gahmuret, one of the greatest knights of his era. She was Queen of Waleis (Wales), Anjou, and Norgals, and the sister of the Fisher King, Anfortas. Gahmuret was a regal born Angevin whose roots tied him to the father of King Arthur, Utepandragon, with the magical strain of the OtherWorld running in his blood.

Gahmuret loved his queen, but he loved fighting more, and he left for adventures serving his former master, the Baruch of Baghdad. He left Herzeloyde pregnant with their son, though it would not have mattered to him, as he had abandoned his previous wife, Queen Belacane, when she was pregnant. When news came of Gahmuret's death, Herzeloyde was devastated. She would have killed herself if not for the life inside of her. As it was, the birth itself had almost killed her, due to the size of Parzival.

Herzeloyde fled her kingdoms to the Forest of Soltane. Everyone was instructed that no mention of knights was to be discussed; her child was to be brought up ignorant of warring. He is not told of his father and heritage. Her names for him were "Bon fils, cher fils, beau fils,"—"Good son, dear son, beautiful son." She did not call him by his name of Parzival.

Parzival knew no unhappiness, until one day he killed a bird who sang sweetly. His weapon was a bow and arrow he made himself. He was compelled by his heritage to listen to the birds singing, but after that, it made him sad. When Herzeloyde saw his sadness, and saw the cause of his sadness, she had many of the birds killed, until Parzival asked what the field hands had against the birds. Her cryptic message implies that it is God's commandment, to which he asks "What is God?" She tells him he is brighter than the day and came in human form and to pray to him when in trouble. There is also the Master of Hell, who is dark and faithless, and who should be turned away from. She explains to him the Dark and the Light.

Parzival learned the javelin and would carry a stag carcass home whole. No matter the weather, he always brought down game.

— *Parzival* Summary, Book I, ¶ 55–56; Book II, ¶ 96–114; Book III, ¶ 116–120

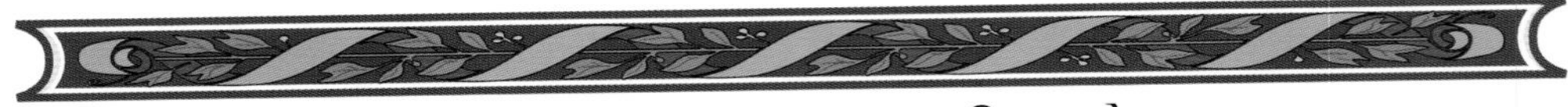

Standing on the Shoulders of Our Ancestors

I have not forgotten my father's face; it has been with me through all.
— from *The Gunslinger: The Dark Tower I* by Stephen King

There is a Chinese philosophy that we all Stand on the Shoulders of our Ancestors. This means that part of what we are today comes from the abilities and sacrifices of those who went before us. Some of us stand on strong, broad shoulders. Some of us feel a little shaky. Some of us even carry on the sins of the father.

An element of the Wasteland that exists in our lives comes from dealing with the problems of other people who are in our lives. Paradise can also be found from the same people through the positive influences they have on us. Part of our enlightenment process is the realization and separation of these influences, so we may choose correct ways of bettering our lives.

Parzival will be dealing with insecurities, immaturities, and lies he has inherited from his parents, but his destiny and the ability to achieve that destiny is also found in his heritage from them.

Let's talk about the bad stuff first. Parzival's mother has been devastated by the death of her husband. This grief has made her give up strength in her life and retreat far from civilization. This would have been fine, if this had been a temporary retreat to reflect on her past and future. Instead, she will lose her kingdoms, which is the birthright of her son. Before her marriage to Gahmuret, she was a confident, strong woman. She ruled three kingdoms alone and it was she who declared the tournament to find a suitable mate to help her. This differs from the traditional fairy tale where the king of the land declares a test to find a fitting mate for his daughter. Herzeloyde is calling the shots, even demanding that Gahmuret marry her. He only wants to be a warrior knight but he is beset by problems with ladies who love him. He is being pursued by the queen of France, who had made him a knight, and he has left his Moorish wife, Queen Belacane, back in the kingdom of Zazamanc. Furthermore, the real tournament had not been fought; he had defeated the best in the practice games. It seems such a man had plenty of excuses not to get married. Herzeloyde is not to be underestimated. She gets a court's decree that anyone donning a helmet for a chivalric cause and wins, gets the queen. She declares his past marriage void, as Queen Belacane is a heathen and baptism has superior power over infidel beliefs. Gahmuret only agrees to the marriage, if Herzeloyde will allow him knightly adventures. That she agrees to.

Standing on the Shoulders of Your Ancestors

Take a few moments to wonder about those people who went before you and the difficulties they went through to get you to where you are. Think of the talents and drive they must have possessed to survive plagues, wars, famines, and dangerous trips across the seas. Realize that the fortitude and skills they possess are part of you now.

The Principle of Life by Frantisek Kupka (1871–1957)

Collections Mnam/Cci - Centre George Pompidou. Aquatint and Colors, 1900–03. 13 ⅓ x 13 ⅓ in.
Photo: Photothèque des collections du Mnam/Cci

It is sad to see such a clever, resourceful woman result to total escape when tragedy comes. It becomes an action not of healing, but of fear. Herzeloyde now fears that she will lose her son the same way she lost her husband. She plans to keep Parzival from his destiny, which is to be the greatest knight of the kingdom just as his father had been. She cannot even call Parzival by his name, but this in itself has a meaning which we will examine in Chapter 4.

Gahmuret, too, has his set of problems: most notably, his inability to be responsible to those he loves. He never stops loving Queen Belacane, and at the time of his marriage to Herzeloyde, he professes love in his heart for Queen Ampflise of France. He takes knighthoods and kingdoms from all of these women, but he is not a man to be tied down. He is like a modern father, who in chasing his career, ignores the need to be present for his wife and children.

Now for the hints of Paradise. Parzival is a member of the Grail family through his mother. One uncle is the Fisher King, Anfortas, while another one, Trevrizent, will be an invaluable teacher. This is his destiny; this is his birthright. It is a right that promises not only material wealth and stature, but a guarantee of spiritual sustenance. To achieve that destiny, he will rely on the talents born to him from his father. From his mother comes Destiny, from his father comes Ability.

These are two important concepts of what we must strive to accomplish in our lives. We must discover our Destiny and we must develop the Talents to achieve that Destiny. Our Abilities will cultivate our Destiny and our Destiny will tell us what we need to concentrate our life on. With Destiny comes Responsibility, but that encounter is further down the path.

Thinking of Destiny

We are all familiar with the idea of setting goals. Now let's change our mind-set to the concept of Destiny. Goals are just a way of fulfilling Destiny, which is grander and more important than check-lists. Envision what your Destiny is, rather than just what your goals are. By doing this, you imbue your life with purpose, which is necessary for those rough times that everyone has.

The KKK and the Knights Templar

We've learned that Gahmuret had been married to the Moorish Queen Belacane. Reading between the lines, we realize that "Moorish" signifies that she is Black. The first chapter of *Parzival* focuses on Gahmuret and Belacane's relationship, which is instrumental to the end of the book.

Wolfram bravely moves from the image of the black and white magpie to the marriage of a black woman and white man. Put yourself in the late twelfth century and imagine what a stir this must have caused. In fact, think back just thirty years. Come to think of it, there are many places today where mixed race marriages are still intolerable.

Wolfram must be applauded for his attacks against racism. It is not only the issue of color, but of religion. I am sure some people deemed him traitorous and sacrilegious. As mentioned, Gahmuret is a great fighter, but he chooses not to fight for a Christian European nobleman. Instead, he fights for the heathen Baruch of Baghdad, because the Caliph was deemed the most powerful man on earth. Gahmuret does not fight for small change.

Gahmuret proves himself under the Caliph, and soon finds himself in the kingdom of Zazamanc where the people are "dark as night," making him uncomfortable. The queen of Zazamanc is as black and heathen as her subjects, but Gahmuret is able to see the good heart of Belacane which overflows with qualities of loyalty, humility, kindness, and—once their eyes meet—desire. He fights for her, and they marry.

Racism occurs in all of the stories we are examining. Blacks are exploited in *Heart of Darkness*. Poverty and the powerless get the most votes as these are issues in *The Fisher King, Siddhartha, The Natural,* and *Good Will Hunting*. Slavery and domination are issues in the *Star Wars* series. Vietnamese are the brunt in *Apocalypse Now. Forrest Gump* covers them all.

Gump innocently talks about his ancestor General Forrest starting the KKK. There's the sepia toned clip of the General with his henchman pretending to be quasi-knights. They wear armor of bedsheets and their horses wear the imitation regalia of knights' horses. Let's not forget that the official name of the KKK is the Knights of the Ku Klux Klan.

This is a good time to tell you that Wolfram von Eschenbach was not just an ordinary troubadour or court poet. He was one of the first poets to consciously engage symbolism, and on top of that, he was a bona fide knight who probably served several noblemen. Though he was not a Knights Templar, he did supposedly go to the Holy Lands and meet with them first hand. The ideals of the Grail Knights of legend reflect the ideals of real-to-life Knights Templar, allowing latitude for artistic interpretation. I feel Gahmuret was probably based on the Knights Templar who, unlike the KKK, had no compunction in mixing with Arab and Islamic brethren.

When I watched my Gump tape, I fantasized that General Forrest, too, renounced being ill at ease with the blacks around him, and found solace in the arms of his Queen Belacane. After all, Gump needs a brother.

The Natural

"What I mean," he insisted, "is I feel that I have got it in me—that I am due for something very big. I have to do it...."
— Roy Hobbs in *The Natural* by Bernard Malamud

Hard to take out of the flesh that is bred in the bone...
— from *Le Morte D'Arthur* by Sir Thomas Mallory

We have all been blessed with natural talents, inklings, desires, and skills. No matter where we go in life, these are the gems that come to us in unexpected dreams, a saved catch, a lucky guess, the ache of what might have been. They release the sigh that says "I remember, I want, I need." For Forrest Gump, it is his athletic ability, especially in running, which enables him to be a football star and war hero. He rescues men by draping them over his shoulders, much like Parzival would have carried captured hinds home. Roy Hobbs is the baseball player who was meant to outshine all who had gone before him and all who would follow. Anakin and Luke Skywalker have natural piloting abilities. Marlow is a seaman who senses the rivers and oceans and goes to any length to be on a boat. He becomes a captain of a steamer, stranded deep in the jungle, just as his own soul is. Will Hunting is the mathematical genius of the century. Parzival has the warrior's blood of his father and the lineage of the Grail from his mother—the perfect intermingling of skill and destiny. This is the basic core that we all must start from. Acknowledging that within each of us lies a special destiny and the character to achieve it is a powerful perception. By embracing that concept, you will free yourself to pursue what will not only make you merely happy, but what will make you joyous. It will give you purpose that goes beyond the duty of the rigors of ordinary life.

Do not misconstrue that this natural ability need be at Olympic competition level, nor fall into lofty realms of poetry and art. It is fine-tuning the hum of an engine, the sizzling aroma of garlic and onions in a down-home kitchen, the tilling of earth to bear simple marigolds, the careful watch of the sleeping child. Anything, no matter how simple or mundane it seems, is noble if it comes from the heart, the wellspring of your life.

It seems that it would be easy to discover the purpose of our lives if we would just look at our natural abilities, but things get a lot more complicated than that. There have been many roadblocks placed in front of us.

Taking Stock of Your Natural Abilities

Make a list of your Natural Abilities. These can range from physical skills to communication skills to mathematics or a fine taste for food. List anything and everything that comes to mind.

Now see how you can tie this into what you believe your Destiny and your Grail is. If you do not see a direct connection, at least find the supporting connection how your skills can support you while you seek out your Grail.

Magic Shoes

Gump tramps around the doctor's office, encumbered by clanking, metal braces on his legs. His mother tells him they are his Magic Shoes and they can take him anywhere. Mom has dutifully done what she thinks is right for her son.

Parzival's mom also places braces on him, though his shackles are of a different kind. Herzeloyde grieved so deeply when she lost her husband in battle that she vowed her son would not become a knight. As soon as he was born, she retreated to a farm, deep in the woods, to raise Parzival without any knowledge of fighting. The trouble was that Parzival was meant to be a warrior. His father was one of the known world's greatest knights, and the blood of the father courses in the veins of the son. Luke Skywalker's uncle did exactly the same thing. He took Luke far away from any mention of fighting, and concealed from him the fact that Luke's father was a great fighter and pilot.

No matter how heavy the braces, the legs beneath them are strong, whether that strength is used for throwing baseballs or flying planes through outer space. Just as Gump's braces make his legs stronger, Parzival's isolation makes him stronger. He uses his natural abilities to hunt stags with a javelin and carry them home whole, without aid of the mules, for which the load was too heavy. Without anybody teaching him, he creates a bow and arrow. Parzival and Gump have been set apart from civilization, but it only prepares them for what is to come.

When Roy Hobbs comes to join the Knights, he is asked why he didn't play baseball when he was young. Roy manages to worm his way out of direct answers to his past, but finally admits years later to Iris what happened. During the years after being shot by Harriet Bird, he lost his confidence. We know from his outstanding play with the Knights in his thirties that he didn't lose much of his ability. So it becomes only psychological shackles that burdened Roy all of those years. In this case, he bound himself, and when he released himself, he was mentally stronger and ready for the challenges.

In *The Fisher King*, Lydia has a fear of relationships, only playing out fantasies with romance novels. After her first date with Parry, she develops a whole imaginary scenario of rejection ending with the comment that she would slowly turn into a piece of dirt. When Parry is injured, she is faced with the most extreme test of love, one of seeing her loved one physically unable to move, and that will break her bindings of fantasy love into real love.

The binding of our natural talents comes from many sources, many of which emanate from a desire to do good for the child. These include parents, teachers, friends, lovers, relatives, and strangers with their own sets of talents and problems. Later in life, we ourselves may place the wrong restrictions and remove ourselves from the society we were meant to be in.

We cannot take this idea too lightly. Our successes and even our joys relate directly to our habits in life. And our habits come from many sources, all with their own agendas. What was so easy to ingrain in a child's mind is difficult to remove in later life.

There have been many times in my life that situations did not turn out how I would have liked them to. When I reflect on why, I often come up with false personal paradigms. Some of my examples may ring true for you. Such as—"I'm not good enough for that," or "If I'm just a good, kind person, he will treat me differently," or "Why bother, it didn't work before." These are the chains that must be broken, no matter the source. Once broken, a stronger warrior emerges, ready for the real challenges.

False Paradigms

False beliefs are hard to break, because they are hard to find and acknowledge. After all, you believe them to be true, so you don't even acknowledge how their falseness is harming you. So, first you must search out false beliefs by listing any suspicious ones. Usually they will reflect a sense of unworthiness or lack of confidence. Others will reflect an extreme view of Pollyanish optimism or end-of-the-world pessimism. Still others rely on "If only..." If you are saying "if only," then you are not recognizing the reality. Don't be dismayed if your list is lengthy. It took a long time to become who you are, both the good and the bad.

Check your paradigms against the real hard truth. For example, you may be saying you are too old to play tennis well, when the real truth is not age, but the willingness to invest the time in practice. Perhaps you are being overly kind to someone who has not been responsive to that goodness. Maybe it is time to admit that the person in question is not ready for your attention, and it is time to turn your energies in a different direction. Confront the real issues behind those scripts you feed yourself. Think of ways to alter your life from the insights you gain.

Heart and Soul (and Birds)

> *So they began to consider how to set out on their quest. The Hoopoe, excited and full of hope, came forward and placed herself in the middle of the assembled birds. On her breast was the ornament which symbolized that she had entered the way of spiritual knowledge; the crest on her head was as the crown of truth, and she had knowledge of both good and evil.*
>
> — from *The Conference of the Birds* by Farid ud-Din Attar

Birds are a major motif that runs throughout *Parzival.* They pop up like a small twittering wren, then immediately hop away, sometimes without much notice. We have already discussed how Wolfram opened his book with the image of the magpie, and that is just the beginning.

Aside from eating a few chickens and turkeys and sometimes keeping birds as pets, most modern people do not view birds as anything significant. We admire their colors and songs, but that is an attitude which says "entertain me." Earlier peoples placed more significance to our avian friends.

Birds were *psychopomps*, soul carriers. Even the souls of gods were carried in the bodies of birds. The Latin root for birds, *aves*, meant "bird" and "ancestral spirit." This was the root of the stork bringing the newborn baby. That stork carried the baby's soul. Angels have the wings of birds and the Celtic fairies flit about the earth as creatures who defy gravity. In various tales, mortals and gods change into swans, ravens, and other creatures of flight.

The word *augur*, a diviner, was someone who foretold the future through the entrails of birds or the flight of birds. To understand the language of birds was to know the intention of the gods. Powerful magic. The most powerful wizard in Arthurian myth carries the name "Merlin," which is a falcon. In T. H. White's *The Once and Future King*, Arthur's first exposure to magic was when he heard Merlyn's owl speak, and in the film *Camelot,* Arthur asks Merlyn to make him a hawk so he can fly away from his problems.

The scene where Parzival shoots the birds lasts only a page, but is so significant. It introduces an important lesson that Parzival will have to thoroughly integrate before he can achieve the Grail. He must learn that every action has a consequence. He shoots the bird, and is amazed that it cannot sing anymore. He loved the birds and thrilled at their singing, but he could not understand how what he did silenced them. There is a saying, "The Road to Hell is Paved with Good Intentions." We may use this phrase when someone's good intentions conflict with our own desires, but we rarely look at what our own actions produce. We will be come back to this focus time and again as Parzival travels through his adventures.

Besides being an insight of not knowing the consequences of our actions, I believe that this is a subtle reference to the killing of the old religions and ways. Herzeloyde believes the desire for the birds' songs comes from the fairy blood that runs in Parzival's veins. This becomes the source of her hatred for the birds. When she orders the birds

Creation of the Birds by Remedios Varo (1908–1963)
Private Collection. Oil on Masonite, 1958. 20 1/8 x 24 5/8 in.

killed, she has ordered the ancient ways killed. Ironically, she has turned her back on her own responsibility because she is an agent of the Grail Castle, which lies in the OtherWorld. The totem of the Grail Maiden is the dove. It is the symbol of love and the open heart.

It sits as a reminder of the erotic love of Aphrodite on our wedding cakes and as a symbol of *agape,* the love of humankind, with the peaceful dove of the Holy Ghost. It started as a representative of the Great Goddess, Astarte. Herzeloyde has strayed far from her roots, as her own symbol would have been a bird of love.

The topic of birds is also found throughout the modern stories. Han Solo and Chewbacca lovingly care for their spaceship, the *Millennium Falcon.* Roy Hobbs will be shot by Harriet Bird, a symbol of the goddess Fortuna, who brings us up the Wheel of Fortune, and as quickly can bring us down. The pitcher in *The Natural* who takes a bribe is named Fowler. The nightingale's voice fills the desert in the poem "The Waste Land."

The movie *Forrest Gump* has a touching scene where birds play an important part. The violation of gentle Jenny by her father is the advent of her Wasteland. Jenny grabs Forrest's hand and they disappear into the corn field to escape her father. She pulls Forrest to his knees, beseeching him to pray with her. Her prayer is to become a bird and fly away. Jenny's prayer is an ancient prayer for many abused children.

As Forrest and Jenny kneel in their appeals, a flock of doves surges to the heavens.

The Lessons of The Mysterious Birth

Whole modern books of psychology have been written on the ideas presented in this small section of Parzival. More and more, people are being told to reflect on their youth to discover both their strengths and weaknesses which direct their adult lives. What we are today is in part determined by our standing on the Shoulders of Our Ancestors.

The most important lesson is becoming aware of how people in our lives have sought to control us and remove us from our personal destinies. Sometimes it is done with bad intention, but often, it is motivated by love and protection, and those are the bindings which are the most difficult to remove.

We must become aware of our natural talents and desires, because they will give us a hint to the path we should take. They are there to make our lives easier and more meaningful. We should utilize them to the maximum.

We recognize that there are people in the world who hate those who are different, and sometimes, a radical, brave stance can plant the seed for future healings. Gahmuret may have had his failings, but his bravery and his willingness to cross over to unwelcome lands will set the stage for the Wasteland's healing.

We begin to sense a connection of our soul to nature. Primitive people maintained a direct attachment of spirit to nature. If we can begin to see our own souls as having similarities to the marvelous birds and creatures of nature, we can expand our own sense of wonder and caring to the world at large.

Now we shall see what will cause Parzival to break the chains that bind him and move him into the "real" world.

The Angels of Night by William Degouve de Nuncques (1867–1935)

Collection Kröller-Müller Museum, Otterlo, The Netherlands
Oil on Canvas, 1894. 18 7/8 x 23 5/8 in.

Chapter 2 - An Encounter with Angels

We're just ambling along, minding our own business, having a reasonably good life, when out of the blue, something extraordinary happens, making us realize the old life isn't as wonderful as we thought it was. A creature appears who has the ability to change our view and way of life. We want to follow that extraordinary being, whom we are sure is an angel, but we don't exactly know where we will end up. We only know that it is time to leave and try a new course.

Knights on the Road

Parzival is out hunting and hears a dreadful crashing of horses' hooves in the brush and thinks it must be the devil. Three beautiful knights emerge, dressed in glittering armor and riding grand horses. Parzival believes they are gods and asks them for help. One knight is perturbed that their journey is hampered and calls Parzival a stupid Waleis. Then along comes another knight named Count Karnahkarnaz, who is lord of the three. They are all chasing two knights who had abducted a lady. The Count asks Parzival if he had seen the knights with the maiden, but Parzival thinks he is God and asks for help. The Count says they are only knights of Arthur's court and not gods. Parzival does not know what a knight is and the Count says that Parzival's looks are fair enough that he may be of knightly stock. Parzival asks questions of their armor, making the knights impatient with him. The knights then see the plowmen, who tell them they had seen Meljacanz stealing away Imane of the Beafontane. The plowmen are upset that knights had entered their land, as Herzeloyde would not be happy with this turn of events.

Parzival goes to his mother, saying he wants to go to Arthur to be made a knight. She thinks of a strategy of dressing him in fool's clothing, hoping he would be ridiculed at court and would return to her. She gives him advice to help him in the outer world—beware of dark fords, only go in clear shallow fords; be polite and greet people; if an elderly man wishes to teach you, accept the learning with grace; win a woman's ring and greeting, kiss her and hold her tight. She also tells him of Lehelin who took two of his countries, Waleis and Norgals, and killed one of his vassal princes. He promises to avenge the crimes. He leaves and she falls to the ground dead.

— *Parzival* Summary, Book III, ¶ 121–128

Synchronicity

A connecting principle,
Linked to the invisible
Almost imperceptible
Something inexpressible.
Science insusceptible
Logic so inflexible
Causally connectible
Yet nothing is invincible
...Synchronicity
— from "Synchonicity I" by Sting

Half a century before Sting sang about it, Carl Jung introduced it by the name Synchronicity. He defined this term to be "meaningful coincidence." It is the coming together of two seemingly unrelated events, but when viewed in a larger context, has significant meaning.

If we were hanging out on a street corner, and some policemen came running by and asked if we saw a suspicious character, we would send them down the right street and that would be the end of the situation. Certainly entertaining dinner conversation that evening, but it would be doubtful that all of a sudden we would leave our old lives and become agents of the law. (OK, some of you might, so pay attention.)

Parzival hears the pounding of horses' hooves, and believes he will face the Devil. He readies himself to stand before the Devil, but instead, he sees three knights. He beholds them as angels and he is right. Here is the coincidence which will change his life and set him on the path of destiny that his mother had denied him. The knights themselves know they are not gods or angels, but any being who wakes up someone to his destiny is truly an angel. The men in the field see three "cops" and send them down the right street, but Parzival's heart leaps at the sight of the magnificent warriors astride Castilian horses. He knows this is the way he has to go.

In *The Natural,* Roy Hobbs is discovered by Sam Simpson, who has arranged for Roy to try out for the Chicago Cubs. This is the impetus for Roy to leave his Midwestern farm life in search of fame and fortune. Marlow and Willard have two men who hand over missions that push them on their individual adventures. Willard admits that his being in Saigon was not an accident, as well as his charge of being the caretaker of Kurtz' legacy. Luke Skywalker's angels literally fall from the sky in the form of droids. For Siddhartha, wandering *Samanas* or ascetics will prompt him to leave a life of luxury for the way of the Buddha.

Jedi Master Qui-Gon Jinn knows that his picking of the planet Tatooine to fix the energy source for his space ship was no accident. He was there to meet Anakin

Skywalker and bring him into the ring of the Jedi Knights. And Anakin recognizes an Angel when one comes into his life in the form of Padmé Naberrie (Queen Amidala).

Another example is the scene in *Forrest Gump* where Forrest is being chased by three bullies, taunting him, as he runs beleaguered by his metal braces. Jenny is there with him and she gives the command which will change his life forever: "Run, Forrest, Run."

Forrest at first runs with his knees welded like the Tin Man, burdened by his metal prison. Then the miracle happens. Jenny's orders sink all the way down to those chained legs. Forrest bursts from his bindings and the steel fragments scatter on the road. He is no longer bound by his mother's limited vision, but empowered by his personal goddess. From that day on, if he was going somewhere, he was running. Appropriately, townsfolk called him a "Running Fool."

He ran straight to the football field where he became a football star. In Vietnam, Jenny's words echoed in his mind and he saves his life and others from that "Run, Forrest, Run." He was able to couple his Natural ability with the event which changed his life. It wasn't just three bullies harassing Forrest, but three angels who where synchronously there to move Forrest on with his life.

The funny thing about angels is that they don't always look or act like we imagine angels should. Luke Skywalker doesn't realize that by taking in C-3PO and R2-D2, he is about to change his life drastically. Dirty beggars impress Siddhartha as they shock him out of the fantasy of the comfortable life into the real world of suffering. In the painting at the beginning of this chapter, *The Angels of Night,* William Degouve de Nuncques presents us with an eerily beautiful vision of sensual angels and petit gardeners of moonlit flowers. He recognizes that these beings have complicated energies that can awaken us on many levels, if only we would let them. We must not judge too quickly the angels who pass into our lives.

The philosophical question for us is whether or not the Universe gives us these events or do we take an event and make it synchronous? The answer doesn't matter. What does matter is our Readiness in life. Just as some of us would only give directions to the police (knights), others would drop their current lives and sign up with the force. What is important for us is to be prepared for the unexpected which reflects our heart's desire.

Angels and Synchronicity

1. Think through past events which you felt were "meant to be." Did you allow this situation to become a milestone in your life or were you unable or unwilling to take advantage of the situation? Were the "angels" involved in the form that you expected them to be? What did you learn from this?

2. How will you prepare yourself for your next encounter of Angels and Synchronicity? Do you have a completed operetta/rock song ready to show the famous Diva if she shows up at your boss' Christmas party? Or do you just have a vague concept like a million other people? Preparedness will save us a lot of energy and disappointment.

3. Note the little synchronicities in your life and expect the big ones. Have an idea of what the big one could be, but keep yourself open to the possibility that it may not quite look like your fantasy. Watch the pattern of your Synchronicities.

Listen to the little nudgings, the little voices that are making you look past where you are now. Someday, an event will come, and you will know the time is now.

Be Ready.

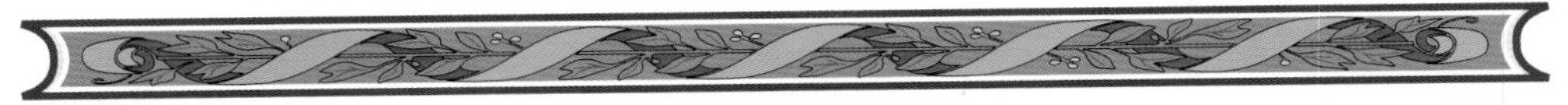

The Abduction

Princess Leia is abducted by Darth Vader's men.
(Leia-Carrie Fisher)

The Synchronicity of Parzival meeting the knights is not only that this meeting will be the catalyst for Parzival to leave his mother, but these men are tied to the adventures of the Grail. The Arthurian legends are scattered with Abduction legends of Queens. The most widely known one is where Gwenevere has been kidnaped by Meleagant. In some stories, she is taken by Arthur's son, Mordred. At this juncture of Parzival, we learn that Meljacanz has stolen Imane of the Beafontane.

Basically, the abduction story is one where the queen is out "maying" with her attendants when she is kidnaped. The kidnapper does not want to demand money for her safe return, but wants to marry her. Eventually, the queen's champion will save her and she is returned home. Some may recognize this story in the film *First Knight.* Though many may play this up as just a man who wants to rape a beautiful queen, the real significance lies in the early powers of the Goddess of Sovereignty, and may even be linked to a time when women had dominion over their own lands.

With what we know about Sovereignty, we can easily see what this represents—an Abduction of the Spirit. It is the first crime that Parzival is witness to, though he is initially oblivious to what is going on. Even in ourselves, we may not initially be aware of the draining and Abduction of our Spirits until we reach a crisis we cannot handle, or one day we just refuse to get out of bed.

Luke Skywalker's adventure gets into gear when Princess Leia has been abducted by Darth Vader. She needs the help of strong heroes to help her regain peace and harmony in her vast empire. Luke initially becomes involved because of the allure of fighting and potential fame. Eventually, he learns that the final battle depends not only on martial skills, but on healing a sick spirit.

The Beautiful Fountain

"Water!" she snapped. "Everywhere you turn here, you're involved with the lack of water!"

— from *Dune* by Frank Herbert

It is no coincidence that the princess who has been kidnaped is of Beafontane, the "beautiful fountain." We've briefly discussed the image of water as the lake where the Maimed Fisher King would fish, but now we will explore the water motif which is omnipresent in world mythologies and importantly so in Grail myths.

Water is magic. Our bodies and our world are mostly water. To be alive, there must be moisture. We float in water in the womb and we attempt to return to the womb at the Fountain of Youth (thus the migration to Florida during retirement?). Isis revives Osiris with magic waters and we are baptized to the higher powers in marble founts. We search for oases in the deserts to quench our thirst and we pray for healing at the Grotto of Lourdes. Moses' wife is Zipporah, meaning "shining wave." The goddess of love, Venus/Aphrodite, emerges from the waters, gorgeous and open to the possibilities of life.

If you approach a fountain deep in the woods in a Grail Legend, you approach life itself. In *The Elucidation*, the Well Maidens nourished the spirit and body with drinks from their well. Once they were raped and their cups stolen, the wells dried up, and the land along with it. In the film *The Natural,* Pop Fisher's drinking fountain is almost like poison as he bends to take a drink. He is spiritually sapped as he complains that in all of his years in service, he can't even be rewarded with a decent drink of water. The water he drinks is of the Wasteland. It is not until Roy Hobbs starts hitting homers that the water is again sweet and refreshing.

In Arthurian myths, the power of water in the form of rainstorms indicate a battle about to happen. This represents a hearkening to a breakthrough in the Spirit which is about to happen. In the story "The Knight with the Lion (Yvain)," knights are instructed to approach a marvelous tree by a cold, boiling spring, upon which an iron basin hangs by a chain. Next to the tree is a stone, and once water from the basin is poured on the stone, a great storm will arise. If the knight survives the storm, then the tree will fill with songbirds singing in harmony. Then the real challenge will come with an angry, great knight charging to defend the sacred site. This is the time that the Soul opens up, and its tests begin.

Roy Hobbs will hit his first home run in a rainstorm, and Forrest Gump will test his warrior's mettle when the rains in Vietnam stop and his war begins. Anakin Skywalker will open his home to the strangers who will change his course in life, when warned by an old woman who feels a sandstorm coming. Sand here is merely earth flowing as water. The encompassing power is the same.

Parzival must cross over a stream to reach his first adventure, and Gawan must ferry a dangerous stream to the Castle of Maidens. In *The Mabinogion,* we find Owein challenging a horseman in black armor at the site of a Countess' fountain. The Lady of the Lake is the one who bestows Excaliber to Arthur.

Because Parzival decided that he will enter the realm of knights, most assuredly, he will again cross paths with Meljacanz, the one who steals Sovereignty, a Lady of the Fountain.

The Birth of Venus
by Joseph Stella (1877–1946)
From the Collection of the Salisbury House Foundation, Des Moines, Iowa Oil on Canvas, 1922. 85 x 53 in.

Hidden Disease

A frozen banana tree, brown and stricken, languished against the front of the porch, the tree preparing to collapse as the iron fence had done long ago. Near the dead tree there was a slight mound of earth and a leaning Celtic cross cut from plywood. The 1946 Plymouth was parked in the front yard, its bumper pressed against the porch, its taillights blocking the brick sidewalk. But, except for the mummified banana tree, the tiny yard was completely bare. There were no shrubs. There was no grass. And no birds sang.

...Stopping by the grave, he read REX in faded letters on the cross.

— from *A Confederacy of Dunces* by John Kennedy Toole

Parzival in all his innocence doesn't know he is witnessing the evidence of the Hidden Disease. It is a cancer of the Wasteland that does not openly rear its head until it is too late. Parzival doesn't even know yet that he is in a Wasteland, as outwardly, everything looks fine to him. He is unaware of King Arthur, whose court has become stale and ineffective. He sees wondrous knights, but does not see their racism as they call him a "stupid Waleis." He does not realize that the code of the knights compels them to rescue ladies in distress, not kidnap them, especially ones of sacred fountains. In John Kennedy Toole's passage above, we see a gravesite for Rex, a dog. The name "Rex" means "king." In this Wasteland, the king is dead.

In *The Natural,* fans hiss and boo their own team. In *The Fisher King,* Jack is a shock jock who listens to the complaints and haranguing of desperate, angry voices all over the city. Queen Amidala must face bureaucratic politics in Coruscant as Senator Palpatine reminisces that the Republic has passed through better times. In the *Heart of Darkness,* the Accountant is perturbed by the moaning of a sick man brought from the Inner Station. The noise distracts the Accountant's attention, causing clerical errors. The king, King Leopold of Belgium, is so far away that he is only known through pictures and has no meaning for the people of the land. In the film version, Marlow is warned of the Wasteland when he encounters a dead elephant, killed for the ivory Marlow was sent for. The lifeless creature, swarming with flies, stares with its unseeing eye. Marlow is also warned that the man sent on the same mission before him committed suicide with a gunshot to the head. In *The Fisher King,* inmates of a hospital wander aimlessly with their private pains and public gashes, uncared for and invisible to most. Once the pizza is delivered, doctors swarm around their lunch, still ignoring the needs of the suffering around them. When Jack sits next to a disabled vet begging for money, Jack remarks that the people throwing in the money don't even look at the disabled man on the ground. The man has no face and no humanness to them. It is a public who doesn't want to be involved with the people they are helping.

These are all clues that something is going wrong.

Long before people leave their jobs, get their divorces, or inflict bodily harm on people, there are hints. The well dressed, wealthy woman can be as beaten as the poor woman in the next community. She keeps it hidden, but the disease which affects her life and her children's, multiplies. She may put makeup over the bruises, but she may not be able to resist shuddering when an arm quickly raises from the table. Her eyes dart down when her abuser enters the room. Always in hindsight we see the indications. Is it that we truly didn't know, or is it that we just chose not to know?

In Buddhism, the first step of the Eightfold Path is to develop Right View. Simply put, we must learn to see the world as it is, unclouded by how we wish the world to be or not to be. So often, we look in hindsight at what appears to be now obvious clues which led to disastrous situations. Were we really uninformed or were we blind? We must make efforts to keep our senses open to all that is around us. We can build a world of hope and goodness, but to do that, we must be aware of the little things that could potentially create larger problems. Sometimes, no matter what we do, a situation cannot be saved, simply because there are other factors or people not willing to also work on solving the difficulty. However, there are times that a gesture of concern, or offered time, may be all that is necessary. Let's be aware of the Hidden Disease around us, and take care of it before it does serious, lasting damage.

Looking for the Hidden Disease

1. Take time to review recent happenings in your life. Look at them with an objective eye and see if there might be small problems which hint at potential larger ones to come. If you do see something that isn't quite right, decide what step you could make to confirm the problem and help the person in need. Remember that the person you may need to help could be yourself.

2. Try to develop the Right View. As you move through your ordinary, everyday world, continually refresh your spiritual eyesight by saying "What am I really seeing here?"

With Friends Like These - Who Needs Enemies

Sean Maguire notes in *Good Will Hunting* that there is a definite difference in Direction and Manipulation. Parzival's mother jumps back and forth between the two extremes. She continues her needy ways, this time with sabotage. She appears to be helpful and supportive to her son, but all the time she is plotting for his ridicule and defeat. If the world sees him as a fool, it will not give him a chance to prove who he is and he will return to her arms. Herzeloyde sabotages at two levels. First, she openly does so with the dressing of him in fool's clothing. Second, she withdraws support by not giving him easy access into Arthur's court. All she has to do is tell Parzival to announce his lineage to Arthur, and Arthur would have to accept him as family. So here we have two examples of sabotage, the active and the passive.

Numerous times we have seen this behavior and been its victim. We may not even know all the times that it had been tried on us. We have seen the failures and successes of this behavior, and we may still be unaware of the ultimate consequences in our own lives. We probably have done some perpetrating ourselves. When it comes to sabotage, our worst enemy is sometimes ourselves. We actively pursue wrong behavior, and when we don't get what we want, blame others instead of looking to our own actions. Other times, we will passively allow opportunities to pass by, by not volunteering information about ourselves or not asking questions when given the opportunity. Silence can be the most deadly form of sabotage.

Sabotage by it very definition is sneaky and undermining. That is why it is so lethal. It is easy to fight the enemy when they wear bright red coats and line up in perfect geometric patterns, but we know it's the guys in the trees that will get you. We don't want to be paranoid, but sometimes, ask the question—"What's REALLY going on here?" We can not sabotage ourselves with doubts, and fantasies that good always come to the quiet and patient. Be active. Question. Turn on the Light.

Friends Like These...

1. I know most of you love and trust your friends and family, but in a loving, kind way, see if there are subtle (or outrageous) ways that they are sabotaging you. Realize that their actions are probably coming from jealousy or fear of loss. If you do see such actions, determine not to fall prey to their petty games, or assure them that you have no need for a power struggle with them. You may have to be creative or even forceful.

2. Now meet your biggest foe, the one inside of you. Look at the habits in your life that have been keeping you from your spiritual and real world achievements. So much of our progress in life can be directly attributed to our habits. Once you have found some of these sabotage techniques you have ingrained, determine what good habit you will use to replace the old, destructive one.

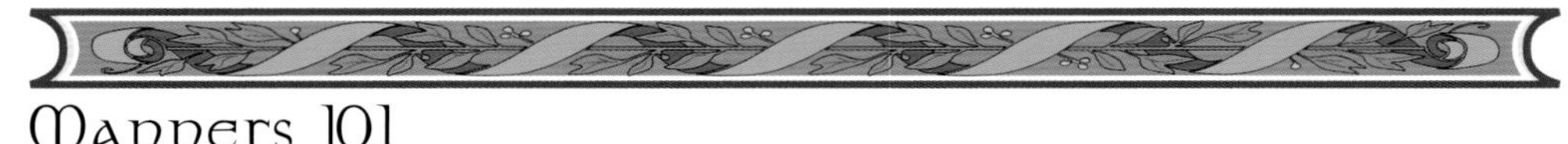

Manners 101

Everyone had behaved splendidly! splendidly!

— Man at Central Station describing the sinking of Marlow's steamer in *Heart of Darkness* by Joseph Conrad

When I go to antique shows, I am attracted to the booths of heirloom silver. The Victorians were masters of etiquette, gracing their tables not only with the usual knife/fork/spoon, but with terrapin forks, toast servers, petit-four tongs, and implements scarier than those found on a dentist's tray. Along with the silver were the rituals and manners that were required for the brandishing of the dinner implements. Knowledge of the correct brandishing meant you were part of the inner circle. A person of a lower caste would flounder in such a world.

Any society you venture into has its own set of rules and laws. How well you play those rules may determine your social standing, your choice of mate, and your wealth. In this sense, mastery of such rules may be necessary to ensure a good life, and all cultures indoctrinate their young with the rules of tribal success. Some people call this "cultural hypnotism" while others call it good manners.

A certain degree of rules is necessary to ensure cooperation within a group and a common framework for all to fairly build on. Throughout the story of Parzival, we shall examine the pull between the rules of society and the heart of the natural man (and woman).

Well trained by his father, Siddhartha will become totally immersed in the rules of the Brahmin society. Gump literally obeys commands and suggestions, while Roy Hobbs thinks he is in the know with the little he learned from his dead agent Sam.

Herzeloyde gives a crash course to Parzival as he prepares to go into the world of courtly affairs. Up to this point, he has lived the idyllic life of anything he does is fine. Herzeloyde knows he will encounter a different world out there, yet she has never prepared him for it. She truly intended to keep him with her. Now she feels a certain obligation.

The rules she gives him have both commonsense appeal and a ring of mystery to them.

The first rule seems reasonable—cross at shallow, clear fords, not in dark fords that have not been tested. For a young boy starting his first journey, such advice is good. But as one becomes more of an adventurer, it will be the untested dark ventures which will give the true tests and rewards. It also speaks to the psychology of the individual, who chooses only the clear, easy routes versus risking going to the darker depths and dredging truths that stayed fertile in the muck.

There is also a mythological significance to the ford, as it is one of the magic water stations of myth. It is at the ford where the goddess resides and often challenges those who are to be tested. In *The Welsh Triads,* Morgan (Arthur's sister) met with Uriens to lie with him and have her twin children, Owain and Morfudd, brother and sister.

Morrighan, of Irish tradition, beats and washes bloody clothes of slain men at the ford. Perceval, in the *Didot-Perceval,* will combat a flock of black birds at the Perilous Ford. When he wounds one, it becomes a woman. In *The Merlin Continuation,* Gwenevere safely leads Arthur's army across a dangerous ford, while their enemies drown. Arthur names it "The Queen's Ford." Marlow will see the Black Beauty along the river in the film *Heart of Darkness.* Roy Hobbs, in the novel *The Natural,* will have a rendezvous with Iris along Lake Michigan.

The second rule is also a reasonable one—that of bowing to wisdom. Though Herzeloyde has the hope of Parzival returning to her, she also knows there is a possibility that he won't. Her Other-Worldly knowledge knows that there are others out there ready to give training to her son. Her description of an elderly, graying man is prophetic, as all of the other rules are.

Old Man Seated in an Armchair
by Rembrandt Harmenszoon van Rijn
(1606–1669)

The third rule of receiving a kiss and ring from a woman appears to be one of courtship, which it is in a convoluted way. Here she is giving rules for dealing with the Women of the OtherWorld, not just regular gals one would meet at the local grocery store.

There are numerous instances of the gifts of the OtherWorld/Fairy women in Arthurian and Celtic legends. In the story of "Owein and Luned," Owein is given a ring of invisibility to escape imprisonment. In "Peredur Son of Evrawg," the hero is also given a ring of invisibility by the Woman of the Mound to kill the feared *addanc.* As we noted before, the *Bean Sidhe,* Women of the Fairy Mounds, ride with the Four Hallows—the Sword, the Cup, the Staff, and the Orb. Arthur will receive his famed sword Excaliber from the Lady of the Lake.

Basically, you are receiving help from Sovereignty when you get these magical objects. And if Sovereignty is looking kindly upon you, you had better love her and hold her tight, because to lose her is to lose a precious inner core.

Heritage

Anakin must leave his mother (Shmi Skywalker) to find his destiny.
(Anakin-Jake Lloyd,Shmi-Pernilla August)

Though Herzeloyde had planned on Parzival returning to her, as she dresses him and gives him advice, she knows she is letting go of him. She acquiesces a bit, telling him he is the prince of lands which have been overtaken, thus hinting at his destiny. He has been given a knightly task of avenging the deaths of those who gave their lives for him, and for him to regain what has been lost to him. At last, she gives him reluctant permission to be who he was meant to be. She also makes him aware that many people have been looking out for him. He is given the charge to honor them by avenging crimes against them.

There is a time in our lives when we must give ourselves permission to move on. Even if we give it reluctantly, we must then jump on it and do it. Even as we venture to a new world, we must never forget that many people have helped us, and that we must still reward their efforts and sacrifices. Sometimes we can only do this through respectful remarks as we recall past events. Sometimes we may actively search out what these people need and help them as they helped us. We continue forward, remaining attentive to those who have helped us in the past.

Permission to Move On

You have some sense of what the Grail means to you. One of the reasons that you may not have achieved your personal Grail is that you have not given yourself permission to truly seek it. You cannot wait for your wife, father, brother, friend to give it to you, though the way you approach your Grail would take into consideration their feelings. Give yourself the Right to Adventure.

Death of Mother

You do not do, you do not do
Any more, black shoe
In which I have lived like a foot
For thirty years, poor and white,
Barely daring to breathe or Achoo.

Daddy, I have had to kill you.
You died before I had time—
— from the poem "Daddy" by Sylvia Plath

Parzival is now ready to ride away, and in doing so, his mother falls to the ground and dies. One interpretation is that the old life is finally dead to him and he is able to proceed on the path he was meant to. Sylvia Plath's poem chillingly and bravely exhibits her own need to ignore the forces placed on her in her exploration of her creative drive—especially since her father had passed away when she was eight years old. Other forces haunted her and as amazing as this poem is, she unfortunately was unable to truly break free of self doubts, inordinate perfectionism, and disappointment in love. She ended her life at the age of thirty-one. She could write the words, but could not live the action. Her tragedy reminds us that we must confront issues which hold us back. These poisons can affect our entire lives.

Letting go of the old life may be not seeing your drinking buddies after work, if alcohol is a roadblock to your dreams. Letting go of the old life may be not using all of your energies enabling others to support their bad habits. Letting go of the old life may be physically moving from the small town to the big city, or vice versa, depending on your dreams.

If we were to use *Parzival* as our only source, the death of the old life would be a fair psychological viewing of this scene. We are now going to look at the Perceval character in Chrétien de Troyes' version. Here Perceval looks back and sees his mother faint at the bridge, but he keeps on riding. This could still be construed to be an awareness of the old life and leaving it behind, but it is more important as an example of Perceval still being unaware of the consequences of his actions, and lacking compassion. His own mother faints, and he doesn't even pause to check if she is well or not. If his departure had not killed her, certainly his indifference would have. We will examine this meaningful issue in more detail in the next section.

Preparing for the New Life

The theme of the Death of the Old Life in preparation for the New is found several times in the Grail legends. Though we are not going to be as calloused as Parzival, we must let go of something before something new can take its place.

If spending more time with your children means less overtime at work, let those involved know that this is going to happen and prepare everyone for that change. If writing a best selling novel means fewer nights out with your partner, be fair and involve your loved one with that decision. Our resources are finite, whether it is energy, time, or finances, so realize that things will change, and prepare accordingly.

Mounted Officer of the Carabineers
by Théodore Géricault (1791–1824)

The Lessons of An Encounter With Angels

- We must develop an awareness of the opportunities in our lives which will set us on the road to our Grail. By overlaying a sense of importance to the people and events in our lives, we give ourselves more of a chance, rather than hardening our hearts to potential experience. The fact that even small directions can be as important as life-altering events makes these people angels in our lives. We just need to be ready for them.

- There are plenty of people around ready to Abduct the Spirit. They not only will abduct, but will rape, cheat, steal, and defame what is most precious in life. These terrible people will attack at the very source of life, represented by the life-giving nourishment of our most basic element—precious Water.

- What is wrong in the world around us may not show up with a cataclysmic event, but as a slow-consuming disease, gnawing away at the lifeblood of ourselves and our community. We must develop the sense of Right View, to see the Truth of the situation, so that healing can be instigated at an early stage.

- We must become aware of the ways that people sabotage us, understanding that they are working out of their own inadequacies and fears. More importantly, we must be aware of how we sabotage ourselves and make a directed effort to change our own destructive habits.

- We can cooperate with rules of society, but we will learn that blind obedience and the ignoring of the compassionate heart can have dire consequences.

- We must give ourselves permission to embark on the Road to the Grail, ignoring sabotage from within and without. As we succeed, we must remember those who have helped us.

- There will be times when we must let go of a stale or destructive life, so that we can begin our journey with a clear mind. We must give up the old life which didn't work to embrace the new.

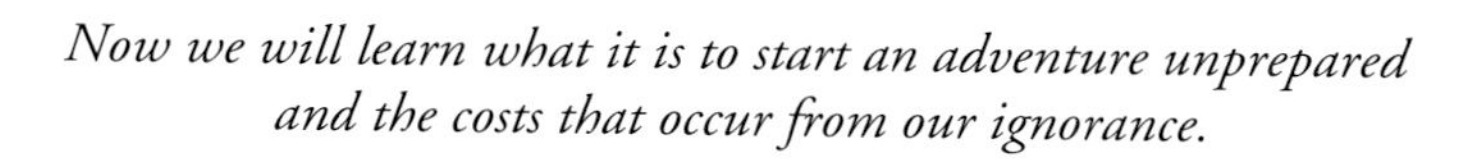

*Now we will learn what it is to start an adventure unprepared
and the costs that occur from our ignorance.*

Lady and the Unicorn: To my one desire (Artist Unknown)

Musée de Cluny, Paris
Wool and Silk Tapestry, ca. 1500. 12 ⅓ x 15 ½ ft.

Chapter 3 - Stumbling into the OtherWorld

At least Dorothy was aware enough to know that she was not in the normal world when she tells Toto they're not in Kansas anymore. Admittedly, Yellow Brick Roads, Witches in fluffy dresses, and Ruby Slippers that don't hurt your feet are good clues. Parzival will stumble into a magical world with no idea of the importance of where he is, whom he meets, or what gifts are being offered to him. More importantly, he still is totally unaware of the consequences of his actions, and his path of destruction becomes wider. Much like a twister churning across the Kansas landscape.

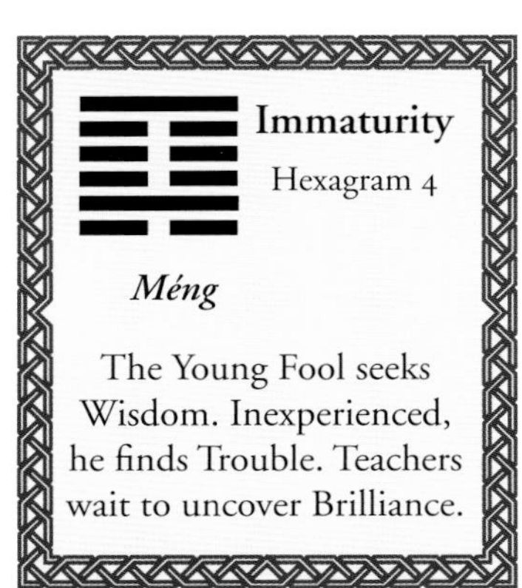

Lady of the Tent

Parzival goes to Brizljan, where he does not cross a dark ford, following his mother's instructions. The shallow water's coloring was from a profusion of flowers and weeds. The next day he finds a tent where the noblewoman, Duchess Jeschute, sleeps peacefully. He lies next to her, forces a kiss from her, takes her brooch and ring, and eats her food. The whole time she protests and says he will have to bear her husband's anger, but he doesn't care. As he leaves, he wishes that God will shield her, just as his mother had taught him to greet people.

Jeschute's husband, Duke Orilus, comes back and accuses her of being unfaithful, though she maintains her innocence. We learn that Orilus was the killer of Parzival's paternal uncle, and that Jeschute denounced being a queen to become his duchess. He has a sister, Cunneware, who lives in Arthur's house and will not laugh until the greatest knight appears. Most of the Round Table Knights do not like Orilus, because he defeated so many of them.

Orilus says he would not eat or sleep with Jeschute. He tears her clothes and would not give her fresh ones. He strips her horse of its trappings. Then they set off to find Parzival, who has no idea he is being pursued.

— *Parzival* Summary, Book III, ¶ 129–137

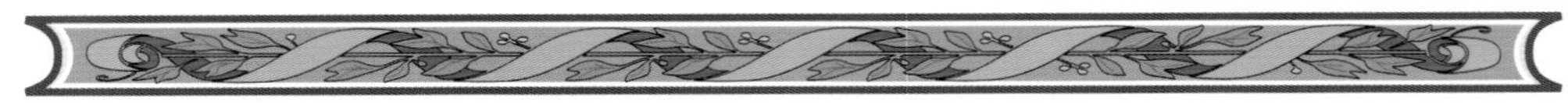

The OtherWorld

Our hero is off to seek fame and fortune in the outer world, but before he gets to Arthur's court, he's going to skim the edge of the world that holds his destiny. It would be easy to quickly read over the first sentence with a funny spelled place—Brizljan. My guess would be as good as yours on the pronunciation (I say *brizlyan*), but I do know where Wolfram immediately put his hero. Brizljan is the forest of Broceliande, a forest of great magic, certainly a portal of the OtherWorld. According to Tennyson, this is the forest where Merlin took Vivienne to seduce her, and found himself surrounded by a sacred oak. Yvain (Owein) fights and wins the Countess of the Fountain, Laudine, at the magical springs in Broceliande.

Here we have Parzival riding his horse along a brook in a magical land, but because he is blindly following his mother's words of advice to only cross at clear fords, he misses a chance to cross over to adventure. He allows his eyes to be deceived by his mother's voice. If he had only looked closer into the water and trusted his own sight, he would have seen that what he feared was merely flowers. If he had been more knowledgeable of OtherWorld terrain, he would have know that where there are flowers, there's a magic woman close by. Wolfram says it was so shallow that a rooster could have probably crossed it. Right out of the starting box, this is the first instance, where Parzival is hindered by rules of his limited society.

Talk about missing chances in our lives. Sometimes we are our own worst enemy. I personally cannot be critical of Parzival, because as I look back now on my own life with clearer eyes, I can see my own brooks that bordered enchanted lands, but I was too rule bound to cross over.

Sometimes the rules aren't even official rules, just cultural assumptions that hinder us. We sometimes think we are too old or too young, too smart or too dumb, the wrong sex or the wrong race. Depending on the situation, we feel we're too good for something, or not good enough. This lesson of not giving in blindly to rules could change our lives immensely. We need to open our eyes to opportunities that are right beside us, and take risks in life, ignoring the destructive voices holding us back.

Missed Chances

1. Think on the times that you have missed chances in your life merely because you had false assumptions based on old rules. Did you fail to try a sport because you are "too old?" Did you pass on organizing an event because you were the youngest one in the crowd? Did you not ask for the raise you deserved because no woman in the company had ever earned so much? Realize that prospects for growth abound, as long as we are willing to cross the river.

2. For future forays into the OtherWorld, prepare yourself with a script that reminds you not to listen to rules which may prevent you from taking a chance. If you really want something, don't let image and others' opinions and rules hold you back.

A Pocketful of Posies

Awake, O north wind:
and come, thou south;
blow upon my garden,
that the spices thereof
may flow out.
Let my beloved come
into his garden,
And eat his pleasant fruits.

— Bible, Song of Solomon 4:16 KJV (Tanakh, Kethuvim, The Song of Songs)

Photography by Don Belobraydich

Solomon attests to the power of the garden as the sanctuary of the goddess. Even today, if we want to show love or reconcile with those we love, a bouquet of flowers initiates a potential tryst. This is a centuries-old custom when flowers were associated with the love goddess or with the mother of the universe. Where there are flowers, there's a blessing of a powerful woman close at hand. While the rest of Parzival's world suffers a Wasteland, the OtherWorld abounds with flowers and lush growth.

There are many allegorical representations behind many different flowers. The two most powerful are the Rose in Western civilization and the Lotus in Eastern civilization.

We saw the Rose in the hand of our Tarot Fool. We will also find it as the Alchemical Rose of the Rosicrucians (Rosy Cross), a mystic Christian organization. We find it as a namesake in the Catholic meditation of the Rosary. The Rose was the symbol of the Queen of Heaven, the Virgin Mary, as well as the love goddess Aphrodite/Venus. In Welsh myth, Blodeuwedd is a woman created from flowers. In the Arthurian myths, we have the Flower Bride, Gwenevere, representing the Goddess of Sovereignty. She exemplifies this in her Maying rituals wearing wreaths of flowers in her hair.

Let us not forget that the apple is of the rose family. It becomes the focal point of that infamous story in Genesis as the fruit of the Tree of Knowledge, eaten first by Eve. Idunn keeps her Norse gods and goddesses eternal with her apples. Hera has a tree of golden apples guarded over by water nymphs, the Hesperides. Paris awards a gold apple as a trophy to Aphrodite which leads to the abduction of Helen and the Trojan War. The usual colors of the apple are Red (skin), White (flesh), and Black (seeds), the three colors associated with a mythological motif known as the Triplicate Goddess. Disney's Snow White has black hair, white skin, and rosy cheeks and lips. And her "amnesia" comes when she eats a poisoned apple. Walt knew what he was doing.

Many of you have seen statues and paintings of the Buddha sitting within a Lotus. The Lotus was the Hindu goddess, MatriPadma, the Mother Lotus. It is her womb that gave birth to the sun. She was the World, just as Gaia in Greek myth was the world, and in popular slang we still refer to Mother Earth. The lotus refers to Lakshmi, the counterpart goddess to Aphrodite, who also was born out of the sea. As Aphrodite floats out of the waters on a shell, Lakshmi wafts in on the lotus. (Note that Anakin Skywalker's mother's name is *Shmi.*) One of the tests of Odysseus is in the Land of the Lotus Eaters where men become forgetful of their lives when ingesting the lotus.

Queen Amidala's name reflects her compassion.

Amidala-Natalie Portman

In *The Phantom Menace,* the young queen's name is Amidala, and her alter ego is Padmé. A sacred Buddhist mantra is *Om Mani Padmé Hum,* the Jewel in the Center of the Lotus. This is a chant of compassion and wisdom. The name Amidala is almost the anagram of Dali Lama (short an "l"). Queen Amidala's quest through the movie is to find a way to relieve the suffering of her people under Darth Sidious' thumb. Compassion is a natural state for her.

The Taoists have an esoteric text called *The Secret of the Golden Flower.* Again, we have the image of the Lotus, this time as a source of Light. At one level of reading, the text teaches of meditation, at another level, it is the joining of man and woman, and at the spiritual level, it is the development and bathing in spiritual light.

Our modern works of art also employ flower motifs. In *The Fisher King,* Parry's battle cry when he rescues Jack is in the name of Blancheflor, who is Chrétien's counterpart to Parzival's Condwiramors. "Blancheflor" means "White Flower." Roy Hobbs' true love bears the name Iris. When she shows up as "The Lady in White," we again have the "White Flower." If we look at the wedding scene between Forrest Gump and Jenny, we see her wearing the wreath of flowers that Gwenevere would have. When Willard meets Kurtz in *Apocalypse Now,* Kurtz recollects the flower plantation along the Ohio River as heaven in the form of gardenias. Siddhartha's love, Kamala, resides in a grove, and he is wise enough not to enter until invited in, as Solomon was beckoned to his love.

Ariadne by John William Waterhouse (1849–1917)
Private Collection. Oil on Canvas, 1898. 35 7/8 x 59 1/2 in.

Meeting Sovereignty

Jeschute will be the first Goddess of Sovereignty with whom Parzival will have an encounter. Not bad to run into a goddess on your first outing to the outer world. She lives in the magical OtherWorld in a multicolored silk tent and sleeps on sable coverlets. Wolfram's description fairly drips with eroticism, her cover being pushed down to her hips because of the heat. But what draws Parzival to her bed is the ring on her finger, not the luscious body. His kiss on her is not prompted by love or even lust, but by the words of his dead mother. Here he has been fortunate to stumble on a powerful queen, but his actions are mechanical and he doesn't appreciate what truly surrounds him. In Chrétien's version, Perceval is more violent, forcing twenty kisses on her, and wrenching the ring from her finger. The Peredur legend has a significant difference in that Peredur doesn't have to forcibly take what is around him. When he asks about the food and ring, the girl of the tent readily gives it to him and addresses him as "Chieftain," a clan ruler. She is recognizing his rights as a future leader and her

> *Loving Our Spirit*
>
> *Think about your Spirit and how you have treated it. Have you held it down and not allowed inner expression? Have you failed to turn to your Spirit in times of need, thinking that you didn't have the personal resources necessary to help you? Love and embrace your Spirit as it is the core of you. Do not mistreat it and care for it lovingly. Start now to express what you find strong and beautiful inside of you, knowing it will always be a source of strength.*

duty to help him. However, his use of the gifts are superficial, just as with Parzival. (As a note, Sean Maguire is always calling Will Hunting "Chief.")

It may seem that the image of a naked Jeschute lying in the tent was just for titillation, but it brings out an important part. You cannot just physically wed or rape Sovereignty, but you must love her. Anything less will diminish the power. She is our psyche; she is our Spirit. She must be openly loved, held, and cherished to receive her gifts. We must love ourselves wholly. Our physical bodies and outward actions must never forget our true spirit, and in turn, that spirit allows us the potency to do what must be done in our everyday working lives.

Impoverishing Sovereignty

With all of this going on, it is no wonder that Orilus is jealous. On the surface, it looks as if Orilus' property is being violated. Jeschute's words to him even reflect this typical view as to how he can inflict pain on her and make her life wretched. This shows us a window of sexism during the Medieval times. He retorts that she is too proud and that her pride must be curbed. But we are dealing with OtherWorldly women governed by a more subtle set of rules. It is not that he owns her, but that she grants him power willingly if he pleases her. Orilus is in fear of losing the right to serve and be with her to an adversary. He must track down this potential usurper or that adversary could return and claim a right to his wife.

We know this to be False Jealousy. He will unfortunately strip Sovereignty down to near death because of misunderstanding. How often have we gone on wrong paths and put much energy into destructive behaviors because of misunderstanding? We do it to our spouses, friends, and acquaintances. We do it to ourselves when we strip our spirits down to nothing.

Poverty of the Spirit comes from misunderstanding who we are and worrying about other ghosts we think are trying to move in on our lives. We must stop and cherish our Spirit and look to the truth that no one is taking anything from us. When others try to claim your Spirit, realize that only you can reduce her to nothingness. They may try to claim her, but they are not the ones to strip her or starve her.

Misunderstandings

1. Think of times when hardships could have been avoided if there had been trust, and time had been taken to understand the circumstances. Were these misunderstandings from your misconceptions or were others to blame? Be honest and look for patterns in your life and those around you.

2. If you have isolated a pattern of mistrust or misunderstanding, make a plan to change the situation. You may have to work on stepping back and working on your own Right View, or you may need to develop more open communications with the people in your life.

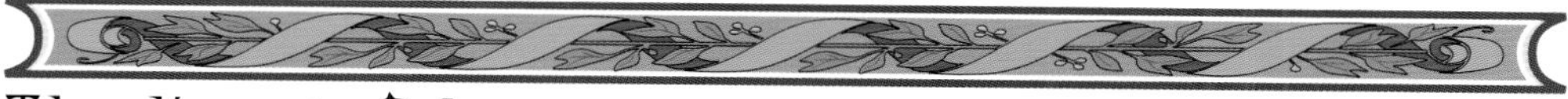

The Karmic Dilemma

Shall the reward of goodness be anything but good?
— The Koran, The Merciful 55: 60

In *The Fisher King,* Lydia confesses to Anne that she believes the reason she doesn't date now is that she was a man in her previous life who used women. It's payback time now.

Cause and Effect. It is the chain of life. It is a chain that sometimes seems unfair, and always seems inescapable. It is the root of Responsibility—the willingness to take on Cause and Effect.

Parzival has just created a horrendous situation for poor Jeschute. He has been an obedient son following the advice of his mother. He is living his life as the Fool who doesn't realize the consequences of his actions. He already had one strike against him with the death of his mother. Now he's got another strike. Throughout the whole novel, Parzival is going to be dealing with the shock waves of the situations in these early chapters. Pay close attention to how everything plays out.

Karmic theory says that your good actions will be rewarded with good returns and your bad actions will reap punishments. Followers believe that it doesn't matter whether your intentions were good or bad, or even if they were in the previous life. All of this rationalizes the good and bad things that come your way.

Luke Skywalker takes in two droids which the Imperial forces are looking for. Because of this, his family will be destroyed as Darth Vader's men burn everything down in the search. Forrest Gump has a whole slew of events that he unknowingly influences, including inspiring Elvis with his awkward dancing, helping bumper sticker and T-Shirt entrepreneurs, and catching the burglars at the Watergate complex. In *Apocalypse Now,* Kurtz authorizes polio shots for native children whose arms get hacked off by tribal men trying to remove the taint of the outside world. In *The Fisher King,* Jack unwittingly causes the death of diners in a Yuppie bar by inflaming an imbalanced man with nasty remarks.

The Judge, in the novel *The Natural,* tries to manipulate Roy Hobbs by convincing him that good deeds may get bad results and bad actions can have good results. The Judge prided himself in paroling a young kid, giving the young man a second chance at life. Yet the boy turned around and killed his parents. The Judge was trying to convince Roy to take a bribe with this Anti-Karma logic.

Karma

Meditate on what your personal view is of the Karmic law of Cause and Effect. Do you believe it is basically true? If you cause problems unintentionally, should you be held accountable? What do you expect from others regarding what they do to you? Can bad come from good and can good come from bad? Do we really have any control over this thing we call Life?

*Nirvana, the Death of the Buddha (*Artist Unknown)

As we watch Parzival make his many mistakes, we should ask if Karmic law truly applies. Should he suffer for problems that he unintentionally caused? Should we?

The second step of the Eightfold Path is to develop Right Intention. We don't always have control over the outcome of our actions, but we can make a real effort to aim for Good. To develop Right Intention, we must think of our lives as a chess game where we try to anticipate the outcomes of various moves. We not only look at the positive results from what we do for ourselves, but the positive gains other people also reap. If we know an action of ours would harm an innocent person, then we must take a step back and try a different route. By keeping in mind how we can positively influence other people's lives, we develop Right Intention.

Right Intention

Look over this past week and think of ways that you did not act with Right Intention. Become aware of it, so you may make different choices the next time a similar situation arises. Think of ways that you did act with Right Intention and see how you can further develop that awareness in your life.

The Lessons of Stumbling into the OtherWorld

We have skirted the realm of our Grail, but have failed to be aware enough to take advantage of the situation. We hold ourselves back with rigid rules and we don't know how to behave once we do try.

Spirit is closely associated with flowers, or the beauty of nature around us. When we are in the presence of what is beautiful, we must honor our Spirit, who lives in that presence.

We cannot just expect our Spirit to be there when we need it. We must actively take the time to nurture and love it. We must learn the true extent of the power of the Spirit.

There are times that we strip our Spirit of power through misunderstandings and jealousies. Our own misconceptions can cause more harm than actual aggressions.

We must be aware that every action we do influences somebody, somewhere. Even the most trivial can send a ripple in the universe. Because of this, we need to develop Right Intention, so we at least try to proliferate good acts instead of bad.

Parzival now rides down the road, looking for this king named Arthur, whom he is sure will make him a knight.

The Wounded Cavalier
by William Shakespeare Burton (1830–1916)
Guildhall Art Gallery, London
Oil on Canvas, 1856. 35 x 41 in.

Chapter 4 - The King's Road

Starting at Buckingham Palace in London is the street known as King's Road. The street angles for several miles towards the Thames and then begins taking on other identities. In days of yore, specifically during Henry VIII's reign, it was simply The King's Road. That road ended at a magnificent castle known as Hampton Court, begun by Cardinal Wolsey. Wolsey gave it as a gift to Henry when Wolsey fell out of favor for not getting a papal annulment of Henry's marriage to Catherine of Aragon. Despite the magnanimous bribe, Wolsey still lost his head (literally) within a few years.

Just as modern politicians work under clouds of stress and burdens, Tudor monarchs also had their woes and troubles. Especially when one has to determine the fates of wives who don't produce male heirs. So the King had his retreat, his own little OtherWorld to withdraw to. Eventually expanding to 1,000 rooms, and boasting the world's first tennis court, the palace was once described as "more lyke unto paradise than any earthlie habitation." It is surrounded by formal gardens, a six foot high maze, water gardens, and a 225 year old grape vine which still produces black Hamburg grapes. During springtime, purple crocuses sprout up like lush carpets, and visitors escaping winter doldrums rejuvenate with strolls along the Thames.

That connection to his OtherWorld was so important to Henry VIII that he made sure that he had a direct route between the business in London and his trysts in the country. Parzival also finds a road that extends from the magical world he just encountered, and the castle doors of Arthur's court. Along the way, he will meet more people who will influence his future.

Road to Arthur's Court

Parzival goes down the road, greeting people aimlessly as he had been taught by his mother, and hears a woman weeping. The woman is grieving over a dead man and Parzival offers to avenge the man's death with his javelins. He has no idea how the man was killed or even if he is actually dead. The woman is his cousin Sigune, and her knight, Schianatulander, has been killed by Orilus. She is touched by Parzival's kindness, and only says her husband was killed in joust. As Parzival starts to leave, she asks his name, but Parzival only knows his name as *"bon fils"*—good son. She immediately knows who he is and tells him his name is Parzival which means "right through the middle." She fills him in of his history including how Lehelin took two kingdoms of Parzival. Lehelin's brother, Orilus, had killed Schianatulander, who had been defending Parzival's lands. She was sorry she had not shown her love more to Schianatulander. Parzival is ready to avenge the death, but she purposely sends him the wrong way, fearing he was inexperienced and would be killed.

Parzival meets the Greedy Fisherman, who only cares about himself and won't give Parzival any food. Parzival offers Jeschute's brooch for food and directions to Arthur's court, which the fisherman gladly accepts. The next morning, the man takes Parzival outside of Nantes, the capital city, but won't go further, as a peasant would offend the knights. Parzival has not had training in manners, so does not recognize the problem here.

Parzival meets the Red Knight, Ither von Gaheviez, who is the son of Arthur's aunt. He had been brought up by Arthur's father, Utependragon. Parzival is so ignorant of the world that he doesn't feel fear when he approaches this formidable knight, entirely decked out in red and riding a red horse. Ither claims hereditary rights to Britain and is returning from Arthur's court where he has taken Ginover's (Gwenevere's) cup. He tells Parzival to go to Arthur and tell him that Ither waits for joust. Ither had taken Ginover's cup as a symbol to his right to the territory. He had not gone so far to turn the torches of the castle upside down, symbolizing setting fire to the fields he wishes to claim, as that would have made him dirty. Ither regrets spilling wine on Ginover, though no one spoke up for her. Arthur's knights will lose their reputation if they don't come and fight. Parzival agrees to deliver the message.

— *Parzival* Summary, Book III, ¶ 138–147

My Name is Gump, Forrest Gump

A good name is rather to be chosen than great riches, and loving favour rather than silver and gold.

— The Bible, Proverbs 22:1 KJV (Tanakh, Kethuvim, Proverbs)

"What's your name?"

Roy Hobbs is asked that after he defeats Whammer and boards a train to Chicago. Gerald Lambeau questions Will Hunting about his name, believing Will is just an obnoxious kid messing with the blackboard math problem. Forrest Gump is asked that throughout his life.

What's in a name? In the Grail legends, everything. We take it for granted that our parents give us a name, and that's that. Grail heroes typically have to have a process of learning or earning their names, and having their lineage revealed to them. You were a nobody until you had your name. Once you had that name, you were proud of it. Gump has that proud part down pat.

The naming of a hero was often done by a woman. Typically the mother did the naming, since in days of past people knew who the mother was, but not necessarily the father. The practice of lineage being passed down through the mother is still evident in the Jewish religion, where children are considered Jewish if their mother was. The Celtic hero Lleu Skilful Hand had to trick his name out of his mother. However, sometimes another woman representing Sovereignty tells the hero his name. If she tells you your name, you can be sure you are something special. Even Lancelot learns his name through the directions of a fairy woman. At the time a young man was to take up weapons, that was when he took up his adult name.

The taking on of a new name is not unusual for initiates in a society. One of the most prestigious is the Pope when he takes on his name. At the other extreme, are entertainers who choose stage names. We know the powerful ones in entertainment because they can get by with a single name. The names of the *Star Wars* characters are allegories in their own rights. Luke Skywalker and Han Solo predict their personalities and destinies.

The power to know a knight's name bordered on near sorcery. There are several tales where knights refuse to give their name to an opponent until after a battle is over, and sometimes not even then. We will see that later in *Parzival.* To us, it seems like a silly practice to keep one's name secret, as if your soul was attached to it. At a practical level, there is logic to it. Someone who was a bit cowardly could save his reputation if he lost a match by not revealing who he was. This doesn't explain why the most powerful knights engaged in this practice, knights like Lancelot and Parzival. One clue is poetically spelled out in a Taoist text, *The Art of War.*

The general who is skilled in defense hides in the most secret recesses of the earth; he who is skilled in attack flashes forth from the topmost heights of heaven. Thus, on the one hand, we have ability to protect ourselves; on the other, to gain a victory that is complete.

— from *The Art of War* by Sun Tzu

What Sun Tzu tells us is that part of winning is keeping a poker face until it is time to show your cards. This doesn't mean that we should just sneak around, not revealing our identities, but it is a toning down of our Pride that could get us in trouble before we have the chance to use our skills. If you brag about your abilities too early, everyone is going to be gunning for you just like gunslingers of the Old West. So when those famous knights do not announce their names, reputation will play no part in the battle, only tried and true skills. Bragging can come afterwards. Not a bad strategy to apply to our personal battles, though admittedly, sometimes difficult to apply in a world of instantaneous information and exposure.

Herzeloyde never told Parzival his real name. He only knew himself to be *"bon fils, cher fils, beau fils,"* —"good son, dear son, beautiful son." It is Sigune who recognizes that the time has come for Parzival to start realizing his way in the world, and she is the one who names him. She tells him that Parzival means "right through the middle." This was based on an interpretation of *perce à val* to be "pierce through the valley." Wolfram is demonstrating a Taoist and Buddhist concept of following the middle way between the extremes of dark and light. In fact, the Buddhist Eightfold Path is also known as the Middle Path or Middle Way. In the Four Noble Truths, the First Truth tells us that life is full of suffering, *dukkha.* The Second Truth tells us our suffering comes about from Craving. In the Third Truth, we learn that *Nirvana,* or peace from our suffering, is possible. The Fourth Noble Truth tells us the path to achieve *Nirvana* is the Eightfold Path. We've already discussed the first and second steps of the Eightfold Path which were Right View and Right Intention. The others are Right Speech, Right Action, Right Livelihood, Right Effort, Right Mindfulness, and Right Concentration. Someone unfamiliar with these concepts may think they connote perfectionism rather than a middle path. The idea behind them is that if you engage in Right Livelihood, Concentration, etc., you will not experience the manic highs and lows that so many of us experience in our lives. If you know you are engaged with the Right Livelihood, you have no worries when problems come rolling in, because you know the end result will still keep you on your right path. This is exactly what we are talking about when we talk about searching out your own personal Grail and doing what your heart knows is right for you. Until you immerse yourself with your right Livelihood, you will suffer. The Middle Path will be a long, long distance away.

The Maimed Queen

"I was foolish not to give him my love!"

— Sigune in *Parzival,* Book III, ¶ 141

The first time I read *Parzival,* I was a little annoyed with Parzival's cousin, Sigune. We will watch her throughout the novel, hunkering over her lost love's body, grieving until the very end. My feminist inclinations wanted her to get up and get on with her life. Not that she should forget the love she held for Schianatulander, but enough is enough, and let's move on. (And I'm the one writing about compassion.)

After meditating on her character, I realized that she was a subtle counterpart to the Maimed King. She was the Maimed Queen who suffers because she had the inability to love when she had the chance. Later we will learn the Fisher King's wound is also caused by love and pride.

What a lesson there. She regrets not showing love to the Prince who loved and served her, and now she will drag his body around the OtherWorld. There is an ancient Indian practice called *suttee* where a widow joins her husband on his funeral pyre. Sigune is performing a living *suttee,* having given up all desires to live in the normal world. One advantage of not throwing oneself on an actual fire is the possibility of learning from your mistakes. Though Sigune seems to be just hauling herself around with her dead love, she will provide an important function for Parzival throughout the story. Whenever Parzival starts to get off track, she links him to what he must do. While the Maimed King is unable to directly tell Parzival what he must do, she is able to fill in missing details to him. Though she suffers, she will continue to open Parzival's eyes and soul for him. She is a Maimed Queen with a Voice.

The Maimed Queen

1. A funeral is too late to tell someone that you loved him or her. In our hearts, we may carry appreciation and love for people, but until you tell them, they may never know the joy of knowing how much they are cared for. Think of the people in your life whom you love, and then let them know that you really care. If at any moment you lose someone, you will at least have the peace of knowing that she did know how you felt. Even if your last remarks to each other were slightly bitter and acrimonious, it doesn't matter as long as she knew the truth that a deep love existed.

2. Perhaps you know of someone who has suffered the loss of someone he loved, and is suffering from a living suttee. Think of some small way that you could help this person back to the living. Make the phone call or write the letter that could go to the heart of that person.

Judging Experience

Parzival is eager to fight, but Sigune recognizes his inexperience. He can't even tell if a man is dead or not, and he assumes everyone kills with the little javelins that he carries around. This situation reminds me of the naiveté of the Tibetans against the Chinese in the 1950s. A peace loving people with little experience in fighting goes out with bows and arrows to confront Mao's gun toting army. The Boxer Rebellion at the turn of the century in China was led by brave men with high martial arts skills, but they were no match to the guns of the Western world. Native Americans also suffered when, because of cultural viewpoint, they could not understand how to deal with the American government, which focused on land ownership, not spiritual bonds with nature.

This is a lesson that good intention and the right to your own land may not be enough. You must educate yourself about the tactics and strengths of your opponent and prepare yourself with the necessary skills. Perhaps Parzival's natural abilities would have carried him through, but Sigune is a wise woman. Her knight trained in war skills could not stand against Orilus and she chooses to send Parzival down another road, until he is ready. In the second installment of *Star Wars*, Yoda consistently tells Luke Skywalker that he is not ready to face Darth Vader, that his confrontation would not lead to a final victory. He is right. Luke will lose his sword hand in that encounter. It's not until the third movie that Luke has developed himself into a Jedi, worthy of the battle in front of him. By the way, in Irish myth, the great king Nuada has his hand whacked off, but it was replaced by a silver hand, much like Luke having a robotic hand attached to his arm.

It is one thing to be willing to take a risk in the OtherWorld and search adventure, but you better have a clear idea of your own strengths and weaknesses. Test the waters of your ambition close to shore until you know you can swim to the other side.

Preparing for Your Grail

1. In aiming for your Grail, think of the skills that you would have to acquire to be able to achieve it. These may include something as rudimentary as typing to be able to write the great American novel to studying stock options to be able to manage your retirement portfolio.

2. Honestly assess where you stand in relation to the skills you need. List your strengths and weaknesses. Make a plan to learn what you need to know and employ what you already do.

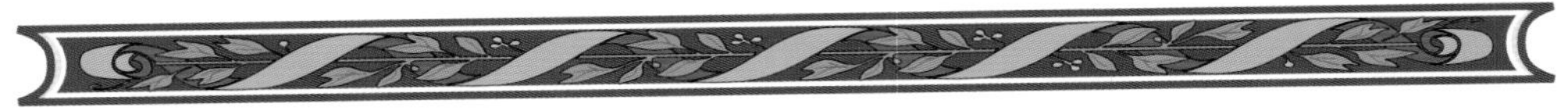

The Taker

Now Parzival meets a wealthy fisherman, but he's not THE fisherman, the Rich Fisher King. In fact, this fisherman would be the Anti-Fisher King. He is so greedy, he tells hungry Parzival that he would not give Parzival half a loaf of bread in thirty years. At least not unless there was money or valuables to be bartered. The naive Parzival offers Jeschute's brooch. A goddess' brooch is just enough to entice a greedy man like the fisherman, and he takes advantage of Parzival's ignorance. At least the fisherman feels a little pang of guilt as he not only offers to give Parzival directions to Arthur's court, but manages to show him the way.

Parzival holds powerful objects from a fairy lady with no idea of their value, and starts giving them away. Luke Skywalker picks up droids that have the secret plans which could bring down the Death Star, but his original plan was to use them to work the ranch as any old hired help. At first, Gump just uses the shoes from Jenny to walk around in regular life. When she leaves him and he is in despair, the shoes show their power by giving Gump the means to go inward as he runs across the country. He rediscovers peace and what is essential in life.

We all squander gifts, not realizing the potential they hold for us. We squander our lives, because we choose not to risk. We squander true power, because we do not know love. We give up our talents and energies for others to use, while we stay stuck in dreary circumstances. This doesn't mean that there aren't times when we do give ourselves to causes and people whom we care for. What it means is that we should be conscious about how valuable we are and make the right choice as to how we use our treasures.

The Greedy Fisherman is a Taker. If anyone is stupid enough to turn her back or drop her wallet, he'll be there to take advantage of her. The trouble is he looks like a Fisher King, so he is mistaken for a respectable guy. Retirees fall prey to phone scams due to the Greedy Fisherman. Young girls wanting to be models end up used in nasty ways because they can't tell the difference between the Taker and the bona fide agent who could help them.

The Gifts You Have

1. Think of the times you've been used in life. You may have given up material goods or maybe it was giving someone too much power over you. Looking back with clear, omniscient hindsight, think of what you learned from that experience and how it will help you make better decisions in the future.

2. Flip the tables and think of how you have used others. No time for guilt trips now, only a clear assessment of how you had acted before. Now think of how you could better handle the situation, so that your dealings with others in the future will be based on a "Win-Win" effort.

3. Inventory the precious gifts you possess within yourself. These are the true gifts you possess which go far beyond any material possessions. These are your abilities, your time, your energy, your love. Think of how you best want to use your gifts for your Grail path.

So, how do you know whom to trust? For some it comes as a matter of experience. Others never learn. This is where you have to look at what you are giving away. You must ask yourself: if I never again see what I am giving away, will it matter? If you spend $10 for a magazine that never comes, no big deal. But if you are handing over your retirement savings for an investment that is a "sure thing," and you have no idea what it's about, think twice. No, think a thousand times. When we know the value of what we hand over, it will help us make the right decision.

We'll have to be honest with ourselves that up to this point our hero has also been a Taker, since he stole the brooch from Jeschute. We, too, have used people and not appreciated what they had to offer us. One of the positive trends in negotiation has been to aim for a "Win-Win situation." This means that whenever we enter into a relationship with another person, both people should come out with something positive. This doesn't always mean that the final outcome is equal, just that both parties have had a benefit. If we all can approach our dealings with people with this type of goal in mind, the world could be a better place.

This scene in *Parzival* is also a further demonstration of the Wasteland. Not only the fisherman's lack of caring, but the fact that peasants cannot enter Nantes. Knights' rules would have previously helped the poor, but now the poor have become an unwanted sight to the knights of Arthur. The court resides in splendor behind the walls of Nantes, ignoring the poor outside the gates.

Challenger to Sovereignty

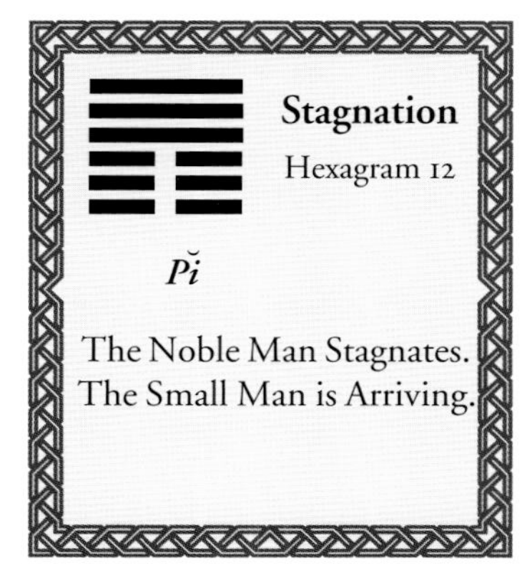

Parzival now meets the Red Knight, who has just come from challenging Arthur's court, but no one has yet ridden out to meet that challenge. Ither's challenge is more than just throwing down the gauntlet. He stands over Ginover, the Flower Bride, and takes her Cup, symbol of the king's right to rule. This is our first hint of the Grail, but demonstrated at a real world, physical level. There are numerous Celtic legends of a king being chosen when the Goddess of Sovereignty offered him a cup. While Ither took the Cup, he "accidentally" spilled wine on her. In "Peredur Son of Evrawg," he is more demanding. He takes her Cup and slaps her. This is no accident. This is the most direct challenge he can make to Arthur, yet Arthur makes no response. This is part of the Hidden Disease, the Wasteland. Arthur is now an ineffectual leader. His days of glory are long past. He and his knights have lived the good life for so long, they are reluctant to take up new challenges. Even Ither holds himself back from turning the torches upside down, so as not to dirty himself. He may want the treasures of the Kingdom, but he doesn't want the hard, dirty work that comes along with it.

In *Good Will Hunting,* Professor Lambeau throws down the gauntlet by offering a direct challenge to the class to solve a difficult problem. We watch the class and get the sense that only half-hearted attempts will be the response. Skylar recognizes Will's brilliance, and shakes him up by telling him he lives in his safe little world where no one challenges him.

In *Forrest Gump,* we see several instances exemplifying the attack of the Goddess of Sovereignty. In one instance, Jenny, nude at a Memphis theater, sings the Dylan folk song "Blowin' In The Wind." A few men make lewd comments, and one throws his drink on Jenny. Later in the film, Forrest and Jenny reunite in Washington D.C., where she is slapped by her boyfriend. In both instances, the men around Jenny do not come to her defense. They accept that women get insulted and hit. She probably deserved it. That's just the way things are. Only Forrest comes to the rescue.

Queen Amidala is forced into a war when Darth Sidious organizes a takeover of her planet Naboo. The Federation has become an ineffectual court, just like Arthur's, bogged down in politics and ceremony. Her Sovereignty will be restored through the effort of Anakin, the Jedis, and the Gungans.

The Red Knight as a challenger to the Sovereignty of Spirit is shown as a horrendous attacker in *The Fisher King.* Parry is unable to escape the attacks on his psyche from this knight who carries the death of Parry's wife with him. Parry, as king of his own soul, does not have the resources to fight back himself, just as Arthur could not accept the challenge of Ither.

This scene represents the danger of the good life. As the goals of our youth are accomplished, and immediate survival needs are met, we want to sit back and enjoy the fruits of our labor. Our arms get a little flabbier, we turn off the alarm clock, we let others do the work that we used to. At some point, a challenge comes to our very heart. We cannot fight back and there is no one to stand and help us. The challenger himself is only offering a half-hearted challenge, but our voice is still meek. We accept unacceptable behavior, hoping others will take up the cause. We have forgotten how to use our sword. The Stagnant Life has become a way of life, and it will take hard effort and courage to revive the true Spirit and Strength.

Laziness of the Spirit

Have you become complacent in areas of your life which could help you on your path? Do you expect others to do things for you without your active participation? Do you look away, even when you know something isn't right? Do you realize that this type of laziness will eat into your Spirit? Record your thoughts and think of how you will prevent laziness from encroaching on your dreams.

The Lessons of The King's Road

- Though most of us won't choose our names in life as we make significant breakthroughs, we should realize that we do build reputations with our name. However, when we are in difficult situations, we cannot let reputation alone determine the outcome. We must learn to rely on the skills that got us there.
- When we have a chance to express love to those we care for, we should do so. It seems elementary, but there are too many "If only I had told…" comments in people's lives. Let's avoid the game playing before it's too late.
- We must learn to evaluate our skills and experience for a particular situation. We neither want to avoid challenges, nor do we want to fail because we have gotten in too far over our heads.
- Let's aim for "Win-Win" experiences in our lives. Let's not misuse our talents and resources, nor others. Let's learn the true value of what abounds within and around us.
- We cannot become lethargic because we've had past victories. We will lose our skills for future challenges, plus our Spirit will become weak and lose confidence. We cannot expect our lives and the world to become a better place if we sit among our rooms of trophies, and fail to move out to the future.

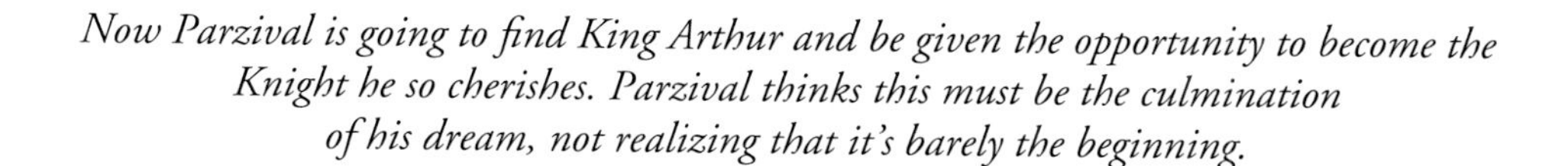

Now Parzival is going to find King Arthur and be given the opportunity to become the Knight he so cherishes. Parzival thinks this must be the culmination of his dream, not realizing that it's barely the beginning.

Chapter 5 - Clowns in the Court

If you ever get a chance to see a performance of Cirque du Soleil, grab the opportunity. These athletes execute seemingly impossible moves on poles, trampolines, bungee cords, trapeze bars, and even terra firma. Flexibility and strength are understatements when it comes to their body conditioning. In spite of their high athletic prowess, their costumes are ragged and offshoots of clown's attire. Take the color off of their clothing, and you may well find the style of a poor street urchin. They are gold hidden in a plain cloth purse.

Parzival will walk into court, dressed in his fool's clothes, ready to take on knightly challenges. The question is—Who are the real fools in the court?

Arthur's Court

Parzival rides into Nantes where a crowd gathers around him. Iwanet comes to help him and Parzival asks which of the Arthurs would make him a knight. Iwanet is amused and tells him the right Arthur is not here, but offers to bring Parzival to the King.

Upon arriving, Parzival greets the court and asks who the king is, because a man in red is waiting to fight him. Parzival says he would surely like to have a red uniform just like that knight. Parzival also says the man wants to apologize for spilling the wine on the queen. In spite of his lack of courtly manners, everyone admires Parzival's handsomeness. Arthur repays the greeting and says he would serve Parzival with his life and possessions. Parzival wants to be made a knight immediately, as he has figured it should have been done a year ago. Arthur says he would do it tomorrow, but Parzival wants the Red Knight's armor now. Parzival says he doesn't care about any other gifts, as his mother was a queen and could have given him many things. Arthur says it is not possible to give him the red armor, but Keie says to let Parzival go get it himself. Arthur says Parzival would be killed.

Parzival is leaving and all gather to watch him ride out to the challenge. Even the queen stands on her balcony with her ladies. As Parzival rides past Lady Cunneware, she laughs. She had said she would never laugh until she had seen the greatest knight. This angers Keie, who beats her with a staff until her clothes are shredded and her skin broken. Antanor, who would not speak until the best knight appeared, speaks, and he too is beaten. This angers Parzival, who would have thrown a javelin, but there were too many people around the queen.

— *Parzival* Summary, Book III, ¶ 148–153

Recognizing Hope

You can't judge a book by its cover.
— Popular Saying

Hope in the Prison of Despair
by Evelyn de Morgan (1855–1919)
Oil on Canvas, 1887. 23 x 25 ½ in.

We may find it unusual that a raggedy dressed boy could ride into town, ask to see the king, then ask to be made a knight, and this is all agreed to. I'm sure bums show up on the White House steps, are asked in to tea, and made a cabinet member. But look at our movie examples. Will Hunting is a janitor, mopping floors, when he is discovered by the professor. Forrest Gump is discovered by football coaches when he runs across the football field in street clothes. Roy Hobbs takes on baseball fame, looking like he just came off the farm, which he did. Luke Skywalker is wearing his inter-planetary "farm" clothes when he is recognized as a potential Jedi knight. Anakin Skywalker wears slave's clothes.

The clue in this story lies in the constant reference as to how handsome Parzival is. If you're a real good looking bum, you might be given a chance. This may seem to be a rather shallow way of judging people, but the courts of handsome men and beautiful women may indicate more than just physical beauty.

With Parzival such a great natural athlete, his physique was probably that of a fighting man, and since he had no fear of anything, he had to exude confidence, even if it was an innocent confidence. In ancient times, those who retained health and beauty had to have special knowledge and practice to fight off disease and the physical wear and tear of everyday life. It would then be no wonder that a beautiful person would come to symbolize someone with special abilities. Even with our modern commercial values, the talented man or woman, even with physical imperfections, is still seen to be beautiful.

So this extraordinary looking man walks in, and the court now has some hope. Perhaps, they think, this is the man who could help us. Maybe there is a dearth of promising men and Arthur is signing up anybody. I remember in grade school, a new boy was transferred into my class mid-year. All of the girls were after the new boy. It's not that he was any handsomer than the other boys in class, but he just seemed to be. We knew all about the other boys and a new one meant fresh possibilities.

So it is with Parzival. Gawan is away from court, and the other knights couldn't do what was expected of them, so maybe this well built young man can do it. Underneath is always a vision of a Messiah, the one who will save us from our troubles. In truth, the court is right about him. He is the Chosen One, but it will be a long time before anyone, including Parzival, is able to confirm it.

Remember that Arthur's court represents the Community. The Community is in a malaise, but it perks up when a potential hero comes riding in, even one disguised in rags. The hero is one who will eventually prove himself in the Spiritual realm. This tells us that even as a nation, as a world, we know at a deep level that it will take values and a sense of Spirit to cure the problems of the Community.

Making Us Handsome

We tend to work things backwards. We think that dress-for-success clothes and Rolex watches make us successful, rather than realizing that it is who we are that determines our real success. The other stuff is just trappings, just fancy fool clothes. Maybe they're fun and beautiful, but they're still just fool clothes. We must remind ourselves of this fact when we enter strange new arenas with everyone staring us down and we start worrying about what we look like, rather than what we have to offer. We must develop the "handsomeness" that comes from a confidence which says "I belong here and I have a mission."

1. Think of the times when you could not take charge of a situation because you spent more time with your clothes/hair/makeup, than practicing your speech or necessary skills. You then walked in hoping your looks would carry you, rather than the confidence that comes from self-development.

2. Now think of future commitments where you want to impress people. Concentrate on the wonderful traits and skills you have to make an impression. I'm not advocating you just walk in as a slob, but let your personality and presence be the real beauty in your life. Make people know that you can make a difference because of your potential, not your "rags," no matter how expensive those rags are.

Hollow Words

We are the hollow men
We are the stuffed men
Leaning together
Headpiece filled with straw. Alas!
Our dried voices, when
We whisper together
Are quiet and meaningless
As wind in dry grass
Or rats' feet over broken glass
In our dry cellar.

— from the poem "The Hollow Men" by T. S. Eliot
(also quoted in *Apocalypse Now*)

Arthur says that he will serve with his life and his possessions. Well, we know this isn't true because he could not even stand up to the insult given his wife, his kingdom. But he has good intentions. At one time, the offering of possessions would have been a truthful statement, because the status of a king was based not only on his warring abilities, but on his generosity. In fact, this tradition exists in many societies. In Native American custom, there are Giveaways. During special celebrations, the party giver hands out gifts of food, blankets, tools, utensils, and almost anything that members of the tribe need. The more you give, the more honor is given. Forrest Gump learned this lesson. After he made his fortune, he set about giving money to the church and charity. He even cut the football lawn at the school for free.

Arthur was known as a generous king, dividing up the goods of war with his men, thus ensuring a strong community. In Triad 2 of *The Welsh Triads,* we are told that Nudd the Generous, Mordaf the Generous, and Rydderch the Generous are the three most generous men of Britain. Except for Arthur, who is the most generous of all of them.

Somewhere along the way, Arthur loses this true generosity. In *The Story of Merlin,* found in the French Vulgate Cycle, we have an interesting story about Arthur and his altruism (or lack thereof).

Right before an important battle, Merlin takes Arthur and several kings to a buried treasure. Merlin tells Arthur not to hold back in his giving because he will then get everything he needs in return. They mark the spot of the treasure, to return to after the battle.

They do win the battle and appear to be very generous as they take the war spoils and divide it among everyone according to their needs. Arthur and the kings seem to have perfected an early social security system. However, they conveniently left out the buried treasure that Merlin had taken them to. It takes Merlin showing up and shaming Arthur to remind him of his true duty.

So, here in the *Parzival* story we have Arthur promising riches as a noble ruler should. However, they are just words of ritual. We don't know if Arthur really has anything to give, or if he has another buried treasure somewhere. Not unlike modern leaders who speak their words of ritual, which could mean something if they are backed by action.

Hollow Words

In our own lives, we sometimes speak with Hollow Words. We often have good intentions when we speak the words, and may even believe that we will follow through with appropriate actions, but we also fail.

1. Recount times that you made commitments which you knew you could not adequately deliver on. Balance the positive and negative results of those promises.

2. One effort we may choose to make in life is to speak fewer of these Hollow Words—only making promises which we are reasonably certain we can or are willing to fulfill. Mentally make a promise to yourself that you will reasonably analyze a demand on your resources when someone asks a favor of you. Don't just let your ego speak too quickly. If you know you can, and are willing to take on a new project, go ahead. Otherwise, gracefully decline, knowing that in the long run, everyone benefits.

3. Now turn your thoughts toward your own gullibility when you listen to other people's Hollow Words. Think of the times you knew someone really couldn't or wouldn't help you with what you asked for, but you held on to their word as if it were an iron-clad contract. We do ourselves a great disservice when we blindly listen to just words and don't take the whole situation into focus. Train yourself to listen and look for the truth of the situation.

The Rash Boon

Something else is going on when Arthur is asked for a favor. It is a custom called the Rash Boon. This has nothing to do with a skin disease on an ape. It has everything to do with our deep fantasies of trust and unconditional love, and what one's Word really means.

The Rash Boon operates like this. A Boon is a requested favor, with its etymological root a word for "prayer." When one asks for a boon, she is asking for a blessing. The Rash part has to do with impetuous behavior, meaning that the person from whom the favor is asked must answer quickly. In fact, in these tales the asker doesn't tell what the favor is, until the promise is made that the gift will be given no matter what. Often, Rash Boons do not have happy consequences. At the least, they create a lot of extra work. It is like walking up to a millionaire, making her promise to give you anything, then asking for a million dollars. And she gives it. In modern day marriages involving many assets, we see the promise to marry, then afterwards a prenuptial agreement is sneaked in. It's also the premise that made "Let's Make A Deal" a popular game show, with participants deciding what they would or would not give up for a hidden prize behind a door.

In *Parzival,* we have Arthur giving a Rash Boon plus. Before Parzival even has a chance to ask for something, Arthur has promised him everything. Some people have theorized that this type of behavior started as drunken challenges, which a man of honor would still have to uphold when he was sober.

There's a possibility that these roots are in something more primal than frosty libations. Whenever we are ready to make a massive life changes, we are, in a sense, asking and giving Rash Boons. When we go into marriage, we extract a promise of love forever, but forget to mention the hidden flaws behind that promise. We send a young man to war with the promise of being a hero, but don't tell him of the hell that awaits in the jungle. When we demand from our mates and our families unconditional love no matter what we do, we are asking for that Rash Boon. When we agree to give a Rash Boon, we are telling people that you can count on us and our word to follow through.

Arthur may be overly anxious to give a promise he cannot keep, but at one time he could. At one time he was strong and could give almost anything anyone asked for. This is the trust that develops between those we love, and this is a test of that love. Sometimes the tests are unfair, but the rewards are greater than imagined.

The Trickster

Keie is an interesting figure in Arthurian myth, because he, like Gawan and most of the women in these stories, degenerated in character as the myths evolved. He is more commonly known as Kay, Arthur's foster brother, whom Arthur went to retrieve the Sword in the Stone for. He is portrayed as sneaky when he tries to claim the kingship for himself, knowing it was Arthur who pulled the Sword of Kingship from the stone.

However, in *The Mabinogion,* we can see hints of his previous greatness. It is found in the story of "How Culhwch Won Olwen," which just happens to be one of those Rash Boon stories. Culhwch (that "w" in there is like the *"oo"* found in n*oo*k) shows up in Arthur's court. He demands that Arthur give him a giant's daughter, Olwen, to marry; otherwise Arthur will face great shame. The whole court gets involved in a complicated quest for this wife when Keie volunteers to save Arthur from the shame. His talents are listed: he can stay under water for nine days and nights, go without sleep for nine days and nights, inflict wounds that can not be healed, and he can grow as tall as a tree. The heat he can generate from his body keeps items dry in a rainstorm and is strong enough to start a fire. Poor Keie goes a long way from being this hero who saves Arthur from shame to the sniveling torturer of later stories.

Blue Whipper Kachina by L. Mitchell
Wood and Various Materials. 6 ½ in.

Keie becomes a nag, a complainer, an insulter. His role, though, is an important one. He is the goading Trickster. He is Loki in Norse myth, stirring up mistrust among the gods of Valhalla by revealing their secret truths. Native American myth has several Tricksters, with Coyote being one of the most popular.

The Trickster forces us to look at the real truths of ourselves, though he may do it in means that are unpalatable to us. The Trickster is different from the Fool because the Trickster knows what is going on. He is very aware, even if he doesn't let on that he knows what's what. All along, the people in Parzival's life have been too fearful for him—his mother, Sigune, and now Arthur, who wants to postpone making him a knight and won't send him against the Red Knight. Keie, though, is downright rude and nasty, beating people who stand up for Parzival. It is his abominable actions which finally give Parzival the anger to goad him into action. We might prefer to think that we operate well just reaching for grand goals, but an element of anger sometimes pushes us into action quicker than philosophical discussions.

Keie's actions are very similar to the Loathly Hag. Both are Initiators, and both use coarse language, but both push people towards their truth. This is different from the negative talk that demoralizes or sabotages. The talk that sabotages is untrue, while the talk that pushes us forward has truth. The language of the Trickster and the Loathly Lady is the language of action.

The Trickster

The people we may usually refer to as our "enemies" or troublemakers, may in fact be Tricksters who are reflecting a truth we don't want to see. Now, some of these people may be Saboteurs, but look to see if there is some truth in the problems they present us.

Think of people whom you could have done without, but when you look objectively at their actions, they tell some truth about yourself. Maybe the athletic jock you were jealous of reminds you that if you want to be that good, you have to work harder. Maybe the obnoxious person who has the boss' ear tells you that you need to develop better communication skills. Maybe those disdained bills that roll into your mail box are a reminder that you shouldn't be spending so much. Just examine the painful situations and see if there isn't some need to make a change in your life.

Greed Gets Us Going

We have a hero who has a calling, but he doesn't know it. He can only operate from the basest of his emotions, which now mean greed and anger. Parzival has no idea what is going on in the court. He is not going to fight to save Arthur's honor and kingdom. He is not avenging the honor of Ginover. He may be angry at how Cunneware and Antanor are beaten for recognizing him as a hero, but he hasn't declared avenging their unfair treatment. He just wants some pretty red armor. And he wants it now.

Christ Purging the Temple
by Giotto di Bondono (1267–1337)
Capella degli Scrovegni, Padua, Italy
Fresco, 1304–06

This is a big motivating stage for most of us fools. Initially, our goals are only based on the material rewards. It is not an uncommon motivator when we first enter the Community at large and must feel our way around. We must recognize that this is only a beginning impetus, and a natural one, but not one which should rule the total path of our lives. It is the focus of the unlearned fool. We must keep this in mind as we develop a path of not only material success, but one of spiritual success.

If nothing else, Parzival's greed has put him on a path of action. This is part of our Yin/Yang paradox where good things can come out of bad, and vice versa. It also reflects how our own lives have evolved. Our initial motivators are based on more primitive needs and desires. As we develop and mature, we can make decisions based on other principles.

> *Greed*
>
> *When examining your Grail, how much of it is based on a Value-Driven Life versus a Greed-Driven Life? If you never receive enormous material rewards from the path you are choosing, will this life give you satisfaction?*

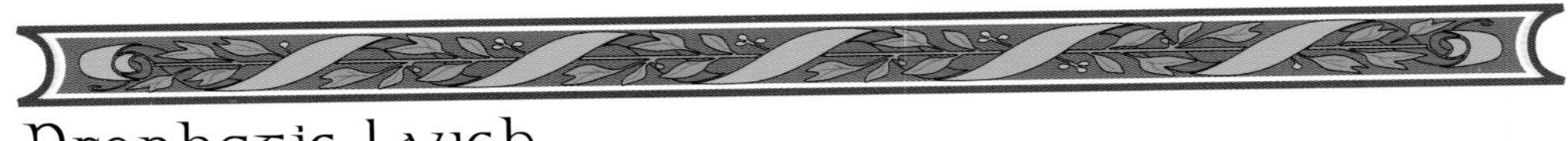

Prophetic Laugh

We have a formerly silent woman sitting in the corner cackling to herself. Most people would have understood laughing at a fool coming into court demanding to be made a knight; but when the woman laughing would only do so when the greatest knight shows up, it becomes a different story. It becomes a sign of the Prophetic Laugh.

The Prophetic Laugh occurs when the most dire of truths is recognized in the face of absurdity. It is the laugh which comes about when a man realizes that his "faithful" wife has betrayed his trust and in an instant, knows his future has changed. It is the hard, uneasy smile that comes when a couple looks out at their tornado-ravaged home and realizes that although there will be the hard work of rebuilding, it could have been worse.

When Cunneware laughs, she has prophesied Parzival's future as well as that of the Sybil who sat at Apollo's shrine. When the silent Antanor finally speaks, he tells Keie that he better be prepared, because Keie will get his own punishment at the hands of Parzival.

Merlin is noted in several stories with his Prophetic Laugh. In a very early tale, his personality is found in the character Lailoken. He, too, has refused to speak, but laughs when King Meldred brushes a leaf from his queen's hair. The king insists that Lailoken tell him why he laughs. Lailoken refuses, saying much harm would come from what he has to say. Only after much coaxing does Lailoken give a prophecy of his own death, but reveals a terrible truth. The leaf in the queen's hair came from an adulterous tryst. Despite her protestations of innocence, the king knows the power of Lailoken's prophecy.

In *The Mabinogion,* Peredur's prophets are a pair of dwarfs, a husband and wife. They had entered Arthur's court a year earlier and not spoken to anyone. Both greet Peredur as the chief of warriors and flower among knights. (Notice the flower motif.) It is important to note that these seers are dwarfs. In myths, dwarfs, like fairies, are representatives of gods who were reduced in stature. They are still power beings, often associated with smith craft, like the crippled god Hephaestus. They make wonderful gifts for the Norse gods, and they have secret hoards of gold as Irish Leprechauns. When you read your fairy tales and myths, remember that these small souls once exemplified truth and power. Even Parry had to listen to the voices of the "little people" who directed him on his Grail Quest.

The Lessons of Clowns in the Court

No matter what we wear, our heroic possibilities must be allowed to shine through. What is most special in our spiritual selves should take a back seat to the mundane paraphernalia we drape ourselves in.

We must not offer promises we cannot keep. This is continuing the language of Hollow Words. Everyone is hurt in the long run and trust cannot be developed. Realize that others also make promises which cannot be kept and learn to differentiate whose word can be counted on.

Rash Boons are tests of our relationships. Sometimes unfair, they make us work harder and challenge us to be greater than we may have thought possible.

Some people who seem to be intolerable, may only be Tricksters in our lives. They cajole and anger us, but give us a shove towards action. Greed also motivates us in early stages of our lives, but eventually we must learn to incorporate other values to encourage us in our endeavors.

The Prophetic Laugh focuses on irony in difficult situations. It is a human response bordering on enlightenment when we see painful truths and can still have an immediate smile.

Parzival will now go out on his first real challenge.
He will be a victor,...or will he?

Chapter 6 – I Was Thinking of Something in Red

The White Cloud,
Head Chief of the Iowas
by George Catlin (1796–1872)
National Gallery of Art,
Paul Mellon Collection.
Oil on Canvas, 1844–45
28 x 22 7/8 in.

Will Hunting scribbles notations on his bathroom mirror. The mirror reflects the work going on inside his mind, while also showing us the meager surroundings he lives in. He is picking up the gauntlet thrown down by Gerald Lambeau. In effect, he will be taking down the Red Knight when he solves that first mathematical problem.

Will definitely has the natural ability to excel, but he also has a major attitude problem. It is only his first success, and if he doesn't change his outlook, that success will eventually mean nothing. He will be the choir prodigy who never cut a CD. He will be the high school basketball star who never worked hard enough to have a chance at the pros. He may just as well keep his back turned to the blackboard and swab the grimy floors.

Defeat of the Red Knight

Parzival goes to Ither and tells him that Arthur knows the spilling was unintentional, and no one was coming out to meet the challenge. However, Arthur has ordered Ither to hand his armor and horse over to Parzival as a gift. The Red Knight is mildly amused at this statement, and turns his spear around to strike Parzival with the blunt end to punish, but not kill him. Parzival is angry at this treatment. He takes his javelin and aims for the open space of Ither's visor. The javelin goes through Ither's eye and brain killing him. Parzival cannot figure out how to get off the coveted armor and his fumbling motions make the horses whinny. Iwanet, Ginover's page, hears the horses and comes to the scene expecting to find Parzival dead. He sees Parzival's troubles and helps him get the armor off. Iwanet tells Parzival to remove the foolish clothes he wears, but Parzival says they came from his mother, and good or bad, he was keeping them. Iwanet won't give Parzival the javelin, as it was deemed a weapon too base for knights, but gives him a sword. Iwanet shows Parzival how to use it, and also explains the shield and spear. Parzival tells Iwanet to return the goblet and tell Arthur that he will avenge the beating of Cunneware. Iwanet grieves for Ither's ironic death and covers Ither with flowers. Everyone grieves Ither's death, including Ginover, who directs in preparing the body. Parzival is now considered a man.

— *Parzival* Summary, Book III, ¶ 154–160

Too Easy Victory

Roy Hobbs strikes out the Whammer.
(Roy-Robert Redford)

While on the train to Chicago, Roy Hobbs meets the Whammer, the best baseball player of his day. The train has to stop by the fairgrounds and the passengers get out to play and rest. Roy is drawing a crowd while he is pitching at milk bottles. The Whammer comes over, which makes Roy nervous, causing him to miss his pitch. Roy's manager, Sam, then bets Max, who is a sports writer, that Roy can strike out the Whammer in three pitches. For Max, this is a no brainer—what country bumpkin could possibly take down the Whammer? Roy sweats it a bit, but strikes out the Whammer. Imagine being a nobody striking out the greatest batter in the world in three pitches. The Red Knight just fell off his horse.

Anakin Skywalker saves Naboo, partly through his skill, and partly through luck. He climbs into a Naboo fighter plane for safety, but after fighting some droids, the plane goes into auto-pilot. It takes him towards the ship which controls the attacking droids. He's thrust into the middle of battle and while trying to shoot some droids, he misses, sending his torpedoes down the hallway, exploding in the reactor room. This sets up a chain reaction of destruction inside the control ship, completely destroying it. His piloting abilities were certainly in play here, but his battle abilities were strictly luck.

Forrest Gump dons a football uniform and waits for a ball to be passed to him. Then he just runs. He stomps over anyone who falls in front of him, and he shoves aside players with more experience and know-how than he will ever have. Touchdown for Gump.

Parry also has a Red Knight harassing him. Jack cannot see the Red Knight, but can defeat him, simply because the knight is afraid of Jack. Talk about a ridiculously easy victory.

All of these scenarios play out Parzival's victory over the Red Knight. He has a victory, but it is a false victory because he has not truly worked for a goal or reward. It is playing the lottery and winning. You have the money, but you have not developed skills, or achieved any wisdom in obtaining it. This is the bane of many talented people, who have early successes in life, built on luck and a certain amount of natural skill,

Kung Fu Calligraphy
by Huang Wei Lun

but who did not take the time to develop what is necessary for long lasting success. Later on, they hit a rough bump, and give up, because they truly don't know what to do. What worked before doesn't work anymore, and they have not gone through the trial and error process that others have. Parzival may even now have the right to demand the kingdom himself through heritage, but he doesn't have what it takes to rule. He may be a fool with natural talents, but he is still a fool. In the film *The Natural,* Roy's father reminds him that gifts are not enough. Success in life depends on personal development.

Kung fu students are taught to recognize the characters and understand the meaning of *kung fu*. The generally accepted definition is "Chinese martial arts," but the core of this word is much more important. The characters themselves stand for "working man" and "time." The real meaning of kung fu is threefold. It is to Achieve Excellence through Hard Work over a long period of Time. If any one of those three elements is missing, you do not have kung fu. I have seen many natural athletes come into class, impress people with their gymnastics, then leave after a short time. They do not have good kung fu because they did not put in the time required to hone skills. I've seen people show up to class many times, but if given the opportunity to talk instead of work hard, they talk. They do not have good kung fu. I have also seen people who put in time and hard work, but don't concentrate on the finer parts to make themselves better. Unfortunately, they miss it also.

> *Easy Victories*
>
> *Have you ever had an easy victory? Did it give you a little too much over confidence and expectations, or were you one of the few who recognized that the road is just beginning? Too many people look for the easy roads in life. It is the hook of "Get Rich Quick" schemes. Reflect on the times of your life that you may have eased up your efforts because of easy victory, instead of working and pursuing a hard earned goal. Think of what you could have done differently, and see how that applies to your exertions today. Determine to learn the necessary skills you need, both physically and spiritually, that complement your natural talents.*

With this definition, you can see that one can have good kung fu in anything you do. It can be art, tennis, the stock market, or knitting. In fact, kung fu masters were typically skilled in several aspects of knowledge, whether it was medicine, calligraphy, or music. The skill was reached through the discipline found in its very definition.

We have looked at the physical requirements for being successful, but the Red Knight represents something else. The battle takes place in a field of flowers, so we are alerted to an Other-

World or Spiritual challenge. An easy victory here can connote disaster in the future if one doesn't actively take the high road approach toward development in life. Will Hunting will maintain his bad attitude for awhile, so will not progress like he should be able to. He stunts developing his abilities, because he shortchanges himself in his spiritual life. Roy Hobbs will have a tragedy happen to him, because his excessive pride will attract the attention of a deranged Harriet Bird. She will shoot him because of his lack of spiritual development.

Easy victories are sweet, but we must take them as only one step in many if we are to succeed in our lives. This is equally true for developing our spiritual skills as well as our physical skills. Integrating spiritual values takes work. There are too many tests out there, and we must not be too self-congratulatory when we leap over the first hurdle.

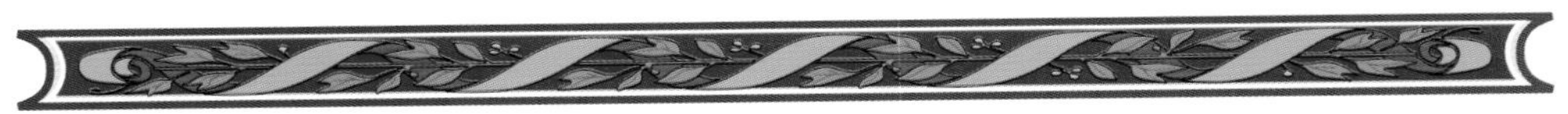

David and Goliath

Some of you may have noticed the same story pattern found in the Jewish and Christian story of David and Goliath. Goliath, champion of the Philistines, has challenged the Israeli court of Saul. Just like in Arthur's court, no one stands to meet Goliath's challenge. Along comes this young sheepherder, David, who says he is willing to face Goliath. Saul tells David that he is too inexperienced, but David is confident because he has handled lions and bears that came after the sheep. Saul "makes him a knight" by giving him armor, but David just wants to use his homemade weapons. David goes to Goliath and is scorned by him, just as Parzival is scorned by Ither. David takes pebbles from a pouch to hurl at Goliath's head; Parzival takes javelins from his quiver. David brings down Goliath and takes his weapons, just like Parzival takes the Red Knight's after killing him.

David also suffers from pride, and though he will become king, he too, will have spiritual lessons to resolve. Like murdering the husband of Bathsheba and the total destruction of villages. David repents his killing of Bathsheba's husband, Uriah, and God forgives him. But God does not walk away. Even though he forgives David, he deals a series of tragedies upon David. David learns Karmic justice—that all actions have consequences. Our initial victories may set us apart from others, but we still must learn to develop spiritually, even if we are a king.

Improper Response

The Red Knight challenges Parry.
(Red Knight-Chris Howell)

Will Hunting is driving around with his buddies when they see a guy who used to beat up Will when he was in kindergarten. The guy is also dating the ex-girlfriend of one of Will's friends. Reason enough to get out of the car and start pummeling the guy with no warning. Of course this leads to Will's arrest—just one in a series of arrests. Even after Professor Lambeau bails him out, Will continues his bad behavior with rude antics toward the psychiatrists brought in to help him.

In *Apocalypse Now,* Captain Kilgore, a man who equates the smell of napalm with Victory, wants to surf a beach held by the North Vietnamese. When you gotta surf, you gotta surf, so he sets about bombing with the cold detachment of a man set upon getting his own way. Nobody else matters as long as he gets his waves which magically break in two directions. (A Taoist metaphor?) He does the strike with the aid of helicopters flying to the music "The Ride of the Valkyries" from Wagner's opera *Der Ring des Nibelungen.* (As a note, Wagner's last work just happens to be considered one of his most profound and intricate—*Parsifal.*)

Benjamin Willard doesn't even know how many people he has killed before getting his assignment to go after Kurtz. He has such little thought about what he has been doing in his life that he can't possibly know what is proper or improper response. This shows up again when he coldly kills a Vietnamese girl wounded by one of his men. Bringing her to a hospital would have slowed down his own mission.

> ䷉ **Treading**
> Hexagram 10
>
> *Lǚ*
>
> He Treads on the Tiger's Tail, but it does not Bite. Careful Treading brings Harmony.

Proper Response vs. Improper Response. So much of our life would be made easier if we could stop and reflect on the line between the two before we make decisions. But we pick and choose a rationalization to justify our actions, sometimes after the fact.

Parzival has come to the Red Knight with a ludicrous proposal, a proposal so insulting that the Red

Knight would have been justified in killing Parzival. In effect, Ither has been challenged, even with Arthur's blessing, but he does see a bumbling boy in front of him. To kill him would have been cold murder, not a courtly joust. He rebukes the challenge by purposely not killing Parzival, instead striking him away with the butt of his weapon. This was Proper Response, at least from a warrior's code.

It is Parzival who behaves irrationally, but he does have all of that natural ability behind him. He kills a great man because of quick anger and his impatience to acquire the red armor. If only Parzival had behaved within courteous bounds, he might have obtained a great mentor and been able to refine his skills under watchful tutelage. Instead, Parzival essentially murders a man for his clothes.

Parzival is feeling rather proud of himself, but the major part of his quest will be learning the lesson that the Power to Heal is more difficult and more noble than the Power to Destroy. Destruction is the easy way out. Giving and restoring life is the true test of anyone's path.

In the Buddhist Eightfold Path, this is an example of Right Action. It is not enough to pursue our Grail with diligence and skill, but we must employ those skills with Right Action. We can choose to evaluate a situation and overwhelm an opponent, or we can meet a force with appropriate force. How often do shouting matches erupt over inconsequential matters in families? How often does road rage fester with an inconsiderate cutoff? How aggressively must we punish children newly learning the ways of the world? How often do we cut ourselves off from future opportunities because we get into trouble with our overreactions?

In the Taoist practice of Tai Chi, there is a way of refining movement by Stopping, Waiting, and Listening to the body to see if it is really in the proper position and moving the energy correctly. This refinement requires great patience and work to learn to listen to what is right and wrong. The more one practices, the quicker one can weed out the imperfections and build a more solid foundation. We have to learn to Stop, Wait, and Listen with the interactions of our lives. Too much hastiness and clumsy movement will never build the life that we want.

In Buddhism, there are the Ten Perfections. The theory is that if we are to

Proper Response

1. Possibly, if you just looked over the events of your life this past week, you can find examples of Improper Response. These reactions might not have been directed towards other people, rather just an emotional overreaction to an incident. So much energy is spent just in worry, anger, and anxiety, even when these reactions won't change the situation. List the events you felt that you did not respond to properly.

2. Now think of ways that you could have responded properly. Maybe you just needed an emotional fine tuning. Maybe an opposite action was the proper response. We know in our hearts what is proper and what isn't. What is proper will achieve your ends, without causing excessive harm to ourselves and others. Take time in difficult moments to Stop, Wait, and Listen to what is really happening and make a decision based on careful evaluation, not one of knee-jerk reactions.

achieve peacefulness and enlightenment in our lives, we need to master the Perfections. The Sixth Perfection is the development of Patience. Many times Proper Response is directly connected to our Patience. We need to make it a practice to take that extra breath before reacting.

Proper Response has to do with Compassion, both for ourselves and those who wrong us. It involves thinking with a clear mind and a clear heart. It does not mean that we should enable others to continually abuse us, but it does mean that we should not excessively use our energies in punishments and hasty reactions.

Second Noble Truth – Craving

The Death of Abel by Gustave Doré (1832–1883)

We spoke of *dukkha,* the first of the Buddha's Four Noble Truths, which says that life is suffering. The second noble Truth says that the reason for suffering is our craving and attachment to things of the world. This battle is a demonstration of this craving, because Parzival's only drive to attack Ither is the wanting of red armor. Ither certainly suffered from this craving, and later, Parzival will understand the magnitude of his crime and will feel guilt.

So much energy in our lives is spent in accumulating objects, rather than our self-development. I'm not against the finer things in life. I enjoy art, as well as a tool that does its job well. Good food, magnificent architecture, and beautiful surroundings are gifts of the universe. We just have to realize that the things of the world are only the icing on the cake. Who we are and what we have to offer as people are more important than what we surround ourselves with. If it means finding a better life, we have to be able to give up whatever we own.

Besides things, we develop attachments to people. I fully believe in the power of love and having those we love in our lives. Sometimes, however, we hold on to relationships which are debilitating and occasionally, devastating. We accept brutality in an attempt to hold on to a myth of being a couple. We endure belligerence from a boss who doesn't appreciate the work we supply. Even if the friendships had served us once upon a time, there is no reason to continue relationships that destroy our Spirit.

We lose loved ones through death or divorce or confrontation. When we lose someone we love, we need to grieve and remember, but we should not give up our lives because of the loss of a loved one. There is still much beauty in the world.

Unfortunately, we sometimes do not even know the true nature of our relationships. I have witnessed one of the more tragic examples of this statement. I once knew a man in his thirties who died suddenly. I sent flowers to his funeral, and within a week, the young wife responded with personalized thank you notes. I did not know the wife and I was very surprised that she could respond within such a short time. It turns out that the day after she had mailed her dutiful notes, she committed suicide. What makes this more tragic is that her husband was surrounded with rumors of dalliances. Rarely did I even hear him speak of his wife. So, a woman in her twenties, who would have had a chance at another life in the future, gave up her life for a man who did not show her much honor. Her attachment, based on what she believed was deep love, became deadly at the physical, and the spiritual level.

We also hold attachments to old beliefs and ideas that no longer serve us, and which may hinder us in development. We entrench patterns that once helped us, and that is why they are so difficult to get rid of. We actually become comfortable with destructive habits, because we fear taking the risk of the unpredictability of new behaviors.

Try this test for attachment. Ask yourself if the pursuit or the keeping of something harms you or others. We've seen the movies where the bad guy won't let go of the stolen money, so he meets his demise. Unclench your fists, if it means improving your life.

Unclenching the Fist

1. The hurricane is coming. You are going to lose everything around you. Your home, your clothes, your vintage comic books. Think of what you have inside you that would give you the strength to carry on. Can you lose everything and still see the potential for a wonderful life?

2. Think of what it would be like to lose the person you love most. Can you imagine life beyond the grieving period?

3. We're returning to the examining of the bad habits in our lives. See how you are attached to old beliefs and habits that have prevented you from achieving your Grail. You not only have to rid yourself of the bad habits, but you need to release the emotional attachment. Meditate on this attachment and how you will release yourself of it.

Old Clothes

I'm wearing second hand hats,
Second hand clothes,
That's why they call me
Second Hand Rose.
— "Second Hand Rose" by Grant Clarke

Parzival's refusal to give up the fool's clothes that his mother gave him is very significant. It is the refusal to let go of old ways and habits, even if those ways are inappropriate for the new way of life. He desires to be a knight, but he still wants his fool's clothes. Will Hunting wants to keeping hanging with his friends, instead of moving on to a new life, though he knows deep down that greater adventures await him

We rationalize that the old clothes are fairly comfortable, and so what if the snow goes through the holes in the shoes, and the coat lining is a bit threadbare? We can last another year, and another, and another. Worse of all, our old clothes were fashioned by someone else. They're second hand and discarded. They're someone else's old clothes.

How often have we clung to old habits, especially destructive ones, when we desire a new life? We have a fairly good idea of knowing what would truly be good for us, but we are always trying to negotiate an exception for us with the universe. We try to bargain to keep our cigarettes, as long as we go running for our health. We run up credit card debt, saying we'll be able to save for a house when times get better. If you want to be a knight, you need to take off the fool's clothes. We have to realize that what worked for someone else may not work for us. And what worked for us yesterday, may not work today.

This is a difficult concept for people, because at one time, many of our habits paid off. That is why we hold on to them. It is also hard to figure out what is necessary to move on in our lives. It requires diligent experimentation until the desired result is reached. It can be an exasperating trial, and we don't always have a friendly knight on the side helping us get the armor on. So, we just have to figure it out ourselves.

Getting Rid of the Old Clothes

We previously discussed the exchanging of old habits for new habits. Take time to see how you are doing in this process. Are there still any remnants of the old habits that prevent you from putting on the new? Do you still try to hide the fool's clothes under the shiny glare of a knight's armor? It'll get pretty itchy if you don't take them off.

Roses Are Red

La Japonaise
(Camille Monet in Japanese Costume)
by Claude Monet (1840–1926)

Courtesy, Museum of Fine Arts, Boston. (56.147)
Oil on Canvas, 1876. 91 ½ x 56 in.

Colors have their own mythology. Artists know this. Designers know this. Children with boxes of crayons know this. Red appears in the flags of the world, on Easter eggs, on Christmas wreaths, at Chinese celebrations, on Indian goddesses, on Native American Medicine Wheels, and on Valentine hearts. It totally covers our Red Knight. It is one of the most primal and powerful colors found in the cultures of the world.

Luke Skywalker flies under the code "Red 5" as he bombs the Death Star. "Red" is the name of Roy Hobbs' assistant baseball coach. Forrest Gump wears red as part of Bear Bryant's Crimson Tide football team. (By the way, the animal totem of King Arthur was the bear.) Gump plays ping pong in Red China. Anne and her apartment in *The Fisher King* glows red. Her clothes, nails, lingerie, phone, and drapes are all red. Professor Lambeau wears a red jacket when he is first informed that his math problem has been solved. Will Hunting gets a red car on his 21st birthday. Sean Maguire misses the World Series with the Red Sox to be with his future wife.

So, what's all this fuss about the color Red? It is the color of Blood. It is the blood of our hearts and veins, of sacrifice, and the blood of the womb where life begins.

As the color of sacrifice, it becomes the Paschal lamb and the blood marking the doors of Passover. It is the blood of Christ drank as wine during communion. World War II men fought with "blood, toil, tears and sweat," as described by Winston Churchill. Because of the menstrual blood association, red is a color of the Feminine principle. Red is the color of the Mother goddess in the Triplicate Goddess of Virgin/Mother/Crone. In Alchemical circles, the male principle is represented by white, the color of sperm. White and red are the colors that bloom in the center of the mistletoe, and this is why we can glean kisses when standing under this "magic" plant.

In Taoist art, red and green are the sacred, balancing colors. These colors are the elements of cinnabar and jade. When the Jedi Knights fight the Dark side, they carry green light sabers, while the Dark side wields the red. Good luck money in China are wrapped in *hong bao,* "red packages." The powerful man-god, General Kwan, is shown all colored in red. With Red a color of Power and Love, it is fitting that our hero will become the Red Knight.

Grief for the Red Knight

The noble Lady Ginover voiced her lamentation, "Alas and alack, the splendor of Arthur has been incomprehensibly broken. That he who should carry the highest fame of the company of the Round Table, lies here slain before Nantes. He demanded his inheritance, but was given death."

— from *Parzival,* Book III, ¶ 160

There is a certain amount of confusion as to why Ginover, Arthur's wife, would grieve for her husband's challenger. One would think that there would be celebration of the death of an enemy, but most of the court is in mourning. My interpretation has been based on my feeling that Ginover is a representative of the OtherWorld. Ither, too, with his red armor and flowers, is a king of the OtherWorld. Ginover has seen a chance for the King of the OtherWorld to take his place in the "Real World." Her current king is passive and she needs a strong king for her to be a strong queen. Otherwise she rules over a court of ninnies. In other Grail legends, Gwenevere is openly critical of Arthur's ineffectiveness. In *Perlesvaus,* she urges him to his own quest, where he meets disdain on the road as a lazy king, until he personally comes to the Grail. In *Diu Crône,* she teases him with an OtherWorld lover named Gasozein, until his jealousy makes him confront this man. Everyone is familiar with Gwenevere taking on Lancelot as a lover in other legends.

This means that the physical being, the person, knows that she needs the Other-World or spiritual world to come and make things right. It will take the king of the OtherWorld to make her kingdom strong, and when he is killed, much hope is lost to her. This is not just a love story of a queen who has quit loving her husband, but a queen who, seeing a failing kingdom, will do whatever is necessary to rebuild her court. By looking to the Spirit for help, she may have been trying to put aside her own old clothes.

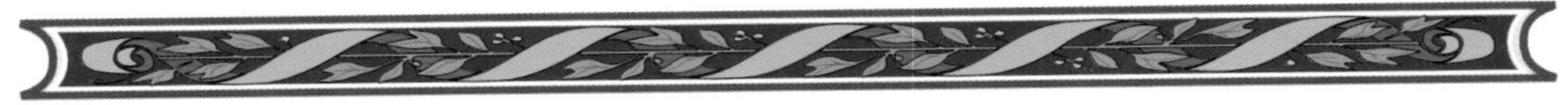

A Touched Heart

Parzival gives Iwanet the red gold cup Ither had stolen to be returned to Arthur. Parzival has won what he wanted, the red armor, but has no need of the Cup of Kingship. He actually has won a kingship, but chooses only the garb of a knight. At this point in the game, Parzival was unknowingly wise to do so. He's still the fool who didn't even know what that cup represented.

What is heartening, though, is the reason why he doesn't go to the court to return the cup. He has a sense of shame. He is wounded to the core when he sees Cunneware beaten for recognizing him with her Prophetic Laugh. He feels that he has been directly insulted by Keie's actions, though he was never directly challenged. For the first time, Parzival's heart has been touched, and it awakens a sense of responsibility that he must make amends. He just doesn't know how to do it. Perhaps he should go back and confront Keie directly, but he senses that there must be more adventure before he can return to Arthur's court. He understands that before he returns he must prove Cunneware's words to be true.

We must learn to appreciate the people who take risks for us. We don't necessarily have to have a whole series of adventures to prove their hopes true, but we can regard their faith in us as an uplifting source of spirit. Ultimately, we must live our lives to our own standards, but if our efforts can benefit and support those who believe in us, then we will achieve a greater sense of purpose.

Appreciation for Those Who Believe in Us

Sometimes we're not too sure how to reward those who had faith in us, especially when they haven't asked for anything. Think of those people in your life who have been there for you, and now think of some small way you can repay their belief. It may be as simple as lunch on the town, or a little note inquiring what is going on in their lives. As you work towards your Grail, note these special people, and when given the opportunity, show your appreciation.

The Lessons of I Was Thinking of Something in Red

We hope and wish for easy victories in our life, but lasting foundations and Excellence can only be built through Hard Work over a long period of Time. This is true for our spiritual lives as well as in our everyday living.

Spiritual choices are made when we develop Proper Response to situations. This is fitting the punishment to the crime, or allowing inconsequential items to not affect us in an extreme way.

We must find a balance between Craving what is superfluous in our lives and Need which gives purpose and sustenance. We must let go of attachments which hinder our personal developments.

Sometimes we hold ourselves back by refusing to put aside the old clothes for the new. We try to hang on to the old way of doing things, rather than taking on the new habits and responsibilities which will put us on our path to the Grail.

There will be people in our lives who believe in what we do and our ability to achieve it. Their good thoughts and prayers do help us along, so we should think of ways to repay them for their goodwill.

Now Parzival will have his chance to learn the skills and code of knighthood. He will be offered a wife and home, but will turn them down.

Midnight Ride of Paul Revere by Grant Wood (1892–1942)

The Metropolitan Museum of Art, New York, Arthur Hoppock Hearn Fund, 1950. (50.117)
Oil on Composition Board, 1931. 30 x 40 in.
Photo: ©1988 The Metropolitan Museum of Art. Courtesy: © Estate of Grant Wood/VAGA, New York

Chapter 7 - Rules of the Road

Luke Skywalker discovers that R2-D2 has taken off. Since the droid was in Luke's charge, he has to find R2-D2. Luke gets in his speeder for the search, but has no idea where R2-D2 went. He guesses that he went towards Old Ben's place. The moment that Luke gets in the speeder, he has mounted the Red Horse of Tao, which will take him to his first teacher — Obi-Wan "Ben" Kenobi.

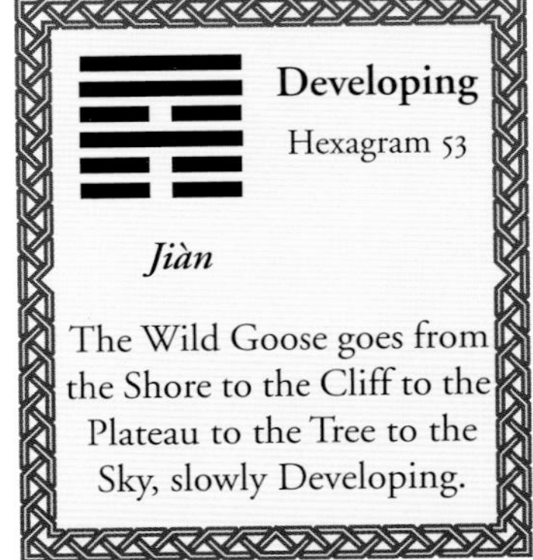

Gurnemanz

Parzival takes Ither's red horse, which never sweated and could ride further than any other horse. Parzival doesn't know how to control the horse and allows it to gallop at will. In the distance he sees towers along the horizon, and he thinks that Arthur has planted these towers and makes them grow. Parzival rides to the castle of Gurnemanz de Graharz, who is leaning against a linden tree. Parzival is willing to take advice from him as his mother told him to take advice from men with gray hair. Pages are summoned and when they undress Parzival, see the fool's garb. At first, people are embarrassed and amused. One knight says the dress could be a guise for a love adventure gone wrong. Gurnemanz cares for Parzival's wounds and feeds him, as no one had fed him all day.

In the morning, maidens help him with a bath and Parzival dresses in fine clothes left for him. Gurnemanz teaches him of the Mass, and asks Parzival to tell where he came from. Parzival relates all of his experiences, and now the court calls Parzival "The Red Knight." Gurnemanz tells Parzival to forget his mother's advice and listen to Gurnemanz' advice. Gurnemanz gives rules that would cover knightly responsibilities, the power of the true love of a wife and husband, and very importantly, not to ask too many questions.

Parzival is then instructed in proper horseback riding and the spear. He easily and soundly defeats five knights. One of the defeated men says Parzival should marry the lord's daughter, and replace the loss of the lord's three dead sons.

That night, Gurnemanz's daughter, Liaze, is instructed to kiss Parzival, but she doesn't have a ring to give. Liaze had been told to give Parzival much attention and the people of the court were told to ignore any intimacies. After fourteen days, Parzival feels the need to leave. Gurnemanz is unhappy, saying he is losing a fourth son. Parzival feels sorry for Gurnemanz and to make him happy, Parzival says he would marry Liaze if he gains renown.

— *Parzival* Summary, Book III, ¶ 161–179

Climbing on the Red Horse

He travels with Fortune's guidance.
— Gurnemanz speaking of Parzival in *Parzival,* Book III, ¶ 175

Dèjá vu. Jenny and Forrest are older, walking that infamous path, when our three "knights" strike again. Jenny hollers her timely lesson, "Run, Forrest, Run!" Again, Forrest takes off running. It seems to be just another replay in another time frame, but serendipity steps in. This time he will leave behind Greenbow, his mother, the taunts of lesser men, and ride a horse which he cannot control. The horse knows exactly where to go; Forrest can only hang on for dear life. Forrest ends up under the tutelage of the infamous football coach Bear Bryant. Gump did not imagine that his running would actually take him somewhere.

Parzival now meets his first teacher on his path of knighthood. He finally will get a chance to start refining that raw, natural talent that he has been splaying all over the countryside. He found his teacher by getting on that red fairy horse which belonged to the Red Knight.

Finding a teacher who will help you in your quest is critical. Anakin Skywalker's pod racer will enable him to hook up with his first teacher, Jedi Master Qui-Gon Jinn. With Luke, Gump, and Parzival, it seems that all they needed was luck; even Gurnemanz says that Parzival rides with Fortune. But Fortune helps those who help themselves. In *Good Will Hunting,* the lottery ticket motif keeps appearing. Sean Maguire fantasizes paying his bar tab with it, but Chuckie knows who has the winning lottery ticket. It's the one that Will Hunting has through his abilities, and he berates Will for not cashing it in. That image of Parzival allowing the horse to take him where he needs to be is a metaphor for keeping your senses aware for possibilities that help you. If you want to be a great knight, get on a great knight's horse.

Once we have an idea of what our Grail is, suddenly opportunities will start popping up everywhere. There are many teachers around us—books, internet, television, or real, live people. They were always there, but now your senses are attuned to them. To really be involved, however, you've got to grab those chances whizzing by you. You have to start somewhere. Get started. Let your Intuition and opportunity open the doors. Find that initial teacher.

Opportunities Around Us

Opportunities to learn what you need to know to achieve your Grail are all about you. Start noting those little "coincidences" which are pointing you in the right direction. Make a list of all of the possibilities to help you get your starting point. Allow yourself to find a teacher so you can actually work towards what lies in your heart.

New Rules for the Road

Obi-Wan "Ben" Kenobi becomes
Luke Skywalker's first teacher.
(Obi-Wan-Alec Guinness, Luke-Mark Hamill)

Gurnemanz is to be Parzival's instructor for this phase of his life. Gurnemanz gives Parzival a new set of instructions and tells him to forget what his mother taught him. Parzival says he will ignore his previous lessons, but the book says he does not forget those instructions in his heart.

Gurnemanz' instructions are the rules which will develop Parzival into a knight. They include courtesy, instructions of the Church, and respect for ladies. These rules are good rules when you want to move within the society of knights, but they are still rules meant to take someone away from their natural state. One of those rules, that of not asking too many questions, will be pivotal in Parzival's life.

Notice that I say that Gurnemanz is the instructor for this phase of Parzival's life. What Parzival learns from him is important, but not the end-all. When Forrest Gump learns to play football, he further develops his physical skills which will enable him to survive the jungles of Vietnam. Obi-Wan "Ben" Kenobi is very instrumental in beginning Luke's training as a Jedi Knight, but even he can't take Luke all the way. Siddhartha and Govinda hear rumors of the Buddha and willingly leave the *Samanas,* much to the *Samanas'* dismay.

Keep in mind that you should learn as much as you can where you are today, but realize that you are probably only getting a partial picture of where you are going. Rarely are people lucky enough to get the ultimate teacher right out of the starting gate.

We must also note that Parzival is working on the skills and manners that help him as a knight in the physical realm. The true tests of his life are based on going beyond those skills and rudimentary rules. He will fail the big test, because he blindly adheres to the rules learned here.

Gurnemanz' Instructions

When Bubba and Forrest arrive in Vietnam, Lt. Dan is ready with a whole list of rules for surviving the war. He starts out telling them not to salute him, since that could put his life in jeopardy if "Charlie" recognizes him as an officer. He tells Bubba to pull his big lip in to avoid any calamitous trips. He tells them to stick close to him. He finishes up with two important rules: one—take care of your feet, and two—Don't do anything stupid like get yourself killed. This seems to be good advice, even if it's a bit incomplete, for two tenderfoots about to be initiated into a bitter war.

The advice that Gurnemanz gives Parzival is worth examining, because it reflects part of the Code of Chivalry. A thousand years later, these concepts make up our own unwritten honor codes.

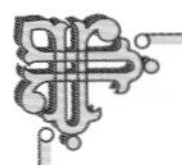

Gurnemanz' Code of Conduct

1. Never lose your sense of shame. Otherwise you could lose your honor.

There are two types of shame we have to deal with. One type is the one forced upon us by outside sources. This is where the child is ashamed of the parent's alcoholism, or the molested teen withdraws to private despair. This type of shame is a crime against the spirit. If you suffer from this, you must realize that you are not at fault, and do whatever you can to heal yourself of this shame.

The type of shame that Gurnemanz gives advice on relates to us being conscious about our own actions. If we take an attitude that anything goes, we will make mistakes which harm ourselves and those we care for. We will not be trusted or honored if we participate in shameful acts.

2. You must be compassionate towards the poor and shield them from unhappiness with generosity, kindness, and humility.

Though almost all of us complain about money problems, most of us do not live in abject poverty. When we do meet those who have less than we do, we should treat them with dignity. If we cannot be generous with money, we can at least be generous with kindness and compassion.

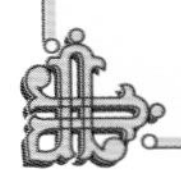

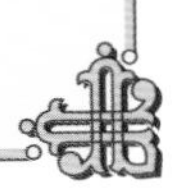

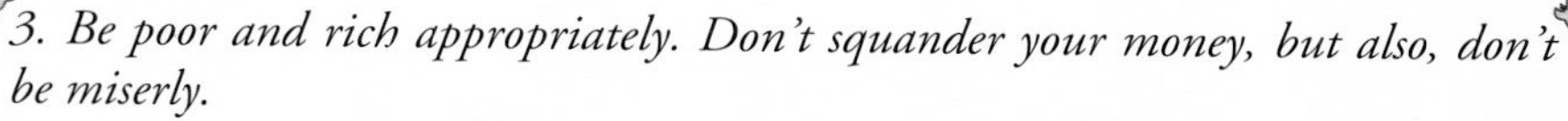

3. Be poor and rich appropriately. Don't squander your money, but also, don't be miserly.

Here is that Taoist concept of moderation applied to financial concerns. (And you thought that knights only thought about fighting and celebrations.) This solid advice could save people so much heartache if they followed those principles. We don't have to get in over our heads in debt to have a good life, and neither do we have to live in bare walled cubes, afraid to spend resources on the nicer things in life. When our finances are balanced, it will be easier to balance the rest of our lives.

4. Leave bad manners and ignorance in the past.

Yesterday, you may have been a jerk and slob, but you don't have to be one today. You have a chance to make yourself better, more refined, and more knowledgeable. Even a thousand years ago they were promoting self-help and improvement.

5. Do not ask too many questions.

WARNING! WARNING!

This simple little rule will get Parzival in trouble later. We need to look at Gurnemanz' intent, though we'll see what really happens later on.

Joseph Campbell has a viewpoint which may offer an explanation to the problem here. He points out the differences in learning and teaching styles between the East and the West. In the West, there is a tradition of the Question. In this case, the student is encouraged to ask questions of the teacher to keep involved with the thinking processes. In the East is the tradition of imitating the master without question. Both systems are valid. The Eastern way keeps students from asking silly questions and being obnoxious and rude before they have a chance to experience what they should be learning. They develop a solid foundation before questioning how things can change. The Western way develops a creative approach to problems, which can lead to early breakthroughs and discoveries. Since this story has a basis in Eastern as well as Western tradition, the admonition to keep your questions to yourself goes beyond a mere courtesy to be quiet, but to make an effort to observe carefully. Parzival will adhere to this rule blindly and not move into a natural level of questioning after the observation.

6. Let your senses help determine the truth.

Too often, we rely on the spoken word and not much else in our evaluation of the truth of a situation. People give clues to us in all senses, so we must rely on more than just our hearing. This rule instructs us to be aware and intuitive. Watch, sniff, feel, look beyond the obvious.

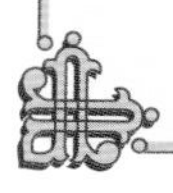

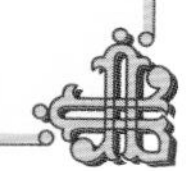

7. Temper daring with mercy. Allow a man to live if he surrenders, unless what he did would give you eternal grief.

This statement is interesting as it sets up a sense of justice that allows mercy without giving up victory. I have an idea that earlier times may have been an all or nothing conquest. Yet, if the opponent did something heinous, the option still existed to do away with the man.

In Tai Chi, there is a system of training called Pushing Hands. It develops sensitivity in reacting to an opponent. The ultimate goal is knowing how to fight through this sensitivity training. There are guidelines and principles while pushing, and what degree of force is determined by the opponent's level of aggression. We can use an example of one's home as a metaphor for determining appropriate aggression in the Pushing Hands environment. If an opponent is using light attacks and maintaining a distance, think of this as someone who has just entered your yard, and you politely, but firmly, ask them to leave. If they move further towards your center and with more intent, that would be like entering your living room, so you push them out the door. They may fall down, but they should have never come into your home. If the opponent uses hard, fast, powerful attacks to your center, that is an intruder who has come into your child's bedroom for evil intent, and you have every right to destroy him.

This rule is the one of Proper Response, which Parzival was unaware of when he killed Ither. From this moment on, this rule will serve him well.

8. When you take off your armor, wash up, so the ladies will like to look at you.

We may snicker at this now, but Medieval Europe wasn't known for its hygiene, so I think Wolfram was ahead of his time. Clean is sexier than armor grime. To be fair, there are still those among us in the 21st century who could heed this rule.

9. Be strong and cheerful.

No brooding heroes in Gurnemanz' court. Knights are expected to win on the battlefield and not come home to kick the dog and yell at the wench because it was a rough day. This is a great message about the Spirit. All challenges in our lives can be tough, but we will face them with strength and still find joy in life. People love cheerful winners, not sulking ones.

10. Keep women in high esteem. You may deceive many with lies, but deception in true love has no honor. Deceit will be found out and you will suffer shame forever.

It seems playing the field with women was a problem then as it is now. Gurnemanz warns Parzival that he can't think that people won't find out about his deceptions because it is like a prowler walking in a park filled with dry branches. The snapping and cracking will arouse suspicions. He may not lose his knighthood for it, but he will suffer the shame.

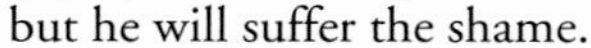

This is one of those rules which some people just shrug their shoulders and say that human nature can't be changed, so we'll just have to live with it. When we choose to manifest our Spirit at a higher plane, we can choose to live a life that does not hurt the ones we love. Some people say "it's just sex," but people are destroyed over indiscretions. Families are broken up, fortunes are dissolved, and long term depressions come out of this type of behavior. Some even lose their lives. It is a root of violence in many homes, and it affects children at levels that perpetuate the problems to our next generations.

Maybe your relationship is not a healthy one. Then work out a way of ending it in a way that does the least harm to everyone. Have the courage, discipline, and patience to end or remain in a relationship with honor.

11. Husband and wife are one, they blossom from the same seed.

This is a very romantic vision for a time when marriage was more economic and political than one based on living with a soul mate. Even today, we can talk of love, and say "we are one," but living it is still difficult. In the modern world, we have so many activities and opportunities that pull a couple apart. Gurnemanz says that the couple should be as inseparable as the sun that shines during the day and the day itself. I interpret this as common values and common goals help keep a couple together, even when the happenings of the day itself are varied.

At the very least, couples must think of this single metaphor as a meditation for life. That way, when either partner undertakes a new project, the couple can give early thought to what it means to them collectively and individually.

Gurnemanz' Code of Conduct

Pick one of Gurnemanz' rules that you think would improve your life. Think of ways you could implement it and integrate it into your life. It may be just putting on that cheerful countenance after a hard day of work, or it may be opening up all of your senses in new encounters. Work with it and make notes about how that rule has changed your life. Then test the other rules.

Warrior Princess

Technically, Jenny was Gump's first teacher. She is the one who teaches him to climb trees, read, and run sprints. As a female kung fu teacher, I'll admit to enjoying the stories of women who were the martial art instructors of heroes. I point out Jenny, because she is playing the role of the female warrior teacher found in Celtic legends. The Irish hero, Cu Chulain, will study with Scathach, and test himself against Aoife. Both women were considered fierce warriors, and Cu Chulain had been told his martial training would not be complete unless he studied with Scathach. Peredur, in the Welsh *Mabinogion,* must study with the Witch of Gloucester. *The Mabinogion* seems to hold many esoteric meanings. The difficulty is that the meanings are sometimes hard to pull from this convoluted saga. Peredur's relationship with the Witch of Gloucester has a meaning that deserves examination.

Peredur has come to a castle where he is warned by the queen not to stay with her, because she has been besieged by the Nine Witches of Gloucester. Peredur, a fearless knight, says "Don't worry, I can handle this." At dawn, he encounters the Chief Witch soundly beating the watchman. Peredur strikes her on the head with his sword, causing her helmet to crack. She calls him by name and asks for mercy. Peredur wonders how she knows him. Her reply is that it was prophesied that she was to be his teacher. She would know him by the harm he would cause her. Apparently, these witches were tough cookies, since nobody had ever harmed her before, much less beat her. Peredur stays three weeks with her, learning how to fight and ride a horse properly. Three weeks doesn't seem to be a long time, but this is a teacher from the OtherWorld. In the OtherWorld, three weeks may be three years or thirty years in earth terms.

Now I am going to cheat and jump ahead to the end of *Peredur* and reveal its fateful ending. Peredur ends up killing this woman who taught him how to fight and ride. This seems terribly tragic, but there is a valuable lesson here for anyone who is a teacher. The Witch of Gloucester knows all along that Peredur is destined to destroy her, yet she teaches him anyway. A teacher is suppose to give a student the foundation to be able to surpass the teacher. Few people are open enough to be able to accomplish this type of unselfish teaching, but this should be the aim of all educators. We cannot progress as a society unless future generations can learn and surpass the current one. Teachers don't have to give everything they know the first day, and they certainly have the right to schedule when they want to release

> *Teachers and Students*
>
> *1. If you are studying something, do you think about how lucky you are to be able to enjoy the fruits of thousands of years of thought and hard work? Do you let your teacher know that you appreciate what you do learn from her?*
>
> *2. If you are a teacher, do you have a clear idea about when you will share higher levels of knowledge with your students, and do you communicate to them what that standard or time frame is? Do you want your students to surpass your own skills?*

information. However, the eventual goal should not be to keep admiring captives for a lifetime, but to give responsible, caring students the ability to evolve knowledge for the next age.

Now for the flip side. We are so fortunate in the developed nations to have access to so much education, that people take it for granted. People believe that they have the right to any knowledge, any time, as long as they have money. Teachers often are treated as hired help, rather than someone who is sharing valuable lessons. Having come from a traditional martial arts background, I understand the difficulty that many Oriental teachers have of finding the balance between this "I have the money—show me" attitude and the traditional way of proving loyalty and patience to earn the right to learn. There must be give-and-take on both sides. Students must appreciate that education is a privilege, not a right. Students can earn the right to learn through diligent study and practice, and teachers have to be willing to teach those who show true interest and dedication.

The Wrong Face

Siddhartha also felt a longing and the stir of sex in him; but as he had never yet touched a woman, he hesitated a moment, although his hands were ready to seize her. At that moment he heard his inward voice and the voice said "No!" Then all the magic disappeared from the young woman's smiling face; he saw nothing but the ardent glance of a passionate young woman. Gently he stroked her cheek and quickly disappeared from the disappointed woman into the bamboo wood.

— from *Siddhartha* by Hermann Hesse

Gurnemanz wants Parzival for himself to replace his three dead sons, just as Herzeloyde wanted Parzival to replace her dead husband. This is an example of the teacher who wants to keep a student around forever for personal reasons, rather than encouraging the student to develop on his own. A person's destiny is being held back because another person is needy. Gurnemanz has given quality knightly training, so now he offers a big trump card to keep Parzival with him: his daughter Liaze.

As beguiling as Liaze is, her face is the wrong face—she is not a Goddess of Sovereignty. She has no ring to give to Parzival, indicating she is not a woman of power and substance. Her father is doing all of the negotiating of her marriage. Where Herzeloyde made her own decision for marriage, Liaze is her father's pawn.

A Very Honorable Courtesan in Springtime by Keisai Eisen (1790–1848)

Jack's first girlfriend in *The Fisher King* was out the door as soon as he ran into trouble. She was along for the ride, just as Liaze would be in Parzival's case. Forrest has a chance to be with some "working girls" on New Year's Eve, but he chooses to hold out for something better. Siddhartha turns down a luscious young woman who is eager to tempt a wandering *Samana,* but he decides to wait on the carnal pleasures of life. (Though he doesn't wait too long.)

Some conservatives may think this is a case for no premarital sex, but the lesson goes far beyond physical pleasures. It is the trapping of oneself in a good life, when a great one might be around the corner. It is disciplining yourself so that you have the opportunity to get on your true road of destiny. These examples happen to be centered around sex, one of the greatest temptations in life. But other baits can be used.

In all of these examples, the inner voice spoke "No." How often do we get ourselves into deep, long lasting, painful trouble by ignoring those nagging voices that warn us? Often, we get off the paths to our Grails because of these temptations. Sometimes, we allow ourselves to be pushed into the situations because of other people's needs. Sometimes we dive head-first into the whirlpool voluntarily.

Just as we need to be responsible in our actions towards other people, we also need to be responsible to ourselves by recognizing that we do not have to settle for less because others want us to. Be aware that the bribes and offers can be staggering. If your inner voice says "watch what you're doing," take heed and take a time-out.

Wrong Face

Many of us probably have a long list of the temptations we've given in to. Just concentrate on the life changing ones which took you off the path to your Grail. Was the night in back seat of the Chevy worth the consequences? Was the Christmas bonus to stay another year at the company worth it? Did your inner voice say "No" even if other parts of you said "Yes?" You may still have to pay for those decisions, but at least determine how wise you have become because of those experiences. Vow to look for similar circumstances so you do not repeat the same mistakes in the future.

Yes Syndrome

Parzival's agreement to marry comes out of that "let me please you" trap that many of us get into, commonly known as the "Yes Syndrome," where we volunteer and agree to do things that neither benefits us or those we care for. We just want to make things nice. The action is there to placate someone else's problems, but in our hearts, we know we're probably not even going to do it or we will do it with resentment. This "Yes Syndrome" can keep you off the path to your Grail for many years.

This is a stage of immaturity when we make promises we are not going to keep. We do it with the best of intentions; we want to make the other person feel good and like us. However, it is fairer to let them realize that they must solve their problems themselves. Sometimes we become enablers who encourage people to keep bad habits by doing their work for them. A Community does not become strong when only a few carry the load. Life is short, and you must learn to allocate your time wisely and towards activities that enrich your life and the lives of those you love. Even Gurnemanz is wise enough to know that Parzival's promise was one of youth, and Gurnemanz continues bereaving as Parzival rides away.

Saying No

If you are someone who fills up your schedule doing activities for others rather than yourself, learn to say "No." When someone asks you for a favor which you are unsure of doing, say "I'll think about it." The bought time will give you the space to decide what you really want to do. If you are still uneasy, learn to say "No." Don't feel guilty. You are giving your life, which is precious. Save your time and talents for projects and people that really matter to you, because that will benefit the world more.

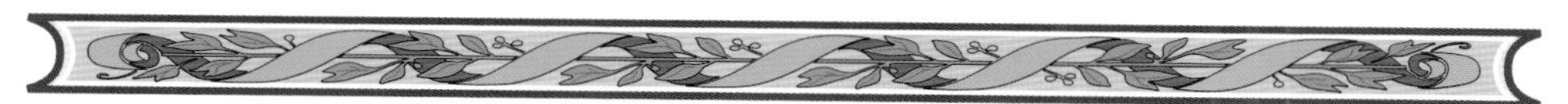

Worthy of Love

> *Sorrow pressed his heart, but only in this one matter—he wanted to have struggled more before enjoying the warmth of what is called a woman's arms. He was of the opinion that worthy striving was the highest goal in this life and the next . These words still hold true.*
>
> — from *Parzival,* Book III, ¶ 177

Parzival has turned down marriage with Liaze for a noble reason. Love is to be earned, not whimsically granted, nor taken. Parry has fallen in love with Lydia. He has not approached her, because he does not feel worthy of her love. Jack views this as quaint, and tries to convince Parry that he doesn't need the Grail to get Lydia's love. Jack says that women are so good at helping men with their goals, he should just go out and get Lydia. Roy Hobbs had a similar idea when he told Iris that he would be back for her, expecting to hit it big with the Cubs in Chicago. He got a little sidelined along the way.

When we first start dating someone, we earn love with kindness and caring. We show up on time, and are generous in many ways. Later on, the difficulties of life can erode a relationship, and we forget that we still need to earn love. We start to expect an illusory perfection of our mates, without looking at our own faults. Parry embraces Lydia's clumsiness as sweet. In fact, when Lydia drops her dumplings and spills her tea, Parry does the same to make her feel comfortable. Parry is willing to learn and share every detail of her life. Jack, however, doesn't even want to kiss Anne because of a pimple on her face, forgetting his own drunkenness and inconsiderate behavior he foisted on her.

Sean Maguire recalls his wife's flatulence with fondness and humor. Acknowledging that she had the goods on him, he tells Will Hunting that the small imperfections are the good parts of life.

There may be times that we need unconditional love, but in general, we should take a stance that the love we receive in life needs to be earned. We need to realize that if we expect love to keep us afloat we need to put effort and caring into a relationship.

There is an acronym popularized by Hugo-winning author Robert Heinlein in his book *The Moon Is A Harsh Mistress.*

TANSTAAFL

It stands for "There Ain't No Such Thing As A Free Lunch." Please note that the grammar rules for double negatives do not apply here. The economic point is that everything has a price and is paid by someone, somewhere. Ask Milton Friedman. You may get a free lunch at the business meeting, but someone paid for it. You may have won a free trip to Cancun, but someone paid for it. Love is the same. Someone is putting effort and, often, sacrifice into a relationship. Both people, not just one, should build the marriage. We need to merit the love we receive.

Worthy of Love

Think of what you have done today to earn the love that your partner gives you. If you haven't done anything yet, get into gear. Take the time to appreciate what your partner does, and let him/her know of your appreciation. Even if you do not have a partner, think in terms of familial love or friendship love. This practice strengthens all forms of love.

The Lessons of Rules of the Road

We must take chances and ride on that Red Horse of Tao, seeking out teachers who could help us achieve our personal Grails. There is a saying "Beginning is Half Done." It is a major step in achieving our dreams.

We must learn the skills that will get us in the fields we are interested in being in. There will be time later to modify and change, but only after we have achieved a certain amount of accomplishment and knowledge.

We should consider if some of Gurnemanz' Code would help us in our lives today. Gurnemanz' advice is a great start for someone wishing to live his life with honor and dignity.

Both teachers and students have a responsibility in the learning process. The student should be open and respectful to what the teacher shares with her. The teacher has the responsibility of giving a strong foundation to deserving students.

Beware of the comfortable life that keeps us from the Grail path. We may find satisfaction in that life, but we won't experience the same purpose and joy which comes from achieving the Grail.

Another deterrent along the path is saying "Yes" indiscriminately to everyone. Time and energy are valuable resources and we must treat them with respect.

The love we have in our lives is earned. It cannot be taken for granted, and we cannot demand it. Our focus must be the same as in any other part of our life where we earn what is given to us.

Parzival has wisely turned down one woman,
because he is about to meet the woman of his life.

The Bride and Groom of the Eiffel Tower
by Marc Chagall (1887–1985)
Collections Mnam/Cci - Centre Georges Pompidou. Oil on Canvas, 1938–39 59 ¼ x 57 ⅛ in. Photo: Photothèque des Collections du Mnam/Cci

Chapter 8 - True Love

Sean Maguire asks Will Hunting if he has a soul mate. In *The Fisher King,* Anne remarks to Jack that as scary as it seems, Parry and Lydia are a perfect couple. True Love is the Quest of many. It builds empires, and when lost, is the source of destruction. Most movies and books incorporate love interests because nature can not be ignored. Even when the Action Hero destroys the Bad Guy, the movie isn't complete until the Hero rides off into the sunset with his Love upon a trusty horse/Ferrari/space vehicle. Usually the Hero has gone through tough times or been separated from his Love, so the new life together seems much sweeter.

Parzival will now find his soul mate. They, too, will be separated before they can ride off together into the sunset.

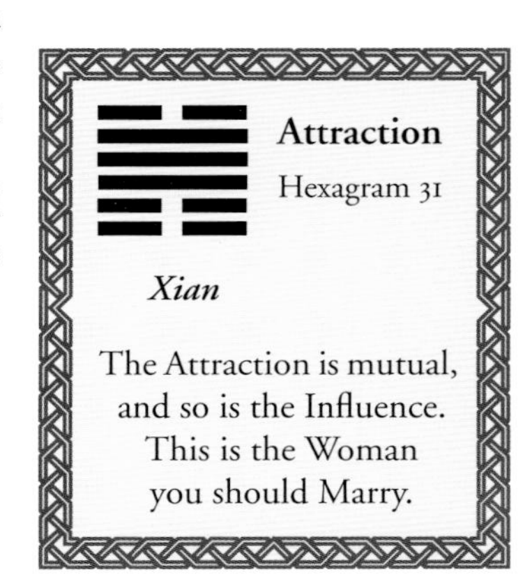

Condwiramors

Parzival thinks of Liaze as he comes to city of Pelrapeire, which belongs to Condwiramors. It was in her service that one of Gurnemanz' sons was killed. At a bridge, men shout at Parzival not to cross over to the town, but he leads his horse across, not fearing battle. The men run away thinking the forces of Clamide are coming, so royally did Parzival ride up. A young woman, expecting trouble, tells him that they have plenty of enemies. Parzival offers his service, so he is allowed in. The people are hungry in the town and armed with primitive weapons. They are ashamed that such a well dressed man would look for lodging with them, but he does not see their distress.

Parzival is taken to Condwiramors, who is escorted by her two paternal uncles. Parzival tries to think of Liaze, but Condwiramors is the most beautiful woman he has ever seen. He sits with her, but doesn't speak, because of his lessons with Gurnemanz. She thinks he is silent because she is too thin from hunger. Finally, they speak. Parzival says he came from Gurnemanz, who is Condwiramors' maternal uncle. She is surprised that Parzival made it to Pelrapeire, as it was a very far distance to cover in one day. As they speak, the two paternal uncles go to get food from their hunting lodge, which is given to the hungry people. Condwiramors and Parzival share their portion.

After Parzival goes to bed, Condwiramors comes to him at night. She tells him her tale of how King Clamide and Kingrun, Clamide's seneschal, are devastating her lands. Clamide wants to marry her but she has refused him. Parzival agrees to meet Kingrun in combat. She stays the night in his room, though neither one has any idea of sex.

The next day, Parzival beats Kingrun, who won't surrender to Gurnemanz because Kingrun had killed his son, nor to Condwiramors because he killed many of her men. Parzival sends him to surrender to Cunneware at Arthur's court. Ships can finally reach the city's harbor with food and the people rejoice.

That night, Condwiramors and Parzival still sleep together as virgins, but she wears her hair like a wife the next morning. It takes three nights of sleeping together to discover what nature means them to do, and neither are displeased.

Meanwhile, Clamide thinks it is Ither who is helping Condwiramors, because Parzival wears the red armor. Clamide attacks and is defeated. He is sent to Arthur's court to surrender and is then given over to Gawan. Kingrun remarks that Clamide was younger and richer than Arthur, yet all of this is happening because Keie beat a princess.

Parzival stays with Condwiramors for fifteen months, then leaves to find out how his mother is doing.

— *Parzival* Summary, Book IV

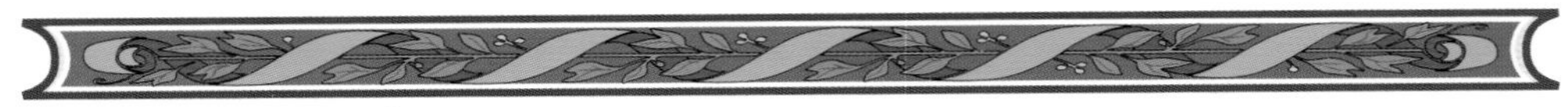

The Tao of Love

A bag of tricks—is it?
And a game smoothies play?
If you're good with a deck of cards
or rolling the bones—that helps?
If you can tell jokes and be a chum
and make an impression—that helps?
When boy meets girl or girl meets boy—
what helps?

— from the poem "Honey and Salt" by Carl Sandburg

Parzival's horse is smarter than he is. While Parzival bemoans not staying with Liaze, his horse knows straightaway how to carry Parzival to his true love.

Forrest Gump is fortunate because he found his soul mate riding on a common, ordinary school bus. Jenny would be the person whom he would be with forever, like peas and carrots. Gump says she is like an angel.

Parry discovers Lydia while she walks the streets of New York, and Will Hunting takes on Harvard bar room snobs to get his Skylar. You never know where you will meet your True Love. All you know is that while you were thinking about the woman in the last city, a radiant woman walks into your life, and all others pale in her presence.

Love is its own mysterious Grail. We can fantasize about the form it will take, but the true form is more wonderful, more weird, and more unpredictable than any Hollywood romance. If there is any giving over to Tao, it is when we give ourselves over to Love.

When we look at the Quest of the Spirit, Love comes in the middle of our journey, not as the ultimate end. Where romantic movies and novels finish with the "boy gets girl," Parzival gets his girl just before the story really gets going. This tells us that Love is the impetus and inspiration that keeps us going as we mature as Spiritual beings.

Though love is highlighted here as a love between couples, there are many ways and people we love. This love can be for our family, friends, and various adopted tribes. At the very root of *Parzival* is Compassion, which is love for the entire human race. What is important is that we take up Love as an integral part of our lives, even when the shape and place it takes is a surprise.

Just as we have to get out and take chances on finding the path to our Grail, we also have to be willing and open to Love. Parzival gets on that OtherWorld horse which takes him to adventure, and ends up with the adventure that will last his whole life. Love as an OtherWorld adventure is certainly an apt description. Too often, after having been hurt by trials of love, we don't want to take that chance again. If we allow one fear into our lives, it will also be easy to let others creep in. If we can be brave in

Love, we can be brave with most other endeavors. Wholeness in life comes from this Courage to Love, and all the wonder and difficulties we experience in Love.

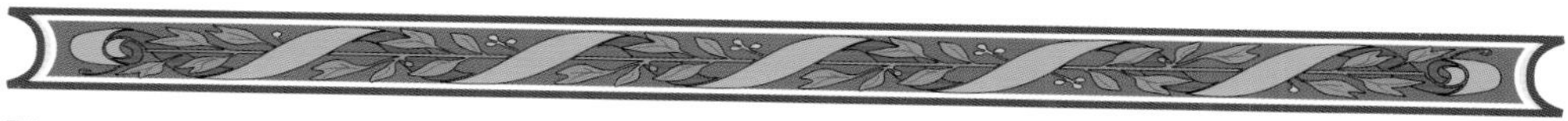

Kundalini and the Rightful Queen

At least Parzival wasn't too far off in his interest of women. Liaze and Condwiramors are cousins, but we can see who is the rightful queen. Condwiramors rules her own lands and makes her own decision to come to Parzival. Liaze is still a woman of the physical world, while Condwiramors is a queen in the OtherWorld.

She is a ruler, but her country suffers as a Wasteland. Parzival is still the fool, because he cannot see the despair of the people. We again see the promise of hope as a maiden correctly ascertains that Parzival may have the mettle that could help her queen. Notice this motif of how women, though nameless and seemingly without power, continue to make important choices for the welfare of their land.

Parzival's love is named Condwiramors, breaking down to *conduire amors,* "conduct of love," with some people interpreting it as "conduit of love." We also have a play on words as the name corresponds to the ancient great Hindu goddess, Kunda/Candi, a form of Durgā. It is the etymological basis for "kin, kundalini, cunning, kind, king" and a slang word for a part of a women's anatomy. In *Parzival,* we meet this goddess four times as Condwiramors, Parzival's love and wife; Cundrie La Surziere, the Grail Messenger; Cundrie (another one), sister of Gawan; and Cunneware, Duchess of Lalant. We see them as the Goddess of Love, the Dark Goddess, the Other Twin, and the Initiator.

And now for a side game of "Six Degrees of Separation" with names. Minnie Driver is the actress who plays Skylar, Will Hunting's love. Minnesingers were the medieval German troubadours who sang songs of love. *Minne* is the word for love. At Ludwig II's castle in Bavaria, Neuschwanstein, a room is dedicated to these singers as the Minstrels' Hall. Ludwig II was Richard Wagner's patron and the decor of the Minstrels' Hall are from scenes of *Parsifal,* which was Wagner's interpretation of *Parzival.* A visitor to this castle was Walt Disney, who based his fairy castles at the Disney theme parks on Neuschwanstein. On top of this, Mickey Mouse's love interest is none other than Minnie Mouse. (I bet you thought Walt was referring to a small rodent.) We've not only gone six degrees, but we've come full circle. It's that Taoist interconnection again. Think of all of that next time you go to Disney World.

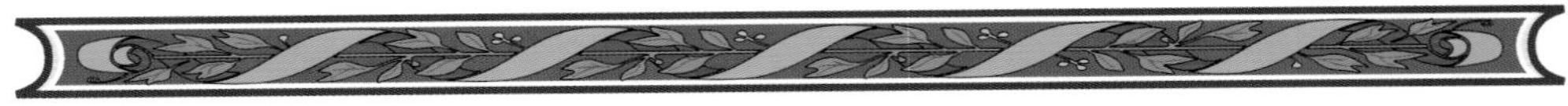

Foreshadowing

Moviegoers know the technique of foreshadowing very well. When we see Forrest Gump's dirty running shoes early in the movie, we know there is going to be a story there. When Jack in *The Fisher King* walks around his apartment practicing the words "Forgive me!" we know there's a theme of redemption somewhere. We get the same clue when the sportswriter in *The Natural* is named Max Mercy, and in *Good Will Hunting* when Professor Gerald Lambeau tells his class to finish Perceval as their homework assignment. I bet most people thought he was referring to a mathematician.

Wolfram also used the technique as he tests Parzival with the rule about not asking too many questions. Though the rules of Gurnemanz have helped refine Parzival to royal stature, Parzival sits in the presence of his true love and is silent. He wants to speak to her, but is reminded that he should not ask too many questions, so it takes her first move to get things going.

We can stand outside the novel and see the silliness of not speaking up when your heart is begging you to. The soul of nature yearns to express and learn, yet silence is the bane of many shy insecure people. When we are evaluating a situation there are times to be silent, but most of the time we are silent for lack of courage. Or we have instilled the classic "Children should be seen and not heard." This archaic rule stems from a time when control of children was more important than the fostering of children. There are times for children to be taught to speak up and times when they allow others to speak. The same goes for adults. We say we have a right to free speech, but then teach people that their voices do not count. There is enough breath and time for everyone to have their say.

One of the most moving battle cries of modern social consciousness comes from the Act-Up group, who labors for AIDS victims. It is very simply, "Silence is Death." We all suffer little deaths everyday when we choose silence.

Raising Your Voice

This exercise is for those of you who have difficulty expressing your opinion or asking questions.

1. Think of five times when your voice could have made a difference, yet you remained silent. These are times when your opinion could have added to a debate, when your knowledge could have helped someone, or a question would have led to a new wisdom.

2. Imagine how in similar situations you could handle it differently. Perhaps you need to practice saying "Excuse me, but I think..." Realize that your voice, your ideas, your words are important.

Silence is Golden

Since we are trying for the "Middle of the Road" approach, those of you who have no fear in speaking up may take the time to allow others to be stronger in their expression.

1. If your usual way of expression is overpowering people with your opinions or a "know it all" attitude, think of ways of how this could backfire on you and cause problems. Determine a way to say what you want inoffensively.

2. If you are generally a give-and-take person in conversation, do you have ways of drawing in a shy person? Think of ways to include such a person by using questions to get their opinion.

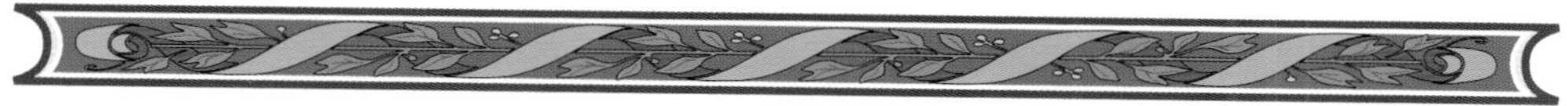

The First Perfection

Will Hunting offers his mathematical expertise to help Skylar do her studies, instead of just using it to show off. Luke Skywalker is willing to take on Darth Vader's forces for Princess Leia. Anakin Skywalker is willing to use his piloting abilities to obtain needed parts for Qui-Gon's spaceship. Parzival is willing to help Condwiramors not fall into the hands of Clamide and Kingrun. This shows how the individual has matured from caring about his small world to extending it into a larger one.

This is not the same situation found in our "Yes Syndrome" where, forced to do work that does not lie on the path of our Grail, we end up being the local doormat. This instance is where we actively give of our services happily and willfully because our heart really wants to. This is following the path of the Grail. This is the way to earn the love we receive, but the first reward comes from following what your heart says is the right thing to do. There is nothing more satisfying than giving our talents to those we care for. The First Perfection is Giving. If we choose to Heal the Fisher King, we heal ourselves by opening our hearts in service, and we heal those we love with our caring and abilities. Open Hearts come from Open Hands.

The First Perfection of Giving

1. Before we learn to give to others, we must also learn to give to ourselves. If you are someone who tends to rush about, ignoring your own needs, take some time to give something you need to yourself. This gift does not need to be a material item. It could just be time to enjoy a book, or walk, or pampering. When you feel better, you are more likely to want to give to others.

2. The next stage is the ability to give to those you love. Again, the gift need not be based on material items, though it should be based on what the person needs. Sometimes it is financial, sometimes it's time to help them with a project. Make a list of people you would like to offer help to and start surprising them with little gifts.

3. After that stage, give to needy strangers through organizations as Amnesty International or the Red Cross. You could volunteer time with Habitat for Humanity or other causes that tug at your heartstrings. Whatever you choose to do, approach it with an open feeling of Giving, rather than a sense of duty. Don't force yourself. Just give a little thought and when your heart is ready, the gifts will flow.

Waiting for Love

Shuffling his feet, Parry will not go upstairs with Lydia on their first date. He assures her that he loves her, but wants only a first kiss right now. Forrest Gump goes to Jenny's bed at her dorm room at the girls' school. That, too, is an unconsummated date. Will Hunting and Skylar share hamburgers and a kiss on their first date. Luckily, Luke and Leia never progressed past their first kiss, as they proved to be brother and sister.

Skylar and Will share a first kiss.
(Skylar-Minnie Driver, Will-Matt Damon)

All of these examples are old-fashioned and sweet, a definite contrast to stories of the post 1950s. They were only following the pattern set in the original story. Parzival and Condwiramors sleep together in bed for three nights before they figure out what the pleasures of being a husband and wife really mean.

The chasteness relates to that earning of love. As Parzival helps Condwiramors, they become closer and closer. Even before they consummate their relationship, she declares him her husband, thereby rewarding him with a crown to the kingdom and all the riches that entails. When they finally join, both have already experienced giving to each other voluntarily and without regret. He has given his skills; she has given her kingdom. Both have earned the right to love and be loved.

The Modern Woman - Circa 1200

Where is the fancy wedding ceremony? Aren't these women suppose to be virgins until a priest proclaims them married? No wonder Jenny and Skylar don't have wedding rings on when they spend their first nights with Forrest and Will. Seems a precedent had already been set. How about Forrest Gump's mother huffing and puffing with the principal of Forrest's school?

OtherWorld women have their own set of rules. They call the shots, especially when it comes to sex. It's important to note that in Grail legends, marriage does not necessarily mean a formal ceremony, but the conscious, joyful consummation of two people in love. These women do not answer to other people's laws. Throughout the legends, especially Parzival, various queens, sorceresses, and maidens wantonly pursue various men and freely choose to have relationships with them. If they are to be formally married, it is with their consent. This very radical concept probably wasn't taken seriously again until the latter half of this century. In fact, Herzeloyde has the power to make Gahmuret marry her, not the other way around. Belacane becomes married by taking Gahmuret into her bed. Condwiramors simply ties her hair up on top of her head and everyone assumes they are married. The marriage of Parzival and Condwiramors is the ceremony of the heart, founded on True Love. When Jack Lucas tells Parry he isn't married, Parry remarks that he looks married. He was, at least in our Grail definition way.

The importance of this issue relates to the independence of women. In this example, we are looking at marriage and sex, but the real focus is freedom of choice, and the power a woman has over her own property/kingdom. The strength of the women and men in this tale can still serve as a role model today.

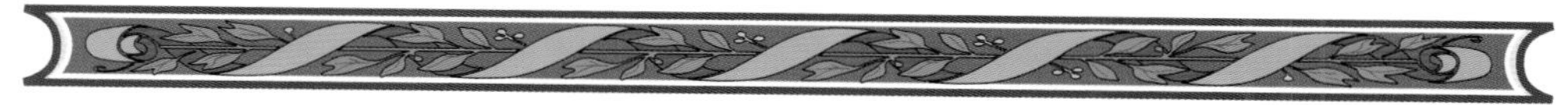

Message to Arthur

I've always been amused at how Parzival sends his prisoners miles away to surrender in Arthur's court, and they do it. It reminds me that I am reading fantasy. Or perhaps this was the start of "being released on your own recognizance." As silly as this seems, there is a very valid message here. Parzival is entering deeper into the OtherWorld, the core of being. He is succeeding at tests along the way and is sending proof back to the King of the Community. It is a message that says "I am doing something right. You were not in error to make me a knight."

When our Spiritual Victories are met, they will be manifested in the Physical World.

As we progress on our own spiritual paths, we will experience victories, which may not be easily visible to those around us. As those positive spiritual victories change us internally, they will slowly become visible to the outer world. As we find peace within ourselves while we work towards our Grail, that peace and happiness will spill over into our other encounters. People remark on the different changes in us, without pinpointing those exact transformations. Eventually, they will understand.

The reverse is true. Suffering on the spiritual plane will also show itself physically—tiredness, weight gain or loss, illness, addictions, depression. These are also the messages that we send to the rest of the world. When we fail with our spiritual battles, they shake the outer world.

Look in the mirror. See what others see. What messages are you sending? And what messages are you sending to yourself?

Messages to the Outer World

Examine how you feel at this stage of your life. Is there a core of happiness or despair inside of you? How is this reflected in your everyday life? Physical clues may reveal hidden truths that you refuse to acknowledge. Are there tensions and aches in your body revealing inner problems? Keep track of how your inner feelings change your physical being. The Inner and Outer Mirror work together.

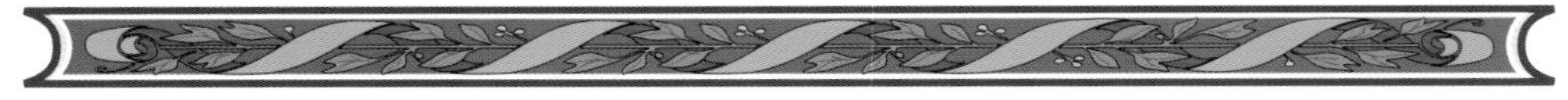

Thoughts of His Mother

It finally takes his love for Condwiramors to make Parzival want to know how his mother is doing. This is not an unusual development. Young people begin appreciating their parents after they start their own families. Though it makes him unhappy to separate from his wife, he knows he must go to his mother and check on her well being. Parzival is truly moving from a world of self-centeredness to a world of concern for those who are important in his life.

After Jack was saved by Parry from an attack of small-minded thugs, Jack could have easily thanked Parry and been on his way. The old Jack would have done just that, unless it could have increased the ratings at his radio station. Now something changes in Jack. He actually wants to return to the makeshift basement hideaway to see if Parry is okay. He questions the Custodian of the building about Parry's past and problems. Jack, still ill-equipped as to how to help Parry, offers him money, but Parry has manifested the First Perfection of Giving and hands the money off to another street person. It is a victory for Jack that he is feeling concern, and yes, a little guilt. He lives and feels and cares.

To put Parzival back on the track to the Grail, he is going from one love to another. What a lesson there! We listen to our hearts and that will dictate the path to the Grail. It is not activated by money, success, or fame. It is ultimately motivated by what is in our hearts.

Absence Makes the Heart Grow Fonder

Or is it "Out of Sight, Out of Mind?" In this story, the heart does grow fonder, but it does bring us to an important point.

Parzival will be absent from Condwiramors for a long time. Gump yearns for Jenny over many years. Roy Hobbs is apart sixteen years from Iris. Jack is emotionally absent from Anne in their relationship, unable to tell her he loves her.

When you go off in search of your Grails, your partner may suffer. This is the time for a heart to heart talk with those you love. Effort and time invested in working towards the Grail is that much less energy available for others. You must be sensitive to their demands, otherwise they may take the "Out of Sight, Out of Mind" approach. No joking. All of the paths of the Grail must incorporate the people we love.

On the flip side, if your partner is engaged in his paths to his Grail, be patient. Be involved in ways that you can, knowing that any absences, physical or emotional, are temporary. Cherish the times that are devoted to the two of you, so that everyone can be happy in their endeavors.

The Lessons of True Love

- To know Love, we must take a chance at Love. We must be willing to engage in the Adventure. It is a Grail unto itself.
- We must learn to question and express what lives inside us. Our whole psyche wants to learn about the world and make its mark. We must rid ourselves of the fears that keep us silent.
- Giving that comes from the heart is a sign of spiritual progress. It goes beyond the mere giving of excess cash. It demonstrates growth in the Soul.
- Waiting for love is the allowance of time to earn the right to be loved and to love.
- Our body and actions reflect our inner progress. By the same token, they can also reflect a spiritual malaise. We should constantly check our spiritual life and physical life against each other. Learn what you are communicating to yourself and others.
- When we take an interest in others, and truly care about their being, we are enhanced spiritually. The Road to the Grail exists between Love. Involve all whom you Love with your Quest. Develop patience and support for your loved ones aiming for their Grails.

Wanderer Above the Sea of Fog by Caspar David Friedrich (1774–1840)

Hamburger Kunsthalle
Oil on Canvas, 1818. 29 3/8 x 37 1/3 in.
Photo: © Elke Walford, Hamburg

Path 11 – The Shadow of the Grail

Are you nostalgic for that time in your life when you were full of hope and potential? Love was as innocent as a Pat Boone movie and we enthusiastically envisioned our future successes in life, complete with overflowing bank accounts, perfect families, and adoring fans. We refer to it as the good ole days, and almost everybody has had them.

Parzival has gone through his good ole days, that first phase of spiritual development, where wonders abound, but the seeds of future problems are planted. We watched him go from a boy fool, with no idea of his place in the universe, to a young man with some sense of responsibility. He knows he has ability, but doesn't know how to use it effectively, or from a moral standpoint. He sees the potential good that he can do, but still hasn't recognized that his actions have also caused harm. His sense of caring and duty is beginning to expand, but as yet, has no deep investment in love. Without that investment, he has not felt the pain of loss.

Life changes—in ways we cannot foretell. We are given incredible opportunities in life, but we ignore and waste them. We take small victories, and pretend they are the large ones. Later on, we wonder why life does not hold joy, and tend to blame our problems on others. Many times, it is we who have turned our backs on ourselves and we live under a shadow of all of the "what ifs" in life. We live under *The Shadow of the Grail.*

Crab Fishing by Winslow Homer (1836–1910)
Painted 1883. © Francis G. Meyer/Corbis

Chapter 9 – Discovering the Grail Castle

I sat upon the shore
Fishing, with the arid plain behind me.
Shall I at least set my lands in order?
— from "The Waste Land" by T. S. Eliot

When Will Hunting first meets Sean Maguire, Will launches into his usual approach of intellectual intimidation by finding what buttons to push. He notes Sean's "Fisher King" painting as a Winslow Homer rip off and proceeds to lambast Sean about being in the middle of storm and looking for a way out. Will first focuses on Sean's field of psychology, then Will finds Sean's real wound when he talks about Sean marrying the wrong woman.

This is Will's first visit to the Grail Castle and he has failed his Fisher King, just as Parzival fails his.

Grail Castle

Again, Parzival rides further than was thought humanly possible. He comes to a lake where there are fishermen. One is dressed richly, with peacock feathers in his hat. He is Anfortas, the Rich Fisher King. Parzival asks where he might find lodging, and Anfortas gives Parzival directions to his own castle, cautioning Parzival against riding astray on the unfamiliar slopes.

Parzival finds the well fortified Grail Castle and tells the gatekeeper of the invitation. Inside live morose knights who do not participate in tournaments, though they do not show their sadness to Parzival. Parzival is cleaned up and given a cloak belonging to Repanse de Schoye, the Queen of the castle. Parzival's armor and weapons are taken, and when he was made the object of a joke, he regretted he didn't have his sword with him.

Parzival goes into the hall and is invited by Anfortas to sit by him. Anfortas is ill and must be wrapped in cloaks to keep warm, even with three grand fireplaces burning. A knight enters with a Bleeding Lance and the company wails in sorrow. Then ladies come bearing a table, candles, and knives. Finally, Repanse de Schoye carries in the Grail. As she enters, all Parzival can think of was that he wore her cloak. Everyone is served a feast by reaching towards the Grail, and whatever one desires, appears. Parzival wants to ask about this wonder, but he remembers that he shouldn't ask too many questions.

A squire brings a sword in, which Anfortas presents to Parzival, saying it had served him before he was wounded. Parzival asks nothing of the sword or Anfortas' wounding. As the tables are cleared, Parzival sees a beautiful old man in a back room, his visage grayer than mist. All during this feast, everyone is sorrowful. Anfortas finally says that it is time to go to bed. Parzival is taken to a sumptuous bedroom, where he is cared for by pages and maidens.

— *Parzival* Summary, Book v, ¶ 224–244

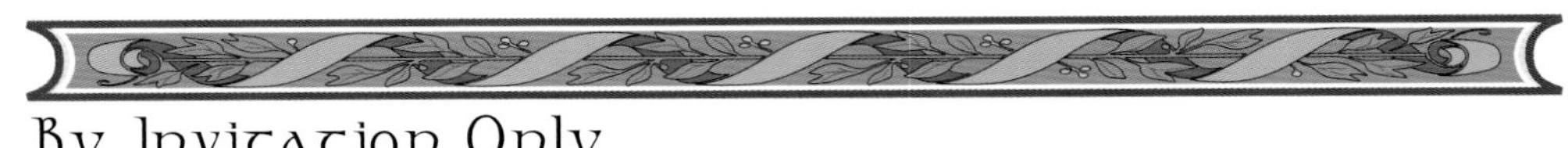

By Invitation Only

I wonder how we learn to live
with our faces?
They must hide so much pain,
so many deep trenches of blood,
so much that would terrorize and drive others away, if they
could see it. The struggle to control it
articulates the face.
And what about those people
With elegant noses and rich lips?

What do they spend their lives struggling for?

— from the poem "I Have Had to Learn to Live with My Face"
by Diane Wakoski

Parzival is now truly in the heart of the OtherWorld, but he doesn't know it. That energetic horse, who has taken him to a Teacher and his Love, has now taken him to his Destiny. However, Parzival is just hungry and tired, searching for a place to rest. The first person he meets is his uncle, the Fisher King himself, out in his boat.

With great hospitality, the king tells him the way to the Grail Castle. Though a generous offer, Anfortas offers it because he must. Only those who have the possibility of achieving the Grail can even find their way to this kingdom. Anfortas gives lodging because he expects Parzival to heal him.

Will Hunting is also a "relative" of Sean Maguire—both are from the same neighborhood. Later they discover that they share similar wounds. This demonstrates a similar connection that Parzival has to his uncle.

Marlow's Congo trek will take him to the Inner Station, the Heart of Darkness. Along the way he encounters hurdles, but when he gets to Kurtz, he knows that he was expected. I love this reference of the Inner Station, because it gives a sense of a directing power, yet we know it to be in disarray, as it is also the "Heart of Darkness." This is such an apt phrase for an ailing spirit.

Willard knew he was at the end of the river when he reached Kurtz' compound. It was a place of slow death and nightmares.

When Siddhartha comes to Gotama, he comes to a land and philosophy that concentrates on the sufferings of the world. Siddhartha recognizes that the teachings of Gotama are good, but acknowledges that there are faults in Gotama's teachings. Suffering will not abate if there are flaws in Buddha's lessons. As cocky as this may seem, Siddhartha realizes that he cannot stay with the Buddha, because he must go out into the world to learn more and judge what is right by himself.

When Jack is saved by Parry and taken to Parry's "humble abode," this was the equivalent of being invited into the Grail Castle. Parry throws out the phrase "Mi Casa, Su Casa," "My Home is Your Home." How true that is! What transpires in Parry's life will be inexorably linked to Jack's life. If we can heal the King in the Grail Castle, we can heal ourselves. Parry offers a feast to Jack—well, just some moldy pie—but that was the best Parry had to offer. There is a mourning court, but it just happens to be invisible, little people. Jack is kept away from the back room, just like Parzival only sees into the side room with the aged man. Parry brought Jack there because he knew Jack was "the One" who could help him win the Grail, just like Anfortas knew Parzival was the one who could potentially help him heal. Just like Parzival, Jack keeps his mouth shut. Here Jack was saved by Parry, and doesn't even have the presence of mind to ask Parry who he is and where he comes from. Jack has been conditioned that bums aren't worth his time, even ones who save his life, just as Parzival has been conditioned to be quiet. He tries to deny that he is "the One" because he was self-centered and weak. Parry assures him that is why he was sent. Only those on the road of learning need such tests.

The trouble with enchantments is that there is a Catch-22. Enchanted people know what it takes to break the curse, but they can't tell the hero what the secret is. Think of the situation where the husband gets the cold shoulder from his wife because she didn't get any acknowledgment from him on their anniversary. If she tells him what he should do, then it isn't an act that comes from his own caring. She is looking for his Free Will choosing the right action. Even the invisible little people in Parry's delusional world say that Jack isn't "ready to know yet." That is because the healing has to come from a Spontaneous Act of Compassion. It is a very important lesson.

IT IS KNOWING THE RIGHT THING TO DO AT THE RIGHT MOMENT.

Willard assumed he would know what to do once he met Kurtz, but he didn't. Parzival also is not able to do the right thing. The reason is his inexperience and the fact he has moved away from his natural self. He is so new at knighthood, he is caught up in its rules and trappings, and can't move beyond the small vision. He is "the One," with a long way to go.

When we look at our own Destiny, we must realize that we are "the One." We must actualize that when we are in the presence of the Grail, we are in the presence of **OUR GRAIL**. This is our life. We must take control of our own future, and know that any healing and achieving done in our lives comes from within us. Others may help us along the way, but we must treat ourselves as the special heroes we are.

Merlin, Anakin, Free Will, and The Force

Merlin by Louis Rhead (1857–1926)

Anakin Skywalker is a Chosen One. In *The Phantom Menace,* Anakin's fatherless conception is similar to a story of Merlin's childhood. Vortigern was a king who was building a castle that always collapsed before it was finished. His sorcerers told him to make the castle stand, they needed the blood of a fatherless child. Sent out to search for such a child, his aides come upon Merlin, who is taunted by another child as being fatherless. Upon questioning Merlin's mother, Vortigern's magicians ascertain that she had been impregnated by an incubus, a demon whose nature is half mortal and half angel. Incubi were known to come to sleeping women to impregnate them. *Jinn,* part of Qui-Gon's name, were an Arabian form of a haunting spirit, who were somewhere in the ladder of creation between the angels and humans.

One theory on the genesis of this story is that Merlin was becoming so popular that Christian priests wanted to demonize him with a birthright belonging to a devil. But it backfired. Instead, we have a story of a magician who knows the future, and understands that his nature is half bad and half good. This endears the character even more to people, as our own lives are always one of choosing between devils and angels. This is a foundation for the Free Will that will be exercised by Anakin Skywalker as he evolves into Darth Vader. Along the line, he will embrace the devil side at the expense of his angel side.

For Anakin, the explanation of his birth lies in the high count of midi-chlorians which exist in the cells of his body. They were the "incubus" who impregnated Anakin's mother. They contain the Natural Abilities and Destiny that make Anakin the Chosen One for the Jedis. The name midi-chlorian sounds like an offshoot of the word "mitochondria." I will rely on my dictionary definition for mitochondria—

> *an organelle in the cell cytoplasm that has its own DNA, inherited solely from the maternal line, and that produces enzymes essential for energy metabolism.*

Note that mitochondria are passed on in the maternal line, so this is an imaginative description when applied to the virgin conceptions of both Anakin's and Merlin's mother.

The other part of being essential for energy metabolism ties in with The Force and Master Qui-Gon's name. In the movie, Qui-Gon's name is pronounced *kwī-gôn,* but in Chinese it would be *chee-gông.* The Pinyin spelling is *qigong,* but in Pinyin nomenclature, *q* is pronounced *ch.* A more common form would be the spelling *chi kung,* related to *kung fu* training, which we discussed earlier.

In *Star Wars,* Obi-Wan "Ben" Kenobi says The Force is the energy field of all living beings and it is omnipresent. *Chi Kung* is a system of exercises which are used to develop our Life Force, which in Chinese is called *Chi.* The easiest way is to understand *chi* is to think of the energy system which runs throughout the whole body. The Chinese characters for *chi kung* are "air" or "gas," and "working man." We are already familiar with the "working man" character from *kung fu,* so let's concentrate on the "air/gas." Sometimes the character can mean an unpleasant gas and other times, it means to bring in fresh air. So *chi kung* exercises are breathing exercises to exchange the bad air for the good. However, they are much more than just breathing exercises, as body movement is involved, and the goal is to relax and open up the whole body. This creates maximum energy flow and health.

For martial art ability, it helps to develop a sensitivity and awareness of your own body and your opponent's. Feeling what your opponent is going to do allows you to react quicker than relying upon eyesight to respond.

Awareness of *chi* gives you accurate readings of your health, so you can monitor potential illnesses coming on and be prepared for them. By using *chi* flow, you can help heal injuries and illnesses in the body. This is part of the theory of Eastern medicine as found in acupuncture and massage work.

Chi development is also credited with opening intuitive channels, so we have a better sense of what is going on around us. I wouldn't use it to bet on horses, but when you are more aware of your own energies, you become more aware of others'. This is just another tool for discovering the truth of situations.

Just as we are all connected at a physical level through our actions, our energies are also connected. "Bad vibes" is not just retro slang, but a recognition of an imbalance within a person, place, or situation. A place of death or bad energy takes much work to reverse its *chi* into a flowering, productive atmosphere. Wastelands are prime examples of bad *chi.*

As you can see, The Force is not some imaginative creation that people can wish for, but it is a state of being, awareness, and skill that can be developed. Everyone can improve their *chi.* The Force is not a fantasy. However, developing it to a high level takes thousands upon thousands of hours of practice. If you are willing, the knowledge is out there to be learned.

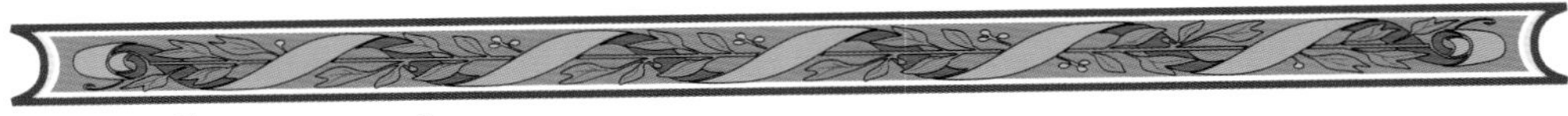

The Eyes of Argus

The bird motif pops up in the form of the peacock feathers decorating the Fisher King's hat. Several cultures view the peacock as representing the soul, fertility, and all-knowing consciousness.

In Greek myth, Hera has her personal henchman, Argus, who has a hundred eyes all over his body, and only fifty close at one time. She sets Argus to watch over one of Zeus' paramours whom he has turned into a cow. It is not recommended to get in between arguments of Hera and Zeus, as Zeus kills Argus. To remember her faithful servant, she places the eyes on the tail of the peacock, which then becomes a totem of hers. The eyes are often viewed as the All-Seeing Eye. As Hera is a goddess of fecundity, the peacock also became a symbol of fertility. This is an ironic twist, since the Fisher King is infertile.

The peacock was also known to be a carrier of the Soul. Brahma and Sarasvati rode on the back of the peacock, and Indra sits on a throne of peacock feathers. In Muslim myth, the peacock represented the cosmos. In early Christian myth, the flesh of the bird was thought to be immune to spoilage and represented Christ in the tomb, who would return from death.

So much for pretty millinery finery.

Axis Mundi - The Mount of Salvation

The Grail Castle is called Munsalvaesche, the Mount of Salvation. It is the center of the Universe. No matter how many books of philosophy we read, each individual is the center of his own universe. More than that, since we are dealing with Salvation, we are dealing with the center of the Soul.

The Center of the Universe is depicted in many different ways in the world's myths. We use the term *Axis Mundi,* the axis which the world moves about. We see it as the Tree of Life, the Sacred Central Mountain, and the Great Tower.

As the Tree of Life, it is known as the Tree of Knowledge of Good and Evil in the Garden of Eden, whose apples also fall in the gardens of the Celtic Avalon. In the East, that tree yields Peaches of Immortality. It is the great tree Yggdrasil, where the kingdoms of the Norse and Germanic worlds reach from its roots to its crown. The Yucatan Mayas have the *yaxché.* Hathor fed people from an Egyptian sycamore. Buddha achieved enlightenment under the Bodhi Tree. The Islamic Tree of Life holds the names of all souls. Merlin is buried in a Sacred Oak, just as Osiris laid in a sarcophagus of the erica tree. The Tree of Life is also the Cross that Christ was hung on.

The Kaballah is built around the image of the Tree of Life. There are many interpretations and devotions around the image. At the base is the Tenth level, which is

Malkuth, representing Earth and the Shekina (feminine face of Wisdom). At the Ninth is *Yesod,* or Foundation. The Eighth is *Hod,* representing Splendor, and the Seventh is *Nezah* for Endurance and Victory. The Sixth is *Tiphareth (Tiferet)* for Compassion and Beauty. Power and Severity is found at the Fifth stage called *Geburah.* At the Fourth step, *Hesed (Chesed),* is Love and Mercy, followed by Intelligence and Understanding at the Third Step named *Binah.* The Second stage is *Hokhma* for Wisdom and the Beginning, and finally at the Top is *Kether* or the Supreme Crown. It is no wonder that this simple, yet totally encompassing symbol has served as a meditation device for centuries. It is worth our effort and time to think of our lives, rooted in the base of everyday life, then moving up the trunk through Endurance and Beauty and Wisdom before reaching a stage of Enlightenment.

Mt. Fuji and Flowers by David Hockney

The Metropolitan Museum of Art, New York
Purchase, Mrs. Arthur Hays Sulzberger Gift, 1972. (1972.128)
Acrylic on Canvas, 1972. 60 x 48 in. ©David Hockney
Photo: ©1977 The Metropolitan Museum of Art.
Photograph by Lynton Gardiner

Sacred Central Mountains abound: Mount Meru in India, Mount Fuji in Japan, and Olympus in Greece. Mount Sinai was where Moses met with God, and sacrifices of fruit were made to the rain god on Mexico's Mount Tlaloc. Chinese Immortals trekked to the Kun Lun Mountains to visit the Goddess of the West, Xi Wang-Mu. Modern adventurers test their physical and spiritual mettle against Chomo-Lung-Ma, "Goddess Mother of the Universe," better known by the modern name of Mount Everest.

In Sufi studies, there are ten stages of personal development, with each stage containing ten attributes. These stages are arranged as blocks in mountain like form in the Chart of Virtues. On the base are the first four stages: I. Gateway, II. Doors, III. Conduct, and IV. Character. Built on these four are the next three stages: V. Principles, VI. Valleys, and VII. Mystical States. The next level are two blocks: VIII. Sanctity and IX. Realities. At the top of the mountain is the Supreme Goal.

The Great Tower is but an earthly mirror of the Sacred Central Mountain. We manifest that mountain at the Pyramids in Egypt and Mexico, and the Ziggurats of the

Ancient Mesopotamians. The Tower of Babel was one monument to the inaccessibility of some magic mountains due to human failings. Every church spire and pagoda imitates this tower which connects heaven and earth.

For the Tower, there is the image of the seven Chakras along the spine of the body. These are a focus of Kundalini Yoga. At the base of the spine is the Root Chakra, *Mooladhara,* controlling feelings of Physical Survival and Being. The second Chakra, *Swadishthan,* exists at the Sacral area and oversees Creativity and Sexuality. Third is located at the Solar Plexus and called *Nabhi,* which regulates feelings of Power. The fourth is at the Heart Center, *Anahat,* where Love and Harmony resides. The fifth is the *Vishuddhi* Chakra at the Throat, which controls Relationships. The sixth is *Agnya,* the Third Eye, which covers Intuition and the Psychic realm. The top is *Sahasara* or Crown, which houses Spirituality and Destiny. Besides being an image of meditation, the work associated with it involves body work, so Health and Spirit are worked on at the same time, much like *chi kung* exercises.

When we get to the *Axis Mundi,* we find Eden, Paradise, Shambala, Utopia, the OtherWorld, Heaven. We know the way to get there, because the Pole Star is our guiding light and it shines as the Star on the tops of Christmas Trees. Sometimes, a fisherman in a boat points us in the right direction.

When Parzival reaches Munsalvaesche, he only sees an extremely well fortified castle that nobody would dare try to attack. The knights inside are not joyous, though they do not reveal this to Parzival. We do the same to our own hearts. We fortify our hearts to avoid further damage, and pretend that everything is all right. However, at some point, we must let in the person who is able to catalyze the healing.

Some people say that the Castle of Montségur in the French Pyrenees was the real Grail castle. Some say it is the Castle of Dinas Bran in Scotland. We know the Grail Castle is wherever your Soul is.

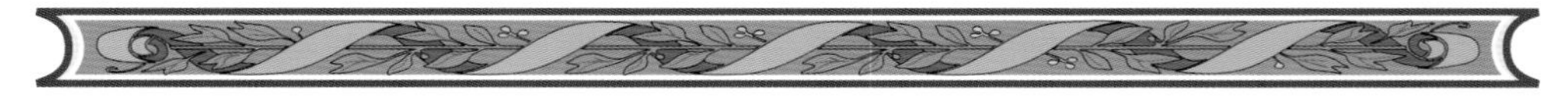

The Bleeding Lance

Some people are too polite to ask someone why he isn't feeling very well. But if they saw a bleeding spear, they'd start yapping right away. The Spear is one of the Hallows and it represents Truth. Like other symbols the Spear that Wounds and Heals has many myths associated with it.

In Malory's version of the Grail story, a knight named Balin goes to the Grail Castle. His sword breaks in a battle with the Grail King, King Pellam. Balin picks up a spear and hurls it at Pellam, causing the wound that won't heal. The Grail Castle falls in pieces around them, and they lie in the rubble until Merlin comes along to save them. The spear that Balin threw was the Spear of Longinus, the centurion who pierced Jesus' side as he hung on the cross. Longinus became a convert, and later on, he was to have been maimed and healed.

In the *Mabinogion,* Peredur earns the name Peredur Long Spear. His name has been parsed to the Welsh words *peri,* which is the plural of *par,* meaning spear, and *dûr,* meaning hard steel. This image of a hard steel spear reflects Peredur's willingness to aim forward in his quest. You can see a similar image in *Lance-lot.*

Norse legend has Odin hanging himself on the Tree of Life, Yggdrasil, and spearing himself. After learning wisdom and magic runes, he returns from the dead, very similar to Christ's Resurrection.

The Celtic god Bran is wounded in the foot with a poisoned spear. This is the same Bran whose name is related to the Fisher King Bron, who had the Cauldron of Regeneration. His head was consulted as an oracle.

Parzival later learns about the Lance that Bleeds when he meets up with Trevrizent, Anfortas' brother. Trevrizent tells Parzival that there are certain seasons and positions of the constellations that cause intolerable pain for Anfortas. He is taken to Lake Brumbane, which eases the pain a bit, but there is also a ritual of the spear. During a time of frost, the wound becomes bitter cold, but the lance has a magical power and heat in the tip. The spear is forced into the open wound, where the poisoned cold coagulates around the spear tip. Only then does Anfortas get relief.

The silver knives carried in the Grail ceremony are the only knives sharp enough to remove the poison frost from the tip. The blood seen on the spear is the fresh blood from Anfortas. That is some heavy duty Taoist medicine. One form of Chinese medicine says that Like Cures Like, so here we see a spear being put into a spear wound. In real life, this usually means something as simple as eating bone marrow to have strong bones, or oysters for increasing male energy. Another Taoist medicine sets up a flow of the Yin/Yang in the body to move energy. A Traditional Chinese doctor might place a bag of ice on one part of the body, and heat at another place, to get this type of energy going. In this story, we have the hot spear tip being placed against the cold wound.

Some scholars think that this ritual could be related to the Hindu god Indra, whose weapon is the Thunderbolt. The theory is that his Thunderbolt's energy draws out the cold of the land, which harkens Springtime.

In *Heart of Darkness* and *Apocalypse Now,* Mfumu/Chief are both killed by a spear. In the first chapter of *Heart of Darkness,* we learn of the strife between blacks and whites when a native chief was beaten by a Dane named Fresleven, who thought he was cheated in a deal. Fresleven had once been a gentle man, but after several years in the jungle he had changed. During the beating, the chief's son made a tentative jab with a spear towards Fresleven, that ended up between the shoulder-blades, killing Fresleven. Shades of Parzival and Ither. Fresleven's body was left to rot, and the village deserted. It became a haunted place—a Wasteland.

Everything comes down to the Truth that Wounds and Heals. When we dispel our fantasies, we can live authentic lives. Sometimes the Truth is very painful, but it takes tough love for us to face reality. We must not live lives with our heads buried too deep in the sand or too high in the clouds. Work with Truth, so it can help us be stronger.

The Spear That Wounds and Heals

Think of times when a painful truth struck a deep wound in your heart. Then look at the strength you had to develop to go beyond the pain. That strength becomes a part of the healing process. Also, look at the information you were missing and how it was sabotaging your life. Without all of the truth, you cannot make sound decisions in your life. Don't cry "If I had only known." Instead, look at how you can move forward with the new information you have.

Perhaps you are now going through a difficult time because of a hard truth. Have faith that you will come out of the experience stronger and wiser. Give yourself the time, and trust that you will heal.

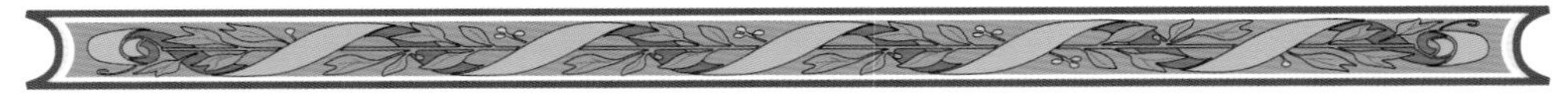

The Unobtrusive Grail

Until now, there has not been a whisper of the Grail in the novel, and Parzival just stumbles onto its presence. He only sees it as one object in many of the Grail Procession, though he wonders at the feeding of the guests. In Malory's *Le Morte D'Arthur,* the best known version of the Arthurian classics, the Grail appears wondrously at one of Arthur's feasts. It is recognized as something holy and prompts the Grail Quest.

Parzival's accidental discovery is important, because the first time we come in contact with our Grail is usually by chance. It may only be one thing in many, though we may notice something special about it. It could be the casual introduction of your future wife, the first glimpse of a Monet in a library book, a passing Buddhist nun in a crowded airport, or a concert on television. These Grails touch us and then move on. Often, there is no fanfare and we are too blind initially to grab it, breathe it and live it. There is no flashing neon sign that says "Paradise here." We come unprepared and unilluminated. This is part of living in the Shadow of the Grail, rather than immediately drinking joyously from it.

First Encounter With Your Grail

Think of the first time you encountered your Grail. Was it so magnificent that you knew right then and there that it would be an important part of your life? Or was it just one of many things that, once you moved away from it, you wished you had held on to it harder? Examine the irony of how the important moments of our lives appear when we least expect it.

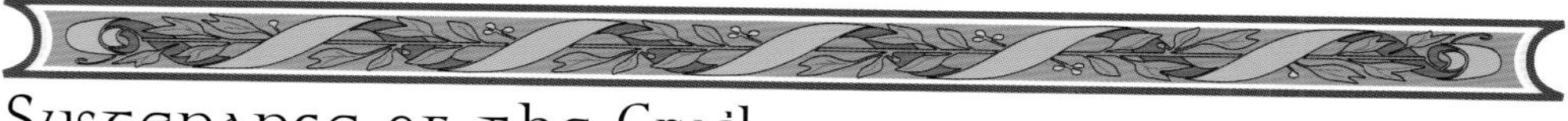

Sustenance of the Grail

In *The Fisher King,* Parry tells his version of the Fisher King story to Jack, which ends with a fool giving a dying king a cup of water. The cup ended up being the Grail, and when the king asks the fool where he found the Grail, the fool responds that he didn't know. He only knew that the king was thirsty. A simple act of Compassion is the act of the Grail.

In *Apocalypse Now,* the Photographer offers the imprisoned Willard a cup of water. With that simple act, he alleviates Willard's suffering. On the flip side, Kilgore acts as the Greedy Fisherman when offering water to a dying man. The wounded man is holding his guts in with a pan, and the soldiers around the man refuse to give him water. Kilgore says a man this brave can drink from his canteen any day, and offers the man water. Then Kilgore learns that Lance Johnson, the surfer, has come to camp. Kilgore forgets the wounded man completely, tossing the water to the side, and leaves to go meet Lance. His offer of water was one of showmanship, not compassion.

The sustenance of the Grail can exist in simple acts of compassion. Everyone in the presence of the Grail is fed what he wants, but this is a simple miracle to give people what they need. As we find success in our own Grail Quests, remember that the nourishment of the Grail can be the giving of simple things to those around us. Look with compassion and see what they need.

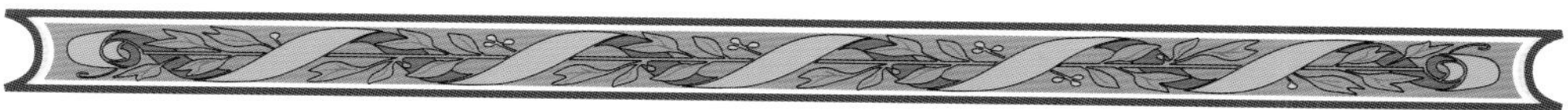

Three Strikes and You're Out

Yes, I did want to stay as an observer. I am not especially anxious to mingle.

— from *A Confederacy of Dunces*
by John Kennedy Toole

Uproot your questions from their ground and the dangling roots will be seen. More questions!

— from *Chapterhouse: Dune*
by Frank Herbert

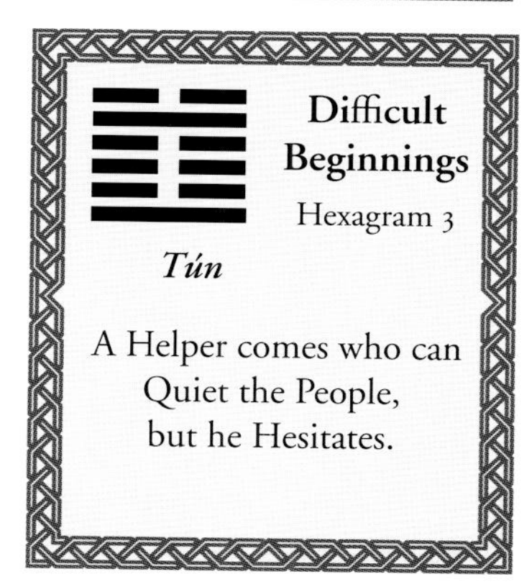

When Willard first meets Kurtz, all he does is answer the questions that Kurtz poses to him. The whole time, the Fisher King does the questioning. Willard must have had plenty of questions about Kurtz, yet he fails to ask one. Will Hunting asks lots of questions, but only ones aimed at harming and pushing Sean Maguire's buttons, not ones of compassion. There are also times that he uses silence as a weapon, ignoring his own healing process.

The reason that we are blind to such wonders and pain is that we cut off our natural selves and instinct. Because Parzival is blindly following Gurnemanz' instructions not to ask too many questions, he sits mute with wonder and pain all around him. He's at a party, but he doesn't ask why the people are unhappy. He sees the Grail feeding people, but he doesn't ask the source of the magic. When he sees the Grail Maiden, all he can think of is "I'm wearing her clothes," not what wonders she possesses that he can learn from. He sees an ancient man in a back room, but doesn't ask who he is. He's given a sword, but doesn't ask the history of it. He is in the presence of a wounded man, and doesn't ask the one question that would cure him—"What ails thee?" He has so many chances to be involved with the people of the court, and he's just lost in a silent haze. It is the searching for common answers, and a small display of compassion that will solve the problem of the Wasteland.

This is the question we must ask ourselves before starting our own healing process. By asking this simple question—"What ails thee?"—we are led to what we need to be truly happy. When we answer the question—and it cannot be answered falsely nor with the voice of others—then our lives will change abruptly. From that moment on, we set ourselves on a path which will deliver rich, full lives with substance. Others around us can moan and cry, but they do not hold the answers. Truth must come from our own self-discoveries.

Unfortunately, Parzival had too many chances at the bat and didn't even take a swing. He's O-U-T. At least, for this inning.

Trying It On For Size

In one of my *Parzival* books, the notes say that it was the custom to make clothing for guests at a castle. I wouldn't mind showing up at one of my friends' homes and have them make me some custom threads. Of course, when castles had guests, they probably stayed for months or even years, and had to help fend off hordes of marauders, so they ended up earning their clothing.

Since nothing was yet made for Parzival, he is given an Arabian silk cloak of Repanse de Schoye, the Grail Maiden. It is a forerunner of the cloak he will wear as the future Grail King. The luxurious gift also demonstrates her hope in him. You've got to admit that the black cloak of Darth Vader's looked daunting as he floated through spaceship halls. When we look at Parzival's clothing, we see him first wearing the Fool's clothes, given to him by his mother. Then he wears the Red Armor from the Red Knight. Now, he wears the cloak of the Grail Maiden—an interesting assortment for hand-me-downs.

Besides representing wealth and power, cloaks have their own magic. They can be sources of Death, Invisibility, and Truth. Here are summaries of three Arthurian tales demonstrating each of these attributes.

In the story of the Strange Mantle, found in Malory's work, Arthur and his sister Morgan Le Fay are at odds. She sends a gem-encrusted cloak to Arthur, but as he is about to put it on, the Damsel of the Lake stops him. The woman who brought the cloak to him is made to wear it, and she dies, incinerated to coals.

The Welsh Triads tells us of the Mantle of Arthur. Anyone who wears it is invisible to others, but able to see everything around him. Harry Potter fans will remember Harry's Invisibility Cloak.

The Mantle of Tegau Gold Breast, mentioned in *The Welsh Triads,* told the faithfulness of the women who wore it. If it touched the floor, the woman was faithful. If it only came to the knees, her husband would be worried.

With these stories in mind, we can imagine what powers Repanse's cloak could hold.

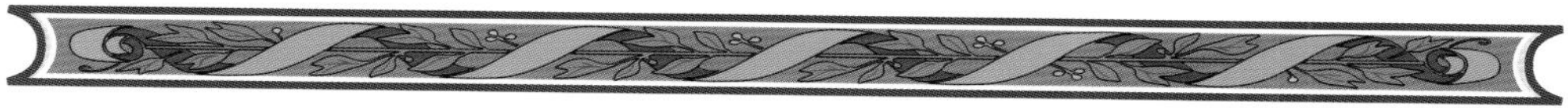

Gift of the Sword

Repanse is not the only one giving gifts to Parzival. Anfortas gives Parzival his own sword. It is a blade of wonders, a hilt made of ruby, and a sheath worth a thousand marks. You can do your own calculations what today's value would be.

More than the value of the sword was its importance in the ritual of the question. When the sword was placed in Parzival's hand, that was the signal for Parzival to Ask the Question.

The Sword is our Skill. It is what we need when we face the battles in the world at large. Whatever Grail we seek requires a skill, whether it is technical or interpersonal. We are handed the abilities to work with our Grail, and we still fail to Ask the Question. We are given a tool from the King of the Spiritual Kingdom, and we still do not ask where it comes from and what it can do. It can protect us and give us strength, but we have to learn how to use it.

> *Gift of the Sword*
>
> *Ask yourself what Sword has been given you. What gift of the Spirit will enable you to charge the talents you have to achieve your Grail? Don't be modest. The world is not an easy place, so we need all the help we can develop. Think of how you will utilize this Skill and make it even stronger.*

Stay Awake!

"For our sakes, please stay awake a little longer."
— Maidens in *Parzival,* Book v, ¶ 244

Parzival is escorted to a luxurious bedroom where pages remove his clothing and maidens bring wine and fruits from Paradise. He welcomes the attention and the care they give him, but when he is ready to sleep, the maidens ask him to stay awake a while longer.

They aren't just trying to have an all night party; they're trying to give him one last chance at Awareness. Maybe if they can get him talking, he'll finally ask them about the Fisher King and the wonders of the Grail. But all he gives them is polite thank-yous for their hospitality.

Perhaps if Parzival could have directed his attentions from just filling his stomach and looking at beautiful maidens, to really being aware of the extraordinary wonders about him, a lot of grief could have been avoided. Often we get caught up in our own personal, safe worlds instead of seeing how we fit in the larger world. If we can Stay Awake and be conscious of all of the possibilities about us, we can actively engage ourselves in lives that have meaning and reward. It is easy to let our minds drift from the greatness of the world because it is easier to go to sleep.

Right Mindfulness is the seventh step of the Eightfold Path. It is Awareness of what you are doing at the moment and fully immersing yourself with what is really happening in the moment. Spiritually, Parzival stood outside an evening of miracles and was not an active participant in the marvels. Up to the very moment he went to sleep he was given a second chance, and he still didn't get it.

Don't wait until the last moment before you sleep to be actively involved with the miracles of your life. Be Mindful. Stay Awake!

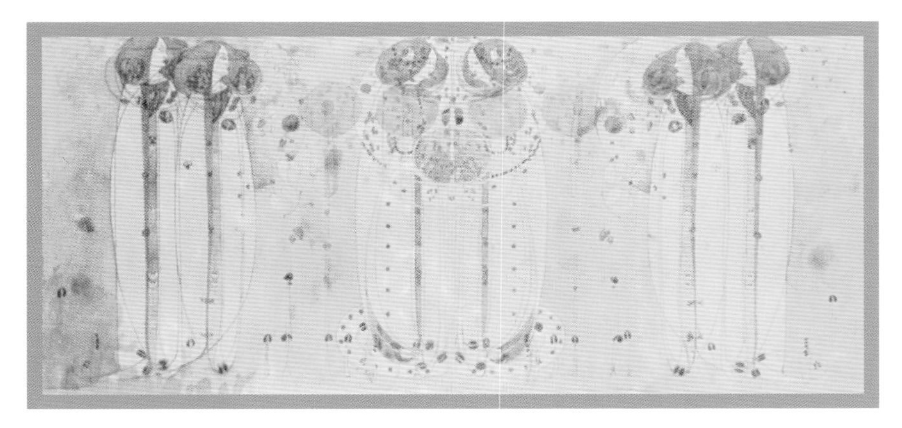

The Wassail by Charles Rennie Mackintosh (1868–1928)

Private Collection. Watercolor, 1900. 12 ½ x 26 ¾ in.

The Lessons of Discovering the Grail Castle

We must take the attitude that we are the "Only One" who is invited to the Destiny that awaits us. We are also the only one who is capable of reaching deep inside us to work on our own healing.

The Grail Castle is the *Axis Mundi,* the Center of the World. Our Grail is the focus that our life revolves around and brings us happiness and peace.

The Spear represents the Truth that Wounds and Heals. Sometimes we feel devastated by a hard truth, but then we'll be able to move on with our lives with honesty.

We usually don't know our own Grail, until we move away from it. The emptiness and nagging feeling when we are apart from it is evidence of this.

Silence is Death. If we don't ask, we will never know. If we don't share our experiences, others will not know. We must express a curiosity which forwards healing the world.

The Sword is our Skill. No matter what Grail we desire, we need the Skill to achieve it. Receiving the Sword is the signal to ask the proper Questions.

Stay Awake! Only through Awareness and Right Mindfulness can we experience the Grail.

If you can't reach out in healing, if you can't react from the source of being a Natural Man, then it is time you move on. Parzival will have to leave the magnificent castle, and begin the true path of Spiritual Discovery.

Katherine Graham and Truman Capote at Capote's 1966 Black and White Ball
© *Bettman/Corbis*

Chapter 10 - You're Not Good Enough For This Party

Have you ever been snubbed at a party? Backs of guests slowly turn away as you are about to give your viewpoint. Waiters hold hors d'oeuvre trays high as they walk by you. Parzival is about to get the ultimate snub. He is going to be completely shut out and then verbally abused. One moment, you're the life of the party, and the next moment, you're not.

Parzival Rebuked

As Parzival sleeps, he has nightmares of fighting, foreboding his own future of suffering. The next day, he cannot find anyone and wonders who will bring his clothes. Finally he gets out of bed and dresses himself. The sword he took from Ither and the one given to him by Anfortas is lying on the floor. Parzival takes both. He runs through the castle, yelling for anybody. He becomes angry and grief-stricken when no one responds.

Outside, he sees an open gate with horse prints leading out. As Parzival leaves the Grail Castle, a gatekeeper pulls the drawbridge shut, almost hitting the horse. The gatekeeper calls Parzival a "Goose" for not asking the Question and winning great honor. Parzival wants an explanation, but gets none. He searches for the knights, wanting to join them. He follows the trail, but it disappears.

Parzival meets Sigune by a linden tree, crying with her embalmed lord in her arms. He does not recognize her because of her haggard appearance. When he tells her where he was, she says he lies, as there is only Munsalvaesche which cannot be found by those who seek it. She then recognizes Parzival by his voice and tells him who she is. She says she would be happy if Parzival delivered Anfortas' suffering. She sees him wearing Anfortas' sword, the Sword of Trebuchet, which will withstand the first blow, but shatter at the second. She tells him it can be fixed at a spring near Karnant, but it requires a magic spell he probably did not learn. She asks him if he asked the Question and he says no. She rebukes him for not healing the Fisher King with the right Question.

— *Parzival* Summary, Book v, ¶ 245–255

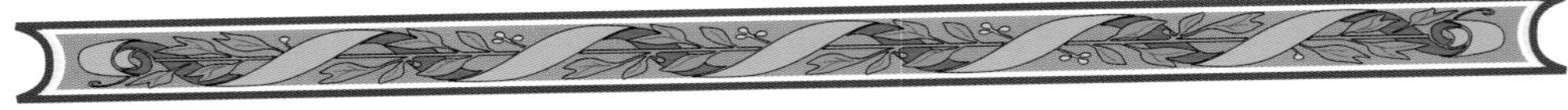

Suffering Begins

Outside of the city limits the heart of darkness, the true wasteland begins.
— from *A Confederacy of Dunces* by John Kennedy Toole

Most of the time, Parzival has been doing deeds because of selfishness or a sense of duty. Nothing has touched him in terms of real pain. Children can watch the most horrific scenes in slasher and action movies because they don't know what it is to feel real pain. Adults are the ones who squirm in movie seats. They understand the true nature of loss.

Buddhist thought tells us life is suffering. Even C-3PO in *Star Wars* notes that he is made to suffer. Now Parzival is going to get a taste of what that pain is. In his sleep, he literally feels the pain of suffering. The passage says that if he had been awake, he would have rather died thirty times. He now knows a little of what Anfortas is going through, and what his mother had experienced in her dreams of Gahmuret's death. Parzival's body knows what his heart should have asked. But even as he suffers, he can't ask himself, "What ails thee?"

When you remove yourself from your Grail, your suffering begins. At first, it may only be night sweats and wistful longings. You don't even have the gumption to ask yourself what's wrong with you. It's just a bad dream. It's just the fish I ate last night. A lot of excuse making is going on.

Parzival is in Exile, though he doesn't know it. No one is around. He has been left behind. There is no food, no conversation, no adventure. He sleeps a little longer, thinking everyone will come back and they will be there to serve him, but he could sleep for years, and no one will come.

It's just like when you decide that you'll hook up with the people you had such a good time with at a party. Only things have changed now. You call, dash off a few emails, looking for someone, anyone, but all you get are answering machines and unknown addresses. Now you are going to get angry. You had such a good time at the party, but now no one wants to talk to you, and you can't figure it out. It must be them.

We do this quite a bit. We want people to act a certain way, to immediately respond because we call them. We want them to dress us and wait on us hand and foot. When they don't, we get angry at them, and never stop to ask, "What did I do to cause them to act this way?" Our anger turns to sorrow and we start to feel loneliness and rejection. Still we think, it must be them, it couldn't be me.

> *Source of Suffering*
>
> *We have many excuses why we are unhappy and why we are not at the Source of our Grail. We get angry at everyone around us when they don't behave the way we want them to, and don't understand why they're not there to do another Grail party. Don't look at how others have prevented you from achieving your Grail. Think instead of how you were responsible for pushing yourself away from it. Realize that where you are today, in whatever unhappiness you are experiencing, has come about because of your own decisions and actions.*

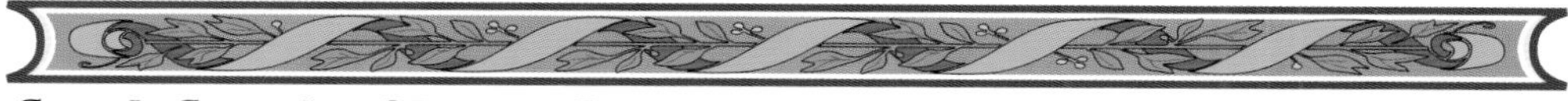

Grail Castle Shuts You Out

The dwarf honked a loud horn at the end of a two-foot walking stick, and it sounded as if a flock of geese had been let loose at the offenders,...
— from *The Natural* by Bernard Malamud

As Parzival leaves, he is hurried out by the gatekeeper, who calls him a "Goose." We're back to the bird symbol, and Parzival has been called by the name of one of the dumbest, slowest waddling birds around, appropriate to his current nature. He is not ready to take flight in the Spiritual world. In the movie *The Natural,* the Judge refers to a lie as being a *canard,* the French word for duck. Parzival's life is a lie right now. He thinks because of his fighting skills he is a hero, whereas a true hero embodies caring and compassion.

Parzival asks for help as to what is going on, but the gatekeeper totally ignores him. He isn't going to help anyone who didn't help his king. This man is like many people around who have their own personal despair which could been solved with a simple act of compassion. If you're not going to help him, don't expect any help from him.

Doors open with simple gestures of goodwill. Those doors will also be slammed in your face if you can't show any concern for the people around you. If you want to get back to your Grail, you must realize that many people will be on that path. Every person is important and deserves a bit of kindness. You are not going to open the door of the Grail Castle if you cannot show compassion to the Gatekeeper. He may just pull the ropes, but that is necessary to get inside. For now, just learn the lesson of acts of kindness to all around you.

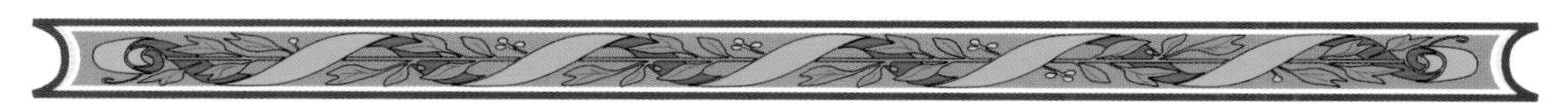

The Cost of Grief

When we watch the movie *Forrest Gump,* we see Jenny go through many transformations. We see her as a beautiful, young, sweet girl, and years later as a drug-addicted worn out woman. Have you ever run into somebody you haven't seen in years and couldn't recognize him? Maybe you once secretly lusted after the high school jock who also happened to be the National Honor Society president, and drove the coolest car at school. Years later you run into a beaten man who slumps when he stands, speaks with a cracked voice and cannot look you in the eye. You're reaction is "Oh, my God! I'm glad I didn't turn out that way. What happened?"

Grief. The grief that comes from losing loved ones and losing dreams. This type of grief is so deep that the mourner will haul the corpse around day and night.

Parzival remembers Sigune as a young woman with long, flowing brunette hair. She is now weak, lackluster, and bald. He sees her dead knight and wants to bury him, but Sigune is not ready to do so.

Recognize what grief does to people. Whatever price it exacts physically is two-fold to the Spirit. You can offer to help rid them of the pain, but realize that they may not be able to do so. People will come to realizations and decisions at their own time, but we must take time to inquire. We may not be able to help them right now, but empathize and offer care.

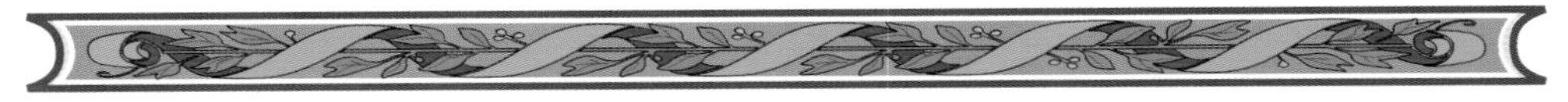

Sacred Trees

Summer by Henri Rousseau (1844–1910)

There is a whole range of divine attributes assigned to the mythology of trees. Anyone who has spent a solitary afternoon enjoying a trek through wild woods will understand the power of trees. It was in a tree that Forrest learned to read from Jenny, and she learned to swing from him, and together they watched stars over the lake.

The Druids were known to have held many trees in sacred regard, especially the Oak, whose groves became their version of a church. Roy Hobbs makes his bat, "Wonderboy," from an Oak tree splintered by lightning. That must be some powerful totem—all members of his team decide to wear it on their uniforms. Robert Graves, poet and novelist best known for *I, Claudius,* made a creative argument about the relationships of trees, myth, history, poetry, and language in his book *The White Goddess.* He speaks of the Oak as being the tree of the great gods—Zeus, Jupiter, Hercules, Thor, Dagda, Jehovah, and Allah.

In this scene with Sigune, we see a popular fairy tale setting with the lady who sits under the Linden tree. Previously, Parzival met Gurnemanz under a Linden tree. The Scythians viewed the Linden as a source of prophetic power, while German myths used it to symbolize the community. Hildegard of Bingen thought a powder from the Linden roots would cure heart ailments. All of these special properties come into play as we study our Futures, our Community, and our Healing.

The Breaking Sword

So now we learn a secret about the sword that Parzival received at Munsalvaesche. It seems to be a lemon. He can use it once, but it will break on his second try.

Failing swords occur in several tales of the Arthurian legends. Arthur will fight Morgaine's lover, Accolon, with a fake Excaliber, which when it breaks will nearly bring about Arthur's death. Nascien tries to fight a giant with Solomon's sword, which breaks, because Nascien was not worthy to handle it. The sword is mended, but it wounds Nascien and maims Malory's King Pelles.

The Peredur version of the breaking sword has to do with his strength. While at the castle of the Fisher King, Peredur is ordered to take a sword and strike an iron column that was as large as a warrior's embrace. Both the column and the sword break in two. The sword and column are put back together again, and he is again ordered to strike the column, which has the same results. Again the sword and column are joined, and for the third time they are broken. This time, however, the sword and column could not be rejoined. Remember, the Sword represents our abilities and skills. Peredur is congratulated by the king who tells him that—though he is the best swordsman around—he only has two thirds of his strength. Only after he works on the other third will he be invincible.

Looking back at the Parzival version, Sigune says the sword will break, but it can be rejoined at a spring. It will be whole and stronger than it was before, if you know the magic words. Sigune is sure that Parzival did not bother with the needed spell.

The theme of healing waters is here, and we are encouraged that the sword will emerge better than before. This tells us that our Skills will serve us, but sometimes they may not be strong enough at the beginning. But have patience. When retempered and reformed, our Skills will become stronger and will be able to serve us better then. What are the magic words? We're not directly told, but I have an idea that it has something to do with Perfect Practice and Perseverance.

Mending the Sword

1. Think of times that you felt your Skills had both served and failed you. Did you become overly confident when they did serve you, and did you retreat when they failed you? Do an honest assessment of your abilities and skills.

2. What are the Magic Words that would help you improve your skills? I've offered two with Perfect Practice and Perseverance. Think of a few more.

3. List specific steps you will take to implement the Magic Words which would improve your skills.

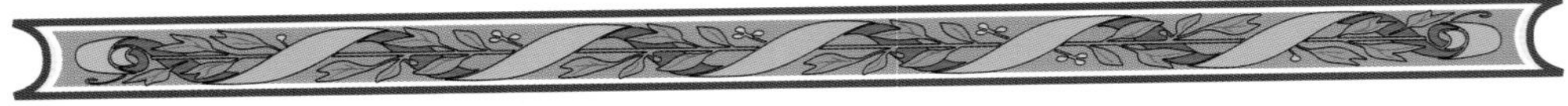

Slap in the Face

Sigune has figured out that Parzival did not get the requisite spell he needed for mending the sword. But she cannot believe that he was so uncaring that he did not heal the Fisher King. She tells him outright that it is his fault that the Wasteland will continue. He squandered a chance at great honor, so is now the scourge of the earth. Terre de Salvaesche, the Land of Salvation, holds the castle Munsalvaesche. It is a place that cannot be sought; one can only come upon it unaware. He missed his chance. Now, instead of being just an inept fool riding through the Wasteland, he is part of the problem.

We complain of all that is wrong around us, but do not take the simple steps that make life a little bit easier for others. In that way, we keep adding to the poison around us. We bicker, complain, criticize, and cajole, but don't ask others—"Well, what is bothering you?" We continue a cycle of destruction. We may not have started the cycle, but we don't do what is necessary to try to end it. So we help it continue.

When Jack first leaves Parry's apartment, he is stopped by the apartment building's Custodian. He tells Jack about Parry's misfortune. Parry is demented because he watched his wife blown apart when a crazed radio listener opened fire in a restaurant. Jack then realizes that Parry's tragedy happened because Jack berated the shooter to do something drastic. Jack has a moment of devastating epiphany on Connection and Responsibility. Jack is a direct cause of Parry's Wasteland. "Sigune" just told him.

Back at his apartment, Jack sheds tears for Parry as he reads about the shooting in old newspapers. Those tears may have been the first ones he ever shed for someone other than himself. He is breaking through, realizing the misery he caused others. He wishes that he could pay a fine that would take care of everything. The Spiritual work in front of him will take more than the few dollars in his pocket.

Sigune's stance may also be seen as continuing the problem. She shows no compassion towards Parzival, and has nothing more to do with him. But her coldness is a push to action. She is not going to tolerate the presence of someone who had an opportunity to do what is morally right and blew it. She's going to rightfully put him back on the road of experience so he will have a chance later of doing what is right. If he just hangs around her and her dead husband, there may not be any hope for healing.

Continuing the Wasteland

1. Acknowledge that we cannot just criticize how other people make the Wasteland. We are part of the problem if we don't include actions of Kindness and Caring in our everyday lives. Think of the activities you were engaged in during this past week. How did your actions contribute to the Wasteland? How did your actions help Heal the Wasteland?

2. Do the same for yourself. How have you contributed to your own Wasteland? How can you make it better?

The Lessons of You're Not Good Enough For This Party

ꕥ When we are apart from our Grail, we suffer. We must realize that it is through our actions that we moved away from the Grail. We cannot blame others for our continuing failure to achieve our Grail. We are responsible.

ꕥ When we do not express kindness towards others, we risk shutting out people who hold keys to the Grail Castle. We are all connected, and these people are part of your immediate web.

ꕥ The Cost of Grief shows in the flesh. Do not be critical of people who do not look as good as they used to. Realize that they suffer from loss and extend a little sympathy.

ꕥ The Sacredness of Trees is a reflection of the sacredness of Nature. Reconnect to these Sacred objects when possible.

ꕥ Our Skills need refining for them to be powerful enough to achieve our Grail. They can be made stronger through Perseverance and Perfect Practice.

ꕥ We get a wake up call when we realize our responsibility in the state of the Wasteland. We have the choice everyday of adding to the misery or healing the Wasteland.

Now that Parzival has been admonished, he has the choice to do something about it. Will he take responsibility for the Wasteland that he has been accused of continuing, or will he continue his haphazard, unconscious traveling?

Chapter 11 - Doing the Right Thing

The Awakening Conscience by
William Holman Hunt (1827–1910)

Tate Gallery, London
Oil on Canvas, 1853–54. 30 x 22 in.
Photo: Tate Gallery, London / Art Resource, N.Y.

Everyday we are given the chance for Atonement through righting the wrongs we have caused. Jack Lucas believes that if he helps Parry get the woman he loves, Jack's life will change for the better. He is right.

It is a big step to go from unknowingly creating havoc in people's lives, to making a conscious effort to repair what we have done. Parzival has just experienced what it is to suffer. Now he will try to ease the suffering he has caused.

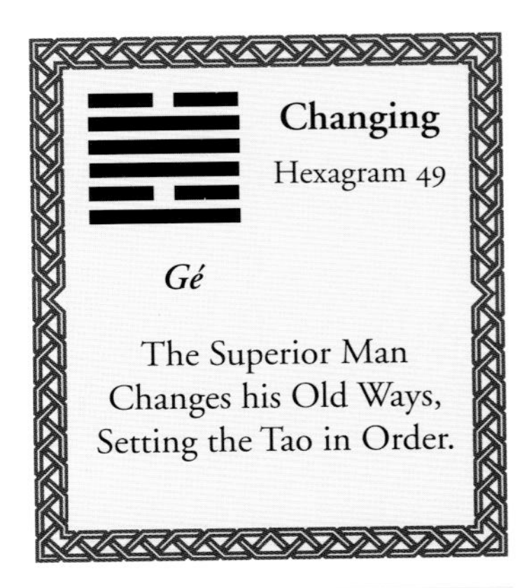

Orilus and Jeschute

Parzival finds tracks which lead to Jeschute, the first woman he encountered whose food, ring, and kisses he took. She is skinny and pale, wearing ragged clothes, and her nag is no better. She recognizes him, telling him he is the cause of her sorrow. He denies having ever harmed her in any way, because a knight would never harm a lady. She weeps and Parzival feels pities her. She will not accept clothing from him and tells him to leave, as six of him could not stand up to the wrath of her husband, who searches to destroy Parzival. Her horse neighs and Orilus finds them.

Orilus and Parzival fight a bold, nasty battle, with Parzival winning. Parzival does not kill Orilus, but tells him he must reconcile with his wife and make restitution to her. Orilus will not do this, because he still thinks he was wronged by Jeschute. He offers his kingdom, possessions, and loyalty, but he won't reconcile with his wife. Parzival says Orilus will reconcile, and then give homage at Arthur's court to the woman beaten for Parzival's sake, or he would die. Jeschute and Orilus finally kiss.

The three then find their way to the hermit Trevrizent's cave. There is a casket there of holy relics and a spear painted in bright colors. Parzival pledges on the casket, admitting his wrongdoing to Jeschute, and that she was totally innocent. Orilus finally accepts Jeschute's innocence and is happy to reunite with her. Parzival leaves Jeschute and Orilus, taking the brightly colored spear which had belonged to Taurian the Wild Man.

Orilus hears that Arthur is camping at Plimizoel and they prepare to go to him. When Orilus presents himself to Arthur, he is unrecognizable because his helmet has been so badly beaten by Parzival, it is unreadable. He pledges fealty to Cunneware, as Parzival had ordered. She recognizes him as her brother by the dragons on his cloak. Cunneware says he has always served her, so she has no need to accept this new oath. Arthur's court hears of the adventures of Parzival. Keie did not wait on Orilus, as he had thrashed Cunneware, so Kingrun did the honors.

— *Parzival* Summary, Book v, ¶ 256–279

Righting the Wrongs

Jack orchestrates a date with Parry and Lydia.

(Parry-Robin Williams, Anne-Mercedes Ruehl, Jack-Jeff Bridges, Lydia-Amanda Plummer)

Parzival now takes a very important step in his development. He is righting the wrongs he has caused and taking responsibility for them. In this situation, although he was offered all of Orilus' kingdom, Parzival only wants to see Orilus reunite with Jeschute. It would have been very easy to take the money and land, and ignore Jeschute. On the material level, Parzival would have made out very well. At the spiritual level, he would have left his past wrongdoings in karmic debt. If he had taken Orilus' initial offer, he would have committed an additional spiritual crime by leaving Jeschute's innocence unrecognized.

When Parzival wronged Jeschute, it was done in total innocence, the act of a fool. Modern courts might have found him innocent of any wrongdoing, because he had no intention or even knowledge of the harm he had caused. Orilus certainly compounded the problem with his own hasty actions. Nevertheless, Parzival consciously makes the decision to put together what he had torn apart, by admitting his own wrongdoing—a definite act of courage that goes beyond knightly codes.

Once Jack learned of Parry's emotional scars, he still could have walked away. Most people would expect this. After all, Parry is just a bag guy. At first, Jack thinks he can just buy Parry off with money. Parry wisely knows that won't help him or Jack. For Jack to truly right his wrong of taking Parry away from his love, he has to help Parry find love again. Jack then becomes instrumental in getting Parry and Lydia together, just as Parzival was insistent on Orilus and Jeschute reconciling.

This profound lesson is played out with a simple battle. On our Eightfold Path it is the sixth stage, Right Effort. We must make a conscious decision to admit what our own wrongdoings are, and make an effort to right them. Even if what we offer is at first refused, try again. In healing the Wasteland, the first step is working with those around us whom we have harmed. It may be those

Righting Our Wrongs

1. Start with the small wrongdoings you've done recently which you can apologize for, or make right through a proper action. Admitting responsibility is a hard habit to learn. We are taught about the consequences of our wrongdoings more than the healing we can initiate through responsibility. Move up to larger issues. Not everyone will embrace your new found willingness for reparation, but many will be touched.

2. Gracefully accept others' apologies and initiations. This doesn't mean that grievous wrongs are not to be addressed, but negotiations can be done with a goal of working towards what is right, rather than heavy punishments.

we love, or those we work with, or some acquaintances in our community. We must learn to take responsibilities for our actions. To build a firm spiritual base that can be trusted, our words and actions must be trusted. We cannot ignore this step in personal spiritual development.

The Spear and the Relics

Viviane and Merlin
by Julia Margaret Cameron (1815–1879)

The admission of guilt and reconciliation is not orchestrated amidst royal settings and trappings, but in the cliff side cave of a hermit. Instead of an artificial landscape, rebirth is begun in a wild, natural, stony womb.

In the hermit's cave are religious relics and a brightly colored spear. Nowadays, we think of religious relics as souvenirs. In olden times, these may be various body parts of dead saints. So it is on symbols of the past that the sins of the past are put to rest. For future adventures, Parzival takes the other object—the spear.

The reference to the spear belonging to Taurian the Wild Man refers to a whole spectrum of Wild Man stories. The Wild Man is the man who has rejected the problems put on him by society and has sought refuge in the healing of nature. Sometimes the Wild Man is referred to as being mad, while other times he shown as fierce and independent. Characters who have shared the Wild Man archetype are Taurian's brother Dodinel, Merlin, Lancelot, Tristan, and Perceval.

We don't have to look far in modern culture to see our desire to be the Wild Man. We see him at Daytona Beach spring break parties, and at the bar. In the original stories, the Wild Man aims towards a healing which will enable a stronger man to bring his talents back to society. Our modern equivalents can stay stuck in a destructive cycle, instead of using it as a purging leading to wholeness.

One of my favorite Wild Man stories is about Merlin and his sister, Ganieda, in Geoffrey of Monmouth's *Vita Merlini.* Ganieda wants Merlin to live with her in the city, but Merlin has chosen a life in the wild with his beloved animals and trees. After pondering the difficulties of obtaining food in the winter, he agrees to return to Ganieda if she builds a special house for him—a castle with seventy doors and windows, from which he could see the fires burn, and observe the stars and the planets. He would need seventy secretaries to record his prophecies and knowledge. So, Merlin lives in the wild during the summer, and during the winter, he spends time with his sister at the castle she built for him. She comes and goes as she pleases. In later stories, Nimue or Vivienne imprisons Merlin in a cave, or crystal, or tree. Nimue and Vivienne could moved freely about, while Merlin remained trapped. The original story has a much more healing, and less devious, story line.

In *Apocalypse Now,* Lance is transformed as the men work their adventure down the river. As he paints his face in camouflage, he appears to be going mad and starts living in a dream world. It is not until Willard and the men reach Kurtz' territory that we see Lance is one of them. His supposed madness was just taking on of the nature of the man who lives in Kurtz' OtherWorld. He is immediately accepted by the tribesmen at Kurtz' compound.

What we need to do is find the balance between our Natural, Wild Nature, and the Disciplined Work required to bring form to creative knowledge, so others may learn from it. Both the Creative and the Disciplined are equally important. We must experience our wild, creative side, then return to the community with wisdom from the creativity.

This story also reminds us that we literally have to get out in Nature. We need to walk among wild creatures, and sky, and mountains, and splash in icy springs. We can return to society refreshed and ready for the work at hand.

As Parzival leaves the cave, he takes the spear with him. We know the spear to be Truth, and this spear is the Truth of the wildest nature. It screams with bright colors, a mixing of many opportunities, choices, and people. It is symbolic of what more is to come, and Parzival's willingness to possess an instrument of the Natural, Wild side—a condition he has misplaced.

The Wild Man

1. If you have ignored your Wild Self, think of ways that you can reunite yourself with that side of you. Allow your creativity and spontaneity to express themselves in as many ways as you can. Then bring that joy and wisdom back to the rest of your life in a way that is productive and healing of others.

2. If you have indulged your Wild Self without discipline, find ways of harnessing your energy so it becomes constructive, yet still maintains that sense of freedom.

Great Love

Great love is joy and misery both.
— from *Parzival,* Book v, ¶ 272

There is no doubt that Jeschute has been treated unfairly. Orilus also has a Spiritual debt for everything he has done to her. The text assures us that their reconciliation was a full and true one. It also reminds us that great love has both joy and sorrow.

People should dispel the fantasies that everything runs calmly in marriages and relationships. Wolfram knew it a thousand years ago. Greek myths had Zeus and Hera warring from the very beginning. Even Adam and Eve had their differences. Yet people are still going into marriage thinking it's a smooth ride. We are real people, living in a real world, with real problems. We need to do our best to help each other along, but we also must realize that the differences that attract people, will be the same differences that can cause people to drift apart. Sometimes, Great Love does require working through real sorrow.

We also can be optimistic and expect joy along with the tough times. After going through difficult times, a couple may settle for the even keel, not expecting Joy to come back to their marriage. Reward yourself with the expectation that you deserve and can create joy once again. Without it, Love will not experience the greatness it promises.

Isolation by
Fernand Khnopff (1858–1921)
Private Collection
Pastel, 1894. 55 1/8 x 17 in.

Darkening of the Light
Hexagram 36

Míng Zhì

The Light has been Darkened, but Persistence brings Reward.

Positive Fallout

The term fallout is usually associated with radiation and corporate mergers. It's usually nasty business. Now we are going to look at Positive Fallout—the fact that doing good can generate more good.

Now that Parzival is making retribution for his mistakes of the past, a wonder of the Tao unfolds. He has set in motion a reverse cycle. Instead of innocently harming people as he goes along, he now innocently brings about greater goodness in life than he intended. He sends Orilus to Cunneware as a liege prisoner, but ends up reuniting a separated brother and sister.

When we do good, we don't know how many ways we affect other lives. It is said that a good (or bad) word spoken to one person affects two hundred others in the same day. One person, who is now in a good (or bad) mood, affects five more people, who each affect five more, snowballing into several hundred individuals. With the advent of email, we may be affecting thousands, perhaps millions.

By choosing kindness and doing the right thing, we reach out with many tentacles to create more decency and healing, even where we are not physically present. By consciously ordering our lives to work from a base of values, we consciously choose to make the world better. Parzival is already changing the Wasteland. We can do the same thing in our lives.

The Lessons of Doing the Right Thing

- To live a Spiritual Life, we must be willing to admit our wrongdoings and make an effort at restitution. Even when we harm people without intent, we need to acknowledge the pain we have caused. We must also allow others the freedom to do the same with us.

- We must honor our Wild Man Nature, and tame it to serve ourselves and others. We need both Creativity and Discipline, and we must make an effort to balance our Wild side with the Focused side.

- Nature is there to invigorate us and keep us in touch with the natural elements which replenishes our spirits. Take the time to enjoy the world.

- Great Love is made up of both Joy and Sorrow. By living in reality and working towards the best, couples can build a lasting, strong union. After any sorrow, be mindful of bringing back the joy.

- Our good deeds generate many more good deeds. Let's make the conscious choice to get this thread of goodness extending far.

There are times when we seem to lose purpose in our lives.
During that time, we need to take time to reflect on what is most important to us.
Parzival will now experience what it is to be apart from his Love.

Dragon ceiling in Hong Kong

Chapter 12 - Trance-lvania

There are tales of blood and maidens that surround a mysterious castle deep in the heart of the Carpathian Mountains in a land called Transylvania. The king of this land was called Dracula, translating to "son of Dracul." *Dracul* means Dragon.

We, too, have tales of blood and maidens and dragons. In this case, blood will send Parzival into a trance about a maiden.

Trance of Parzival

Arthur leaves Karidoel to search for the Red Knight who keeps sending him prisoners, intending to make this man a knight of the Round Table. Arthur has also instigated a rule that all who wish to fight must ask his permission, so he can keep men close to his side for his own protection. Arthur is considered a man of May, and significant events involving him happen at Pentecost. In this case, it snows in May. Arthur's falconers lose their best falcon from overfeeding and it is not going after its prey. It flies into the forest, finding Parzival, and stays near him to keep warm. Both nearly freeze during the night.

At daylight, the falcon follows Parzival. Coming upon a large flock of geese, the falcon attacks one fiercely. Three drops of blood fall on the snow, causing Parzival to go into a trance, thinking of Condwiramors. He sees the pure colors of the red on white as symbols of Condwiramors purity. The triangular fall of the drops resemble her face, and Parzival knows his love for her is strong.

Cunneware's squire rides out on an errand, and sees Parzival with his spear standing up. The squire reads this as a challenge to fight. He does not know that Parzival is in a trance, nor that Parzival also serves the Lady Cunneware. The squire returns to camp and shames the men to fight this challenger. Sagremors is hot headed and always looking for a fight. He petitions Ginover as kin to get Arthur to allow him to fight. Arthur allows it, though he warns they are close to Anfortas' Munsalvaesche. No one knows exactly where the castle is, and its knights defend the forest.

Sagremors challenges Parzival, who does not hear Sagremors because of his trance. As Sagremors charges, Parzival's horse turns so Parzival does not see the blood, thus awakening him. Parzival defends himself with the spear, knocking Sagremors off his horse. Sagremors returns to camp defeated, and Parzival returns to gazing at the blood. He thinks of Condwiramors and the Grail.

Keie then rides out and challenges Parzival with insults. Keie too is defeated, and ends up with a broken arm and leg; thus Parzival avenges the beatings of Cunneware and Antanor. However, Parzival's spear is destroyed in the battle. Keie returns to camp and is met with concern. Though Keie has a sharp tongue, he is known as a brave and loyal man.

Keie shames Gawan into going after Parzival. Parzival's trance now focuses on the suffering of his parents and ancestors. Gawan approaches Parzival, but recognizes the trance, as he too has experienced such trances. Gawan breaks Parzival's trance by tossing a yellow silk scarf over the blood. Parzival cries to Condwiramors, who seems so far away, and he does not know where his spear is. Gawan introduces himself and offers friendship. Parzival at first does not want to go to Arthur's court, because he has not avenged Cunneware. Gawan tells him all he has done and shows Parzival his broken spear. They ride to Arthur's camp.

Parzival is joyously greeted by Cunneware and rewarded with a jeweled studded belt and clothing. He meets with Arthur and becomes a knight of the Round Table. The custom of the Round Table was that an Adventure must take place before one could eat, and the joining of Parzival was considered such an adventure. Ginover joins them and Arthur teases that he will allow Ginover to kiss Parzival, if Arthur can get the same at Pelrapeire with a kiss from Condwiramors. Ginover does kiss him and forgives him for the death of Ither.

— *Parzival* Summary, Book VI, ¶ 280–310

The King Looks for the Red Knight

Gerald Lambeau is ambushed by students wanting to know who has solved the challenge of a complex mathematics problem. No one takes credit, so Gerald has to lure this genius out by presenting another problem. He does catch a glimpse of Will Hunting solving the second problem, but isn't quick enough to get to him. After all, Will is just a janitor, and no way can a janitor do such complicated math. Then, Gerald recognizes that Will is one in a billion, and a potential protégé like that can't go unrecognized. He launches his own search for Will.

King Arthur finally admits there is weakness in his court, but he still does not look to himself as part of the problem. Instead of making himself stronger, he forbids his knights to go on adventure, keeping them for his own protection. If a man wants to go out, they go to the queen first, who knows the strength of the empire is the individual strength of the men. Arthur will never have any honor if his men do not have honor. Ginover speaks on the knights' behalf in getting Arthur's permission. The knights of Arthur's court are the fat falcon which has become lazy and does not go after its prey. Miracles of Arthur occur during May, but this year it is a cold miracle. Instead of spring, there is ice and snow on the ground, a frigid Wasteland. For the falcon to desire the hunt again, he must venture into this Wasteland.

At least Arthur is smart enough to look for the best knight, whose prisoners keep showing up on Arthur's doorstep. He is also smart enough to know this man could dwell along the edge of a magical forest guarded by the Grail Knights.

This is a stage that many of us go through before we break through to another level of consciousness. We recognize that something is wrong in our lives, but then set about surrounding ourselves with old habits, not allowing new tests to help us solve our problems. We forbid any changes or new adventures, because we fear that what we do have could ultimately be lost. We fail to make ourselves stronger, relying on others to do our battles. On top of that, we only allow them to perform duties in a manner we conscribe, thus tying up their own creative thinking and problem solving. The pattern we are stuck in has failed us, but we are afraid to make the leap that is necessary to save us. In spite of all of our self-sabotage, at least we are smart enough to search out another creative solution. And we know it lies somewhere in the OtherWorld.

Trances and Right Concentration

That fat falcon knows the source that could save it and readily finds Parzival. In fact, both need each other to stave off the cold. The knights of the court must awaken in the presence of Parzival to their duty, and Parzival must recognize his role in the kingdom. As yet, he does not see how the suffering of the Grail Castle is tied into the suffering of Arthur's court. The falcon needs only to see a thousand geese, a thousand potential tests, to know its mission. Once the blood of its attack is on the snow, Parzival goes into a trance, turning his sight away from this world into the inner one.

Parzival's trance is the trance of his love, what lies deepest in his heart. He vacillates between thoughts of his wife, his family, and the Grail. His heart knows they are connected, but only as a source of sorrow. He has come a long way from the fool who left his mother lying on the ground, but must still discover that to fulfill the ailing of the heart is to find true love.

Parry's trance of blood would throw him into a coma as he relived the murder of his wife. It would take the "vision" of Lydia to help heal his wounds. He imagines her as his potential partner in New York Central Station, where everyone dances and everyone smiles and everyone gets along. Gump always thinks about Jenny, whether away in the army, running the roads of America, or alone in his house at Greenbow. Sometimes his vision materialized as a Playboy magazine layout. Roy Hobbs senses Iris in the bleachers, but the glare of the sun off her white dress dims his vision of her. Princess Leia reveals herself through R2-D2's holographic image of her. Siddhartha's vision was a dream of Kamala's songbird lying dead in the bottom of its gold cage. He throws the tiny corpse away on a road. His vision was one where he felt he had thrown away "all that was good and of value in himself."

Now some might view Parzival as being spacey and totally unaware of his surroundings in his trance, but what it really illustrates is our Eighth step of the Eightfold Path, Right Concentration. One part of Right Concentration is the ability to focus on a project or activity so you are able to perform well and complete your task. This is a very practical application of this step. Another is the total concentration on matters of the Spirit. Parzival is focusing on what is in his heart and what it means to be connected to the Spirit of what he loves. Parzival is handling the material world just fine, defeating the knights who challenge him. It is the questions of the Spirit that he must resolve if he is to find peace in his soul.

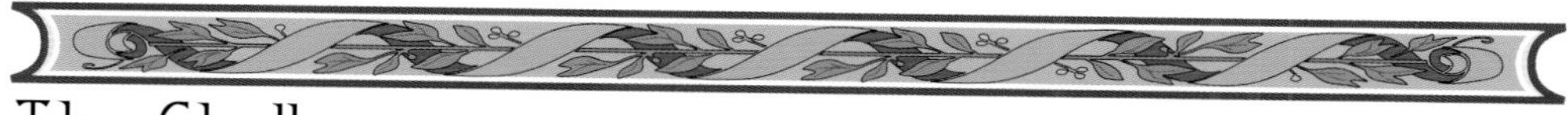

The Challenge

> *It happened that a woman who lived on the sixth floor of an apartment house overlooking the stadium was cleaning out her bird cage, near the end of the game, which the Knights took handily, when her canary flew out of the window and darted down across the field. Roy, who was waiting for the last out, saw something coming at him in the low rays of the sun, and leaping high, bagged it in his glove.*
>
> *He got rid of the bloody mess in the clubhouse can.*
>
> — from *The Natural* by Bernard Malamud

In this quote, Roy unknowingly kills a bird while playing baseball. It is representative of him "killing" Bump Bailey, who was his nemesis since he arrived to play for the Knights. When Roy started to show his talents on the ball field, Pop Fisher warned Bump that he better try harder. Finally having some competition, Bump goes all out and does not see the field's wall as he catches a ball. Seriously injured, Bump is sent to the hospital. The next line following the above quote tells us Bump is dead. Roy has met his challenge in a trance similar to Parzival's, by unknowingly defeating his opponent.

In his trance, Parzival is oblivious to the fact that he gives a symbol of ready combat. This is a true challenge, because the voice of the OtherWorld—his subconscious—allows it to happen. The physical world of Arthur's court must be initiated to begin finding and confronting the hero who can help the court. Otherwise, they will pass by men on horses, not searching permission from the king for tests. A man ready to fight with a brightly colored spear deserves some sort of attention.

Parzival's fighting technique is a little unorthodox, because he keeps communing with the OtherWorld until awakened to a battle. This is a reminder that no matter how important it is to enter into your own private, meditative world, you must wake up and deal with the realities of the world around you. Once you have taken care of the work you have instigated in the first place, you can always return to the necessary work of finding your heart.

We all know people who live in the dream world. Maybe we are one of those people. They may have wonderful dreams and good intentions, but they never leave the dream world long enough to do the tasks to make the dreams real. If we are lucky, we may have a smart horse that turns its head long enough to wake us up. If there is no one to help us, then we must devise the cues ourselves to remind us it is time to leave the OtherWorld, and go face the challenges of the Physical World.

How to Meditate (One Way)

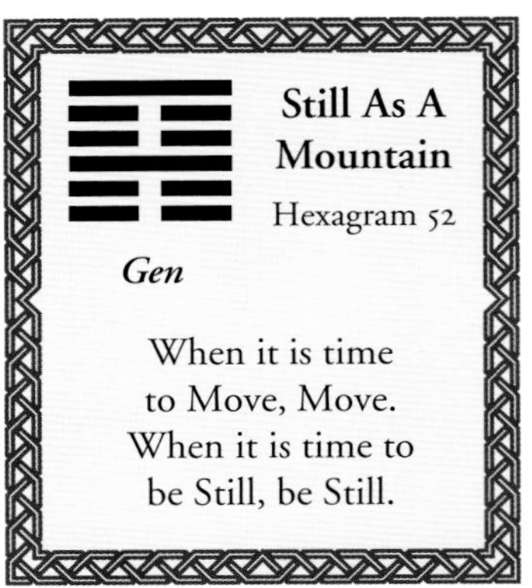

In the film *Camelot,* Guenevere asks Lancelot if he has reached perfection. He responds that he has physically, but the soul's work is endless. Meditation can aid in perfecting the body when it needs rest and concentration. It can perfect the soul, by giving it needed reflection.

Meditation is a way of exploring your Inner World. It is a way of choosing a Mindful Trance to regain balance and focus in your life. The Fifth Perfection is Insight. We must know ourselves before we can truly know others and the world. Until we understand ourselves and our own weaknesses and strengths, we cannot assume to know others.

There are many ways to meditate including prayer, journaling, mindfulness in action, and calming the body to a place of stillness. You can run, sit, or bend yourself into contortions. Though most people think of Eastern practices when the word "meditation" is used, all religions have their way of meditating.

Since many of us lead stressful lives, one important way of meditating is giving yourself the luxury of calming yourself and going to a place of peace within yourself. Here is one way to work on stilling your body and mind.

1. Wear comfortable clothes and be in a comfortable environment. Turn off the phone, TV, spouse and kids. You may choose to sit or stand, but do so in a comfortable way. Sitting can be done on the floor or on a chair. Whichever position you take, be sure your spine, neck, and head are straight.

2. Choose something to focus your attention on. The most basic way is to focus on your breathing. You may count your breaths in repetitions of five or ten. This is more difficult than you think, because often your mind wants to wander to problems or other sensations. Try to come back to your breathing. What you are doing is developing your Mindfulness, the ability to keep focused on what is at hand.

3. Another way of focusing is to pick a phrase which is meaningful for you, at either a personal or universal level. If you have been feeding yourself negative scripts about yourself, reverse this pattern by repeating a phrase that counters this. Pick a phrase that hooks you to your personal belief system, and the goodness of your God, Buddha, Beloved, Goddess, or Tao. You may wish to affirm the goodness of the people in the world. If you start to mentally wander, reel yourself back to the concept you wished to meditate on.

4. Or pick an object of art, literature, devotions, or music, and immerse yourself in its beauty and truth. When you take the time for such study, you are wiser and have more depth than you realize.

5. At the beginning of this practice, limit yourself to just a few minutes if you become physically uncomfortable and fidgety. As you learn more about yourself and reap benefits from the practice, extend your time frame. Some people like to start their day with such work, while others like to wind it down. Experiment to find what works for you.

Moving Into the Trance

Use whatever form of meditation you are comfortable with, whether it is one of the exercises above, a walk in the woods, or prayer. Use it to calm your mind and body, then allow yourself to reflect on those you love. Then reflect on your own personal Grail. Realize that all that you love are connected. Think of the dreams of your life and what they mean to you and others.

Moving Out of the Trance

After spending time in the dream world, return to the physical world. Think of specific ways you can achieve your Grail, remembering that those you love are part of that Grail. Use your wisdom and invigorate yourself to real action.

The Balanced Trinity

In the Welsh story of Peredur, there is more than just the contrast of the Red Blood and White Snow. Here the hawk has left the dead duck, and a raven alights on the duck. Peredur sees the Black of the Raven as the jet black hair of the woman he loves best, the White of the Snow as her skin, and the Red Blood as the color of her cheeks. In this version of the story, Peredur hasn't even met his true love yet, so he is only seeing a vision of the Goddess of the Land. These three colors represent the Triplicate Goddess.

Queen Amidala wears the colors of the Triplicate Goddess—Red, White, and Black.

(Amidala-Natalie Portman)

In the movie *Apocalypse Now,* there is a scene where a helicopter delivers three women to entertain the troops. Rock entrepreneur Bill Graham introduces the ladies who happen to be a Blonde, a Redhead, and a Dark Haired beauty. Francis Ford Coppola, no stranger to mythic symbols, presents us with three sexy goddesses. The three major women in the movie *The Natural* all wear these colors. We first meet

Le Destin by H. Siddons Mowbray (1858–1928)

Courtesy, Museum of Fine Arts, Boston. Tompkins Collection. (1979.39)
Oil on Canvas, 1896. 30 x 40 ½ in.

Harriet Bird in a black and white suit with a red rose pinned to her jacket. Queen Amidala wears fantastic gowns of red, black, and white.

The Triplicate Goddess is a recurring motif in many mythologies. She is the holy feminine triad, represented by the Maiden/Virgin, Mother, and Crone. These are symbolically the powers of womanhood as she moves through her passage of life. You have heard of her as the Three Fates who spin the thread of life, or the Three Witches who stir that bubbling, boiling cauldron in *Macbeth*. The Greeks had the Three Gorgons and the triad of Hera/Hebe/Hecate. The Norse had the Three Norns. The Irish had the Triple Morrighan. India had Parvati/Durgā/Kali. The Grail myths had several with the sisters of Arthur, Elaine/Morgause/Morgaine, and the Three Damsels of the Fountain. Parzival has had his experience with the Triplicate Goddess as Jeschute, Liaze, and Condwiramors. His father, Gahmuret, is loved by Belacane, Ampflise, and Herzeloyde. Later on in our story, Gawan will have his own encounters with the Triplicate Goddess in the form of three women. The list goes on and on.

In *Forrest Gump,* Jenny will fulfill each of these three roles. She starts as the innocent young girl whom Gump first falls in love with. Later, she will be the mother of his child. Finally, she will come to him with the mask of the Death Crone, and teach him the hardest lesson he will ever learn.

There are also Triplicate Gods in religions and myths. Norse myth had Odin, Tyr, and Freyr. The Christian religion has God the Father, God the Son, and God the Holy Ghost. The Hindu faith has the One God, Ishwara, representing Brahma the Creator, Vishnu the Preserver, and Shiva as the Destroyer. Sometimes a goose is depicted with Ishwara. The goose is comfortable in the air, the land, and sea. He is master of the three worlds, so this gives insight into Parzival, and later Gawan, being called a "Goose." Rather than just considering Parzival and Gawan as having been insulted, we can now view them as apprentices learning to master the realms of the world.

Notice that throughout the *Parzival* story, male and feminine principles are balanced, following a true Taoist doctrine. The Sufi philosophy, a mystical sect of Islamic and ancient world beliefs, also deals with dualistic notions. Sufi also believe in a concept of male/female balance—the feminine is called *Jamāl* or Divine Beauty, and the masculine is *Jalāl* or Divine Majesty.

When the Male and Female principle have failed, we have a Maimed, essentially Castrated, King. By the end of the story, we will have a healthy kingdom again when Arthur and Ginover find peace together, Parzival rules as the new Grail King with Condwiramors, and Gawan rules as the King of the Land of Wonders with Orgeluse.

This further emphasizes how important it is to find balance in everything we do and with everyone we know. We have to balance what goes on in our Inner lives as well as our Outer. Part of us likes aggression, part of us likes peace. Part of us creates, part of us destroys. The balance comes about when we recognize that both have valid times of power. There is a time for the Goddess to rule, and there is a time for the God to rule. When you can acknowledge the power of all of your conflicts and give them their own space, your life will become balanced.

The Balanced Trinity

Choose one conflict in your life that seems to reoccur. This could be an Inner or Outer conflict. Think of ways that you can balance it by allowing space to each side of the conflict. Do you feel like you are too passive? Take a stand on an issue and voice your concerns. Maybe you tend to overpower people around you, so they end up disliking you. Tone down, and give others a chance to be stronger. Realize that the power of both the Male and Female is necessary to find balance.

Return to Transylvania

You may think I was just making a play on words when I used "Trance-lvania," but there was method in my madness—another game of Six Degrees. Many people have different theories about the source of the Arthurian legends. One idea is that tribes of Scythia, an ancient area in southeast Europe by the Black Sea, carried these legends as they wandered and battled across the continent. One of these tribes was the Sarmatians, loosely translated to mean "Lizard People," who had serpentine or dragon-like banners. One of these Sarmatian tribes did invade what was later known as Transylvania. Dracula's father was supposedly a member of a secret society called The Order of the Dragon, allegedly sanctioned by the Catholic Church and Emperor Sigismund to fight the Turks.

In the previous chapter, Cunneware recognizes her brother from the dragons on his cloak. Passages on the fight between Parzival and Orilus hold a description of dragons on his shield and helmet. In both the Eastern and Western cultures, Dragons have stood for Power and Primeval forces.

Arthur's father was known as Uther Pendragon, the Head of the Dragon. His kingship had been foretold by a dragon image in the sky. Merlin was still a child when he dumbfounded the sorcerers of Vortigern's court with his revelations of red and white dragons warring under an incomplete castle. These dragons have been interpreted to be Vortigern vs. Uther, the British vs. the Saxons, the alchemical blood and sweat of Christ, and the balance of female and male energies. The Welsh flag bears the sign of the Red Dragon.

Oftentimes, dragons in Western myth displayed unruly primeval energies, so the destruction of dragons was a test of the Hero. St. George kills his dragon and dwarfs' treasures are guarded by fire breathing dragons. The *Ouroborus,* Earth Serpent, of Norse myth is Jormungand, born of the trickster Loki. This serpent is so large, he circles the earth and bites down on his tail. These unruly dragons are the unruly wild selves, which must be controlled and tamed, so treasures can be revealed.

In the East, the dragon is a positive symbol, representing the Taoist Way. It is a powerful being, always coiling around itself, conquering the sky and earth. Emperors and Immortals used the dragon as their symbol. The Earth itself is a dragon and the mysterious forces that *feng shui* (Chinese geomancy) seek out come from the dragon veins of the earth. When you look at Chinese landscape ink paintings and see the contours of the mountains, you are looking at the dragon veins. The mists hanging among mountain passes and cliff side temples are the dragon's breath.

The family of Orilus and Cunneware work under this powerful sign of the Dragon. Parzival's mastery of Orilus, his homage to Cunneware, and his recognition as a hero of Arthur's court represent his beginning mastery of Primeval Power.

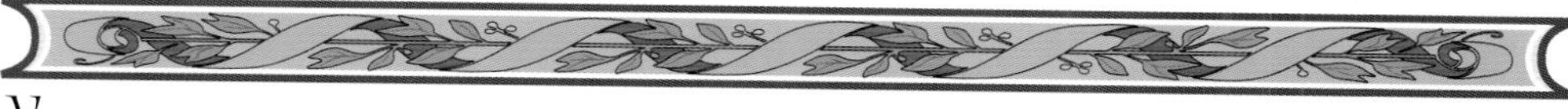

Vengeance

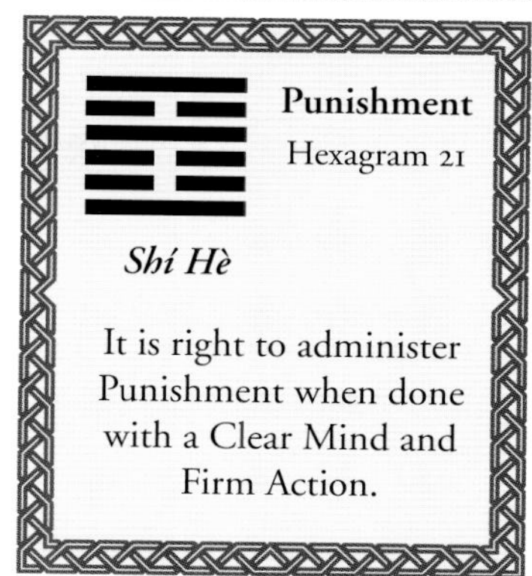

One of the tasks of Parzival is Vengeance. It seems to be a strong, negative goal in a book that is heading towards the necessity of compassion, but the philosophy of *Parzival* lives in a real world. In Christian theology dichotomies also exist. One passage says "Turn the other cheek," while another says "Beat your plowshares into swords." Because we treat those who are suffering and innocent with compassion, it does not mean that a wicked person is to be treated with the same charity.

In the Peredur legend, the "Grail" is a head of Peredur's cousin on a platter. The cousin was killed by the Witches of Gloucester, also responsible for the maiming of Peredur's uncle, the story's Fisher King. It was foretold that Peredur would exact vengeance, and he does so with their deaths.

Chrétien's version of *Perceval* may be one of the first written accounts of the Grail legend, but he died before finishing it. The book ends in mid-sentence. This may have been the inspiration for the abrupt cutoff in Monty Python's film of the Holy Grail. Several authors wrote finishing stories which are called *The Continuations. The Third Continuation,* known as *Manesier's Continuation,* also uses vengeance as a theme. In this story, Perceval kills a man named Partinial, who had been the cause of the Fisher King's ailings. Perceval brings Partinial's head to the king, which is the action that heals the king.

In the films *Apocalypse Now* and *Heart of Darkness,* both Kurtz characters use the heads of members of Willard's/Marlow's crews to incite a need for vengeance. Chef's head is thrown into the lap of Willard, while Marlow looks out the window to see the head of one of the young boys in his charge. Kurtz also shocks Marlow by snapping the head of a pet monkey, a totally trusting creature. In *Heart of Darkness,* Kurtz is looking for a man who can face hard truths and understand the insanity of the racism in the Congo.

Earlier, Parzival killed Ither because he wanted his armor. There was no tempering of the situation, and Parzival behaved improperly. In meeting Sagremors and Keie, he has met the challenges with appropriate punishments, even while he was in a trance. Sagremors, hot blooded and vain, has his rear end planted on the ground. Keie has administered two beatings, and in compensation has received two injuries. The laws of Karma say that crimes can be met with equal punishment, thus delivering proper restitution to the victims. If someone commits a wrongdoing, and has not lived up to his or her responsibility in that wrong doing, then proper vengeance is allowed. It is a continuing process of showing compassion to the victim, and not to the perpetrator of crimes.

Mirror Spirit

We now meet Gawan, Arthur's nephew, for the first time. His relationship is significant, because he would be the heir to the throne, since Arthur does not have any sons. Gawan is known as a great warrior, lover, and a paragon of courtly manners. In Chrétien's version, he is sent to meet Perceval because of his witty and polite way of words.

Gawan does not seek Arthur's permission to ride out. He acts on his own accord. He responds to his own nature as a warrior. From this point on, Gawan's path runs parallel to Parzival's, as he is Parzival's Mirror Spirit. He is the knight who will run the tasks of the Physical Quest while Parzival runs the Spiritual Quest. Some scholars theorize that Gawan may have been one of the original Grail Heroes. In *Perceval, Parzival, Perlesvaus,* all but the first of the *Continuations,* and Malory's version, Gawan's story is intertwined with Parzival's. In *Diu Crône* and *The First Continuation,* he is the primary Grail winner.

Arthur may be the king of the Physical World of the Community, but we have learned that he is an ineffective king. Instead, the best knight, Gawan, rides out to the challenge. The passage tells us that Arthur is considered a man of May—his nephew's name in the Welsh tales is Gwalchmai, interpreted as Hawk of May. At the beginning of the story, Gawan is absent from the court at the time of Ither's challenge. Now, he is here to help, and will circle Parzival just like a Hawk.

When Gawan approaches Parzival and taunts him, he is wise enough, from his own personal experience, to recognize a man who communes with Love. Immediately he knows that such a man is his kindred spirit, and knows the proper way to approach him. As an acting king of the real world, Gawan awakens Parzival from his trance with a weapon as innocuous as a yellow scarf—yellow being the color of transformation. He is the proper person to bring Parzival to his senses. Their tasks together will form the healing of the kingdom.

Completion of Tasks

The password was given to me by a man who died in the dungeons of Arrakeen. You see, that is where I got this ring in the shape of a tortoise. It was in the suk outside the city where I was hidden by rebels. The password? Oh, that has been changed many times since then. It was "Persistence." and the countersign was "Tortoise." It got me out of there alive. That's why I bought this ring: a reminder.

— *Tagir Mohandis: Conversations with a Friend*

— from *Children of Dune* by Frank Herbert

Parzival, who believes he has not finished avenging Cunneware's beatings, is at first reluctant to go to Arthur with Gawan. It would be dishonorable for him to return to court, because he has not completed the adventure he has chosen.

The completion of an important task is a valuable lesson to learn. So often, we bog ourselves down in the mundane and trivial, using those small completed tasks as evidence of growth. It is not until we complete the important tasks of life that we obtain the honor we seek. Until we focus on what is necessary, we will not achieve much in our lives. Our reality will be a dead end. Parzival has chosen his task, goes around announcing it, and now works to complete it. He will not go back until he has earned his own self respect through doing the best he can. He feels he cannot receive the accolades of the court until he has earned them.

We often stray far from the goals of our lives. Sometimes, it may be due to outside forces. Sometimes we have had to make decisions that concerned the welfare of those we love. Sometimes we just made bad decisions. No matter what the past reasons are, we earn our own self dignity by completing those events and goals which we have chosen for ourselves. Announce your intentions to the world, then strive to complete them, and receive the respect due to you. It may come from the outer world, but most importantly, that respect must be what you give to yourself. Parzival goes to Arthur for honor, but Arthur himself is past the stage of earning honor. He sits on the laurels of his past. Ultimately, it is the honor that Parzival gives to himself which will count.

Completing the Task

This is a very important multi-task exercise that will take a bit of thinking. It involves analyzing what tasks are necessary in achieving your Grail. Don't fool yourself by doing busy work which only puts you further away from what you want to accomplish.

1. Meditate on what you want to achieve with your Grail, then brainstorm and list the major tasks that must be completed along the way.

2. Choose one of the major tasks and break it down into manageable parts.

3. Now choose one of those tasks and work on it.

4. Once it is completed, pat yourself on the back, because no one else is going to. If you are going to receive any type of accolade, it probably won't be until you finish your whole project, so in the meantime, reward yourself. I don't recommend spending large sums of cash or indulging yourself in a whole cake, but small rewards you find pleasurable add that much more to the satisfaction of having completed an important task. Now begin work on the other tasks.

Broken Spear

> *The Broken Spear*
>
> *Have you had times when the lure to receive praise became more important than doing the work that got you there? So often, we keep the image of the reward in so much focus, that when we do receive it, we turn our back on the things that got us there. Have you given up skills and a natural spirit to only bask in congratulations?*

In *The Natural,* the Knights are on a winning streak and the team starts celebrating as if they were already the champs. Roy works on a path of indulgences which include Memo Paris and food, ignoring warning signs from his old bullet wound. All of this will end up as trouble, since Roy is forgetting what baseball is all about, and more importantly, what he is all about.

Parzival has succeeded in avenging Cunneware, evidenced by the broken spear belonging to a Wild Man. Parzival was beginning to follow his true nature, but now he is going to accept the praises of the court. He will leave his natural world, the one of adventure, and go to Arthur, who only wants those who will stay close by and serve him. The spear of the Wild Man is shattered, and Parzival will forget his wild nature to indulge in the ways of the court. He has stalled himself from achieving his Grail.

Kisses of the Queens

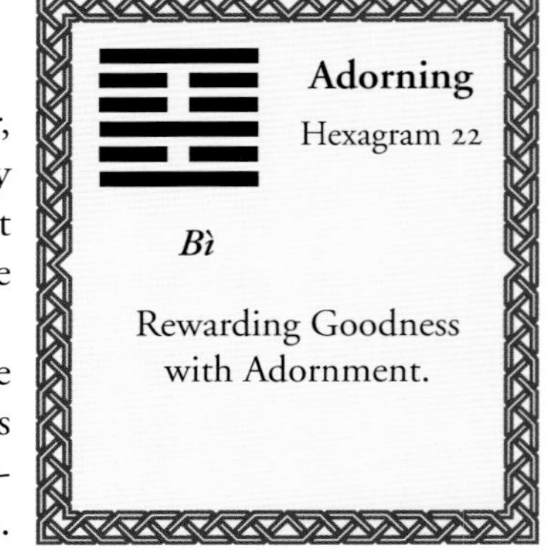

Cunneware recognizes what Parzival has done for her, and rewards him with a kiss, a green robe, and a ruby clasped girdle. A girdle in those days was a thick belt like a boxing champ would wear, not one a lingerie model would parade in.

More importantly, Ginover forgives Parzival for the death of Ither. In kissing him, she recognizes that he is the Red Knight—the representative of the Other-World—who will right the wrongs of her kingdom. Arthur may tease of a kiss from Parzival's wife, but only because he knows a fairy wife when he sees one. Ginover's power has been indispensable to him in helping his kingdom, and another goddess looking over him would serve Arthur well.

Another thing to keep in mind is that sometimes a kiss in medieval stories can be more than a kiss where kings are involved. Some stories are referring to *droit du seigneur,* or "The Lord's Right." In *Braveheart,* there is a scene where the lord of the land has come to claim his right to bed a new wife before her husband. Historically, Edward I probably did not have *droit du seigneur* as a law on the books. In fact, the use of such a practice was believed to be very limited, and possibly a payment for debts.

Miracles and Adventures

Gump quotes his mother as saying miracles occur everyday. King Arthur would agree. His court had a custom that no one could eat until an Adventure had happened. This may seem a little harsh, but it is a wonderful idea that every day we should expect and look for Adventure. Small miracles happen everyday if we would only recognize them as such. Each bit of learning we do, each insight we acknowledge, every bit of positive news are Adventures we should cherish. If the Adventures are not coming to you, then go out and create them. When you sit down for your final meal of the day, ask yourself what Adventures you have experienced. It's up to you if you get to eat or not.

The Lessons of Trance-lvania

- The Community knows that strength will come from a hero who has been winning battles in the Spiritual world. When in doubt of what to do next, we should look to answers on the Spiritual side.
- There is a time to examine the love of people and our Grail in the form of meditation. However, we cannot always stay in the dream world, and there is a time to come out and use that learning for action.
- We should seek balance in our Inner and Outer worlds with the balance of our Male and Female attributes. Both deserve power and space, and the balance will strengthen your whole being.
- There is a proper place for retribution, as long as it is equal to the insult or crime. We should come from a place of the Spirit to enforce the punishment.
- We have Mirror Spirits which represent different aspects of our lives. We have a Spiritual side that concentrates on our Inner conflicts and we also have a part of us who is willing and strong enough to meet Individual challenges.
- We must learn to complete our tasks if we want to succeed in reaching our Grail. Beginning strong intentions must be carried out to the end.
- We must not forget our Wild Natural Self as we meet our challenges. Otherwise, we will find ourselves stuck on the path, unable to go forward.
- Look for Miracles everyday. Adventures not only come in big packages, but appear as small, but important milestones.

The Scream by Edvard Munch (1863–1944)

Lithograph, 1895. 14 x 10 in.

Path III – The Grueling Road

How many roads must a man walk down
Before you call him a man

— from the song "Blowin' In The Wind" by Bob Dylan
(also sung by Jenny Curran in *Forrest Gump*)

Each station should be like a beacon on the road towards better things, a centre for trade of course, but also for humanizing, improving, instructing.

— from *Heart of Darkness* by Joseph Conrad

At the beginning of a project, everyone is very excited and committed. Volunteers rush forward offering hours of work, a few extra dollars are thrown into the pot. But then hurdles get in the way, and people start to drop out. Then a crisis happens and you find yourself standing alone in the road. On top of that, there's a hailstorm, the road is partially washed away, and quicksand traps border the way. This is the Grueling Road.

Parzival was presented with great opportunity. He had been in the presence of the Grail, but because he ignored his natural state of curiosity and compassion, he was unable to heal the Grail King. He began to experience suffering himself, developing a sense of empathy. He realizes that he has to take responsibility for his actions, even when he has unintentionally harmed someone.

Parzival did start to do the right thing, but his congratulations have come too early, from a court which has become lethargic. Despite his successes, the Loathly Lady reminds him that his True Quest is yet to come. Parzival's Mirror Spirit, Gawan, will take charge of quests along the path of the Individual, as Parzival searches out the Spiritual.

Now Parzival will learn how truly difficult Destiny can be on *The Grueling Road.*

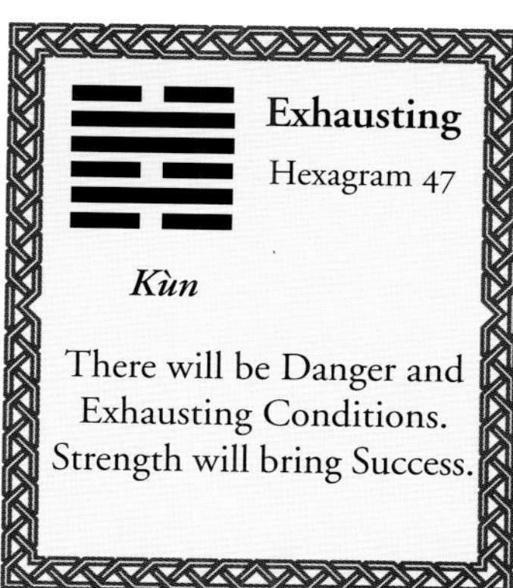

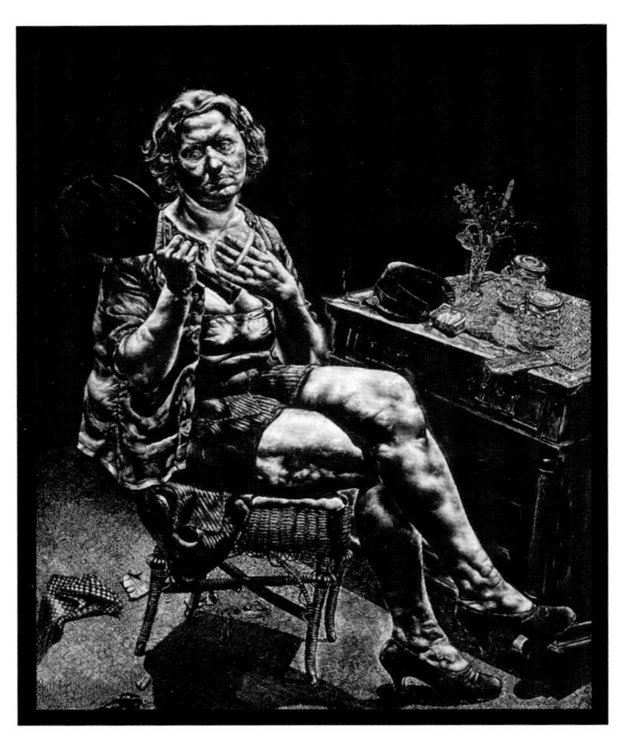

Into the World There Came a Soul Called Ida
by Ivan Albright (1897–1983)

The Art Institute of Chicago, Gift of Ivan Albright. (1977.34)
Oil on Canvas, 1929–30. 56 ¼ x 47 in.

Chapter 13 – Loathly Lady Pays a Visit

"I once met an ugly woman."

"How ugly was she?"

"Well, she was so ugly, she had two nine inch boar's teeth sticking out of her mouth (which was blue), a dog's nose, yellow eyes, bear's ears, a hairy face, monkey skin hands, lion claws for fingernails, and braided eyebrows that met the long, wiry braid of her black hair."

"I think I once had a blind date with her."

— description of Cundrie the Sorceress played out in the style of *The Tonight Show with Johnny Carson*

Jack Lucas is starting to feel real good about himself. He has called his agent, and the two of them are going to hit the town, setting up interviews to get Jack's career in gear again. While entering the building for one of the interviews, he is stopped by the Homeless Cabaret Singer who had helped him get Lydia and Parry together. Though Jack ignores the man, the truth of his desperate situation reminds Jack that he has unfinished business with Parry. Even while Jack is climbing that ladder of success again, Parry still suffers. On top of that, the producer has conjured up a sitcom about homeless people—a happy show, depicting the freedom of the poor living in the streets. They don't have to deal with problems that successful people like themselves do. Jack has seen real poverty. His guilt gnaws at him, and he knows he has to get out and do something.

Cundrie the Sorceress

While the court is celebrating, a most awful looking woman rides in on a diseased branded mule. She is Cundrie the Sorceress, who despite her ugly appearance is dressed in costly fabrics and speaks Latin, French, and Arabic. She tells Arthur that his court is in disgrace, and now it is worse that Parzival has joined it. She admonishes Parzival, calling him a monster who did not free the suffering of the Fisher King, though he had the power to do so. She curses Parzival, and tells of his brother Feirefiz, son of Gahmuret and Belacane, whom she considers flawless and has won much honor. Cundrie weeps as she delivers these attacks. She faces Arthur and challenges the court to find adventures at the Castle of Wonders. Though it is an arduous journey, she will be there tonight. As she leaves, she bemoans that there is no one to help the suffering at the Grail Castle. Parzival is now ashamed, and the ladies of the court weep for him.

Just as Cundrie the Sorceress leaves, a famous man named Kingrimursel rides up. He challenges Gawan for the death of his lord. They are to meet in forty days at Schanpfanzun before King Vergulaht of Ascalun. Beaucurs, Gawan's brother, wants to take his place, but Gawan does not even know why there is a challenge, and refuses his brother.

Clamide asks Parzival for help in securing Cunneware's love. Eckuba, the heathen lady of Janfuse, says Belacane was her aunt. She confirms that Feirefiz is a very noble king.

Parzival vows to find the Grail again, and laments that he had listened to Gurnemanz's advice on knightly courtesies. Parzival says that the knights could renounce his fellowship if they desire, but no one is happy to see him go. Gawan wishes God to give Parzival a good hand in battle, but Parzival renounces God. He tells Gawan to turn to a woman's love as his shield in battle. Parzival leaves to find the Fisher King again.

The other knights go to find the Castle of Wonders. Clias the Greek once said he was detained there, unhorsed by the Turkoite (Florant of Itolac), and said there were four queens there. They are Itonje, Cundrie (different from sorceress Cundrie), Arnive, and Sangive.

Gawan goes to fight his challenge. Clamide and Cunneware are married. All of those gathered at Arthur's court now go their separate ways.

— *Parzival* Summary, Book VI, ¶ 312–337

The Truth Hurts

Ganesha

The Loathly Hag is one of my favorite characters in Arthurian literature. She is the Crone, the Dark Woman, the Cailleach, the Witch at the edge of the Forest. She is Motivational Truth and she is as tough as they come. She is the one who has mastered the Seventh of the Ten Perfections—Truth.

In *Forrest Gump,* Lt. Dan and Forrest are partying with two prostitutes when Forrest pushes one away because she tasted like cigarettes. The other woman ridicules Forrest for being stupid. This angers Lt. Dan, who defends Forrest. He tells the two women to get out, and they respond with calling him a "loser" and a "freak." Those two ladies of the evening are acting as the Loathly Lady. They are telling it like it is, a harsh wake up call for Lt. Dan.

We have seen how Parzival broke his brightly colored spear—the spear of the Wild Man, the Natural Man. He had fulfilled what he thought was his goal, and was ready to settle down in Arthur's court and accept the accolades and rewards of his prowess. The only problem is that this was not the culmination of his Destiny. This was just the warm up for the real test.

Stage Right—Enters the Loathly Hag Riding her Mule. Truth is not always pretty, even when it wears riches and fine silks. The mule should not be considered as something lowly, but the opposite. In the *Perlesvaus,* there are various references to Joseph of Arimathea, who reputedly carried the cup of Christ, while riding around the land on a white mule. It is the animal that Jesus rides as he enters Jerusalem. As lowly as we may view the mule, it is ever enduring, it will carry heavy loads over rough terrains, and is even accessible by the poor.

In the *Didot-Perceval,* Perceval meets an ugly woman riding with a knight, whom she kisses most tenderly. When Perceval sees this, he crosses himself and laughs, offending the knight. The knight, who loves the woman deeply and finds her beautiful, is happy that she didn't hear Perceval's insults. The shame would have killed her. Here is a knight who actually loves and embraces the Ugly Truth, and finds her beautiful.

In Hinduism, Ganesha, the Elephant God, is a reminder that unusual outside appearances are but shells for beautiful spiritual beings inside. He is the God of Knowledge, Wisdom, and Obstacles. He is sought out for success in undertakings, *siddhi,* and to pray for intelligence, *buddhi.* In *The Phantom Menace,* the Gungans are not the most handsome creatures in the universe, but they live in an exquisite, delicate underwater and have qualities of courage and cooperation. The same is true for our Loathly Lady. Her unconventional features hide a soul who tirelessly works for Healing the Land.

Cundrie's words to Parzival are not just a slap on the wrist. She is nasty and hard, criticizing Arthur and his court for their ineptitude and for congratulating themselves on their new-found hero. Most importantly, she wakes Parzival up to his failures and sets him on the road he was truly meant to ride. Not only will the Wasteland never end without the appropriate actions, but she knows that Parzival will never know true peace without this accomplishment.

> *The Loathly Lady*
>
> *1. Tell yourself some harsh truths about your progress towards your Grail. Have you allowed yourself too much self congratulations in areas that do not move you towards your goal? Have you opted for procrastination, instead of constantly working on necessary tasks?*
>
> *2. Now that you have spoken some harsh words to yourself, what are you going to do to rectify the situation? If you find yourself going off course, have a very definite means of getting back on track.*

Very few people would know what your path should be. They may see certain attributes and encourage or nag you to use those talents. They may have their own personal agendas and feel that your talents might be beneficial to them. So trusting those people, no matter how good their intentions, may not be the best path. Ultimately, the Loathly Lady is someone you must cultivate for yourself. Develop the voice that is the harsh truth which says, "You are wasting your time. You know what you have to do, so start working towards it. Don't settle for your old rewards. There is Healing to do, and Adventures to experience."

The Mirror Has Two Faces

We have already learned that Gawan is the Mirror Spirit of Parzival. Parzival just got his challenge from one of the ugliest women in the world, and on the other side, Gawan will get his challenge from one of the most elegant men. It's that Yin/Yang balance again. While Parzival is off on a quest which represents the Spiritual World, Gawan is attending to his quest in the Physical World of the Individual. It will take the efforts and testing of both to achieve the Grail.

Gawan already shows a reflection of maturity in his willingness to take on his challenge. He honestly doesn't know if he has caused the death of the lord or not. He is mature enough to say, "I don't know if I have truly harmed anyone, but if I have, I will make restitution." This is the opposite of the current trend of keeping our mouths shut about possible guilt, and calling the lawyer.

Gawan's adventures serve as an important reminder that we must always be cooperative in our working, outer, physical lives and our inner, contemplative, spiritual selves. Both must be successful, because both help each other.

The Dark Brother

The court first hears of Parzival's lineage through Cundrie's tirade. She also speaks of a magnificent, dark brother who rules in the mysterious lands of the East. It is so refreshing to find a sibling story where the other brother is not an evil twin, especially since he is the darker one. Instead, the brother, Feirefiz, is given a description that would make anyone jealous and envious. He is the personification of honor and beauty, brought about through the joining of two cultures and two races. I again applaud Wolfram's vision, which still has not found roots in many places of the world today.

Saracen Reclining on a Divan
by Benjamin-Constant
(1845–1902)
Oil on Panel. 9 ¼ x 12 ½ in.

Determination

I will never allow myself to know Joy until I see the Grail, no matter how short or long the time. My thoughts drive me to that destination, and I will not be put aside from it my entire life.

— Parzival in *Parzival,* Book VI, ¶ 329

Roy Hobbs was apart from the game of baseball for sixteen years before he is given a chance to play in the majors. He was hired by a scout sent by the Judge on a mission to find a loser, giving the Judge an opportunity to steal the team from Pop Fisher once the pennant was lost. Roy ignored the jabs about his age. Even though Pop Fisher benched him constantly in practice, Roy came prepared everyday because he knew what he wanted in life. He wasn't going to lose his chance this time because he wasn't ready and determined.

Yoda tells Luke that there is no such thing as trying; you either do something or you don't.

Parzival now clearly sees what his Mission in life is. He will not give up, no matter what happens. He knows he will never be happy until he succeeds in finding the Grail and Healing the Fisher King. This virtue of Resolution is found as the Eighth of the Ten Perfections.

In Chrétien's version, more is added to the determination of Perceval on his Quest. Perceval will not spend two nights in the same place for as long as he lives. He will cross any dangerous passage and fight any knight necessary until he learns whom the Grail serves and why the lance bleeds. I really like Chrétien's passage because it is so specific. There is no challenge in the world that is going to stop Perceval. Forget any danger, forget any man—he's going forward. He will not stay in the same place twice. He will always be moving towards the Grail.

We have so many excuses for not achieving our goals that we stop trying to see what we can do. We are not going to succeed in every task along the way. Sometimes our successes are determined by what we learn from our failures as well as the successes in life. We learn what not to do, or how

Determination

1. Are there any challenges you have been avoiding because of their difficulty? Remember to approach the challenge by breaking it into smaller tasks. Amass needed resources or increase your skills, so that you have a good chance at succeeding in the long run.

2. Are there people who appear to stand in the way of your goals? Find a way to approach them, even if you feel uncomfortable. Muster the courage and the skills to approach these people.

3. Each night before you go to sleep, ask what you did today to move you towards your Grail. Be in a different place everyday.

to do something better. If we shy from risk, we will never gain the experience required for success.

Do not be intimidated by people along the way. Watch them, and learn from them. If it is necessary to compete against them, do so. Take whatever you can glean from the experience. Being afraid, and avoiding people who have authority in the field that you are interested in, is to forever ban yourself from achieving that power.

That passage of not staying in the same place twice is excellent advice, as it tells us that everyday we should take steps towards our Grail. When we go to sleep at night, we should be in a different place in our progress than we were when we woke up. Even if we only take little steps, we need to take those steps everyday. When we finally place our heads on the pillow, we should ask ourselves, "What did I do today to move me closer towards my Grail?"

"Alas, What Is God?"

In *Forrest Gump,* Lt. Dan asks Gump if he has found God. Gump replied that he didn't know that he was looking for him. Parzival faces this question several times on his quest, though in different forms. At the beginning of his adventures, he asked his mother what God is. He has come to a crossroads, where that question again presents itself in Gawan's good wishes of God's help. Parzival answers with a denial of that help. Many times our toughest battles and triumphs come from our own internal struggles of questioning what higher deities exist, and what our relationship is to those powers. Doubt becomes one of our strongest questioners of finding a truth. Parzival's lament is the cry of many good people who have set out to do the right thing, but are still not rewarded for it. Parzival, who has tried to do a good job since he left the Grail Castle, is dismayed to learn that it just wasn't enough. It is so frustrating to do your best, and receive a slap in the face. He says that he has done his work for God, yet he is not appreciated for his work. He is willing to bear God's anger with his words. In *Forrest Gump,* Lt. Dan openly challenges God to come and get him as he rides out a hurricane. He is ready to face his doubts, and he is ready to release his anger for all of his years of suffering. This is a turning point for Lt. Dan.

Feminists acknowledging a Great Mother will applaud that Parzival has chosen the Woman over God. Monotheists will declare him sacrilegious. Taoists will appreciate the fact that Gawan chooses God and Parzival chooses the Goddess, as together, they form an incredible team.

In his story, Wolfram bounces back and forth between the male and female principle. Sometimes I have the feeling that he was aiming for balance. Other times he seems to embrace a return to seeking knowledge through the Feminine. It may have been a desire for peace rather than war. His passages throughout *Parzival* comment on rules of courtly love, and he seems to have had personal problems in securing favors with a lady. Perhaps he had a Christian bent towards the feminine, finding solace in the Virgin Mary, a common belief during those times. At the time he was writing *Parzival,* Notre Dame (Our Lady), a church dedicated to the Feminine principle in Christian religion, was being built in Paris. Some people believed the wastelands of Arabia had come about from the turning away from the Great Goddess, and the same would happen in Europe. Some say that this theory was even the root of the Grail legends. Wolfram may have faced varying degrees of political and religious pressures at different times of the writing, thus resulting in conflicting views.

Still another way of looking at this is found in a problem as true today as it was thousands of years ago—Rhetoric versus the actual Living of our creeds. Our religions talk of Love, but don't always live it. For Parzival, the word "God" has been associated with lists of rules which turned people away from their natural goodness and spirit. His failure at the Grail Castle has come about from people purporting their lives are influenced by God's wishes. God has become only a concept to Parzival, one which did not support him in his trial of need.

What Parzival does understand is what it is to do something for the woman he loves. He does this with a free heart and his reward is a life that she offers to him. He will take the physical proof which comes from his Love rather than the promise of empty words coming from priests. At the root of it all, Love and caring is what will heal.

The Face of God

Examine your own view of Spirituality and your relationship with your Spirit and/or Higher Power. Have you reconciled doubts or do you accept that you will learn as you go? Is your path to your Grail a path of developing a stronger bond with your Religion or Spirit? Do you have a clear view of the Face of Your God?

Castle of Wonders

The Loathly Lady has not only spurred Parzival on his proper path, but has ignited the rest of the Court to do what they must do. Arthur has lost control. His men are excited at the possibilities of adventure, and they set out on a course to the Castle of Wonders, also known as the Castle of Marvels and the Castle of Maidens. It is here that four hundred women and four queens are held captive. At this point in the story, no one in the court knows that the four queens are Arthur's and Gawan's relatives. Itonje and Cundrie are Gawan's sisters. Arnive is Arthur's mother and Gawan's grandmother. Sangive is Arthur's sister and Gawan's mother. Denied adventure under Arthur, the knights now are going to set out to find Sovereignty herself. They are ready for proper adventures. But they are less prepared than even Parzival to attempt the Grail Castle, so they must start at a beginning point. It is Parzival's need, not Arthur's, which is the catalyst for the rest of the court.

When you awaken yourself to the path you must follow, the whole body becomes excited and wants to be involved. The Spiritual Self may know what it needs to do, but the Physical World may be lacking in necessary skills. It has a like mind. Just as Parzival has chosen the way of Sovereignty, so has the court; only it's a few steps behind. That is the way of your own Destiny. Your own inner life will visualize the life you are meant to live, and the physical world will agree to it enthusiastically. To make the Quest successful, the real world must gather its resources and start with the small, necessary steps towards the common goal.

Man Contemplating His Destiny by Émile Fabry (1865–1966)
The Montreal Museum of Fine Arts, Marjorie Caverhill Bequest
Oil on Canvas, 1897. 20 ⅞ x 26 ⅛ in.
Courtesy: Succession Fabry-Deleslcuze. Photo: The Montreal Museum of Fine Arts, Bernard Brien

The Individual's Path

> *...every knight took the way that him liked best.*
> — from *Le Morte D'Arthur* by Sir Thomas Malory

Malory's Grail Quest has a slightly different way of taking off. While Arthur and his knights are gathered at a feast, there is a clap of thunder and a great light. The Grail comes into the room, covered by white silk, so the Grail itself cannot be seen, nor who carries it. The court has the experience of being fed what they desire, then it disappears. Gawain desires to see the actual Grail, so he is the first knight to say that he will go search for the Grail. The other knights follow suit with their pledges. Arthur grieves that he will not see many of the men again, and that this is the end of the glory days of the fellowship of the Round Table. Arthur counts 150 knights who leave him. Once the men hit the road, they split up so that each could take the road he liked best.

Despite what legends of the Crusades tell us, the search for the Grail is an Individual Quest. Even Princess Leia says that no one can choose Han Solo's path for him; he must do it himself. There may be people who will help you along the way and be involved with your projects, but ultimately the Quest is really your own. You will have to depend on your skills and your vision to see you through to the end. You will be the last say and you will be the one whom you must count on. When you start leaning on others, or trying out their Grail, your own path will become lost in the brambles.

When Forrest Gump makes his run across the country, he eventually picks up "disciples" who form running packs behind him. When the day comes that he is done running and it's time to go home, the cry is "Now what are we supposed to do?" All along, they were supposed to be on their own Quest, not Gump's. Now they must switch gears and find the path they were suppose to be on.

This is sometimes a lonely path. Though we share what we learn with others, the most significant progress will come from those late nights, poring over the angles and facets of your own dreams. The rewards come from that inner journey, building confidence and faith in the possible.

Path of the Individual

Acknowledging that we all need help along the way to our Grails, do you lean too much on the support of others? Can you complete your path, even if others withdraw their support? Do you try to latch on to others' visions instead of following your own? Along with taking responsibility for how we treat others, we must also take responsibility for the success and vision of our own paths. Make that commitment to yourself to see it through because of your own vision and efforts.

Gawan's Preparation

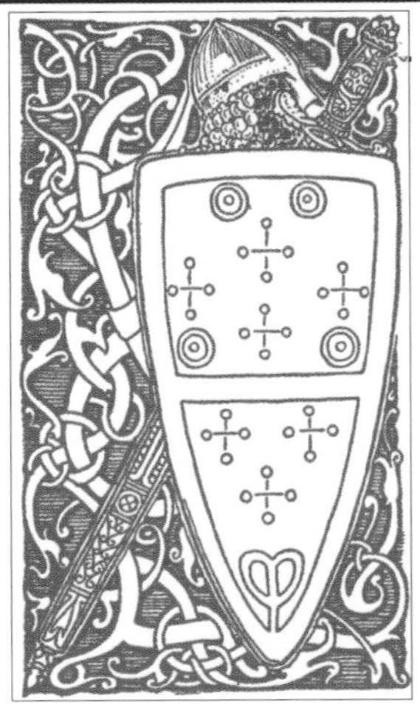
by Louis Rhead (1858–1921)

Gawan has been such an exemplary model of knighthood that he has people who want to help him. The merchants give him three pack mules loaded down with equipment. Others give him seven horses and twelve spears. Arthur gives him gold and jewels. People are generous because Gawan is a good guy.

The shields are noted as being "old, firm and well seasoned." Gawan doesn't care what they look like. He appreciates the tried and true. A seasoned veteran of battles, he willingly accepts the help of others who offer tools for his challenge. Often people will give you advice as you go out on your path. We've already seen some of the bad results of

that. But once you have acquired some experience, as Gawan has from his travels, you will be able to discern what works and what doesn't work. You will be able to choose what advice you can heed and what you have to let go. The best way is to look at the accomplishments of those who choose to help you. Look for the "old, firm and well seasoned." If there are teachers and people who have accomplished similar goals you desire, those are the ones who should be high on your list of people to listen to.

The Lessons of Loathly Lady Pays a Visit

- The Loathly Lady is the hard truth which reminds us that we must get on with our Quest if we want to succeed. We have to develop her advice as the true wisdom that is tough, but done with the Grail in mind.
- Our Quests in the Spiritual and Physical World are both equally important. They are both vital parts of ourselves. Success in achieving our Grail depends on how we excel in both, and coordinate the two.
- Do not lack Determination. Each night ask what progress you have made towards your Grail. Work on your Grail everyday, even if it's just for a few moments.
- We each have a special relationship with our Spirit and views of Higher Powers. We must realize that our doubts can be a source of searching out the truth. Examining our Souls leads to developing a source of strength and restoration, and in dire situations, may be our survival.
- Realize that the path of the Grail is an Individual path. We have to take responsibility for our own visions.
- We can prepare for our Quests by carefully choosing the tools that others offer us. If we look to those who have experience, our path could be well armed.

Our Spiritual and Individual paths are similar, yet have their own unique trials and practices. Gawan and Parzival will head in different directions to complete different duties, yet both are doing the necessary work that promotes the final healings of the Community.

Chapter 14 - Cloning

Han Solo is Luke Skywalker's Mirror Brother.
(Han-Harrison Ford)

Chuckie and Will decide to play a joke on the recruiters who are actively trying to grab Will for their organization. Chuckie goes to the interview, pretending to be Will, and plays mind games with the recruiters. The recruiters probably just thought they were dealing with an eccentric genius. Chuckie was even able to scam money off of them for his "expenses." Chuckie is Gawan. He takes Will's place, just like Gawan runs corresponding adventures to Parzival's.

Han Solo runs alternate adventures to Luke Skywalker's. Han's tests have to do with "down to earth" problems, solved by laser guns and fisticuffs, while Luke will win his final battle with spiritual means. These paths are the same as Gawan's and Parzival's, with Gawan running courses in the Physical World, and Parzival in the Spiritual World.

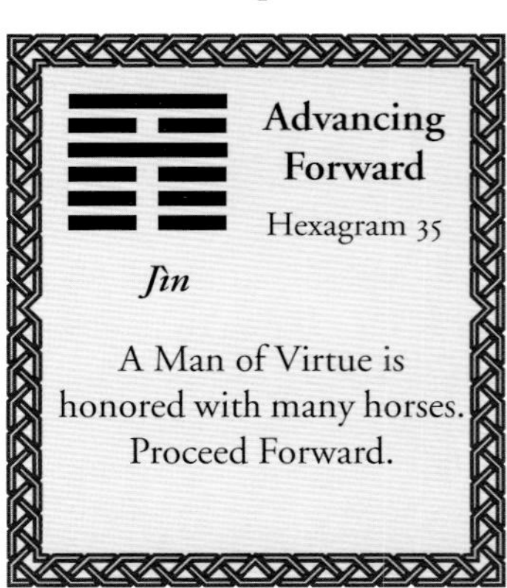

Gawan's Adventures

Gawan rides Gringuljete, a white horse with red ears from the Grail Castle. The horse was given to him by Orilus, who had received it from his brother, Lehelin. Gawan comes to a mighty host, which has two armies. King Meljanz leads one force, while the King of Gors (Meljanz' uncle) leads the other, with his son, Meljacanz. Meljacanz is the knight who kidnapped Imane of the Beafontane, and was chased by the knights who were Parzival's first encounter with knights. King Meljanz of Liz was raised by Prince Lippaut of Bearosche, who has two daughters, Obie and Obilot. Meljanz wants Obie's love, but she refuses him, so he leaves in anger. Obie loves Meljanz, and was hurt when he left. Meljanz returns with the armies to punish Obie. Gawan decides to go to the jousts at Bearosche and delay his own trip.

Gawan rides to the battlefields, but no one welcomes him, and the town itself is fortified. He comes to camp by Lippaut's castle, where the two daughters openly speak of him. The elder daughter, Obie, surmises he is a merchant and of low class, while the younger, Obilot, wants him for a knight.

Obie needs to take her anger for Meljanz out on someone, so she picks on Gawan. She first taunts Gawan by treating him as a merchant. Then she sends a burgrave (sheriff), Scherules, to arrest Gawan for stealing horses. Scherules sees that Gawan is respectable and invites him as a guest. Then Obie sends a minstrel woman to her father, saying Gawan is a counterfeiter with booty. Lippaut goes to him for the illegal goods, but also sees that Gawan is well bred. Lippaut invites Gawan to fight for him, but Gawan says he is on his way to his own battle, and must think about it. Obilot decides that she is going to ask Gawan to be her knight. Gawan at first says he is pledged and she is five years too young, but he remembers Parzival saying it is better to trust a woman then God. Gawan agrees to be her hero, commenting that if she has this power over men now, imagine how she will be when she is grown. Obilot promises a token and goes home. Her mother arranges for a great silk dress to be made. The sleeve is presented to Gawan as the promised token.

At night, there is a great battle where many people are injured and die, including Arthur's son. "The Nameless Knight" in red (Parzival) had joined Meljanz' army three days before. Gawan defeats Meljanz, then Meljacanz. Gawan and Parzival are deemed the best knights of the battle. Since Parzival had been fighting for Meljanz, who was captured, he decides to continue on the Grail quest. He takes the horse, Ingliart, which had escaped from Gawan when he took Meljanz.

Gawan sends the sleeve back to Obilot, who parades it in front of her sister. While Gawan and Lippaut meet with Meljanz, Parzival's squires come, announcing Parzival is off for the Grail. Gawan is glad they did not meet on the battlefield. Both keep each other's identities secret. As Meljanz surrenders to Obilot, she hands him over to Obie. Obilot knows that the two love each other. They marry and there is great celebration. Obilot begs Gawan to take her with him, but he refuses and he leaves in grief.

Gawan goes to Schanpfanzun. He sees King Vergulaht of Ascalun, Parzival's first cousin. The King is hunting, and sends Gawan to the castle where his sister, Queen Antikonie, will entertain him. Gawan goes to the castle and the lady's kiss is more than a greeting. Gawan wants more, and though she acknowledges the attraction, she refuses. When the servants leave, they get a bit closer. A gray haired knight accuses Gawan of murdering his master, and attempting to rape the daughter. Men are called to fight. Gawan and Antikonie retreat to her tower. Gawan uses a chessboard for defense, and both of them use the pieces as weapons. Vergulaht comes back from hunting, and dishonors himself by fighting his guest. Kingrimursel shows up, and is appalled that Gawan is being attacked, as Kingrimursel had guaranteed safe passage to him. Kingrimursel helps Gawan and Antikonie. Finally, a truce is called. The story reveals that Gawan is innocent of Kingrimursel's charges, but no one knows that. Their master had actually been killed by Ehcunat, as he captured another man. At the time Ehcunat took the prisoner, he was by Gawan's side, thus the confusion. Antikonie thanks Kingrimursel, then upbraids her brother. Kingrimursel says he had granted Gawan battle with one man and safe conduct, now Kingrimursel's reputation could be ruined. A vassal, Liddamus, still accuses Gawan. Kingrimursel says he would give Gawan reprieve for one year, and they would meet before Meljanz. Liddamus and Kingrimursel argue until Vergulaht stops them. Vergulaht says they must take council.

King Vergulaht says he had been charged to go on a Grail quest, after losing a battle to a knight, whom we know to be Parzival. Liddamus suggests that Gawan should do it for him. Gawan agrees, and leaves alone to great peril.

— *Parzival* Summary, Books VII and VIII

Service to Others

Willing Submission

Hexagram 57

Xùn

The Wishes of Heaven are carried out in Willing Submission.

Gawan is known as a good guy who doesn't make waves. While Parzival has to work on fixing the problems he caused, Gawan will go about fixing situations he did not cause. Gawan has been wrongly accused of killing a man, yet he is willing to meet a challenge. He has nothing to do with the love squabbles of Obie and Meljanz, yet he will put off his own agenda to represent Obie's family by being her sister's hero. Gawan exhibits the Third of the Ten Perfections, that of Duty.

Spiritually, we have a Duty to make sure that our own house is in order. That is Parzival's Quest. Success as an Individual in the real world will depend on our Service to Others—that is Gawan's Quest.

Service does not mean that you have to run about offering your talents and time for free—knights often rode away with jewels, gold, and kingdoms. Whether you are paid or not is your choice. Some Service you donate, some you will expect just rewards. You don't have to be obsequious and fawning like C-3PO. This service is done with a sense of dignity and pride.

Service is based on a simple notion that success will come about when you are able to gratify people's wants and needs. Parzival's Grail Quest is fulfilling one's own needs in a way that other people are also served. Gawan's Grail Quest is fulfilling the needs of others which then brings about what he needs. In both instances, the world at large will be served.

When we speak of your quest of the Individual, we are talking about the immediate circle of people with whom you are actively involved. This is your family, your friends, and your business and work concerns. Doing well at this level will spread out to the Community at large, but first you must focus your talents on your immediate concerns.

Service to Others comes down to the fifth stage of the Eightfold Path—Right Livelihood. This is choosing a career or job which benefits everyone who touches your path. We choose whether we will be a nurse or a drug dealer, a teacher or a thief. We choose whether we want to help others, or open doors of destruction. We also choose how mindful we will be when performing work for others. Do we give our best, or just enough to get by? These are all elements we must consider when choosing our life's work.

Right Livelihood

Look at the work that you do in your life. Is it work that positively helps others, or is it one which preys on people's weaknesses? Is it work that does not try to hurt others? When you work, is it done in a way that you are proud of what you do and deliver? Think of ways that you can improve the way your work serves others.

More Magic Animals

> *Creatures will abandon the man who thinks that creatures are apart from the Soul.*
>
> — from the Brihad-Aranyaka Upanishad

Here's that red horse again, or to be more precise, the white horse with the red ears. Gawan rides the horse, Gringuljete, which has come from the Grail Castle. White fairy horses and other unusual animals are found in other myths, also related to Arthurian stories.

In the *Mabinogion* story, "Pwyll Lord of Dyved," Pwyll* encounters the Hounds of Annwvyn (the UnderWorld) which were bright white with red ears. Pwyll later sits on a magic mountain which guarantees that you will be beaten, or a wonder will appear. I think this refers to how people view life, similar to our modern saying of making lemonade out of lemons. Others think this is similar to the Siege Perilous, which will either destroy you, or give a sign indicating you are the Chosen One. Pwyll takes a chance and plops himself on the hill. He sees a gorgeous woman, dressed in gold brocade, who rides a grand white horse. The only problem is that though she appears to be moving slow, the faster he chases her, the further away she gets. (Another comment on life?!) The only way Pwyll can stop her is to yell at her to stop for the man she loves best. This woman is the goddess Rhiannon in human form, who has a mythical relationship to the horse goddess Epona. Rhiannon and Pwyll marry, and have a son, Pryderi. When the boy disappears, she is framed for his murder. As her punishment, she is forced to carry guests to the city on her back, just like a horse. At the same time a couple's mare is giving birth, Pryderi mysteriously shows up. The couple cares for Pryderi. Years later the man hears of Rhiannon's misfortune and realizes Pryderi is Rhiannon's son. The man returns Pryderi and the family is happily reunited. The name of Perceval has been interpreted to be "Per-cheval," meaning "by the horse," thus possibly linking the Pryderi/Perceval legends.

The Cult of the Horse stretches back to caveman days, where horse pictures were painted inside the dark passages. The goddess Demeter had a form of a white mare, and in England today, an ancient white chalk horse still reigns the countryside.

Leonora Carrington, a surrealist artist who understands the power of the horse motif, utilizes it in her *Self Portrait.* Here we see that grand white horse of Rhiannon/Epona as it gallops across a mythical scenery. Leonora waits uneasily in a room with a shadow of the mare in the form of a white rocking horse, and a hyena that certainly doesn't come from this world. Her immediate environment is uncertain, but at least she can glimpse at those possibilities outside her window.

It is not unusual to find story lines in which an animal, usually a horse or dog, is born at the same time as a hero. The theory is that the same magic is present at the time

* "w" has an *"oo"* sound and "y" has an *"i"* sound—if you want to cheat just say "Paul"

Self Portrait by Leonora Carrington

Oil on Canvas, 1938. 25 ½ x 32 in.
©2001 Leonora Carrington / Artists Rights Society (ARS), N.Y.

of the birth, and now the two will have intertwined lives. In this case, it would seem that animals not only have souls, but share souls with us too.

There are several tales involving Perceval and Owein, where a lion befriends the hero after being saved by an attack. The lion then becomes literally a trained pet, sleeping at the feet of its master, ready to do battle when the hero is threatened. It's not bad having a lion soul mate. Han Solo was probably on the right track when he hooked up with Chewbacca.

Early Flight

Any coward who turns and flees before he is pursued, is too quick for his own honor.

— Gawan in *Parzival*, Book VII, ¶ 340

When Gawan first encounters the hosts of warriors heading to battle, he has second thoughts about approaching them. Strangers are viewed with hostility. A man with all his horses and arms might prompt challenges. Being outnumbered, Gawan could have been construed to be a practical man if he chose to turn back the way he came, at least until all of the armies had passed.

Instead, Gawan decided to press on by putting aside his fear. He tells himself that only a coward turns back before he is even challenged.

Many of us are self-defeating. Once any possibility of conflict arises, we will think of every excuse as to why we should not proceed along our course. In the film *Heart of Darkness,* Kurtz lectures Marlow, saying the worst creature is a man who runs from his demons. Gawan could have turned around, but instead he stayed to find out what was going on. Most of the army did not notice he was there. Sometimes, we imagine that we are going to encounter severe problems, and choose not to go ahead. However, if we would allow ourselves a proper dose of courage, we may find only small obstacles, or none at all. We defeat ourselves before we give anyone else the chance. We take early flight from a situation instead of finding out what is going on. How many personal battles are lost because of this crippling behavior?

The Fifth of the Ten Perfections is Courage. Courage means having a choice. You can either take the course of turning back and letting someone else make decisions that affect your life, or you can choose to face whatever lies in the path in front of you. It does not mean that you do not face the unknown without fear, or doubt, or full knowing. It only means that you are willing to face the potential challenges, whether they prove to be real or not. Each time you make that choice to face those large armies, you strengthen your courage for the real tasks. You become a hero instead of a coward.

In the movie *Heart of Darkness*, Mfumu wears a small, sharpened bone from his enemy as a pierced cheek ornament. Since Mfumu is a cannibal, he may have also consumed his enemy. He proudly tells Marlow that his enemy was very strong, and now his enemy's spirit protects him. Around his neck is a whole pouch of enemies' bones. He made his victories of courage part of his own being.

The Fifth Perfection—Courage

1. Courage is not allowing yourself to be defeated by your own inaction. Think of times when you defeated yourself by not allowing yourself to face a challenge. Were you set back even further in your goals in life because you did not take a chance? In hindsight, were the situations as stressful as you had imagined them to be?

2. Is there a difficult task or situation that you don't want to face looming in front of you? Gather the courage to face the adversity. It may be breaking a difficult problem into smaller manageable problems, and successfully solving those smaller tests. It may be envisioning what a brave person would do, then acting in a manner similar to that "braver" person. It may be evaluating what the downside and upside would be. In many situations, the downside may only be some temporary embarrassment associated with some rejection. Reminding ourselves of the ultimate desired outcome is a great way to push through with our needed actions. Building courage becomes a habit, as with anything else. We must be consistent in testing ourselves and finding ways not to turn aside from the goals we need to accomplish.

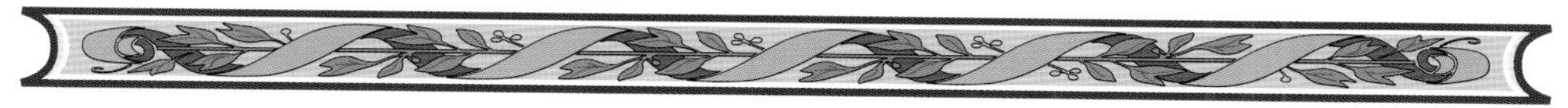

Sovereignty Speaks

> *Freedom's just another word for nothin' left to lose.*
> — from the song "Me and Bobby McGee" by Kris Kristofferson

> *I have set a higher goal. I do not want to hold a fief from anyone: my sovereign freedom is greater than any crown an earthly head has worn.*
> — Obie in *Parzival,* Book VII ¶ 347

Obie's words are strong fighting words for a woman to be speaking almost a thousand years ago. Looking at the plight of women around the world today, not too many could speak those words today. When Janis Joplin crooned "Me and Bobby McGee," she spoke of a freedom that comes from losing everything material. Obie is willing to turn her back on the material for her own sense of freedom. In Obie's case, we have a woman who tells a man she loves that she desires freedom more than a crown. Shallow minded that he is, he thinks she is being rude, so he starts a war with her father. He doesn't pay attention about playing the game of love. If at that moment he had declared her sovereignty as beautiful and worthy as she was, and still pledged his love, he would have immediately gotten his bride and saved a lot of bloodshed.

This story is so apropos because there is another Arthurian story of a woman and her sovereignty. It involves Gawan himself. Gawan is often thought of as a ladies' man in Arthurian literature, figuring prominently as a lover and a husband. In fact, he will encounter a few love interests in this story alone. A higher view is that he is the ultimate hero of the goddess, and he knows his strength lies in his service to her. One of these stories is about Gawain (spelled a little different in this tale) and Dame Ragnall.

In the story, Arthur has a run-in with a man who will kill Arthur unless Arthur can tell him by a deadline what it is that women want most. He runs into an ugly old hag, Dame Ragnall, who says she can help Arthur. Her fee is marriage to the handsome knight Gawain. Arthur tells Gawain he doesn't have to do it, but Gawain is loyal and agrees to the marriage. When everyone in court sees the horrendous-looking bride, they only have pity for Gawain.

The night of the wedding, Gawain enters the bridal chamber, gives Ragnall a kiss, and is very pleased when the hag turns into a beautiful, voluptuous woman. After getting to know each other a little better, she gives Gawain a choice. She can go around court in the daytime as a beautiful, young woman, and return to their home as the ugly woman. That way he could be the envy of everyone in the day, but keep the lights low at night. Or she can stay ugly around the castle and gorgeous in bed with the obvious rewards.

Gawain gives the smartest answer of them all: "I'll let you choose." Gawain gave this woman sovereignty over her life, which was the answer to Arthur's riddle. Women want power of choice over their own lives. Now it turns out that the man who posed that riddle to Arthur was Ragnall's brother, who had also put that ugly hex on her. When Gawain spoke those words, he not only saved Arthur, but broke the spell, making her beautiful all of the time. They marry and have a son together. Some of you may have noticed the same story line in Chaucer's "Wife of Bath's Tale" in *Canterbury Tales.*

For me, the real moral of the story is that we all want to have sovereignty over our own lives, men and women both. We want to have room for searching for our individual Grails, and yet we also want to love each other. When Gawain gave Ragnall her freedom to be who she was, it became a Win-Win situation for Gawain and Ragnall. Because of his respect for her, he got a wife who was beautiful all of the time.

That beauty is something more than physical beauty. When partners are happy, there is the beauty of peace in the family. It is always better to be greeted with smiles and happiness, rather than a bitter sullenness born from a stifled mate. There are times when one has to bend a bit for the other, but as long as both are aware of what is important to each other, the small bends will lead to a long, healthy relationship.

Respect for each other's sovereignty is a basic spiritual right that can only enhance a personal relationship. Asking what each other wants—what each other's Grail is—gives life and hope to a marriage.

Sovereignty in Marriage

If you are in a serious relationship, marriage or otherwise, when was the last time you asked your partner what she wants out of life? What are his dreams and aspirations? How you can help her achieve individual goals? Sometimes this can be as simple as standing out of the way. Other times, volunteering to watch the children or doing extra chores can free up space and time for your partner. If you want support to follow your heart's need, you also need to allow your loved ones to do the same.

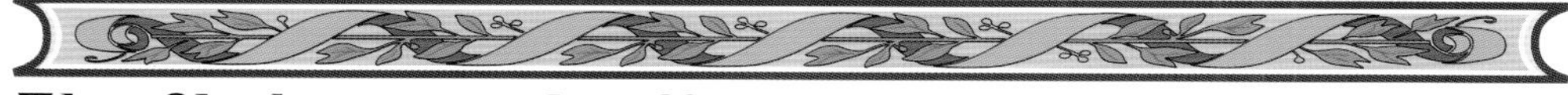

The Shelter of the Mind

Speech is the shelter of the mind.
— Obilot in *Parzival,* Book VII, ¶ 349

Rarely do we reflect on how speech influences our ways of thinking. Language develops from our need to express what is in our mind, but it also can bring the mind to a new way of thinking. Anyone with friends from another country and culture can recognize these differences. People from snow cultures look at the land differently from people surviving at the equator. Their languages and deities reflect those differences.

Obilot's comment on speech shows this relationship of a structure which filters the inner and outer worlds. Parzival is in a process of learning the speech of Compassion by now learning to Suffer. Gawan is learning the speech of Service, with his tests of the Individual. On the Eightfold Path, the third step is Right Speech.

In our own lives, we want our speech to reflect what lies inside of us, and we want to influence our inner lives by allowing the proper speech to come into us.

Sometimes we may use off-color language for shock value that gives us a sense of power. This technique never works as well as carefully constructed arguments and persuasive words, which require practice as much as any other skill. It also means having faith and truth in what you speak. You spiritually erode yourself if you must sell items or ideas that you do not have faith in. Work towards your language of the outside matching the language of your inside. Your language must have the conviction and power of truth.

We must also realize that every single word spoken to us makes an impact. We must learn to separate the truth from emotion, and what empowers or destroys us. Sometimes we don't have a choice about what is spoken to us. As a young child, you may have had to listen to various levels of criticisms, ranging from screaming and swearing to constructive corrections. You may have ingrained a destructive language which affects your actions today. Counter that destructive language with a more positive one. You must talk to yourself, and you must talk honestly. Recognize your flaws, then tell yourself that you will work to do better. As you make small successes, remark on how well you are doing. If we speak words of truth and compassion to ourselves, we can only do better in life. We should also surround ourselves with friends who speak the truth to us in caring, compassionate ways, and give them the same positive feedback.

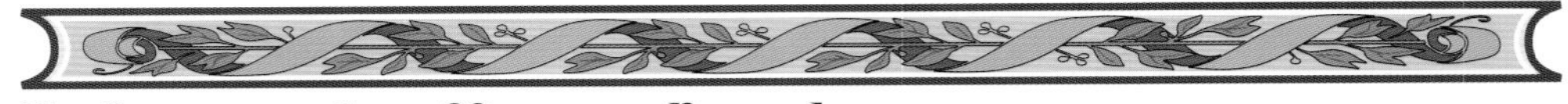

Fight of the Mirror Brothers

It is myself I have defeated.

— Parzival speaking after discovering he is fighting with Gawan from *Parzival,* Book XIV, ¶ 689

If anyone doubted that Gawan is equal to Parzival, this chapter clarifies it when Gawan tells Antikonie (who is Parzival's first cousin) that his ancestry can match hers. It is even illustrated to a greater degree when he is charged with carrying out the Grail Quest of Parzival through Vergulaht's decree. An interesting situation develops when Parzival and Gawan are involved with the same battle. They appear to be on opposing sides, but in effect, they are playing out the reuniting of the Summer Maid and the Winter King. Specifically, Meljanz and Obie love each other, but are angry at each other. The kingdom won't have peace until their odds are put aside. One of the armies involved with the fight is from Jamor, a play on the French words *Je amour,* "I Love."

In Greek legends, Hades, the Lord of the UnderWorld, kidnaps Persephone, the joyful, spring daughter of the Earth Mother, Demeter. In the story of Iseult and Tristan, another Arthurian myth, there is the constant struggle of Iseult going to her husband, King Mark, or to her lover, Tristan, who is the nephew of Mark. In one legend, Arthur actually tells her to stay six months with Mark and six months with Tristan. In the movie *Legends of the Fall,* Brad Pitt's character is named Tristan. Julia Ormond's character, Susannah, is always torn between the affections of Tristan and other male members of the family.

We can easily see several Taoist struggles here. There is the basic conflict of the feminine and the masculine who need to be brought together. There is also the struggle of winter and summer. The winter needs to retract and withdraw, to conserve and reflect, highlighted against the activity of summer, exploding with creativity, putting into practice all that has been learned in the winter months. This is just like the situation where Merlin goes to be the Wild Man during the summer, and at wintertime comes back to reflect on what he has learned at the side of his sister.

So, Parzival fights on Meljanz' side and Gawan on Obie's side, but the two will never meet directly with each other. They do connect concretely though, when Parzival takes one of Gawan's horses as he leaves. This is the hero of the Spiritual World taking the tools and strength of the Physical World on his Quest. In addition, the horse named Ingliart, whom Gawan loses and Parzival retrieves, was originally one of the Grail horses. Here you see a trading back and forth of Wisdom and Tao between the two worlds. Parzival leaves instructions to a servant to deliver a message to Condwiramors that he is always thinking of her and the Grail. Both motivate him.

The two armies are described as the Outer Army and the Inner Army, but in battle, there is almost no difference between the two. Even in the middle of battle, Gawan thinks that the two armies are the same. The Taoist concept is not just two opposite forces, but two powerful sources coming together to make a whole. Armies that have

Tristan and Isolde by Edmund Blair Leighton (1853–1922)

Painted 1902

Parzival on one side, and Gawan on the other, are surely utilizing this principle. Eventually, Meljanz is captured, and apologizes for his behavior, though saying it was because of Obie's taunting. Gawan wisely decides there must be a reconciliation which only "death can sever."

With Gawan as winner, he hands Meljanz over to Obilot, who in turn makes Meljanz and Obie reconcile. They put aside their differences and marry.

This story continues to emphasize that the Outer and the Inner Being work towards a common goal, even when it may seem to be coming from opposite directions. The two are not in direct conflict, but add their own special strengths to each side, so there may be a unification of the whole. The two sides may bicker and quarrel, but at one point, there must be a demand for reconciliation. There is again balance in life.

For our own life, we must make our Inner and Outer life work towards a common goal and truth. Sometimes they may seem to be at odds, but the debate should always orient itself towards what you need and want most.

Relationships with loved ones should also be developed with the aim that peace and love is the final goal. Summer Maids and Winter Kings find ways to be with each other. Petty differences in our own lives should fall to the wayside when the bigger picture is clear.

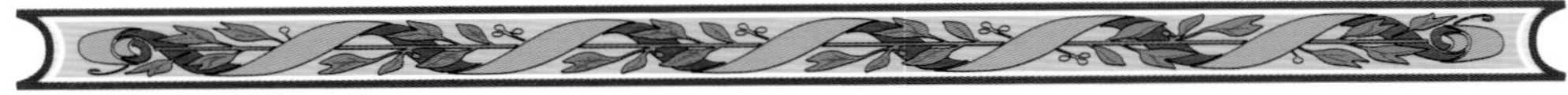

The Virgin

Mäda Primavesi
by Gustav Klimt (1862–1918)
The Metropolitan Museum of Art, New York. Gift of Andre and Clara Mertens, in memory of her mother, Jenny Pulitzer Steiner, 1964. (64.148) Oil on Canvas, 1903. 59 x 43 ½ in. Photo: ©1986 The Metropolitan Museum of Art

Gawan has now started his relationship with the Triplicate Goddess by pledging his service to Obilot, the Virgin. When Gawan receives her dress sleeve as an amulet, we are told that he has three shields, and he nails the sleeve to one of them. Whenever he passes the road where he first met her, he bows, noting the blessing of their meeting. Gawan's service to Obilot was directly related to Parzival's admonition to serve a Woman, not God. She is a representative of natural Spirit, not the cultural form which entailed rules and customs. In Gustav Klimt's painting, Mäda Primavesi, Mäda epitomizes the self-assured, wise beyond her years, young lady who lives her natural strong Spirit—much like Obilot.

Gawan's Quest is at its beginning. His relationship to Obilot is based on pureness and a service based on being virtuous. Since we know Gawan is operating in the Physical, Individual World, this is the pureness which exists as we take on a new adventure in life. At the beginning, when we are interested in something new, we easily focus on a new task. We see all of the possibilities, and hardships seem non-existent. Our commitment is minimal. Though Gawan agrees to help Obilot, his real task is elsewhere, so he has no real deep attachment to this battle. He could walk away at any moment. If he had, I'm sure the story would have fared a different way.

Our Spirit does have the pure, exhilarating feeling with new encounters. It is an excitement that piques our interest, not unlike a period of dating, when it is easy to make time and effort for a new love interest. We bend over backwards to rearrange our schedule and invest in new clothes. And if it doesn't work out, we move on.

This is the stage of our initial dabbling in our Grail. If our interest is in cooking, we take a few cooking classes, have fun, and if the soufflé falls, who cares? If we want to sail to a tropical island, we rent a Sunfish to try our seamanship. Sinking in six feet of water is no big deal. We swim to shore and laugh about the story over drinks. At this stage in our Grail, our relationship to our Spirit is basically one of fun. Everything is Virginal and untested.

Just as Gawan must leave Obilot, we too must leave behind the Virginal to make real progress in our development.

The Land of Ascalun

For, as I say, the world itself has changed. There was a time when a traveler, if he had the will and knew only a few of the secrets, could send his barge out into the Summer Sea and arrive not at Glastonbury of the monks, but at the Holy Isle of Avalon; for at that time the gates between the worlds drifted within the mists, and were open, one to another, as the traveler thought and willed. For this is the great secret, which was known to all educated men in our day: that by what men think, we create the world around us, daily new.

— from *The Mists of Avalon* by Marion Zimmer Bradley

Gawan has been ordered to the land of Ascalun to fight for his honor for the death of Kingrisin. So what's so special about Ascalun? We will look in Chrétien's version for a more definite clue. His Perceval legend says the land was Escavalon. You may recognize "Avalon" embedded in the name.

Avalon is the Paradise island which darts in and out of the Arthurian legends with various guises. It is the island where King Arthur is taken to by three Queens to be healed, one queen being his sister, Morgaine. In *Parzival,* Vergulaht is said to come of the same fairy stock of Parzival, which existed in a mountain in Famorgan. This name is but a twist on the name Morgaine Le Fay, Morgaine of the Fairies. Avalon is an island associated with women, including the Lady of the Lake, Argante. In the *Vita Merlini,* Morgaine is said to live there with her eight sisters. You'll recognize the Triplicate Goddess times three here, becoming the Ninefold Goddess, which you commonly see as the Nine Graces or Muses in Greek myth. In the Celtic poem, "The Spoils of Annwfn," nine maidens safekeep a magic cauldron. Geoffrey of Monmouth tells us that this is the place where Arthur's sword, Caliburn (Excaliber), was forged. It's probably not a coincidence that Roy Hobbs picked number 9 as his jersey number. His whole life revolved in appeasing that Triplicate Goddess in the form of Iris, Memo, and Harriet. And Forrest Gump waits for the Number 9 bus to get to Jenny.

Avalon is known for its apple trees. This is partly due to various Celtic words which mean "apple" and sound similar. In Middle Breton, "apple" is *avallenn,* and in Old Welsh, it is *afall.* After our previous discussion of the apple, and knowing it is an island inhabited by powerful women, we can see the connections.

Some legends say it was the home of King Avallach and his daughter Modron. Avallach is also found in the Grail legends as King Evelake, who happens to be a Maimed King. In the Vulgate Cycle and in Malory, Evelake takes the baptized name of Mordrains and is eventually healed by Galahad on his Grail Quest.

Avalon is associated with Glastonbury. Since Avalon is of the OtherWorld, it would exist in the same spot as Glastonbury. The association may have been with Avalon being called *Ynys Witrin,* the Isle of Glass. In several legends, Joseph of Arimathea is the founder of Glastonbury, and this is the site he first brought the Grail. His staff was a

Jerusalem Thorn bush, which he planted in the ground. To this day, an Eastern style thorn bush blooms on the ground. A sacred well is found there called the Chalice Well, whose cover has the symbol of *Vesica Pisces* on it. The *Pisces* is the fish and its shape is formed by the overlapping of two circles. This symbol represented the overlapping of two worlds as well as intimate spiritual conjoining. The water that runs there is red, stained by iron in the water, but it is also affiliated with the legend of Christ's blood carried in the Grail.

Going to Avalon is going to a Paradise of Healing. In this story, it is just a casual half-referenced mention of a city Gawan must go to. In other legends, it is a land of plenty and rejuvenation. It is Sanctuary.

No one is actually going to come and take us in a boat to a nirvana that nurtures us when we need it, but we can try to create one in our own homes. This is a long term project for many of us. First, you must get beyond just being able to have enough around you for a survival level, then you can get on with the creation of a place of Sanctuary. You may start with a corner in your bedroom, or it may be your whole house. You may start with a few potted plants, or you may design a whole garden. It may a comfortable chair with a few good books, or a mahogany shelved library. We all need an Avalon after long tough days, especially when we are not feeling up to par. Careful thought and planning may give us the island of Spiritual sustenance we need for our long journey in life.

Creating Avalon

1. Start a notebook of what you can do in your living environment which would create an Avalon for you. Think of the simple things as well as those major remodeling jobs. Dream of a perfect place of healing, then modify it to your current real world situation.

2. Choose a project from your list to actually start creating your Avalon. Once that project is completed, take time to appreciate it before heading into the next task.

Birds of Prey

The Heron Hunt by Eugène Fromentin (1820–1876)
Musée Conde, Chantilly
Oil on Canvas, 1865. 39 x 55 7/8 in.
Photo: Réunion des Musées Nationaux / Art Resource, N.Y.

There are many references to birds throughout this chapter of *Parzival.* Gawan is separated from his squires before his fight when they chase a sparrow-hawk hen. When Gawan is trying to seduce Antikonie, he thinks of how a weak eaglet can catch a large ostrich. This gives him the confidence to run his hand under her cloak and onto her thigh.

However, it is Gawan's first encounter with Vergulaht and his falcons which I find most revealing. Vergulaht sets his hunting falcons on water birds—cranes and herons. Once falcons grasp their prey, they do not let go until they are forced apart. The falcons wound a heron. As the heron falls into the water, the falcons are on the verge of drowning because they do not let go. Vergulaht gives up his horse and clothing to wade into the water and rescue the falcons.

Here we see powerful creatures of the air, risking death because of stubbornness. They have ventured into a realm they are unfamiliar with, and in an attempt to bring down weaker creatures, almost destroy themselves. Primates can be just as stupid. Monkeys have been known to insert their hands into small holes of termite mounds, searching for delicacies. When they grasp the termites, their clenched fist becomes too big to remove from the hole, so they suffer in the African sun for hours, instead of letting go of their prize.

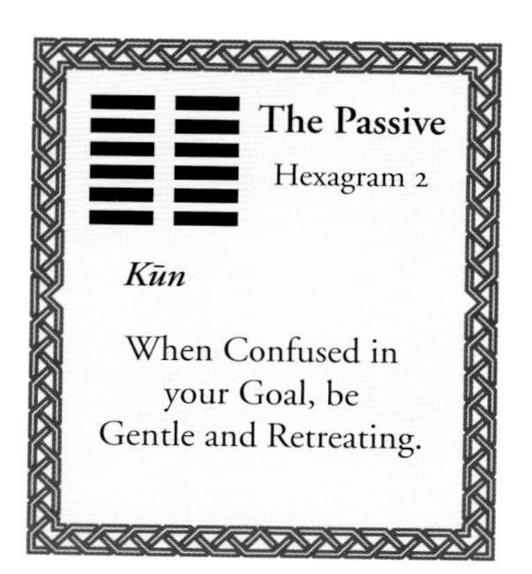

Of course, the other primates known as *Homo Sapiens* do the exact same thing. Sometimes we stubbornly attach ourselves to an idea or material item we don't need, something that could actually destroy us. We hang on so long, we find ourselves drowning, or dying of dehydration. Both examples are extreme opposites that end with the same result—death. Another check mark in the plus column for finding the Middle Way.

In these cases, letting go would solve the whole problem. The falcons could fly and the monkeys could find another termite mound with bigger holes. In both instances, there are plenty of other good things to eat. Focusing on the one dangerous prey has disastrous results. We must learn in our own lives how to "let go" of the inconsequential problems and superfluous objects of our lives, so that we can continue to strive for the worthwhile. We know what these problems or objects are. They are literally drowning or depleting our strengths. Once we let go, they are rarely missed. Don't destroy yourself with the small things of life.

Letting Go

Many of us have petty ideas and actions that we keep hanging onto, even when they lead to debilitating results. List a few of these habits and consciously work towards letting go of them. Look at the destructiveness they cause in your life, and envision the payoff in time and energy available when you finally Let Go.

The Mother

Now, Gawan and Antikonie are not going to go so far as to have children in this story, though Antikonie does marry a king and give birth to a hero, Tandereis, in another legend. What we do have is an escalation of carnal feelings. Given more time, Gawan would have been more intimate with his second representative of the Triplicate Goddess. In these legends, the more intimate you are with these fairy women, the more power you receive. This is far from a later viewpoint, where sex becomes the crippler of power. Both Parzival and Gawan wed and "know" (a biblical term) the important women in their lives. Once we get to Malory's version with its three Grail heroes, Galahad and Perceval are virgins, and Bors only sleeps with a woman once. Perceval gets tempted by a woman who steps off a mysterious black ship. Of course, she is a devil and just as Perceval is about to get in bed with her, he sees a crucifix on his cross, and stops. She disappears in a dark smoke, and he maims himself through the thigh with his own sword—the same wound as the Fisher King's. This temptress as troublemaker is found in Memo's and Harriet's characters in *The Natural.* While Memo is in bed with Roy, she touches the scar from his shooting, which causes the nightmares of Harriet Bird. When Memo says she felt like she and Roy had met before, they had—she and Harriet are the women who turn Roy from his path. The up side is that survival of the tests from these women means inner growth.

In Gawan's relationship with Antikonie we see the development of difficulties the farther down the road he goes, and the more he wants the woman. Probably many men would agree with that statement—the more a guy wants a woman, the more trouble she

Goddess Durgā Fights Buffalo Demon by Bikaner School, Rajasthan
National Museum of New Delhi, India. Watercolor, ca. 1275. © Angelo Homak/Corbis

is. In terms of personal Individual development, the more committed we are to a project, the more it inflames a necessity to be involved, and the more challenges we face.

We are at the stage of the Mother, the stage of Birth and Creation. There is no birth without work and adversity. The attacks become more personal. Before, Gawan's involvement with Obilot was voluntary. Now at this stage he must actively defend himself from attacks directed at him. Luckily, despite her elegant manners, Antikonie has Durgā's warrior spirit in her. Her natural fighting spirit aids Gawan.

As we work towards our own Individual development along the Grail path, the obstacles will become greater, and we will find ourselves needing to defend our path from a more personal view. On the opposite side, our successes will have more exciting rewards as we accomplish our goals, just like Gawan's involvement with Antikonie is a more heightened experience than the one with Obilot. We will bemoan the troubles, but celebrate the successes more.

Gawan will be given the charge to go on the Grail Quest. Prior to this, Gawan had his squires to help him handle his equipment and accompany him, but they are sent back home. As Gawan is now officially on the Grail Quest, he must leave Antikonie and go on alone. His encounter with her has been one more learning step which moves him to the time he will be a King in his own right.

The Chessboard

The Chess Players
by Jacques Clément Wagrez (1846–1908)

When you don't have a good sword and horse around, the next best weapon is a chess set. The game of chess traveled from India to the Middle East and then into Europe. The Celts had similar games, one called *gwyddbwyll* and one called *Brandubh* (Black Bran). Chewbacca and C-3PO play interstellar chess, moving unusual creatures as the chess pieces, relying on the game to hone strategy skills. Harry Potter's Wizard Chess was inspired by the many chess games found in the Arthurian legends. Perceval, Lancelot, and Gawan all play matches on a board which plays itself. The Chessboard usually belongs to someone called the Empress or Lady of the Chessboard Castle. Arthur and Owein play a magical chess game, while Tristan and Iseult drink the fateful magic potion while moving knights and pawns. One of the Thirteen Treasures of Britain is the Chessboard of Gwenddolau. Elen, whose fame were the roads of Britain, has a father who carves chess pieces while sitting on a magnificent throne. Peredur throws his Chessboard away, then has to have a quest to retrieve it. It seems that knights have a lot of free time if they can sit around all day playing chess.

As you can guess, the Chessboard represents something more. It is the Land of the Goddess of Sovereignty. It must be defended. It must be cherished. If you throw it away, you must retrieve it. If need be, it will come to your aid. The most powerful piece on the Chessboard is the Queen, and the next piece which can make the most variety of moves is the Knight. Though Antikonie is considered a refined woman, she takes on a fierce battle spirit as she uses the pieces to defend Gawan. As she fights, Gawan finds her inspiring and beautiful.

The Chessboard's shape is reminiscent of the Stone, the form of the Grail that Parzival searches for. The Healing of the Land is the foremost reward at the end of the Grail Quest. Peredur must find the thrown away Board of the Empress, just as Parzival finds and restores the land's strength.

Honor of Word and Honor of Hospitality

If we associate any overall theme with the stories of Medieval Knights, it is one of Honor. People created a higher, spiritual law of conduct that goes beyond mercenary fighting. A Code of Ethics developed and much of how we view events of the world today can still be linked to the ideas formed in these legends. Forrest Gump reminds Lt. Dan that a promise is a promise, never to be broken.

Two important issues of Honor of Word and Honor of Hospitality are debated. They are considered as important as Gawan's possible guilt for the killing of King Kingrisin.

Kingrimursel had given his Word to Gawan that he would receive safe conduct and a one-on-one fight to the challenge. Kingrimursel is so ashamed when he sees Gawan being attacked that he comes to Gawan's aid. It would be easy to let Gawan be killed, and thus get rid of a supposed dishonorable enemy, but Kingrimursel stands by his Word. He not only enforces his own actions, but has the power to make others recognize the seriousness of the promise he gave Gawan.

There would be little need today for complicated contracts if people stood by their Word. Trust is almost totally built on the matching of our actions to our pledges. If we go back on our Word to our children and our friends, how can our adversaries expect a fair treatment? We cannot heal a Land unless all people, friend and foe alike, can trust our promises.

The Honor of Hospitality—to give safe rest to guests and wayfarers—was begun in a time when mountain passes and desert stretches claimed lives of people unable to find refuge. Whether it was a Northern European custom of Guest-Right, or an American rite of Southern Hospitality, the gist was to make strangers and friends feel a comfort greater than they knew at home. The best food, the best blankets, three dogs on an icy Eskimo night, a few draughts of libations, and pleasant, often vital, conversation was de rigueur. Travelers were often sources of news of the world to those living far away from major cities. We offered protection and warmth and extended a reach into the outer world. Even in early America, relatives stopping by for a chat meant weeks of travel and weeks more of stay. Vergulaht is upbraided by his sister for his involvement with the nasty treatment of their guest, and he rightfully acknowledges his guilt. I'll have to admit that I might have also battled Gawan, thinking he had killed my father, but the story is illustrating the importance of the care extended towards guests.

We now have so much access to so many forms of instantaneous information, that we do not need to rely on backyard fence gossip and weary hikers for our news. And that is a certain loss. We have internet communities instead of block parties. We schedule quick business lunches instead of leisurely dining. We lose touch with what it is to entertain and care for others, even at a simple level. At one time, to some travelers, that care may have meant life or death. We lose touch with what it is to be gracious and accommodating, and wonder why human contact becomes less and less. This is just another way in which we have created a Wasteland.

Illustration by Arthur Rackham (1867–1939)
© Courtesy of the estate of Arthur Rackham / The Bridgeman Art Library

We can take an attitude of treating people we meet with the respect we would give an honored guest. We can be wary of those very few people in the world who take advantage of us, and still extend a feeling of kindness towards others. All people on the street are guests, whether from another country, another state, or another neighborhood. They should leave our presence feeling they were treated as such.

The Lessons of Cloning

It is through offering Service to Others that we will achieve success in the Realm of the Individual. If we offer what is best in ourselves, we only make ourselves better.

We can only achieve our Grail through developing courage. This may never become an easy goal to achieve, but by striving for it, we rid ourselves of self defeat. Courage is a habit as much as any other practice.

Just as we desire Sovereignty for our own lives, we need to create an atmosphere where others can also search for their own Grails. Mutual respect for our loved ones will reap the support that we need in our Grail search.

We must watch the quality of our language as it affects our own actions and those around us. We must learn to develop a language of truth and persuasion, not one of intimidation.

There are times when our Spiritual and Individual worlds seem to be at conflict, but we must have the presence not to have them war directly. Look for ways to bring the two together on a peaceful, yet powerful path.

The Virgin is the easy, innocent view of beginning new projects, while the Mother represents the difficulties, but joy of the actual birth of our endeavors.

We can create our own Avalon, a place of healing for ourselves. We can appreciate the little things we do for ourselves as well as the grander visions. A personal Sanctuary will aid in developing our Spirit, and understanding our Inner Self.

We must learn to Let Go of petty problems and notions that could destroy us if we hold on to them too long.

We must develop the Honor of keeping our Word and the Honor of Hospitality. How we treat others, and the trust we develop, is critical to the Healing of the Wasteland.

We will now check in again with Parzival, who has been futilely searching for the Grail Castle. He will run into another uncle, who will give him valuable lessons as to how to get back on track.

Luke Skywalker continues his training with Jedi Master Yoda.

(Luke-Mark Hamill)

Chapter 15 - Direct Experience

Siddhartha said: "You know, my friend, that even as a young man, when we lived with the ascetics in the forest, I came to distrust doctrines and teachers and to turn my back on them. I am still of the same turn of mind, although I have, since that time, had many teachers. A beautiful courtesan was my teacher for a long time, and a rich merchant and a dice player. On one occasion, one of Buddha's wandering monks was my teacher. He halted in his pilgrimage to sit beside me in the forest, I also learned something from him and I am grateful to him, very grateful. But most of all, I have learned from this river and from my predecessor, Vasudeva. He was a simple man; he was not a thinker, but he realized the essential as well as Gotama. He was a holy man, a saint."

— from *Siddhartha* by Hermann Hesse

"Open!"

To whom? Who are you?

"I want to enter your heart."

Then you want too narrow a space.

"So what then? I can manage with only a little trouble—you have no need to complain of my pressing in. I come to tell you of wonders."

Oh, is it you, Lady Adventure?

— opening lines of *Parzival*, Book IX

Anakin Skywalker was not long with his first teacher, Qui-Gon Jinn, before Qui-Gon was killed. He now must turn to Obi-Wan Kenobi for further development in the Jedi ways. In the next generation, Luke Skywalker will studiously train with Obi-Wan until Obi-Wan is killed by Darth Vader. Luke will now be directed to search out Yoda for his advanced learning. This is the same pattern as found in Parzival, where Parzival now turns to his second teacher, the monk Trevrizent, to aid him in his adventures.

Until this chapter, Wolfram has given no explanation as to what the Grail is, nor what was Parzival's failing at the Grail Castle. Wolfram says he was not allowed to speak of these things until Lady Adventure was ready to tell the details.

This is the chapter where many questions get filled in, both for Parzival and the reader. It is also the chapter where real issues of religious spirituality are brought to the forefront. As stated before, Wolfram seemed to vacillate with his Christian message. Here he will affirm Christian values, with a few surprises. In his spirit of trying to accommodate the varying degrees of religious views, we will take a broader view as to how the lessons here can be applied to any form of spiritual and personal practice.

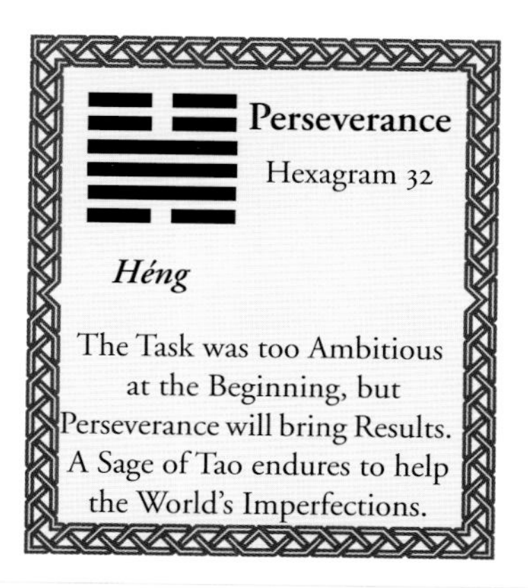

Trevrizent

Parzival comes to a hermit's cell where Sigune has been constantly praying over Schianatulander's corpse. Sigune is fed by the Grail from Cundrie the Sorceress every Saturday. Parzival tells Sigune how he still looks for the Grail, and Sigune tells him that Cundrie just left on her mule. Parzival tries to follow the mule's path, but loses it.

Parzival is challenged by a Templar protecting Munsalvaesche. Parzival unhorses the knight, but Parzival's horse plunges over the cliff. He is saved by jumping off his horse and holding onto a tree branch. The Templar runs away, so Parzival takes the knight's horse.

On his travels, he comes across a family of pilgrims—a father, a mother, and two daughters—all dressed in gray. The man is Gambenis, a prince from Punturtois. He chastises Parzival for wearing armor on Good Friday. Parzival says he once served God, but no longer. The man points him towards the direction of a holy man, saying Parzival should seek his guidance. The daughters think their father should point Parzival to hospitality, as it is very cold. The man does offer food, but Parzival declines to stay with them. He feels a little guilty about riding on horse while they are on foot.

Parzival lets his horse lead the way, which goes to Fontane la Salvatsche, where Orilus received Parzival's oath. Trevrizent is the holy man who lives there.

The reader learns more of the background of the Grail. Wolfram claims a man named Kyot was his source. Kyot speaks of Flegetanis, who was half heathen, a scholar, and astrologer, who read in the stars that the angels had left the Grail. Kyot researched the Grail and how Titurel and Frimutel bequeathed the Grail to Anfortas. Anfortas' sister is Parzival's mother, Herzeloyde.

Parzival finds Trevrizent, who says that he was once a knight, so he is not afraid of men who wander to his home. Inside, Parzival sees the casket of holy relics he pledged on for Lady Jeschute. The casket is carved of a green stone, given to Trevrizent by Parzival's father. Parzival says he was the one who took Taurian's spear. Trevrizent says Taurian left it four and a half years ago.

Trevrizent tells Parzival to turn to God. Even as a layman, Trevrizent says he found solace in God. Parzival says his sins are longing for the Grail and his wife.

Trevrizent said longing for his wife is understandable, but the Grail is only for those chosen of heaven. Trevrizent tells of his experience with the Grail and of the Templars who go out because of their sins. The Grail is the *lapsit exillis* (stone from heaven), and its powers will keep even the sickest man alive. He tells of the neutral angels and the children meant to serve the Grail, whose lineage is written on the stone, though the writing disappears as soon as one reads his name. Maidens can leave freely from Munsalvaesche, but men must do so secretly. The children of the people of the Grail Castle are to serve the Grail. When serving the Grail, the men are supposed to forsake women, which Trevrizent did not do at first. Anfortas lives there in grief, and only those who are bidden can go there, except for one who did not ask the right question.

Trevrizent tells of the son of Lehelin, who jousted and killed Lybbeals. He took Lybbeals' horse, leaving the corpse to rot. He asks Parzival if he is Lehelin, as he has a Templar's horse with the turtle dove insignia. Parzival says he is Gahmuret's son, not Lehelin, though he once in ignorance left Ither to rot. Trevrizent reveals he is Parzival's uncle, that Ither was his relation, and his mother Herzeloyde died from grief when Parzival left her. Trevrizent had two other sisters, Schoysiane, mother of Sigune, who died at childbirth, and Repanse de Schoye, who tends the Grail. Anfortas is their brother and Frimutel was their father.

Anfortas was interested in love as a young man. In a battle with a heathen from Ethnise, Anfortas was wounded in the thigh with a poisoned spear engraved with the Grail's name on it. Trevrizent became a monk at that time, and Anfortas was taken to the Grail. He would not die, but could not be cured. Writings on the Grail said a man would ask the question for the cure, but he could not be prompted. If the man does not ask his question on the first night, then the question would not have power.

They broke to search for food, though they would not eat until after Nones (3 P.M.). Parzival finally admits he was the one who did not ask the question. Trevrizent asked if he saw the spear at Munsalvaesche. He also tells that at certain times, frost hurts Anfortas immeasurably as ice forms on the wound. When the moon changes he suffers more and is taken to Lake Brumbane for relief. That is how he earned the name, the Fisher King, though he doesn't fish.

Parzival tells how he received the horse, and Trevrizent equated it to theft, though Parzival viewed it as battle earnings. Parzival learns that the gray man by the Grail is his great grandfather, Titurel, who is lame, but cannot die. After fifteen days, Parzival leaves.

— Summary of *Parzival,* Book IX

Direct Experience

> *Mankind by nature has wild, strange manners. Sometimes it is youth who chooses the way of wisdom.*
>
> — Trevrizent in *Parzival,* Book IX, ¶ 489

Parzival now actively seeks the Grail, but it continues to elude him. He comes across Sigune, who just happens to be there when Parzival is reaching a turning point. Wolfram remarks that Sigune heard no Mass, yet was always in prayer. This alludes to the importance of Direct Experience. Sigune has no need of formal ceremonies or intercessors to give her spiritual nourishment; she knows what to do without others telling her the right or wrong way. She listens closely to her heart, and instead of riding miles and battling useless skirmishes in searching for the Grail, its blessings are brought directly to her. This is the lesson that Parzival is meant to see—to listen to what lies closest and deepest in his heart. Still, he bemoans that he can't find the Grail. All she can do is send him back out with a few clues. Cundrie rides her mule, which drinks at a spring (magical, no doubt), and Parzival goes to pick up the trail there.

So it is with our lives. I mentioned before how our first initial contact with the Grail is chance. Once you know what it is you want, you should go for it. But we usually go on a trail of many forked turns. We haphazardly work our way back to what we need, now expending much effort, and despairing when we don't quite get it right. We need to take Sigune's example of completely focusing our energies on what is important, and reach for that direct, inner experience. At that point, the blessings of the Grail would come to us willingly.

Forrest Gump had to run many, many miles, trying to extinguish his personal pain caused when Jenny left him. He ran for over three years, much like Parzival being lost for five years. Though he couldn't experience Jenny directly, Gump wore the running shoes that she gave him, so he was close to his Grail all of the time. It was only after he stopped running that she could come to him. Once he experienced the hard times of desperately searching for her in his heart, then she could reappear.

What Forrest did accomplish on that run is reaffirming his natural self. When he was hungry, he ate; when he was tired, he slept; when nature called, he went. By going through the process of rediscovering the natural self, you are able to discover pure, unrehearsed vitality. When you are confident in who you are, compassion towards others will be automatic.

Sean Maguire reminds Will Hunting that he is an inexperienced kid, who doesn't know what he is talking about. Kurtz, in the film *Heart of Darkness,* tells Marlow that if you only look at the world with the opinions of others, you will lose your originality.

In meeting Trevrizent, Parzival is repeating the lesson that he should have learned when he last met Sigune. He again encounters a man whose religious studies did not follow the way of the church, but of the heart. He is again in the presence of Direct Experience. Trevrizent has retreated into the wild woods, and has discovered his personal way of communing with God. His wisdom is renown, and pilgrims now come to him for penance and advice.

> *But there is one thing that this clear, worthy instruction does not contain; it does not contain the secret of what the Illustrious One himself experienced—he alone among hundreds of thousands. That is what I thought and realized when I heard your teachings. That is why I am going on my way—not to seek another and better doctrine, for I know there is none, but to leave all doctrines and all teachers and to reach my goal alone—or die.*
>
> — Siddhartha to Gotama Buddha in *Siddhartha* by Hermann Hesse

Siddhartha recognizes how important it is to go out and find Direct Experience. He even has the audacity to tell Gotama the flaws in Gotama's Buddhism. Though he is convinced Gotama is the Buddha, Siddhartha will not follow Gotama. Siddhartha knows that true Enlightenment will only come about when he gets out and searches for it personally.

Direct Experience is important whether we speak of Spiritual experience or the experience we need to develop in achieving our Grail. When Trevrizent tells Parzival about the wild nature of man, he is telling him to return to the root of who he is and not fight his own Nature. We are back to the young cowherd trying to force his way to spiritual attainment, rather than allowing his own Nature to achieve it.

All professions have standards and methods of achievement. If you want to follow the rules of the establishment and can maintain a fair level of ability, you will be rewarded. However, the geniuses are the ones we remember. It is the Daniel Boones who forge the brave, creative path that we want to emulate. This can only be achieved by going into the wilds of the woods and directly facing bears and black flies, not just reading a book.

There is no advancement in civilization without this step. It takes a person who says that maybe the rules worked in the past, but only to a certain extent. It is time for something new and different. Whether the name is Bach, Salk, Dali, or Olivier, the accomplishments come from Direct Experience, not second hand knowledge. To step into the future, the step must be away from the constraints of those who only follow the rules of the past.

Understand how important Direct Experience is. Get your direction, get your base instruction from others, then allow yourself the freedom to explore and delve deeply into what is important to you.

Need for Spiritual Guidance

Parzival was close to his goal, but he has lost direction. He is primarily on a spiritual mission, but has somehow lost his track. He meets pilgrims along the road who make an annual trek. The father directs him towards a hermit, where Parzival can receive forgiveness for his lack of religious attentiveness. His daughters, who seem rosy and inviting in the cold, remind their father of the first lesson, to show compassion. Parzival is given food, though he wishes for a kiss of atonement from their sweet lips.

Since Parzival has been unhappy in his journey, he thinks that perhaps he should try God again to see if it will help him. He even allows the reins on his horse to drop, so he can again experience what it is to give himself over to Tao and Faith. This Spiritual giving over is portrayed in Wassily Kandinsky's painting *Lyrisches.*

Sometimes we need to shake up our lives, and allow ourselves to search for Spiritual Guidance. I believe that there is not a person in this world who has not experienced doubt and anguish in examining their spiritual beliefs. It is not because the initial teachings were bad. But in the process of religious evolution, politics and personal agendas become entwined, leaving a shell of the original spiritual intent. Just as you have legal rights to search out justice with man-made laws, you have the spiritual right to search for a truth that serves your higher purpose. When you sense that you need new direction, allow yourself the freedom to explore. It could be that you are like Parzival, and decide to try your original faith again, or it may mean investigating other religions and philosophies. It may mean keeping the faith you have now, but reevaluating certain tenets which no longer speak to your way of living. All religions evolve, so you have the right to allow it to evolve within yourself. Give yourself the freedom to search for a direction which can help you.

Lyrisches (Lyrical)
by Wassily Kandinsky (1866–1944)
Städtische Galerie im Lenbachhaus, München. Color woodcut, 1911. 5 7/8 x 8 1/2 in.

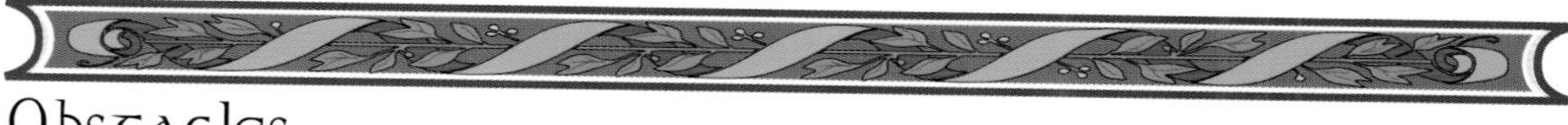

Obstacles

Parzival now meets an important obstacle: an encounter with a knight from the Grail Castle. This means that he is close to his goal. He jousts with the knight, with chaotic results. There is no noble win. After knocking the Grail Knight off his horse, Parzival lets his own horse get out of control, and very nearly kills himself. His OtherWorld horse does die, careening down a cliff. He cannot even get an acknowledgment of defeat from the losing knight, who runs off into the forest. The only saving grace is that Parzival now takes the defeated knight's horse, another stallion from Munsalvaesche.

This is typical behavior when we search for our Grail. We are heading in the right direction and are close to our goal, when we meet a difficult obstacle and behave erratically. Instead of getting closer to our goal, we now set ourselves further away. This is the time when many people give up on their dreams. They meet what they think is a formidable opponent or obstacle, and because they almost lose everything at that encounter, they think it is time to give up. It is really only a sign that they are getting closer to their goal.

When you are approaching your goals, and the mountain gets steeper and more treacherous, don't give up and turn back down. This is the time to anchor those ropes, swing the little toe over the ledge, and pull yourself up further.

Return to the Right Path

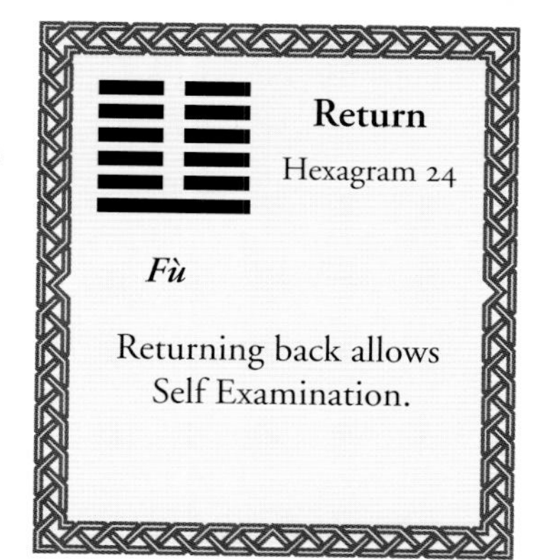

Parzival goes to the cave of Trevrizent, which was the place of reconciliation between Orilus and Jeschute. When Parzival was originally traveling the right path, he found Trevrizent's cave with ease. Now he has to be shown the direction. Of course, the first time, he didn't really understand who Trevrizent was.

When you have lost your way, reflect on where things were right, and look for direction there. Understand that things will not be exactly as they were before. Just look for a clue you may have missed before. Too often, we try to recreate memorable events by staging the environment exactly as it was before. The laws of Tao say that things may repeat themselves, but not exactly as before.

While you are examining the past for clues, do not get too hung up on staying there and chastising yourself with "If only." That time is past. Look at your mistakes and learn from them; don't dwell on them. Take what is right, and find your way back to the right path.

Noble Company

It sounds snobbish when the point is driven home that Grail servers are chosen by heaven. They are considered the noblest of initiates with the highest of duties assigned to them. They are protectors of an object which receives its power from a dove of heaven once a year.

On the negative side, it's the same system that allowed kings and queens to rule with a tyrannical fist, justifying their actions believing they were chosen by God. On the positive side, there is something empowering about knowing that the highest authority of the cosmos has searched you out to tell you your mission. God has endowed you with a purpose and he gives you a way to know it. Your name is engraved on a sacred stone, and the writing only disappears when you read your own chosen name on that stone.

We should view our own personal Grail search as something noble and blessed. We should surround ourselves with a like nobility, defined by the nature of our Grails. Whatever you search for, should be searched for with the best. Do yourself the honor of finding the best teachers and support teams that you can. Build your own Noble Company.

The Chymical Grail

> *"I always ask leave, in the interests of science, to measure the crania of those going out there," he said. "And when they come back, too?" I asked. "Oh, I never see them," he remarked; "and, moreover, the changes take place inside, you know."*
>
> — conversation between the Company Doctor and Marlow in *Heart of Darkness* by Joseph Conrad

> *By the magic of the Stone, the Phoenix burns himself entirely to ashes, but the ashes give him new life. And so molts the Phoenix, with afterwards his plumage being as fair and gleaming as ever.*
>
> — Trevrizent in *Parzival,* Book IX, ¶ 469

The Grail may represent what we are in exile from, but the whole journey, to the point when we stand in front of our Grail, is our Transformation. At the beginning of our journey, we are the Phoenix dying to the old life: we are Odin hanging by the neck on

Yggdrasil. At the end, we will be reborn, with greater knowledge and understanding. It is the most magic of Alchemies—that of developing Wisdom.

The Phoenix myth is found in many cultures from Egypt to Europe to China. In China, it is called *feng-huang*, and has a plumage of the five colors of the Taoist Five Elements. It only bathes from a spring in the Kun Lun Mountains, one of the Sacred Central Mountains. Legend says that it had appeared to the Yellow Emperor, Huang Ti, shortly before his death at the age of 111. This emperor is credited with the development of a civilized China, and notably, the birth of Taoism. Perhaps the Phoenix' presence heralded a possible rebirth, just as Arthur is supposed to return from Avalon as the Once and Future King.

In Chymical circles, the Phoenix, a bird of the air, is also paired with the Pelican, a bird of the water. In Medieval tales, the Pelican represented Christ. This relates to a legend that the pelican has such loyal love that it will bite at its own breast and feed its young with its blood. The pelican then dies soon after. Some stories say that the young birds are dead and brought back to life. This is akin to Christ unselfishly giving his own blood for mankind. Indeed, when Trevrizent tells Parzival about the many cures tried on Anfortas, the blood of the Pelican was one.

Trevrizent speaks of another Chymical aspect of the Grail: From the day a person sees the Grail, he will look the same the rest of his life—except for some graying of the hair. There is a Taoist tale that demonstrates similar benefits from Taoist studies. A scholar named Hsieh worked on his practices everyday. As he grew older, his face did not change, and after many years, his middle-aged grandchildren even looked older than him. The Emperor summoned him to learn his secret. Hsieh told him his meditation. When the Emperor learned that the practice would only keep him at his present age, and not reverse the aging process, Hsieh was imprisoned. After the death of the Emperor, the new young Emperor released Hsieh, who told the new Emperor about his work. This Emperor practiced what he was taught. Legend says that even several centuries later, people would come across two men drinking wine together, one in his fifties, and one in his twenties, who would laugh and disappear when spoken to.

In real life, working with your Grail does promote a youthful energy and desire to keep you going strong into your golden years. Creative work, whether it is managing a business, harmonizing a family, or creating art, gives purpose and direction. Looking forward to days filled with working on what's dearest to you creates an energy and joy that keeps you young.

If It Was God's Right to Judge

Trevrizent tells of the Angels who brought the Grail to earth, choosing the Middle Way between God and Lucifer. They were no dumb angels. They knew that there has to be communication between all worlds. To only know of good is to live in naiveté. To only know of evil is to live without hope. To achieve, we must accept that both exist, and strive to do what is best in a precarious world. The Grail is the ability to know what is spiritually correct, while living in a world which constantly challenges that goodness.

Wolfram sneaks in a surprising comment here. He says that after everything was over, he did not know if God forgave or condemned them. And if it was God's right to choose, he chose to take them back. Here Trevrizent allows a possibility that God had no right to judge these angels.

There may be some obvious situations in our lives where judgment is called for. We can live by values, and determine our stance on an issue by these values. There are times, however, when we need to step aside and cease unwarranted judgment. If the God of this legend had no right to judge angels who refused to side with him, who are we to constantly judge those different from ourselves?

This all ties in with our ability to "Let Go." If a difference of opinion between yourself and others has no high moral consequence, don't create a negative atmosphere by judging the trivial. Save your energy for defending important issues. Stop criticizing the unimportant.

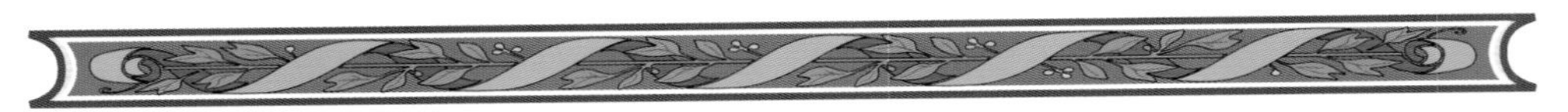

The Right Question

Parzival gets his final dose of shame when Trevrizent prattles on about the incompetent knight who didn't ask the Right Question. Trevrizent even says that all the knight had to do was ask about the king's suffering. What was worse, he says, is that the knight only gets one chance. If he didn't ask the question the first night, the healing would not work. Parzival finally admits that he was that incompetent knight.

This is a turning point for Parzival: admitting that he was the one who could have healed the Grail King. He didn't cause the king's wound, but he still had the responsibility to heal him. Providence had brought Parzival to his place of Destiny, and he had failed. Even when you are not the cause of the problem, it is a big step to admit responsibility to help fix something.

The world is one bundle of joy, and one bundle of pain. It is great to commit yourself to adding to the joy of the world, but it is even better if that joy comes about from healing the pain. If all of us could take a responsibility towards healing, even when we did not cause the problem, this would certainly be a more gratifying and optimistic world. We will be giving ourselves and others a chance at a better life.

The Right Question

Let's examine what it is to ask "What ails thee?" We'll do it by looking at all Three Kingdoms.

1. Kingdom of the Community: Look for some void or suffering that is in your community. This could be at either a small, immediate level, or a larger political level. Think of ways you can help heal. This could be with cash or time donations to causes you believe in, or simple gestures such as watching some neighborhood children, so a tired mother can have an afternoon breather.

2. Kingdom of the Individual: Are any friends or family in need of attention or help? Even a gift of a book or day trip can bolster hidden, lagging spirits. Sometimes money is needed, but often time is the key.

3. Kingdom of the Spirit: This is for yourself. Does any part of your life need extra healing? Give yourself the time to work on it. Once you feel better, it is much easier to work on the healing of others.

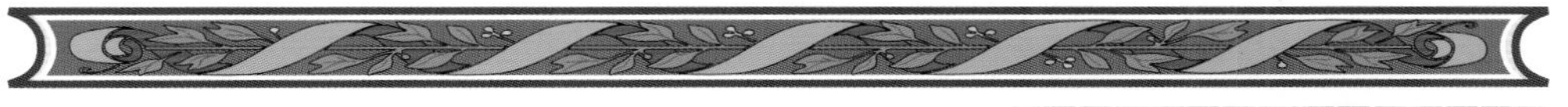

Hubris

"Sometimes when I walk down the street I bet people will say there goes Roy Hobbs, the best there ever was in the game."
She gazed at him with touched and troubled eyes. "Is that all?"

— Roy Hobbs and Harriet Bird
in *The Natural* by Bernard Malamud

First, your meekness must protect you from your arrogance. Your youth could mislead you from self-control. Pride has always sunk and fallen.

— Trevrizent in *Parzival*, Book IX, ¶ 472

Harriet Bird carefully questions Roy Hobbs about who is the best in baseball. He acknowledges that the Whammer is the best, but she notes that Roy just beat the Whammer. That gets Roy's ego going and he brags about the future where he will have fame and fortune. The only problem is that he is bragging to Lady Fortuna, Lady Luck, who rules the Wheel of Fortune. She is the one who decides to spin the Wheel, causing those at the top to fall to the bottom. In this case, Harriet has been shooting the best athletes in several sports, and Roy just marked himself as her next target.

Wheel of Fortune
by Edward Burne-Jones (1833–1898)

Musée D'Orsay, Paris
Oil on Canvas, 1875–83. 78 1/3 x 39 3/8 in.
Photo: Erich Lessing / Art Resource, N.Y.

At the beginning of *The Fisher King,* Jack Lucas is so caught up in his success, which appears to be on an upswing with a possible sitcom contract, that he busies himself with deciding the title of his autobiography. He originally thought that it should be *Jack Lucas, the Face Behind the Voice,* but now he might have to choose *Jack Lucas, the Face and the Voice.* This is Hubris. We know he is going to be in for a downfall. Lady Fortuna wouldn't have it any other way.

One of the most dramatic myths demonstrating fall due to Hubris, or pride against the gods, is from the story of Daedalus and Icarus. King Minos is keeping the inventor Daedalus from leaving Crete by blocking the roads and ports. Daedalus creates wings of wax and feathers, to allow him and his son, Icarus, to escape. Daedalus tells Icarus not to fly too close to the water, because the wings will become water logged and weigh him down. He is also told not to fly too high, or the wax will melt. (Notice the theme of the Middle Way here.) Once they started flying across the sea, Icarus feels such a surge of power by being able to fly, that he imagines himself as powerful as the gods. He decides to dare the heavens with his flight, melting his wings, and he plummets to his death. This is Hubris.

Anfortas' wound has also come from a hubris which said he was so good that he could ignore the love for the Grail, and misplace it with love for a woman who wasn't meant for him. As chivalrous as it sounds, a battle cry of *Amor* is only appropriate when battling for the right woman. Though Grail knights were suppose to refrain from women, the Grail King was allowed to marry, so Anfortas only had to find the right bride. Instead of choosing a woman from the Grail Realm, he went after Orgeluse, a Queen in the Land of Wonders.

Trevrizent says that if any Grail King wants a love other than what the Grail allows, he will suffer extreme misery. That we already knew. If you don't love and hold close your personal Grail, you will suffer. Since Anfortas in his pride ignored his Grail, he is poisoned by a spear that magically has the name "Grail" inscribed on it. It would forever pain him and yet not let him die.

People often get confused about the Oriental viewpoint of "losing one's ego." This does not mean losing the pride which keeps your standards high to do good work. It means losing the False Pride that stands in the way of what you really want to achieve. When we start daydreaming about the accolades that come to us, and the adoring fans who scream for us, we move away from spending the time necessary to make ourselves better. As good as you are, you can always be better. When we brag about how good we are, we must be prepared to meet the challenges we stir up.

Disdain and arrogance are prides that invite a downfall. True measure of our abilities and self-esteem moves us forward in our lives. Do not confuse the two sides of Pride. Eliminate the Hubris, increase the Self-Respect.

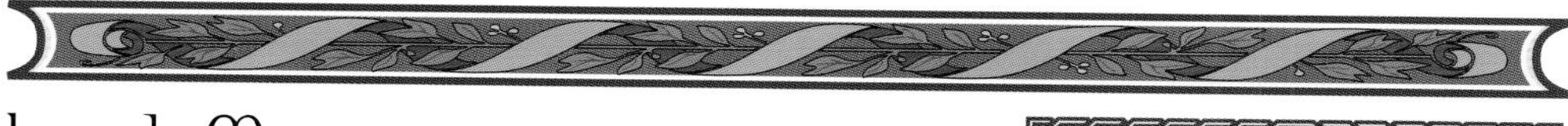

Less Is More

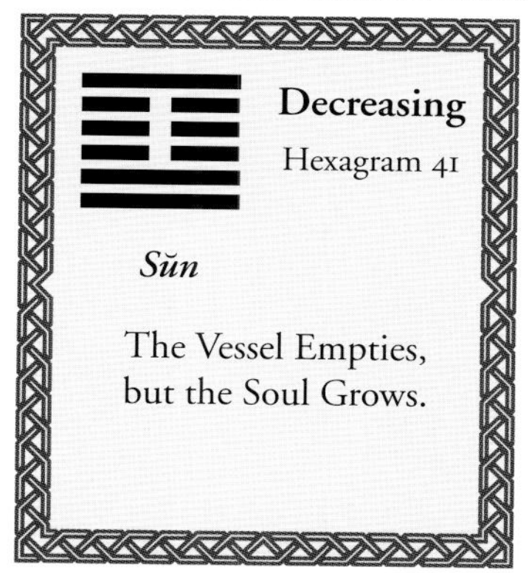

Less is More.

— Ludwig Mies van der Rohe

Trevrizent lives in poverty. This was his choice. When most of us fall on hard times, we develop stress, anger, and shame about our lack of funds or material items. This *I Ching* Hexagram serves as a reminder that there are times when actively decreasing our use of resources preserves energy for more important growth. In the Ten Perfections, the Second Perfection is Renunciation. Many of us live with excess, and much of our energy is spent towards acquiring even more. It is not that material items themselves are bad—they are often the products of hard work and creativity—but when all of our efforts are directed towards them, we run out of time for growth of the Soul. Less time striving at work means more time with your family or interests. Less accumulated debt means not worrying so much about the future. We do not have to do the extreme Renunciation of a Buddhist or Catholic Priest, but we can find a wisdom in reducing our wants. The Body, the Mind, and the Spirit rest easier when we can empty the big vessels we carry.

Less Is More

Take an honest look at your finances and material items that surround you. Does any debt you have justify what you have? If the answer is no, develop a plan to reduce your debt. Don't accumulate more things until you have balanced your life to a comfortable level.

Are you prepared financially for the future? Do you have time to do what you really want to do? Do you have time and energy for those you love? If any of these are answered "no," find a way to "empty your vessel" so that you will have a less stressful present and future.

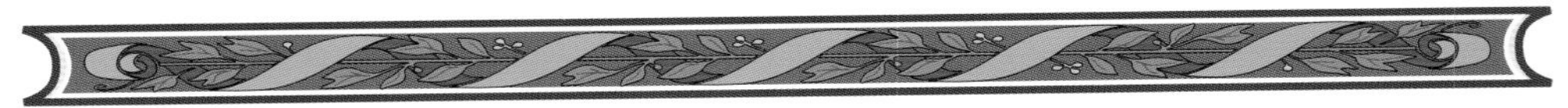

Atonement and Redemption

What if you have done something really horrible in your life? Jack Lucas practices the line "Forgive Me!" as he soaks in his bathtub in his expensive New York apartment. He has no idea what it is to harm someone in such a way that he would need forgiveness, so his hollow words must be practiced until the insincerity sounds like a punch line. Halfway through the movie, forgiveness becomes a real issue for him.

We've discussed that we need to take responsibility for wrongdoings we have intentionally and unintentionally committed. We've also looked at taking responsibility for healing the harms we have not done. What happens if you are willing to take responsibility, but what is required to make things right goes beyond merely donating time and energy to right your wrongs?

This is where matters of Atonement and Redemption come into play. The whole spiritual being must immerse itself in going beyond an eye for an eye concept. It is the giving of the eye, hand, and tooth to begin making things better.

Parzival jokes about taking an atonement kiss from the lips of the two young women he met on the road. Once he meets Trevrizent, the issue of Atonement becomes a reality. Parzival learns that when he killed Ither, he murdered a kinsman, and that he caused the death of his mother. Trevrizent volunteers to take Parzival's sins before he leaves, but true steps of Atonement require more work.

If you have grievously harmed someone, you must apologize to that person, even if the victim screams at you and your family tells you to mind your business. There will not be any healing on either side until an apology is made. Even if it is not accepted, you must communicate your regret.

If you are offered forgiveness, be gracious enough to accept it, even if you have not yet forgiven yourself. You cannot ask for forgiveness—that is falsity—but forgiveness freely extended is a precious gem not to be discarded. This is again a stage of Healing.

If you cannot directly help the person you harmed, find another way to give to people who have been similarly harmed. If you hurt someone in a car accident, volunteer at a hospital rehabilitating injured people. If you have hurt someone in a drunken rage, get professional help, then you can help others who have the same weakness.

Redemption, a state of personal clearing and forgiveness, can only occur when the heart has been totally involved in the remedy of spiritual crimes. You are not redeemed until you can wake up one morning knowing you have helped many others, and that you will never harm another person in such a way again.

What if you are the victim? The Ninth Perfection tells us to develop Loving Kindness, even to those who have hurt us.

Perhaps you can accept an apology, perhaps not. Perhaps you can offer forgiveness, perhaps not. Perhaps you have the right to fight back. Then do so. No matter what happens right after the incident, most assuredly you will be angry. At some point, you will have to focus on eliminating the anger and find healing alternatives. Mothers who lost children to drunk drivers formed MADD (Mothers Against Drunk Drivers). After the death of their abducted child, John and Reve Walsh formed the Adam Walsh Foundation (later combined into the National Center for Missing and Exploited Children) to help missing children. Many people set up charities to help victims of the New York and Washington D.C. September 11th attack. If these people had only wallowed in anger and hate, they would not have done the good which has helped others. You must eventually move beyond anger. Otherwise, you continue being a victim. Find projects and tasks that take your mind away from pain, something that totally engrosses the energy you have allocated to it. If you can work with others who have gone through similar experiences and who have been successfully healed, then do so. Their experiences will help you move away from your anger.

Redemption for you is when you no longer wake in the mornings loathing the perpetrator, and maybe—yourself.

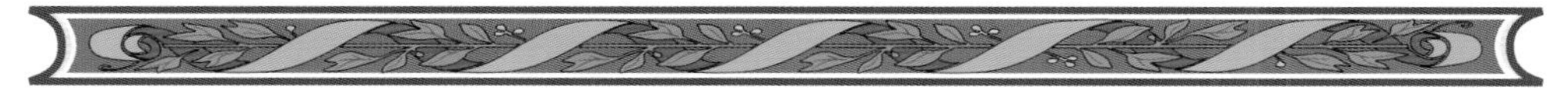

Titurel

Titurel—the father of Herzeloyde, Anfortas, Repanse, and Trevrizent—suffers a similar fate as his son Anfortas. He is crippled and old, yet cannot die because of the force of the Grail. The people of the Grail Castle keep him alive because he is valued for his counsel.

Deep down, in the very back of our psyches, is an old, wise man unwilling to die, and continuing to feed us counsel. When all else is falling apart around us, his wispy voice can get us back on track. He won't fight the battles, or smack us on the head to deliver instant Zen enlightenment, but he will continue to offer wisdom, and we keep him around for that reason.

Accessing this wisdom can only be done with absolute stillness and a willingness to listen to voices that speak truth, even if they speak words we don't want to hear. There is a certain Truth to situations that are obvious to others, but hidden to ourselves. Until we take time to listen to this Wisdom, we will rationalize and make excuses. Make a practice of searching out this Truth, especially during difficult times.

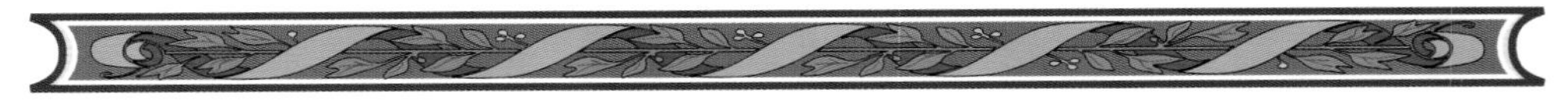

Ritual of Spirit

Parzival joins Trevrizent in his custom of not eating until after Nones. This is in observance of the time Christ died. Trevrizent has created his own personal, spiritual ritual that links him to his God, by Prayers of the Hours. Muslims take time in the day to bow towards Mecca. Buddhists turn prayer wheels and hang malas around their necks. Jews don prayer shawls. Catholics pray on rosaries.

Ritual is important as it can bond families, countries, and people of faith, as long as the meaning of the ritual still resonates in the heart of the participants.

Perhaps you go to a church that has a whole series of various rituals, which you follow, but leaves you feeling spiritually disengaged. Does that mean you must abandon your faith? No. There are two possibilities to help you.

First, research the genesis of the ritual you participate in. Your spiritual leader can guide you towards books and studies of history of your faith. The more you understand, the more meaning the ritual will have.

The second thing you can do is create your own personal ritual. Trevrizent is not attending any formal mass, yet he has created his own special way of concentrating on his spirit during the day. This may be accomplished by a specific prayer at a particular time of day, taking time to walk outside to enjoy the magnificence of nature, or taking five minutes to think of people and things you are thankful for.

You may even want to consider creating a personal ritual for your family that several members can participate in. For some families, this may simply be having family dinner together. For others, it could be evening walks or prayers. If we can share something small, yet significant, with those we love, we can heal the Wasteland.

Spiritual Ritual

1. Develop a personal ritual that reminds you of how you are connected to your Spiritual world. This may be a personal mantra or prayer. It may be done by creating a shrine as simple as a table with objects that remind you of those you love.

2. Create a ritual with those you love, which nourishes all in that love. Forcing people to artificially get together will not work, but finding common joys and ways of sharing spirit will.

The Lessons of Direct Experience

Nothing will replace Direct Experience. No books, no movies, no second hand opinions. We must get out there and live life. This applies to our Skills we develop, as well as our Spiritual life.

The closer we get to our Grail, the more obstacles we will encounter. Accept this as part of the process. Do not use obstacles as excuses to quit your Quest.

There are times we will need to seek out Spiritual Guidance. Do this with an open heart and mind. This will be a process of rejection, as well as affirmation.

When things aren't going right, return to the point where positive results were beginning to happen, and see what you can learn. Look for both the good and the bad. Do not expect things to be exactly as they were. The Tao always changes.

The Grail is Transformational. The whole process of working towards the Grail creates the change. This is the image of the Phoenix being reborn after immolation.

We need to treat ourselves to Noble Company as we aim for our Grail. And we need to treat ourselves as nobility also. We must surround ourselves with the best, to make ourselves the best.

If God did not have the right to judge the Neutral Angels, then we too must step back from some of our judgments. Let petty differences fall to the wayside, and let's save our energies for important issues.

Hubris can be the downfall of the most talented of people. We must work to be the best we can be, without inviting too much challenge early in our development. Do not confuse Hubris with Self Respect.

The Right Question is always "What Ails Thee?" When in doubt about a situation, start with this question.

Atonement and Redemption is reserved for the worst of crimes. It is a path that works on apology, forgiveness, giving, and the releasing of hate and anger.

We must create our own personal spiritual rituals to help revitalize our energies. A little time each day focusing on what is important to us can create harmony in life.

Deep down inside, we have a Voice who knows the truth. Take time to listen to it, especially during the most difficult times.

Now we will find out how Gawan is faring. He will have an encounter with the third face of his Triplicate Goddess—Queen Orgeluse.

Neuschwanstein Castle, Germany

Chapter 16 - Castle of Wonders

In the beginning of their friendship, Princess Leia and Han Solo have the same love/hate relationship as Gawan and Queen Orgeluse. Leia uses sharp words to push Han on and keep his ego in check, just like Orgeluse verbally attacks Gawan. Leia denies any love, until Han almost dies in his test of the "Wonder Bed," the one made of carbonite. Gawan will have to survive his Wonder Bed, and another battle, before his love will acknowledge him.

Orgeluse

A year passes, and Gawan meets Vergulaht to battle over Kingrisin's death. It is called off when they are found to be kinfolk, and Ehcunat is discovered to be the guilty person. Gawan and Vergulaht both go for the Grail. It is noted that whoever goes for the Grail approaches it with the sword.

Gawan finds a lady grieving over a dying knight. Gawan takes a linden branch to make a tube to withdraw the bad blood from the injured man and revive him. The man says he was knocked down by Lischois Gwelljus in Logrois, and this lady rescued him.

Gawan follows the bloody trail to Logrois, and finds Orgeluse de Logrois. Gawan is smitten with her, but she says to move on; love with her would be a test. Gawan wants the test, so she sends him to bring her horse, so they could go riding together. When he reaches her horse tied in an orchard, the people there are sad for him, knowing the harsh tests of their mistress. Gawan brings her the horse, and she berates him as they start out. As they ride, Gawan sees a medicinal root. He retrieves it, hoping to use it on the wounded man if their paths cross again.

Orgeluse's squire, Malcreatiure, rides up and warns Gawan not to mess with his lady. Malcreatiure is Cundrie the Sorceress' brother and is as ugly as she is, with tusks of a boar and short, bristly hair. Cundrie and Malcreatiure belong to Queen Secundille, who rules a land where such creatures exist. She had sent them to Anfortas as gifts, hoping to learn about the Grail. Anfortas then sent Malcreatiure to Orgeluse. Gawan flings Malcreatiure away, but the bristles cut Gawan's hand. Malcreatiure follows Orgeluse and Gawan as they ride along.

They find the wounded knight, and Gawan helps him. The man tells Gawan that his trouble came about from Orgeluse, so Gawan should be wise and leave her. While Gawan is helping the wounded man's lady mount her horse, the man jumps on Gawan's horse, Gringuljete. The wounded man and lady ride away. Orgeluse chides Gawan, saying he has gone from knight to page since he met her. She asks if he still wants her love. Then the wounded man comes back, saying he ate with the dogs for four weeks at Arthur's because of Gawan. Gawan recognizes him as Urians, who would have been hung for rape if Gawan had not interceded. The man doesn't care that Gawan saved his life, and says he was taking Gawan's horse anyway. After hearing the whole tale, Orgeluse says she will make the man pay for his crimes. Gawan then takes Malcreatiure's nag, and Malcreatiure goes on foot. Gawan ends up leading the nag because of its poor shape, and it carries his weapons. Orgeluse continues to tease him, now as being a merchant.

After negotiating a deep forest, they see a castle across a river bank. Many women, including four noble women, watch from the windows. The knight Lischois Gwelljus, who serves Orgeluse, waits by the bank to challenge all approachers. Orgeluse taunts Gawan some more, then gets on the ferry to be taken to the other side. Gawan and Lischois fight, with Gawan getting the upper hand. However, Lischois refuses to surrender, preferring to die. Gawan cannot kill him, as he knows they both fight for love of the same woman. Instead, he takes Lischois' horse, which turns out to be Gawan's stolen horse, Gringuljete. Gawan thinks that if Orgeluse has witnessed the fight, she should be his.

The ferryman, Plippalinot, demands Gringuljete as his fee as it was his custom to take the loser's horse from the jousts. Gawan negotiates, and gives Lischois and the nag to the ferryman. The ferryman then offers his home to Gawan. He tells Gawan that Clinschor is the lord here, and this is a land of fantastic adventure.

Gawan goes to Plippalinot's house, which is equal to Arthur's palace in Nantes. All of the ferryman's family help care for Gawan that night. The sons catch larks for dinner, and Bene, the young daughter, is Gawan's dining companion.

Gawan asks who the ladies are who watched them, and he is reluctantly told that he was in the Land of Wonders. The women in the Castle of Wonders are captives and an adventure exists there with the Wonder Bed. The mage Clinschor has kept the women imprisoned until a knight can break the charm of the Bed.

Plippalinot says he ferried Parzival, who was looking for the Grail. The ferryman did not ask Parzival where he was going, nor did he tell of the adventure in the Castle of Wonders, since that information is only volunteered to one who asks. Gawan wants to go to the castle and the ferryman insists on giving his shield. Plippalinot tells Gawan to leave his horse with the Trader at the castle, and buy anything from him. Inside he would find the place deserted, and then Gawan should find the Bed.

Gawan finds the Trader, whose wares are more costly than any Emperor or ruler can afford. The Trader confirms that the ferryman had directed Gawan to him. Gawan asks to see "reasonably priced" brooches or girdles. The Trader offers to watch Gringuljete.

Gawan enters the Castle of Wonders. He finds the main building and the chamber with the Wonder Bed. As Gawan approaches the Bed, it swerves away from him. Gawan jumps on it, and it slams him against the walls as he rides it. After it subsides, five hundred rocks are slung against him, but his shield holds them. Then five hundred crossbows shoot arrows at him, followed by a burly man saying a devil must be keeping him alive. But it's not over yet. A lion attacks, but Gawan is able to kill it. After all that, Gawan passes out.

The Castle of Wonders is inhabited by Gawan's grandmother, Arnive; his mother, Sangive; and his two sisters, Itonje and Cundrie. Neither Gawan nor his relatives recognize each other. Gawan looks dead, so Arnive sends two maidens to see if he is alive. They resuscitate him, and Arnive uses medicines from Cundrie the Sorceress to help him.

Gawan is well cared for by the ladies in the castle in sumptuous surroundings. In the tower there is a Pillar, stolen from Queen Secundille, where he watches various marvels. The Pillar reflects the happenings of the countryside for a range of six miles. From the Tower, Gawan sees Orgeluse riding with a Turkoite, and Gawan wants to fight him.

Gawan is in pain, but is determined to fight. He meets the Turkoite, Florant of Itolac. Gawan wins the joust, and Orgeluse allows him to accompany her. The inhabitants of the castle are not happy when Gawan rides off with Orgeluse.

Orgeluse wants a bough from a tree in Clinschor's forest. Gawan has to jump the river Sabins, but Gringuljete falls in and the two barely make it to the opposite bank. Gawan plucks the branch from the tree, and King Gramoflanz, son of Irot, comes to defend it. He carries a falcon that Itonje sent him. Gramoflanz does not want to fight, especially since he only fights if there are at least two men. Instead, he asks Gawan to bring a ring to Itonje. He said the only one he would fight would be Gawan, as Gawan's father, King Lot, had killed his father. Gawan reveals himself and they plan to meet in battle.

Gawan returns to Orgeluse, who is now repentant for her treatment of him. She says she needed to test him, as she had previously lost another knight, Cidegast, to Gramoflanz. She agrees to go with Gawan to the Castle of Wonders, but is sad. She tells Gawan that Anfortas was wounded in service to her after Cidegast's death. Anfortas had sent the booth of wares that the Trader sold, as token of love. She gave Clinschor the goods, so he would not wrought black magic, but it backfired. She had another knight, Parzival, whom she tried to enlist, but he only wanted his Queen of Pelrapeire. They arrive at the castle, and Gawan asks Orgeluse not to reveal his name.

They are greeted by Clinschor's men and the ferryman with his daughter. Orgeluse wants Lischois and Florant of Itolac taken care of. Gawan has a message sent to Arthur to come witness the joust. Arnive questions the messenger of the contents, but the messenger won't tell anything.

— Summary of *Parzival,* Books x, xi, & xii

Sword Necessary for the Grail

One of my favorite lines in *Parzival* occur in the first paragraph of Book x. "For whoever desires the Grail must come alone with his sword. So should glory be striven for." It is an appropriate phrase to occur in the chapter about the tests of the champion of the Kingdom of the Individual.

In other stories, Gawan's quest is finding a Sword. In the *Perlesvaus,* he is sent to find the sword that was used to behead John the Baptist. At noon time, the hour John was beheaded, the sword starts to bleed and turns a bright green. This mysterious occurrence is tied to other stories of Gawan. Gawan's strength was known to increase before noon, and decrease after that time. Just as the sword bled, so did Gawan's abilities. It is surmised that at one time, Gawan was associated with a Sun God, which explains the increasing and decreasing in his strength during those times.

So, in between all of this talk of compassion and spirituality, we talk of needing a sword. This reminds us that achieving the Grail is not an easy process. We must approach it with a warrior's determination and spirit. Otherwise, we will be easily dismissed.

When Cundrie the Sorceress rode into Arthur's court to criticize Parzival, she also instigated the other knights on the quest which would take them to this castle. They must not have been successful, or they were lagging far behind, because the spell wasn't broken until Gawan showed up. Perhaps they lacked the needed determination and spirit.

It reminds us that we must develop the appropriate skills necessary to achieve the Grail. In recent years, a popular trend emerged claiming that if you just wish and visualize for a certain life, it will come to you automatically. Visualization—that first accidental discovery of the Grail, and being in its presence—is part of the process. But getting back to the Grail takes a lot of hard work and effort. We must come prepared, not only with the proper questions, but with the proper spirit and skills. The wishing and dreaming part of your life should be less than ten percent. Striving is going to be the other ninety percent.

Picking Up the Sword

If you find yourself spending more time daydreaming about your future, than developing the skills needed to shape the future, now is the time to pick up the sword. List the skills you need to work on, and spend time each day working on at least one of them. Your Grail will not be achieved if you do not have your Skills and Determination ready to fight for it.

Tests of Love

> *"What I started to say," he went on, "is that although she is not really a bad person, yet she is unlucky and always has been and I think that there is some kind of whammy in her that carries her luck to other people. That's why I would like you to watch out and not get too tied up with her."*
>
> — Pop Fisher in *The Natural by* Bernard Malamud

> *My service needs no cowards.*
>
> — Orgeluse in *Parzival,* Book x, ¶ 511

The difficulty in finally achieving goals is emphasized in this chapter. Parzival had a willing Goddess of Sovereignty appear to him, but he ended up failing at the Grail Castle; maybe because it was initially too easy for him. Gawan's situation will be more difficult and he knows it right away. His goddess shows herself as a combination of Lady Fortuna, a Flower Bride, and the Loathly Lady. She tells him up front that loving her is going to be a tough decision. Her own people warn Gawan not to go with her. In *The Natural,* Pop Fisher warns Roy not to date Pop's niece, Memo, because she is bad luck. Jenny goes through many relationships, always pushing Forrest Gump away, until she finally accepts his love.

Orgeluse, however, must be a glorious goddess, this is the woman whom Anfortas was wounded for, and other men keep vying for her. She has gone through a series of lovers. Some died for her—all failed her. Her tests are tough, but the rewards must be great.

Gawan's path is mirroring Parzival's, with its own little twists. Both knights helped ladies whose castles were besieged, then left them behind to find the women they will love. Both find women grieving over knights, who are somehow connected to the heroes. Orgeluse even calls Gawan a "Goose," reminding us when Parzival was also called a "Goose."

Orgeluse's name means "Pride." She is also called the Duchess of Logrois, commonly spelled Logres, which refers to the territory we know as England. Arthur is known as the King of Logres. Some say the name came from an old Welsh name *Lloegr,* meaning England, however, some scholars opine there is already a Latin influence on that word. Some translate it as *l'ogres,* which certainly puts a spin on the name as being a land of ogres, or giants. With all of the stories of giants popping up in the legends, this may not be so unlikely. Speaking of names, Princess Leia's last name is *Organa.*

Orgeluse is, of course, our third face of the Goddess of Sovereignty—the Crone. Though Orgeluse is a gorgeous Crone, she nevertheless displays the arrogance, wisdom, and no-nonsense approach afforded a wizened Crone. Immediately, she tells Gawan that loving her is difficult, and he shouldn't do it. He should run from her if he can. But he is hooked. He tells her that he only wants love that is earned. Anything else is for sinners.

Madame X (Madame Pierre Gautreau)
by John Singer Sargent (1856–1925)

The Metropolitan Museum of Art,
Arthur Hoppock Hearn Fund, 1916. (16.53)
Oil on Canvas, 1884. 82 ¼ x 43 ¼ in.
Photo: ©1997 The Metropolitan Museum of Art

Orgeluse represents the demanding parts of a project that can only be stuck to because we love it so much. The trials and tribulations will drag us down, but we are willing to take on anything, because we anticipate the rewards at the end of the trail. Orgeluse tells Gawan that her service has no cowards, so only the bravest need apply for this job. This only happens with goals that are dear to our hearts.

Orgeluse's tests go beyond ordinary obstacles. They are the final mountain that must be climbed before we begin our downhill strides.

This painting was the model for Kurtz' painting of his fiancée in the film *Heart of Darkness.*

Creatures of the Boar

In *The Fisher King,* an irate radio listener calls Jack Lucas a pig. The listener isn't too far off in her evaluation.

Malcreatiure and Cundrie are more interesting than one would think—they have boar tusks. They both belonged to Queen Secundille, the patroness of Parzival's brother, Feirefiz. Supposedly, the creatures were made by the daughters of Adam dabbling in herbs. (Certainly a warning against women who worked with medicines, who would later be branded as witches.) The boar references go back to a time when the Boar God and Sow Goddess held a high position in mythologies. In Norse myth, it was Freya riding the back of her lover in the form of a golden bristled boar. In Celtic myth, we have Cerridwen, the Sow Goddess, who also has a magical cauldron. A potion from her cauldron became the poetic wisdom and vision of the poet Taliesin. There is also Henwen, the great sow described in *The Welsh Triads,* who terrorized the Welsh, British, and Irish lands while giving birth to magical animals. *The Mabinogion* gives us the story of Arthur hunting the dreaded boar Twrch Trwyth. In Indian stories, Vishnu was incarnated as Varaha the Boar. He also gave birth to three boar sons.

The Boar was a sacrificer and sacrifice. The beautiful Adonis was sacrificed by Ares disguised as a boar. Sacrifices of boar were made to Demeter and Atalante. Vishnu's boar sons were also sacrificed.

When Gawan tries to push Malcreatiure away, he his cut by the bristles. Undoubtedly, Gawan has been marked by the Boar, a form of a small sacrifice.

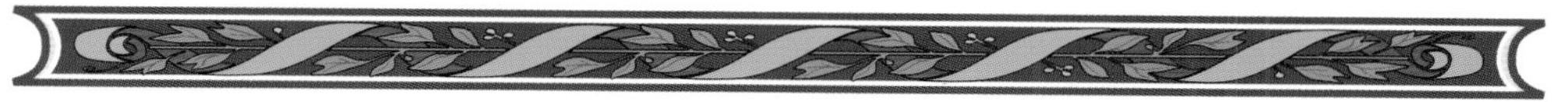

Doubtful Justice

The charade with the wounded man, Urians, points out the dubious nature of the world around us. Here Gawan shows compassion towards a man, who happens to be someone who holds a grudge against Gawan. Gawan's reward? His horse Gringuljete is stolen, and replaced with a miserable nag. The unfortunate fact in life is that sometimes, especially when under the spell of Lady Fortuna, we may do good deeds, but are rewarded with harshness. This becomes the excuse of many people to give up. Why should kids say no to drugs when drug dealers are driving BMWs? Why should somebody work hard at a blue collar job, when scamming old people reaps millions? Murderers get reprieves because they can afford the best lawyers. The answer is that eventually justice is done. The drug dealers die young, dishonest con men go to jail, murderers must still look behind their backs for those wanting revenge. As Harold Kushner noted, Bad Things Do Happen to Good People, but we do not give up because the Wheel of Fortune has turned. Have faith that it will come back up.

We can also take another view of a Karmic law. Gawan brought it on himself. Arthurian law stated that Urians should have been hanged for raping a woman. Even now, Orgeluse says she will have to give justice to the woman, since Arthur's court did not. Gawan had helped Urians, because he had surrendered himself to Gawan. Now the price has come back to Gawan, because he had wronged the victim in the first place. He must make amends for that crime.

When you are handed a raw deal, try to make the best of a bad situation. Look for the positive possibilities that come out of bad times. Riding a miserable nag isn't so bad. Often, we are rushing so quickly towards our goals, that sometimes we need to change horses to get a different perspective. Sometimes it just forces us to slow down and reevaluate. Sometimes it makes us more efficient. Sometimes it makes us appreciate what we do have.

The Ferryman

Don't pay the ferryman!
Don't even fix a price!
Don't pay the ferryman
Until he gets you to the other side.

— from the song
"Don't Pay the Ferryman"
by Chris de Burgh

Apocalypse Now's Ferryman—
the Freelance Photographer.
(Photographer-Dennis Hopper, Willard-Martin Sheen)

"Yes," said the ferryman, "it is a very beautiful river. I love it above everything. I have often listened to it, gazed at it, and I have always learned something from it. One can learn much from a river."

— Vasudeva in *Siddhartha* by Hermann Hesse

Siddhartha takes a few turns in life before realizing the value of the lessons of life along the river. He ends up living in a hut with Vasudeva, the Ferryman. The first time he meets Vasudeva, he was but a young ascetic beginning his life on the road. At that time, Vasudeva knew Siddhartha would return. Vasudeva correctly predicts the first lesson that Siddhartha would learn along the river. The lesson was one of Being and Returning.

The Freelance Photographer who instructs Willard how to enter Kurtz' territory, was *Apocalypse Now's* Ferryman. Without the Photographer, Willard's entire crew could have been killed. And in the middle of all of his hallucinogenic rantings, there is a

certain wisdom that emerges, such as revealing "if" is in the middle of "life."

The most famous Ferryman in myth is Charon—the decrepit, hunched figure who brings souls across to the UnderWorld. He has to be paid if you expect to get past Cerberus, the three headed dog who loves to chew on souls, and not drown in the poisonous river Styx which winds about the UnderWorld.

The Ferryman is an Initiator. He is the Shaman. He is the Priest who intercedes on your behalf. He is the one who will carry you across to the Mysteries on the other bank, the OtherWorld that holds secrets of life and death. Sometimes he is depicted as a Watchman at a Gate, sometimes a One-Eyed Herdsman looking over a flock of wild animals. Our Trader at the Gate, with his array of costly jewels, is an Initiator. Before you can go any further, you must pay, appease, cajole, negotiate, bribe, use magic words, or intimidate the Ferryman. If he likes you, be prepared to meet the hardest challenges of your life.

We are dealing here with aspects of the Eleusinian Mysteries, which center around the Greek Goddess Demeter and her daughter, Persephone, a Summer Maid who had been dragged to the UnderWorld of Hades. The background makes more sense with the study of Gawan's adventures, and how he experiences a death, then returns to life.

Demeter is a Great Mother figure who is a goddess of Fertility. Her daughter is Persephone, also known as Core/Kore. Some say Kore was the root name of the Koran, pertaining to an early goddess-based religion in the Middle East. She is also noted as being the "core" found in the apple. With a little imagination, you can see the connection of the apple in the mouth of the Yule roasted pig, as Demeter was one of our Sow goddesses mentioned earlier.

Hades is the Lord of the UnderWorld, and the brother of Demeter and Zeus, the chief god. One day he sees Persephone frolicking among the flowers, and he desires her. He opens a chasm and kidnaps her, carrying her away in his chariot. Heart-broken when she cannot find her daughter, Demeter is shocked to learn that other gods looked the other way during the abduction. She disguises herself and searches earth, finally collapsing, weeping by a well in Eleusis. There she is befriended by a family, who takes her in as a nurse to the baby son. Demeter decides to make the baby immortal through a ritual of holding him over a fire each night, but the spell is broken when the horrified mother discovers the ceremony. Demeter reveals herself, and says that she will return to teach her mysteries, as one of the family's sons had given her information about Persephone. Despite Demeter's pleas to the gods at Olympus, Persephone is not returned to her. Demeter withdraws her fertility, and the land becomes bare—a Wasteland. Everyone, even the gods and goddesses, suffers. Finally, Zeus says Persephone could return from the UnderWorld, as long as she had not eaten anything. Persephone reunites with her mother at Eleusis, but when it is discovered she had eaten seven pomegrante seeds from Hades' garden, the deal is called off. Rhea, the mother of Zeus,

Return of Persephone
by Frederic Leighton (1830–1896)
Oil on canvas, ca. 1890–91. 80 x 60 in.

Demeter, and Hades, is called in to arbitrate, and they reach a compromise: Persephone will spend half the year above ground, and half the year in the UnderWorld. While Persephone is with her mother, the world is in blossom, and while she is below, there is cold and barrenness. This is our cycle of the Summer and the Winter, of Death and Rebirth.

Demeter did return with her Mysteries, and a shrine was built at Eleusis. We can only make reasonable guesses at the rituals during the Eleusinian celebrations—revealing the Mysteries could result in death, and certain aspects were kept secret. It is reminiscent of the secrets of the Grail mysteries. It reminds me of Branwen's Cauldron, which could bring dead heroes back to life, but they could not speak. It is also reminiscent of the Grail Castle Court who remains silent in the presence of its potential hero.

We do know that these were nine-day rituals, and that initiates were not allowed to arrive by chariot. There were three main stages of initiation—the *Dromena,* the Things Done; the *Legomena,* Things Said; and the *Deiknymena,* the Things Shown. Those who passed the initiation and returned, participated in a separate ritual, the *Epopteia,* Having Seen. Other stages of the ritual have been theorized, such as the rituals being presided over by a High Priest and Priestess, with a ritual of *hieros gamos,* the Sacred Marriage. Priestesses carried the *Heira,* or sacred objects, similar to the Grail Maiden in the Grail procession. Initiates fasted, then broke their fast with a drink known as *kykeon,* similar to a barley mint beverage that Demeter drunk. Participants enacted going into an UnderWorld environment, then being reborn into the new world. Sophocles has assured us that the ritual was emotionally satisfying.

When Gawan passes that first joust and proves to be a tough negotiator with Plippalinot by giving him an appropriate fee, Gawan has formally started his initiation process. He will be able to cross over into the Land of Wonders to a Castle inhabited by women, just as an Eleusian initiate goes to pay homage to two goddesses. The women in the castle are held captive by a powerful mage, just as Persephone was held prisoner by Hades. While Persephone stayed with Hades, the land was bare, just as Clinschor was a barren man in a Wasteland.

When the Ferryman insists on giving Gawan his shield, he is the Initiator who gives a totem of safety to the student. When I read this passage, I imagined the shield to be that of Heracles (Hercules), another hero who successfully passed over the River Styx into the UnderWorld, and returned. In Hesiod's poem, "The Shield of Herakles," many magical scenes are depicted including one of a Fisherman in a boat fishing. The final blow that Heracles wields upon his enemy is a strike to the thigh.

This Ferryman as Initiator gives us the instructions to approach our upcoming tasks with Strength. As we move higher up the Ladder of Success, we must anticipate more frequent, and more vicious attacks. These may be personal, financial, maybe even physical, so we must come prepared.

The warning not to approach the Castle of Wonders with a horse parallels with the taboo of Eleusinian initiates riding in on a chariot. The ban comes from several possibilities. Hades abducted Persephone in his chariot, so perhaps they do not wish to offend Persephone. Or, this shows respect for another aspect of Demeter, which was Demeter-Mare, a horse goddess. It is also another reminder to approach our work with an air of Humility. Rich and poor alike walk to their ritual, a reminder that we should all be humble, even as we strive for greatness.

The Trader with his wares is the one who oversees the Gifts for the Goddess. The gifts originally came from the Grail King. It is a reminder that we must come with the best we can offer. We have so many natural gifts to bring to our friends and family. We do not need to keep others outside of the Castle, but we should bring them inside to be shared.

The Ferryman

1. You may need the help of someone in the inner circle of your desired goal. Determine who this is and make an effort to befriend him or her. Do so with a true willingness to be a friend who is interested in the same arena. Don't be sneaky or manipulative. You are two people who have the same interests and your friendship must be respected. Honor the wisdom of your newfound friend.

2. At an individual level, you already have an intuitive voice of wisdom who can give you the directions to cross over to your next level of involvement. Listen to that voice. It is more than just talking to yourself, it is learning to listen to yourself.

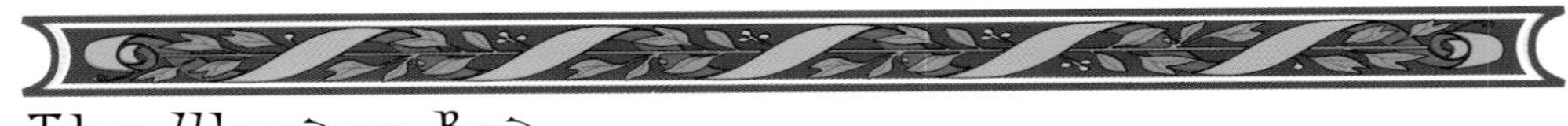

The Wonder Bed

When you are going after a woman, what could be more of a test than a bed? Especially this bed. A bucking bronco bed, arrows and stones, and a hungry lion. If you can survive this bed, a lady is no problem. There is some irony that this bed was created by Clinschor, who is castrated. Another sexless mage, Jabba the Hutt, receives Han Solo captured in a Carbonite Bed. Han's test is strictly body conditioning and survival. He will come back from the dead, just like Gawan did.

When Gawan conquers the Wonder Bed, he frees the maidens of the castle. It makes you wonder what those secret Sacred Marriage rites were like. No wonder Sophocles said participants in the Mysteries were emotionally satisfied. It is no surprise that this Perilous Bed is found in the Castle of Wonders. Sex, certainly one of the most powerful wonders of the world, keeps everything going, and going, and going.

There are many rituals of the male and female energies that are played out in spiritual practices, both physical and symbolic. In the East, *Tantra* and Taoist practices combined sex and meditative practices that were to promote health as well as heighten a sense of spirituality. In an effort to focus all energies towards devotion, some religions forbid their priests and nuns the sexual experience. Even with those type of situations, there are marriage rites, such as the nun's vow of commitment to Christ with the Church as her husband.

Another Bed in Arthurian literature is found in Malory's *Morte D'Arthur.* Galahad discovers this bed with a sword on a floating ship built by King Solomon according to the instructions of his wife. She ordered a bed made from a tree planted by Eve, and under which Abel was slain. As it was being cut, the tree bled, but Solomon's Wife ordered the carpenter to keep going under penalty of death. The magnificent bed was covered with silk, and King David's Sword was placed at its foot. Everything about the ship was opulent, except for the sword's sheath, which was made of hemp. This angered Solomon, but his wife said an appropriate sheath would be made at the time that the greatest hero found the sword. The sheath was to be made by Dindrane, Perceval's sister, woven from her hair. The ship was set adrift, and was untouched through the centuries, until Galahad retrieved the sword. Though both Galahad and Dindrane are virgins, the underlying message of a sword from a sacred bed being placed into a sheath of hair, is a roundabout form of Sacred Marriage. Later in the story, after both have died, they are buried together in Sarras, just like a married couple.

The Bed is a place of Love and Truth. People can play games there, but eventually Truth is revealed. While in Skylar's bed, Will Hunting has to face his feelings of potential loss and rejection. When Roy Hobbs sleeps with Memo Paris, his nightmares and pre-dream images emanate hard, painful truths. Forrest Gump knows true love with Jenny, and it is when she leaves the bed empty that he faces his worse loss. Jack's depression keeps him from totally accepting Anne's love.

We live in a world where sex sells everything from cars to toothpaste. We are as guilty of banalizing the power of sex as the Puritans were of hiding it. Sex is a force which everyone must deal with, whether it is from a range of abstinence to obsessive bed hopping. It is a test which everyone encounters—some pass, some fail.

We must remember that Gawan came to this bed because of Love. He was certainly tempted into others, and there are plenty of Arthurian tales where casual sex is condoned, but in this story, commitment is the value in the forefront. The toughest tests of real Love are often tested in the bed. Gawan has multiple tests, all of them difficult, but his worst injuries came from this adventure. Yet he still fights on, because he is in service to Love. This is a practical, and a spiritual lesson to be learned of life.

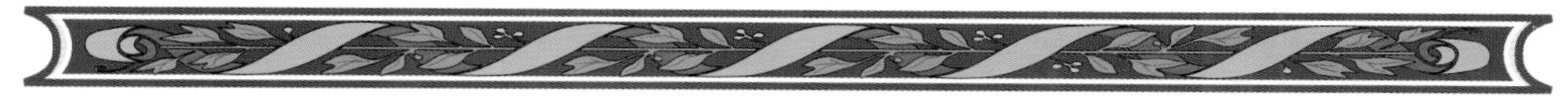

Almost Death

I dream of journeys repeatedly:
Of flying like a bat deep into a narrowing tunnel,
Of driving alone, without luggage, out on a long peninsula,
The road lined with snow-laden second growth,
A fine dry snow ticking the windshield,
Alternate snow and sleet, no on-coming traffic,
And no lights behind, in the blurred side-mirror,
The road changing from glazed tarface to a rubble of stone,
Ending at last in a hopeless sand-rut,
Where the car stalls,
Churning in a snowdrift
Until the headlights darken.

— from "The Far Field" by Theodore Roethke

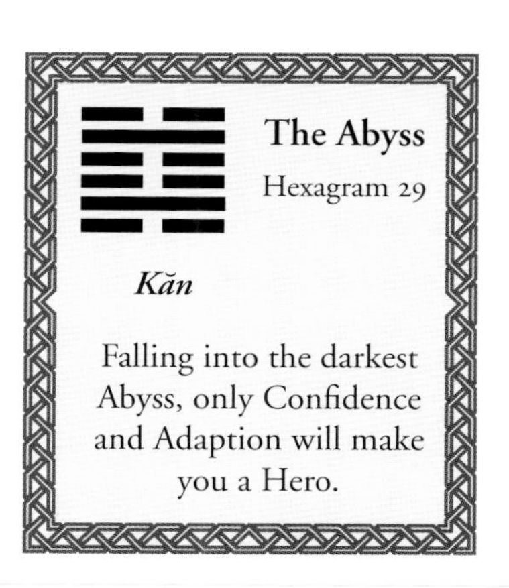

My life closed twice before its close;
It yet remains to see
If Immortality unveil
a third event to me,

So huge, so hopeless to conceive,
As these that twice befell.
Parting is all we know of heaven,
And all we need of hell.
— poem by Emily Dickenson

Roy Hobbs has to constantly deal with his maimed mage in the form of the Judge, who curses the team with bribes and tricks to keep them losing. Roy is surrounded with perils in the form of Max, Gus, and Memo. Meetings with the Judge and his henchman take place in a room devoid of light. Eventually, at a party given by Memo and Gus, Roy takes his second brush with death. Luckily, he awakes in a Castle of Maidens in the form of Tower Maternity to receive his necessary healing.

In other Grail legends, the test of the knight is in his ability to handle the difficulties of a Perilous Bridge which must be crossed to enter a castle. Sometimes there are battles with lions or giants at the end of the bridge, but often it is the bridge itself which holds the peril. In *Apocalypse Now,* there is a bridge where Willard must choose to turn his boat around or go forward. The bridge is so dangerous and its surroundings so out of control that no one knows who is in command. Directionless soldiers are continuing to play the game of death. They are lost souls who do not know how to go forward, or how to come back. Crossing that bridge is crossing over into the OtherWorld. There is no turning back and no one to rescue you.

The Judge bribes Roy Hobbs
(Judge-Robert Prosky)

In Chrétien's story, "The Knight of the Cart (Lancelot)," Gwenevere has been abducted by Meleagant, and both Lancelot and Gawain go to rescue her. There are two bridges entering the land of Gorre. One is the Sword Bridge, and the other is the Underwater Bridge, also known as the Lost Bridge in the Vulgate Cycle. Lancelot crosses the Sword Bridge, which is a deadly sharp blade planted above a turbulent river. To go across, he must remove his protective boots and gloves to be able to hold the blade as he inches his way across. He manages to cross the bridge, but his hands and feet are cut up. Gawain goes on the Underwater Bridge, which has an equal amount of water above and below it. During the crossing he slips and almost drowns. When he is found on the banks of Gorre, he is half dead. The message here is that no matter what path you take in rescuing the Goddess of Sovereignty, the tests are challenging to the point of Death. That must not deter you. Anything worthwhile is difficult and demanding.

In *Parzival,* Gawan almost dies trying to reach his quest. His healing comes from Cundrie the Sorceress' medicines, ones also used at the Grail Castle. In fact, hearing her name makes him believe he is close to Munsalvaesche, and it gives him hope that he is close to the Grail. He comes back, ready to take on more challenges.

The Eleusinian Mysteries and many other religious practices enacted the myth of dying and rebirth because that is the cycle of our living life. We always look to be Renewed. Every time we walk into a Church, a Synagogue, a Mosque, a Tree Grove, we are looking for renewal. Every time we enter a Sweat Lodge, a Sauna, Mineral Springs, or our Daily Shower, we wash away the grime and problems of the day. We call it Rebirth, Resurrection, Reincarnation. We want a second chance at a new day and a new life.

Whenever we go out to new adventures, a part of our old life and old illusions must die. This is not done without pain or effort. Sometimes the pain is so terrible, we fool ourselves with false adventures into the OtherWorld using drink, drugs, and other addictions. We awake thinking we are renewed, but we are only pulled back to more suffering and real death. And I mean Real Death. We must learn to deal with the problems of true adventures involving ourselves and our loved ones, because that is the natural course of working towards the Grail. There will be difficulties, and there will be tests. We will experience a form of death many times before we actually cross over. But we will hold on and fight as well as we can. The reward is the Awakening to a New Life.

Being Reborn

In addition to any religious services that give you a sense of rebirth, develop your own rituals that cleanse you of the difficulties of life, and renew your Spirit. You may have small rituals that prepare yourself for finishing the old day, and ones to start the new day. You may have more elaborate ones to celebrate surviving very difficult times. Do them with the sense of a joy and excitement that brings new life.

Beyond Brotherly Love

In *Parzival,* Gawan kisses his mother and sisters, then compares his maiden sisters to Orgeluse. He decides that it is definitely Orgeluse in his heart. Gawan doesn't know yet that he is in the company of his family, so the observation is innocent. In *Diu Crône (The Crown),* Gawein's grandmother offers Gawein the choice of his mother or sister as a wife, in reward for freeing the castle. Again, this is done in total innocence of everyone's identities. Even Luke Skywalker kisses his sister, Leia, with romantic inclinations, before he discovers the truth.

This leads us to the uncomfortable presence of incestuous relationships in myth. I chose not to ignore this side of myth, because as a grade school girl reading the Bible and books of myth which had these stories, I had confused, conflicted feelings, and did not feel comfortable talking about it with adults.

In Arthurian myth's most famous example, Arthur mates with his half sister, Morgause, which brings about the birth of their son, Mordred. In other myths we have Zeus and Hera, and Isis with Osiris. Sometimes in myth, it's only close sharing of powers between brothers and sisters, as with Apollo and Artemis, or Merlin and Ganieda. Even the Bible carries its stories of inappropriate relationships. Lot slept with his daughters, Abraham was married to his sister, and Moses' mother was also his great-aunt. The Egyptian dynasties of Ptolemy, which included Cleopatra who married two of her brothers, may have enforced regal incest to continue their solar god blood lines. Other European and Middle Eastern tribes and monarchies had their own sanctioned, close bloodlines. Some royal families today still require marriage within the approved royal family. In the case of Arthur and Morgause, there is an interesting twist in terms of the recognition of inheriting kingship. In a matriarchy, succession is determined by the mother, in a patriarchy, by the father. In this story, the son is guaranteed kingship through both lines. Mordred, however, will bear the taint of his parents' relationship and that guaranteed kingship will only bring about doom.

In some interpretations, these stories represent the balancing and joining of the male and female energies, both within ourselves and in our real life. In the myths, the male and female partners share equal power or responsibilities and it is the co-mingling of these powers that presents a whole, the balancing of the Yin/Yang. It may also represent the splitting of one character into two, further demonstrating masculine/feminine attributes, and then the rejoining of the single identity. When you read stories of this kind, try to understand if the story has an inner meaning that goes beyond sensationalism.

Pillar of the Soul

Wisdom hath builded her house, she hath hewn out her seven pillars.
— The Bible, Proverbs 9:1 KJV (Tanakh, Kethuvim, Proverbs)

Gawan has been able to recuperate. He then expands his horizons by climbing into a Great Tower which houses a Pillar of Marvels. That tower is an *Axis Mundi,* a Center of the Soul, and within it is a Pillar which reflects truth of all that goes around it. It is the Mirror of the Soul which only knows Truth.

Pillars have long had symbolic meanings of strength and wisdom. They represent male power, often balanced by female power. In this story, we have a Castle of Maidens, with a Pillar in the center of its tower. Even in the United States, we see this balance of powers on the Mall in Washington D.C. At one end is the round Capitol Dome, and at the other end is the majestic obelisk of the Washington Monument. Don't think for a moment that this was a coincidence in urban planning. Our founding fathers were Freemasons who understood the nature of Sacred Geometry. This was Western *feng shui* at its finest. At the Masonic Memorial in Alexandria, Virginia, you can still see Masonic artifacts belonging to George Washington.

Pillars flank Egyptian temple entrances and the Temple of Solomon. In India, the Pillar is found in the phallic form of the *lingam.* Both Hercules and Samson are tested with Pillars. Sophia speaks from a Pillar of Fire.

When we think of the image of the Pillar, we think of a supporting foundation for a great building. When we speak of someone being a Pillar of the Community, we mean that person is a source of strength and stability. When we bring together all of the attributes of the Pillar—Wisdom, Strength, Truth, and Stability—we see what we can possess within ourselves. The development of Spiritual Strength relies on the ability to reflect Truth and Stability. Our words and visions will have meaning. We are able to count on ourselves during spiritual crises, and others can also turn to us during difficult times. For these reasons, we hold the image and the concept of the Pillar close to our hearts during our reach for the Grail.

Washington Monument

Leaving the Castle

Sagrada Familia Church by Antonio Gaudi

Gawan has passed a major test and is rewarded for his efforts, but there are conditions to becoming the hero of a castle. Namely, the inhabitants don't want him to leave. The ladies there, already dependent on him, don't want him searching adventures as an errant knight.

Many people empathize with that situation. You have worked hard building your own company or establishing yourself in a corporate environment, and you are rewarded for those efforts—so rewarded that you cannot get away from the castle when a true sense of adventure calls. For many financially successful people, their dinners, play, and family life are dictated by their work. This is no problem if this work is your true Grail, but if your yearning is elsewhere, then you must decide to break away.

Gawan still has not won Orgeluse's heart, and when he sees her with a another man, he is inflamed with jealousy. When his love is out riding with another, no Castle of Wonders is going to hold him back. So it is with our Grail. When we see others accomplishing what we desire, we become jealous. Sometimes we are jealous of the accolades of the Grail, but often it is just envy at being in the circle of the Grail. It is the Doing and the Being that really matters. Orgeluse is merely riding with another, but that is enough for Gawan. He must be in her presence and there is nothing he won't do to be with her.

The Tree Branch

Orgeluse sends Gawan to retrieve a branch that comes from a tree representing the Tree of Life. No jewels, no gold, no material wealth. She desires a wreath from a magical forest. It was said that fruit from Yggdrasil would guarantee fertility, so we have Orgeluse craving new life.

There will be no Ferryman to help Gawan across the river this time. It will be his own courage, strength, skills, and a horse of Destiny which gets him safely to the other side. Gawan and Gringuljete almost drown in the trip, but manage to retrieve that sacred branch. Once Gawan has the wreath, coming back is easier. Once you pass the hardest parts of your test, doing them again becomes easier and easier. Your skills and your experience are honed.

Gawan finally passes Orgeluse's big challenge. She admits that all her nastiness and challenges were tests. Others had died or were seriously wounded in the process, so she can only enlist the best and the strongest. Her signal of acceptance means the most difficult tests are behind, and the final goal is around the corner. Gawan, King of the Land of Wonders, will marry his Queen. The King of the Individual has achieved enough experience to be successful, and will serve those he loves.

When we approach our Grail, we are plucking from the Tree of Life. Our hardest tests will come during this time. They are ones we must face alone. We have had many teachers and initiators to help us get this far, but the final efforts must come from ourselves. When we achieve this, we unite with a side of us that knows boundless love, and that is what we share with others.

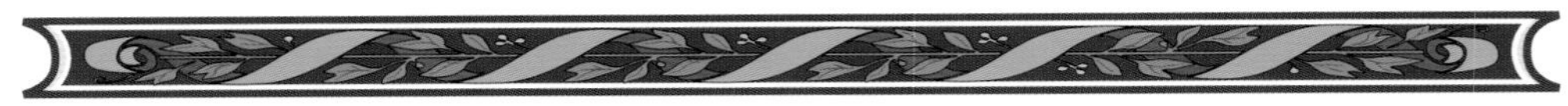

Sins of the Father

Gramoflanz is a major key in learning to let go of punishments and revenges exacted by the "sins of the fathers." It is the coming together of the Hatfields and McCoys with feuds that go back generations, and have nothing to do with the people of the present. We are still plagued with these problems—just look at the border and civil wars around the world.

At one time, Gramoflanz tried to win Orgeluse's love, and it was he who killed Cidegast. Now his thoughts have turned to loving the daughter of his enemy, à la *Romeo and Juliet.* But because of the old feud, he cannot directly approach her. Ironically, Gramoflanz doesn't even know what his enemy looks like when he stands in front of him, yet still feels he must fight Gawan for revenge.

There is a need for reconciliation, and now there is a King who is strong enough to bring it about. Gawan will again take responsibility for acts he did not commit.

Sending the Message

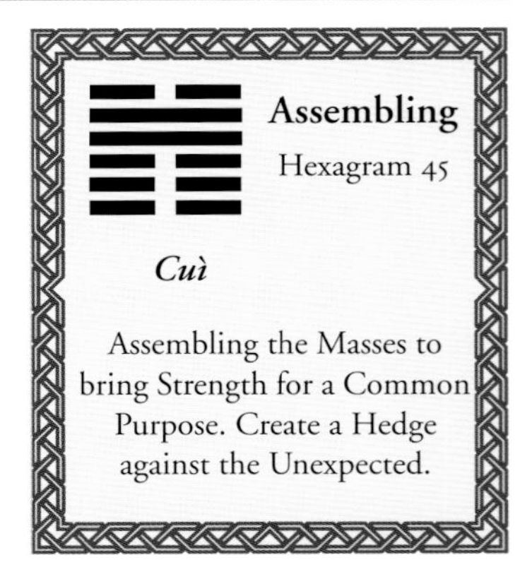

The messenger will not reveal Gawan's message for Arthur to anyone, not even to Queen Arnive. He is setting a great plan in motion, but until the right time comes, he will not involve extraneous people or activities. This is like our unconscious mind working out problems, while our conscious mind is unaware of what is going on. When we are close to a breakthrough or insight, the unconscious mind will start bringing everything together and notifying the conscious. Until then, the message is only directed to the inner core which has to resolve deeper problems.

It may be that we have decided that a situation is not as outrageous as we originally thought. Perhaps we have had an anger which has cooled down, and dialogue can begin. Perhaps a new interest has been subtly sparked, and is slowly surfacing in your life. In due time, what is important will be revealed. It may only be a feeling or an intuition, but when the time comes, the message will be announced and the motivations understood.

The Lessons of Castle of Wonders

- To approach the Grail, we must approach with the Sword. This means we must develop our skills to achieve our Grail.
- The closer we get to our Grail, the more difficult and threatening our tests will be. Only the focus on the Love for our Grail will enable us to go on.
- Sometimes, good things happen to bad people, and bad things happen to good people. No matter what, we should have faith that eventual justice is done.
- The Ferryman is the Initiator who takes us over to the land of our Grail. He gives us important messages to help us along our journey.
- The Bed is a place of Love and Truth. Without a foundation of love, the tests and truths found here are crippling. Success will be a glorious union of a growing relationship.
- We will endure tests that almost take our lives. This is all part of the cycle of dying to the old way of life, to be stronger for the next life. After we survive these tests we will be renewed and reborn.
- There are times when we must leave the comforts of our current successes, which hold us back if we let them. Keep on the path of adventure, and keep after your love.
- On the path of the Grail lives the Tree of Life. Being courageous enough to pluck a branch from this tree means getting closer to your goal.
- We may not be aware of problems we are working on in our inner lives, but we can trust that this process leads to the lessening of pain and healing of old wounds. When the proper time comes, all will be revealed.

Gawan knows it is time to heal old wounds and start a reconciliation among families. Many healings begin as families and foes find unification.

Peaceable Kingdom by Edward Hicks (1780–1849)
National Gallery of Art, Washington, Gift of Edgar William and Bernice Chrysler Garbisch
Oil on Canvas, 1834. 29 3/8 x 35 1/2 in.

Chapter 17 - Reconciliations

When Lt. Dan comes to Forrest's and Jenny's wedding, he brings his fiancée with him. A woman of Asian descent, she is the one who has allowed him to embrace love. As important as it was for Dan to deal with his physical limitations, it was more important for him to look beyond the emotional pain he suffered during the war. It was a big step for him to welcome a woman who might have easily been associated with the enemy. The magnitude of Lt. Dan's step of reconciling his anger towards the enemy must be appreciated. It is a microcosm of the possibilities of what can be done at a larger scale in the world today.

Gawan and the Courts

Gawan allows Lischois and Florant to be set free. The four queens of the castle come out, and Gawan asks to sit by Itonje. He lets her know Gramoflanz is interested in her, and gives her the ring. She admits Gramoflanz is her love, but asks Gawan not to tell the others. She hates Orgeluse for wanting him dead. She is candid about her secrets, but Gawan still does not reveal he is her brother. A great feast ensues, and that night Gawan and Orgeluse get together.

The squire brings Gawan's message to Ginover, who is happy to hear that Gawan is well. She tells the squire to go secretly from her and present the message in court with great fanfare. The message is for Arthur to come to Gawan who prepares for battle. The court is happy to hear from Gawan and prepares for the journey. The squire returns to Gawan, and delivers the message that Arthur will come.

Gawan asks Arnive how the Castle came to be enchanted. She tells the story of how King Ibert castrated Clinschor after catching him in bed with his wife, Queen Iblis. Clinschor went to Persida, where magic was invented, and learned to control the good and bad spirits. He took over the Castle of Wonders from Gramoflanz' father, King Irot. He then placed a curse preventing anyone found on the land and castle from leaving. Gawan broke the curse by surviving the test of the Wonder Bed.

Arthur arrives and sets up camp. As Arthur's host passed through Orgeluse's lands, her men jousted with Arthur's men, not knowing Arthur was coming at Gawan's request. Gawan reunites Arthur with his mother and sister, and introduces his nieces. Everyone now realizes that Gawan is related to the four queens. Orgeluse releases the men she captured from Arthur. Arthur then sends a message to Gramoflanz, asking if he still wants to joust now that Arthur's army is there.

Gawan rides out alone for a practice ride, and encounters a knight along the river Sabins. The knight, all dressed in red, has a bough from the same tree where Gawan took his wreath. Gawan thinks this knight is Gramoflanz, and the two fight. Meanwhile, Gramoflanz, in a tent, receives Arthur's message. Bene, the ferryman's daughter, has also come with Itonje's ring. Gramoflanz still plans to fight. As the messengers return, they come across Gawan battling the Red Knight. When the messengers call Gawan by name, the Red Knight, who is Parzival, realizes who he is fighting and stops the fight. Parzival reveals himself, and Gawan, still recovering from his previous wounds, faints from battling hard. A squire revives him.

The jousts are set against Gramoflanz's army. Gramoflanz arrives, but Gawan is tired from fighting Parzival. Bene notices Gawan's weakness, and tries to help him. Gramoflanz postpones the battle, but Parzival offers himself to fight. Gramoflanz insists on Gawan, which upsets Bene. Gramoflanz wants to send a message of service to Itonje, which also upsets Bene since he will fight her mistress' brother. Gramoflanz leaves.

Parzival is introduced to the four queens. Gawan tells Bene not to tell Itonje of the impending joust. Bene knows it is a disastrous situation, because the death of either Gawan or Gramoflanz will devastate Itonje. Parzival is reunited with Arthur's court and he asks permission to do the joust with Gramoflanz the next day. Gawan will not allow it.

Parzival spends part of the night repairing his armor, and sneaks out early the next day to fight Gramoflanz. When Gawan and Arthur arrive at the battlefield, Parzival is about to win, but the fight is halted. Gawan then offers Gramoflanz a night of rest. Gramoflanz wants Arthur's assurance that the right man shows up.

Itonje hears about the joust, and admits her love for Gramoflanz to Arnive. Arnive then sends for Arthur, and Itonje says she and Gramoflanz have loved each other sight unseen. Gramoflanz' love is confirmed when he sends a letter of love and ring to Itonje. Arthur sends Bene to Gramoflanz with a message for Gramoflanz to come meet him. Arthur secures a truce from Orgeluse, whose heart was softening due to Gawan's embraces.

Gramoflanz comes with King Brandelidelin, his maternal uncle. They sit with Ginover and Itonje, until Bradelidelin leaves to meet with Arthur in another tent. Brandelidelin and Arthur decide there should be no battle. Everyone is brought together for reconciliation. Itonje and Gramoflanz are to wed, as are Lischois and Cundrie (Gawan's sister), and Florant and Sangive. Orgeluse pledges her lands to Gawan publicly. Amid all this revelry, Parzival thinks of his wife and leaves.

— Summary of *Parzival,* Books XIII & XIV

King of the Realm of the Individual

Our mirror world is converging even faster now. Gawan's pursuit of Orgeluse has resulted in massive changes in the Land of Wonders. The bitterness and curses of the land came from a maimed king, a castrated mage. Because this infertile mage will never have a son to rule, the new king is determined by tests and trials, instead of a birthright. Gawan has succeeded, and is now King of the Land of Wonders. Technically, Gramoflanz should be king, as the lands originally belonged to his father. As mighty as he was, he wasn't great enough to break the spell, or gain Orgeluse's favor. We may have fantasies of inheriting wealth, but most of what people own are from their own efforts. Fortunes change hands many times. The Kingdom of the Individual is ruled by strong action.

Gawan could have decided to just ride against Gramoflanz. Instead, Gawan decides it is time to start reconciliation. He wants more than just wearing a crown in his own lands. He wants a better life for all involved.

It is the King of the Individual who forges a way for the Spirit and the Community to start coming together.

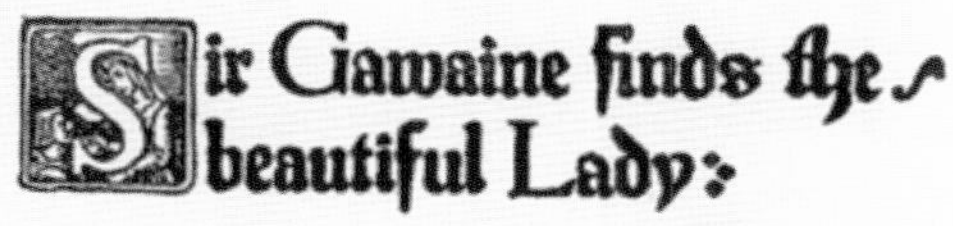

"Sir Gawaine finds the beautiful Lady"
by Howard Pyle (1853–1911)
Illustration, 1903

Path to Peace

The Tenth Perfection is Serenity. That is a Peace which is so pure and calm that all other troubles fall by the wayside. Peace is determined by careful thought and orchestration. Gawan has carefully brought together the King of the Community with the Queens of the Land of Wonders, who are all related to each other. The Queens are themselves representatives of the three stages of the Triplicate Goddess, who now reunite with the world which has been cut off from them. Gawan also knows to send the message requesting Arthur's presence to the Queen of Sovereignty, Ginover, before approaching Arthur. It is Sovereignty, the representative of the Psyche, whom the heroes must first get approval. Gawan will also reconcile his Queen, Orgeluse, with her past enemy, a king and Other-World guard over a Paradisal Garden. "Coincidentally," Parzival also shows his face at this most critical time. He is the representative of the Spiritual World, who will make his mark as the Community and the Individual work out their difficulties.

Reconciliation brings together people who are supposed to be united. It cannot be one-sided. Both sides must be armed with forgiveness, and lay aside stubbornness. With the goal in mind that the two sides have a shared Destiny, concentrate on how the reunion will bring positive benefits for both. Pave a Path to Peace by being a focal point for battling forces to find a new purpose and future.

Path to Peace

If there are people around you who constantly battle, or refuse any contact with each other, think of ways that you can help in Reconciliation. Only expend this energy on people you really care for. Otherwise you'll just be a nosy busy-body. Find a common ground that they both view as being advantageous. Envision a Win-Win situation for both sides.

The Guardian of the Tree of Life

All reconciliations revolve around Gramoflanz. Why is he so pivotal? Isn't he just another opponent for Gawan?

As guard of the Tree of Life that both Gawan and Parzival have taken boughs from, Gramoflanz is justified in fighting both men. There is a reason that Gramoflanz is used to fighting two men at once. That is because Gramoflanz is the knight who fights Love and Hate at the same time. He guards the Tree of Knowledge of Good and Evil. That is why he is Gawan's final test.

Gramoflanz exhibits involvement in classic examples of Love/Hate relationships. He hates Lot's family because Lot killed his father, yet he loves Lot's daughter. He once loved Orgeluse, yet he fostered her hate by killing her love. Gramoflanz respects Gawan, yet he must fight him because Gawan has dared to challenge him. These are common situations in real life. Those we once loved can become our bitter enemies. Our enemies may have attributes that we aspire to and love.

Bene is right to cry for Itonje. If the hate side is allowed to exercise its force, no one comes out a winner in these situations. Either the Knight Who Guards the Tree of Life dies, or the King of the Individual dies. No winner here.

When we battle in situations where there are justifiable opponents, and good reasons to love, reconciliation is the only victory. We love our children, yet hate the drugs they take. We love our spouses, yet hate their actions of indifference. We love our friends, yet hate them for being too needy. If we only lean towards destructiveness and hate, we will lose the parts we love. We must put aside the past, and start anew with fresh understandings and forgiveness.

Love/Hate situations are the true tests of the Individual. It is easy to fight the bad guy. Taking a pure moral stance to fight him is no problem. Our real test in life is how we handle the tough situations with those we love.

Love and Hate

Are there situations in your life right now which you could classify as a Love/Hate relationship? Realize that Hate will only result in destruction. Reconcile the opposing views, and communicate with Love. The down side is the loss of Love without some unification of both sides.

Surrendering

All along, we've spoken of personal development and winning battles. There are times, however, when we must learn to Surrender.

Fans of *Monty Python and the Holy Grail* are familiar with King Arthur exhorting his men to "Run Away" at the least bit of trouble. This is not the type of surrendering we are speaking of. This is not about giving up or cowering in fear. It means taking a defeat knowing that a long term victory will be obtained. It means handing yourself over to a higher power when you have no other means to solve your problem. It means trusting in the Universe when your previously tried-and-true methods have not worked. It is when Obi-Wan "Ben" Kenobi tells Luke to trust The Force. It is knowing that the root word of "Islam" is "Surrender to God."

Orgeluse can keep demanding that Gawan fight Gramoflanz to revenge the death of Cidegast. Gramoflanz can keep insisting he fight Gawan for Irot's death, and the theft of the wreath. All involved know that no matter who wins, there will still be a loss. Gawan, Orgeluse, and Gramoflanz have all taken a road of Surrender. They give themselves over to a judgment that says a battleground victory would yield very little.

In *Apocalypse Now,* one of the mantras is "Never get out of the boat." Willard adds—unless you are willing to go all the way.

In myth, the Ship can designate the Surrendering of oneself to one's Destiny. In Malory's Grail legend, Galahad, Bors, and Perceval are mysteriously transported to the Grail in a floating ship. In the Tristan and Iseult legend, Tristan is wounded in a battle against Iseult's uncle. The wound festers and smells so disgusting to all around Tristan, that he sets himself adrift in a boat, totally committing himself to Fate. He lands in Ireland, and is cared for by Iseult. In an attempt to kill his son Mordred, Arthur orders children of Mordred's age placed in a ship and pushed to sea. The ship wrecks, but Mordred's Destiny is to survive and return years later to the father who had tried to kill him. Lancelot finds a drifting ship with the corpse of Perceval's sister on it. He lives a month on the ship, then is reunited with his son, Galahad.

Ships represent our voyages in life, with all the mysteries and eddies around each bend. Marlow and Willard float down dark rivers to their Destinies. Ships were named after women, in order to not tempt the Mother of the Sea from claiming seafarers. Even Forrest names his boat after Jenny. For final voyages in life, Viking burial grounds were ship caskets outfitted with necessary implements for the next trip. At Lindholm Høje, Denmark, a necropolis of 200 ship graves can be seen.

Surrendering becomes a noble act when you know you protect your future with the losses of today. Surrendering is eminent when you recognize a wisdom greater than your own. Surrendering is faith in powers greater than yourself. This goes beyond physical strength. It can be a power of a Higher Being. It can be Love, Wisdom, Knowledge, Justice. It can be the power of Life. It is Tao.

Surrendering here is to Love and a Peaceful Community—not a defeat in the least.

Surrendering

1. Think of times when you ended up with a dubious victory. If you had taken a stance of Surrender, could you have made a victory for both sides?

2. Think of ways that you can Surrender to Love, to Wisdom, to a Higher Spirit. How do you think this will make your everyday life more rewarding? How will this help those around you?

3. If you are currently involved with a dispute, is there a way to Surrender so that the future will be better in the long run?

Illustration by Ivan Bilibin (1876–1942)

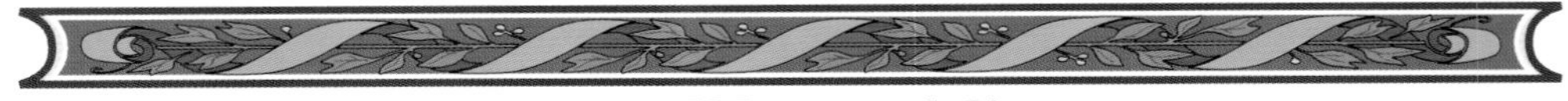

Spiritual Knight and Physical King

When Gramoflanz fights Parzival, he says it is like fighting six men. This is because he is fighting Spirituality. But this battle belongs to Gawan, since Parzival's final battles are yet to come. Gawan has been successful in his endeavors and for a brief moment, the King of the Community, Arthur, is able to reunite with his Spiritual Knight, Parzival, after many years. Success in the material world has been achieved, and for many, the book could end here. However, finishing tasks in the physical world is not the same as finishing a Quest. For final victory, the Healing of the Spirit must be completed. So Parzival must take his leave.

Illustration by N. C. Wyeth (1882–1945)

The Lessons of Reconciliations

Being King of the Realm of the Individual means being responsible for bringing the Community and those in our immediate circle of influence together. More than just personal achievement, it means using skills and achievements to build a bridge from our lives to the world at large.

We need to take the energy to reconcile friends, family, and work partners and build a Path to Peace. Make it a Win-Win situation for everyone.

The most important test we take is dealing with our Love/Hate situations. We need to learn compromise. We need to examine what the downside is when we do not lean towards Love.

We need to learn to Surrender. This can be to Wisdom, Love, a Higher Spirit. We do this now to build a better future.

Complete victories allow for the Spiritual Self, as well as the Physical Self, to know success. Otherwise, only part of the battle is completed.

Parzival also has a final battle before he is able to meet the Grail King again. He must face his Darker Nature.

Lt. Dan asks Forrest and Bubba if they are twins.
(Forrest-Tom Hanks, Bubba-Mykelti Williamson, Dan-Gary Sinise)

Chapter 18 - Are You Twins?

Two souls, alas, dwell in my breast.
— Johann Wolfgang von Goethe

Lt. Dan asks Gump and Bubba if they are twins, because they act so much alike. Forrest and Bubba look quizzically at each other, as if trying to figure out the question—and the truth. They could be asking themselves if this Lieutenant is crazy to even ask such a question of a white man and a black man. Or they could be pondering if somewhere along the line they do have intermingled blood. I can tell you right now that they are long lost brothers with the names of Parzival and Feirefiz. Now let's find out what happens in our story when the two finally meet.

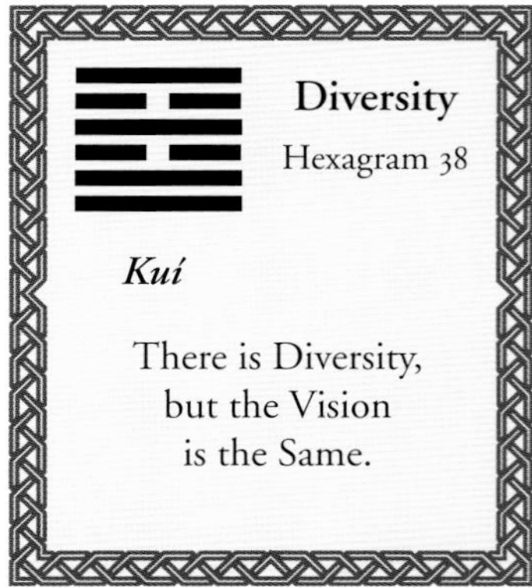

Feirefiz

In battle, Parzival meets the heathen Feirefiz, whose battle attire is more costly than any treasure in Arthur's lands. Feirefiz fights for Queen Secundille, and yells "Tabronit" whenever he strikes, as that is where she is. Parzival is losing, and Wolfram wonders why he does not think of Condwiramors. If she or the Grail cannot help him, then he should think of his two sons, Kardeiz and Loherangrin, who were born when he left. Parzival finally thinks of Condwiramors and calls the name of her city, "Pelrapeire," but at that moment, his sword breaks. The blow makes Feirefiz fall to his knees. He stands up, but decides it would be ignoble to attack the now unarmed Parzival. They decide to call a truce while they rest. Feirefiz decides to take the loss, and reveals his name as Feirefiz of Angevin. Parzival wonders about him coming from Angevin, since Parzival would be the ruler of Angevin, as the son of Gahmuret. That clue leads them to discover they are brothers, and Feirefiz removes his helmet to show his mottled black and white skin. He has come searching for their father. Parzival tells him their father died in joust, which saddens Feirefiz, but he is happy to have found Parzival. He thanks his god, Jupiter, for having brought them together unharmed. Feirefiz offers to take Parzival to his armies, but Parzival says they should go to Arthur, who is close by.

When Arthur hears they are coming, he prepares for them. Feirefiz recounts his adventures, including having served three queens—Olimpia, Clauditte, and Secundille. Then Parzival tells of his conquests. Feirefiz becomes a member of the Round Table, along with Gramoflanz, Lischois, and Florant.

Cundrie the Sorceress shows up. She welcomes Feirefiz, as she also serves Queen Secundille. She weeps and begs Parzival's forgiveness for her past recriminations. She then tells him he will be the Grail Lord, serving with Condwiramors and his son Loherangrin. His other son, Kardeiz, has another destiny. Cundrie will lead the way to Munsalvaesche, but Parzival must choose a man to accompany him. He chooses Feirefiz. Feirefiz then distributes many costly gifts to Arthur's court.

— *Parzival* Summary, Book xv

Forces of the Spirit Meet

You have struggled here with yourself; you have ridden in single combat against myself, and would have gladly slain myself, but you defended my life from me.

— Feirefiz in *Parzival*, Book xv, ¶ 752

Combat de Cavalier (Knightly Combat)
by Salvador Dali (1904–1989)

Private Collection
Color printed etching with aquatint, 1971. 13 x 20 ½ in.
©2001 Kingdom of Spain, Gala-Salvador Dali Foundation / Artists Rights Society (ARS), New York

Just as Parzival's sword breaks as he fights Feirefiz, Roy Hobbs' bat breaks when he faces the young upcoming left-handed pitcher. Roy Hobbs is facing himself. The bat was named "Wonderboy," and it had to break at this time—Roy is completing his journey, and his boyhood is behind him. Parzival is completing the tough tests of his quest, and is finally able to leave his life of a Fool behind.

The breaking of Parzival's sword is more than just divine intervention to save two brothers from each other. Recalling the Peredur story where the breaking and mending of his sword represents two-thirds of his strength, we can see Parzival as only having two-thirds of his strength. His last third will be achieved when he has the power to Heal the Fisher King.

Parzival and Feirefiz are of the same flesh—one of the Dark and the other of the Light. Often we are directed towards Light as good, and Dark as evil. If this were a television show, we would see the Good and Evil Twin themes. People of darker races have suffered from this image. Light became superior to Dark, forgetting that the two balance each other. Wolfram again emphasizes the Taoist view where the Light and the Dark are one.

Feirefiz is a magnificent man, whose armor blazes with light from all of the encrusted jewels, mostly given to him by women (three in particular). Feirefiz' coat was woven in the fire by salamanders. Ancient folk myth viewed the salamander as a creature that could live in fire, without being destroyed by it.

Feirefiz' name conjures an image of Fire—a fire that will burn the old phoenix to give life to the new. His Fire can give life and illumination, or purify evil with destruction. If you are not careful, he will burn what is in his path. He is Agni, the God Fire, who is wedded to Kali, the Dark Mother. He is an element that lives in the moment, and a test of him is a test of the Now.

When Parzival faces Feirefiz, he is facing the Darker aspect of himself. This is not an evil side. It is a side that is merely Different. It is the side that chooses to sometimes walk with the Moon instead of the Sun. It is a side that appreciates what is foreign instead of what is common. It is a side that sometimes holds terrible secrets, but uses that knowledge as a source of creativity and compassion. The embrace of the Dark side is the embrace of a complete person who loves what is commonly acceptable within himself, along with the marginal. It is a side of what may not be perfect, yet adding to the wondrous complexity of who that person is.

If you refuse to face your Darker side, you will not be able to reach your Grail. When Parzival confronts Feirefiz, he is taking the last adventure necessary for Cundrie to bring him to the Grail Castle. Two Forces of the Spirit meet, and at the time that the Light Spirit could kill the Dark, his weapon shatters. The Dark side in turn has the opportunity to destroy the Light, yet recognizes a Master when he sees one. When dialogue is begun, the two sides know that they are one and the same.

In Jungian psychology, this Darker aspect is referred to as the Shadow, the repressed self. Jung stated that enlightenment comes from making the dark side conscious, not just forcing it into the light. In ancient times, a person's shadow was considered to be one of his souls, so Jungians are not too far off from this concept. Issues lying in the Shadow can be very painful, but Jung knew that attempts to destroy the Shadow creates a two-dimensional person. Instead, he chose a therapy which brings the Shadow to the Light in a way that the valuable resources still found in the Shadow would not be demolished. The Fire that burns can be quenched, and the Fire that illuminates can be saved. This is precisely what Parzival does with Feirefiz. Instead of going with his brother to his ships, he brings Feirefiz to Arthur's court, the Kingdom of the Community. There Feirefiz will also meet Gawan, King of the Individual. Feirefiz is adamant in bringing the people of the court wonderful gifts, signs of his own personal wealth. Parzival then chooses Feirefiz to accompany him to the Grail Castle.

With the confrontation of Parzival and Feirefiz, we see a return of the Circle. Parzival's life begins with activities that happened long before he was born. That history produced his faults, which prevented him from achieving his Grail at his first encounter. By bringing his Shadow into the Light, he is ready to rediscover the Grail Castle and Heal the Fisher King.

The Shadow Side

Meet your own Shadow. It may try to hide from you and say "No one's home," but keep knocking. Your Shadow is complex and multi-faceted. It has destructive components and creative inspiration. It is linked to memories that embrace someone you loved who hurt you.

1. Review the side of your Shadow that is destructive. How can you change the habits that come from your destructive side? These are the characteristics that have kept you from achieving your Grail. Recognize how they have done this.

2. Now see the side of your Shadow that is magnificent. This is where creative truth can speak to others unable to meet with their own Shadows. This side has gifts to bring forward and inspire others.

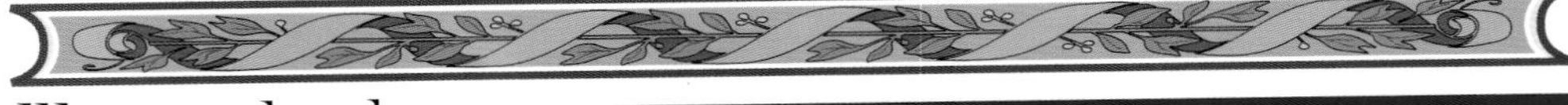

Win with the Name of Love

Following the Example of the Gods
by Henryk Siemiradzki (1843–1902)

Lvov Museum, Ukraine
Oil on Canvas, 1879

Ultimately, to win, you must win with the name of Love. Parry knew that when he called "Blancheflor" as he rescued Jack from street thugs.

Feirefiz is winning the battle because he calls the name of where his love resides. Parzival strays from his strength when he cannot think of Condwiramors. Parzival's skill is not enough. Love will give him the power to survive. Wolfram is quick to point out that the love of his wife, the power of the Grail, and the love of his children, are all equal and bring success.

Purpose in life gives us determination and the grit to see things to the end. When that purpose is fueled with love, we can survive almost anything and be successful in our Quests. Many people would have thrown in their towels on work they didn't like, if it wasn't for the fact they were responsible for their families. Their next goal is to work towards their Grail, so that their purpose has the love of family and self behind it.

Whatever you are working on—even if it is something you dislike—should be hooked to a purpose that involves love. Remind yourself about the benefits for your loved ones when you finish the chore. The task then goes beyond just work. It becomes an active meditation of Love. The Spirit wins as well.

In the Name of Love

1. At a simple level, love can help us through the dreariest tasks. Think of the task that you like the least, and determine how it helps those you love (including yourself). When you perform this task, keep this benefit in mind so it eases the tension in your body and spirit. When you've accomplished decreasing your tension at this particular task, try another.

2. At a higher level, our larger projects must be motivated by an even bigger vision of how our loved ones are involved. This time you will need to share this vision with those you love, so they understand how they are part of the inspiration and purpose.

Finding Joy in Sorrow

I have in this hour, lost joy and found joy.

— Feirefiz in *Parzival,* Book xv, ¶ 752

Feirefiz and Parzival exchange stories and realize they are brothers. Feirefiz has come to this land to find his father, Gahmuret, but now learns Gahmuret is dead. He finds sorrow when he learns of his father's death, but discovers joy in the serendipitous finding of his brother.

Sometimes we start out with expectations of what we want or need. Along the way, we discover that our expectations are impossible. When that happens, we must learn to make the best of a bad situation. We cannot grieve over the loss of something that was not to be, but we must honor what we have learned and discovered along the way. In that way, all experiences in our lives will have meaning and depth.

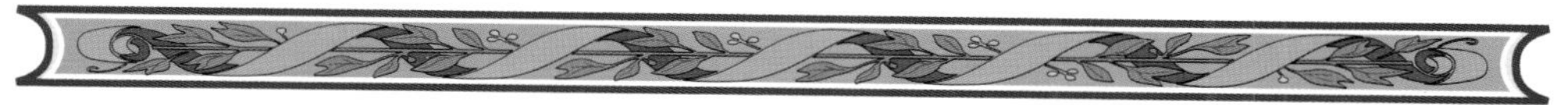

Secundille - Shekina - Shakti - Sophia

For Wisdom, which is the worker of all things, taught me: for in her is an understanding spirit, holy, one only, manifold, subtle, lively, clear, undefiled, plain, not subject to hurt, loving the thing that is good, quick, which cannot be letted, ready to do good.

— The Apocrypha, The Wisdom of Solomon 7:22

Queen Secundille is an enigma. We are never directly involved with her, yet she plays an important part in the Parzival story. We know that Cundrie the Sorceress, Malcreatiure, and Feirefiz all serve her, and they are powerful representatives. We know that Gawan was able to see for miles around the Castle of Wonders because he stood in her stolen, brilliant Pillar. Feirefiz' wealth stands as evidence of the riches of her land. She influences many things, yet we never see her, because she is the Veiled Goddess. We do not directly gaze on her, but we know her through Spirit. We know her through the names Shakti, Shekina, Sophia. She is the Feminine Spirit of the Godhead, and she is the World Soul.

Secundille's name gives us a little clue—we see Cunda in there, and almost Kundalini. As Shakti, we know her as Cosmic Energy. It is her servant, Cundrie the Sorceress, who is able to travel through all of the realms of the world, running on that current of Energy. Cundrie can even go in and out of the Castle of Wonders delivering medicine, whereas anybody else becomes entrapped in its magical spell. Shakti is a female guardian angel who can be a spirit-wife to a deserving man, as well as the wife of the greatest deity. We know Shekina as the central base pillar of the Kabbalah, being the Kingdom or Earth. She is the spirit in the Pillar of Fire who leads Moses by night, and the Pillar of Clouds who leads in the day. Secundille's protege has the name of Fire, and her Pillar at the Castle of Wonders is so bright that a person can see for six miles. As Sophia she is Wisdom, and her symbol is the Dove. Sophia is the All-Seeing Eye that sees everything in the world. She carefully watches the progress of the Grail Quest, and when Parzival's and Gawan's tests are completed, her servant fetches Parzival for the final healing.

Secundille is the web that ties everyone together. She brings East to West, she brings Male to Female, she brings the Quester to the Grail. Her methods may seem coincidental, but they are anything but. She plants her agents with full intentions, and she allowed her pillar to be stolen; then she lets people's natures do what they will. She is Wisdom and she gives the tools for learning. And still remains Unseen.

The Last Battles

Parzival and Gawan have now finished their final and greatest battles, which ended up being non-battles.

Gawan's battle did not involve a final, deadly fight, but a forum for Reconciliation. Throughout all of the legends, Gawan is a man of refinement, polish, and courtesy. This side of him is highlighted when he successfully brings together the Kingdom of the Individual with the Kingdom of the Community. He successfully puts aside old family wounds, and brings the warring parties together as a family. This becomes his final, greatest achievement.

Parzival's final battle ends in a draw. There is a joyous union of two brothers from two different parts of the world. Parzival brings the Darker Brother into his life, and allows the Community to benefit from the rich gifts he offers. This is not a final achievement for Parzival, but a prerequisite for his final task.

Once Parzival has accepted his Dark Brother, Cundrie the Sorceress comes back to Parzival. She originally rode into the court as the Dark Loathly Lady with biting words to spur on Parzival. Now she kowtows and begs for forgiveness for her harsh treatment. She seems pathetic with her obsequious actions, but this is just another test for Parzival. She must confirm that he has learned forgiveness as a part of compassion before she takes him to the Grail Castle. Granted, he gives his forgiveness at the urgings of others and without a kiss, but he has toned down his pride. Only after he offers forgiveness, does she tell him that he will succeed. He is now within reach of his heart's goal. Not only that, he will be with his wife, and he learns that he is the father of two twin sons.

Upon hearing the good news from Cundrie, Parzival cries for joy, a prototype of the strong, sensitive man. At this point he admits that her nastiness towards him came

because of his own shortcomings. He recognizes her faithfulness and confirms her relationship with Munsalvaesche seeing the doves on her garments. He now asks the Question of her, "What do I do next?"

Parzival's last tests are ones of Acceptance, Forgiveness, and Humility. If he fails at any one of these, he would still be looking for the Grail Castle and would never see his wife or sons. Rather than rushing out to get to the Grail Castle, he finally has learned to stop and ask critical questions. Because of that, she will be his guide. This is true in our lives, where Acceptance, Forgiveness, and Humility are critical to our relationships. Without those attributes, we can never truly see the ones we love, and whatever goals we achieve are meaningless.

Final Tests

The Achievement of our Grail does not have meaning unless we pass tests of Reconciliation, Acceptance, Forgiveness, and Humility with those around us. See how you can better incorporate those attributes into your life. Make your own little tests to see how well you fare, and how you are changing. Your reward will be a deep satisfaction as you achieve your Grail.

The Lessons of Are You Twins?

We all have a Shadow side which we must learn to bring forward and accept. We can heal the parts that are most painful, but also use the resources of the Shadow to enrich our lives.

We can only truly win in life if we do it in the Name of Love. Love gives us the strongest purpose to carry on in life. This is love for those around us, as well as ourselves.

We can find Joy in Sorrow. To do so is to strengthen our souls and prepare for future battles.

Wisdom is the Pillar of the World Soul. It is the energy which binds all together. It is the Balance of the Universe.

Our most important battles rest on learning Reconciliation, Acceptance, Forgiveness, and Humility. Our success will not mean much if we cannot have Peace in our personal lives.

Sunlight on Mountain by Jens Ferdinand Willumsen (1863–1958)
Thielska Galleriet, Stockholm
Oil on Canvas, 1902. 82 ¼ x 82 in.

Path IV – The Healing

I am blind and do not see the things of this world; but when the light comes from Above, it enlightens my Heart and I can see, for the Eye of my Heart sees everything; and through this vision I can help my people. The heart is a sanctuary at the center of which there is a little space, wherein the Wakantanka (Great Spirit) dwells, and this is the Eye. This is the Eye of Wakantanka by which He sees all things, and through which we see Him. If the heart is not pure, Wakantanka cannot be seen.

— Black Elk

The journey has been long, but the lessons—as painful, as rigorous, as demanding as they've been—have given the Wisdom and Skills needed for the Healing. At Munsalvaesche, the Mountain of Salvation, the sun breaks through, illuminating the landscape with fiery energies. The Soul is ready to accept the Compassion it deserves, and it will strengthen the Spirit for future endeavors.

The most difficult times are past for our heroes, but there still must be a final Closing, *Healing,* and Preparation for the Future.

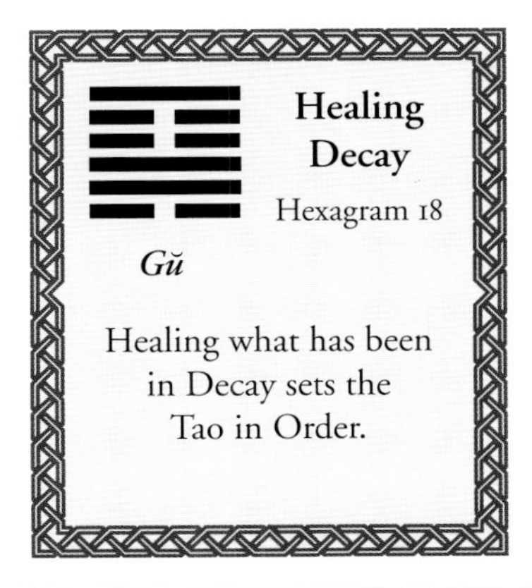

Chapter 19 – Second Chance

Galahad and the Dying Amfortas
by Edwin Austin Abbey
(1852–1911)

Painted 1895
©Burstein Collection/Corbis

After years of searching and trials, Parzival is brought to Munsalvaesche for a Second Chance at Healing. Without hesitation, he does what is right, and a new era begins. We now examine the deeper aspects of The Healing.

The Healing

Anfortas still suffered, because his people continually showed him the Grail to keep him alive. He begged them for death, and they would have let him go, but Trevrizent read on the Grail that there would be a second coming of the man who would release him. True to the prophecy, Parzival, Feirefiz, and Cundrie arrive at Munsalvaesche, and to great celebration. Immediately, Parzival asks Anfortas what ails him, and Anfortas is healed. Condwiramors is on her way, because she was told of what was to come.

Parzival goes to Trevrizent, who says that Parzival successfully defied God by taking the second chance. Trevrizent says he lied to Parzival about how things stood as a test to divert him from the Grail. He now asks forgiveness and Parzival says he still values Trevrizent's advice.

Parzival then goes to meet his wife and sons, Kardeiz and Loherangrin, at Plimizoel. Kardeiz is to be made king of Parzival's lands, and in later years he would recapture Waleis and Norgals. Condwiramors and Loherangrin are escorted to the Grail castle. Parzival then goes to Sigune, who has died in a posture of prayer over Schianatulander's tomb. She is placed beside Schianatulander. Both of them look alive, though there is no life in them. Parzival then returns to the Grail castle.

— Summary of *Parzival,* Book XVI, ¶ 787–805

Another Try

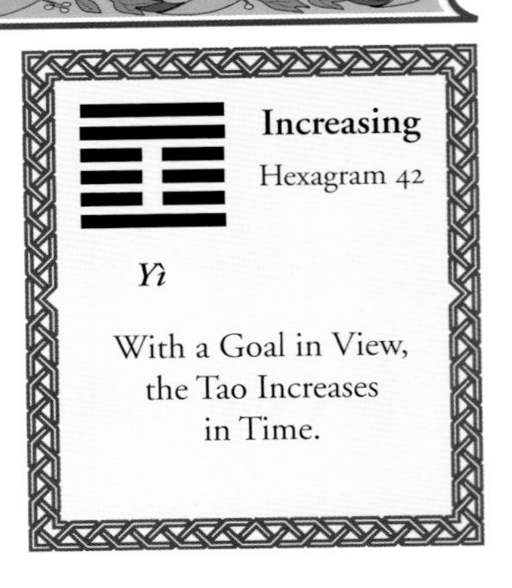

The Grail can be very cruel. It will keep you alive forever. It keeps Roy Hobbs going for sixteen years, before he is given a second chance with odds and age still against him. The Grail doesn't care whether you are gazing upon it with joy or suffering. It will pump life into you, no matter what. As Parzival returns, the stars are in such a position that Anfortas is suffering the greatest pain he has ever experienced. Anfortas is begging his court not to show him the Grail. He wants death. Trevrizent has read in the Grail that there would be a Second Coming of the man who could cure Anfortas. Now the court endures the cries of suffering with the faith that relief will be soon.

It is not an accident that Wolfram used the term Second Coming, hinting at the Second Coming of Christ. There are comparisons in the characters of Parzival/Perceval and Galahad as representing Christ returning for a second chance at redeeming mankind since the Fall of Adam. The Wound of the Grail King is viewed as the Fall of Adam, and the advent of the Wasteland is the Expulsion of Adam and Eve from Paradise. When Parzival fails at healing the Fisher King the first time around, that would be considered the First Coming. He succeeds at the Second Coming, and Paradise is restored. Though this is presented as a Christian tableau, a Second Chance at rebuilding Paradise is a common theme in many religions.

The Adamic Myth centers around another try at life. Even Paul in 1 Corinthians refers to Christ as being an Adam. Whenever we are striving for a new life, we take on the innocence and fresh possibilities that Adam had in Eden. Settlers in America pushing their way across the continent were relying on this myth. When life did not work out in Europe, there was hope for a better life in the burgeoning country across the Atlantic. Wherever refugees cross borders, it is the same myth pushing them. The old life has failed, and now a new paradise must be born. The old sins and the old way of life are dissolved, and we start over. In the film *Forrest Gump,* even the prostitutes enjoyed the New Year, because they get a second chance at starting life over.

Adam-Kadmon was a Gnostic character referring to the Primordial Man. He was made of mud and considered the Unenlightened Man. He was also called The Prince of Fools. This all fits in with our theme of the Great Fool, who eventually becomes Enlightened, and is able to Heal the Fisher King and the Land. Our Parzival becomes another Adam, ready for his Second Chance.

In the chapter on "Direct Experience," Trevrizent told Parzival that the knight destined to cure the Fisher King had to do it on the first night he visited the Grail Castle. Because it was foretold that a second chance would not work, Trevrizent is amazed that Parzival has defied the heavens and insisted on completing his task. Trevrizent further admits that he lied in saying he didn't know whether the outcast angels were in God's favor, as God had declared them eternally lost. The book says that Trevrizent admits this as a test to throw Parzival off the trail. However, in my opinion, Wolfram was made to get in line with the Church's orthodox view at that time. The idea of angels taking the middle ground between Lucifer and God would be considered heretical.

Sisyphus

The essential matter is that even though Parzival was told he had no chance at healing the Grail King, he didn't give up. He continued his search for Munsalvaesche to give it one last try, even though Trevrizent had told him that it wouldn't do any good.

If you truly want to get to your Grail, you cannot give up, even if representatives of Heaven tell you that it is impossible. For if you do quit, you will suffer forever. There is no win if you give up. Not only that, those around you will not enjoy paradise if you continue to suffer. We already know that whole connection.

Destiny points us towards the right place to go. When that Horse of Destiny throws us, then we must be sure we get back on, and this time direct the Horse if we have to. Mrs. Gump told Forrest that he is the one who makes his own destiny. He picked up that white feather and he did.

So—Don't Give Up. Don't Give Up. Don't Give Up.

The Impossible Dream

Everyday you can take another chance at your Grail. There will be times that it seems impossible, so develop a clear sense of how your Grail will enrich your life and others. This will give you the confidence and strength to work towards your dream even when others tell you it's impossible.

The Attainment: The Vision of the Holy Grail to Sir Galahad, Sir Bors, and Sir Percival
by Edward Burne-Jones (1833–1898) and William Morris (1834–1896)
Birmingham Museums & Art Gallery
Stanmore Hall Tapestry, 1898–99. 8 ½ x 30 ft.

The Question Asked

What Ails Thee?
Why Does the Spear Bleed?
Whom Does the Grail Serve?

In the Parzival story, the crucial question to Heal the Fisher King is "What ails thee?" We've explored the importance of asking this question of ourselves to apply direction and focus to our lives. What is also important is that we do it with true empathy; it must come from the soul. When Jack Lucas first enters the "Grail Castle," he hallucinates hearing galloping horse's hooves when he sees the Red Knight insignia on the stained glass. In the hallway, he sees Edwin, who had shot Parry's wife on that fateful night, shooting at him. Some may call Jack crazy, but he's actually empathetic. He now hears and sees the source of Parry's pain. Now the healing comes from the Soul.

Jack is now able to do the right thing spontaneously and compassionately. He sees the comatose owner of the home, Carmichael, slumped in his chair after overdosing on pills. Jack purposely sets off the burglar alarm so Carmichael can get the help he needs. By awakening Carmichael from his coma, he also awakens Parry. You heal one Grail King, you heal the other.

In *Good Will Hunting,* Will, Sean, and Gerald all suffer from an inability to love. Gerald is always trying to pick up young co-eds in his classes. Sean has been deeply wounded from the death of his wife. Will, an orphan, suffers from abandonment issues compounded by physical wounds, including a stabbing at the hands of foster parents. By Sean reiterating to Will that his childhood problems weren't his fault, he is essentially asking him "What ails thee?" The healing process of Will's soul is directly tied to Sean's. Now Sean, urged on by Will, is willing to play another hand at life.

Forrest Gump asks the question by writing a letter to Lt. Dan, telling him to come out and be first mate on his boat. Dan's experiences on Gump's boat allow him to confront his purpose in life and his spirituality.

Luke Skywalker is able to heal his father, Darth Vader, by believing that goodness still exists within him. His refusal to attack his father, and his near destruction by the Emperor, brings Darth Vader out from his deepest wounds. What ailed Darth Vader was that he forgot how to love.

In other Grail legends, the question is different. One question is "Why Does the Spear Bleed?" and another is "Whom Does the Grail Serve?"

Let's face it, there are lots of bleeding objects in these legends. We have a platter with a man's head on it; we have a cup that catches Christ's blood; we have a sword that bleeds; and of course, we have the infamous Bleeding Spear which appears in almost all of the versions. This is truly a myth that attests to Suffering and Loss.

The usual answer to the Spear bleeding question is the one that it is Longinus' spear used to gore Christ's side. This reference then is to the blood of Christ, and it becomes a symbol of Redemption.

In the *Perlesvaus* version, there is a very strange passage about the lance being brought in to Gawain, with a bleeding head stuck to it. Three drops of blood fall on the table in front of Gawain. When he gazes on the drops of blood, he is sent into a trance. Déjà vu. Gawain tries to kiss the blood, but the drops move away, not letting him touch them. Is the head the same one we saw on the platter in the Peredur version? Is the head female, and another statement being made? Is the blood still the blood of Christ, as this Grail procession includes a vision of Christ on the cross? I will leave you to your own interpretation.

In one of the *Continuations,* Gawain asks the question about the Bleeding Lance, but not about whom the Grail serves. Gawain heals the land because he asked the question about the Spear. But because he failed to ask about the Grail, Joy will not return.

In the Parzival legend, we know that the Spear bleeds with the blood from Anfortas' wound. Now that Anfortas is healed, the Bleeding Spear is no longer part of the Grail Procession.

Still, the Spear is Truth. It bleeds because Truth can inflict its own pain. It also Heals as it moves one closer to revealing the True Self. When you get to your Grail, the Spear no longer needs to bleed, as you have found the Ultimate Truth of yourself.

The Grail may be what lies deepest in our hearts, but Whom does it Serve?

Everyone.

The Grail serves us by keeping a promise of Hope, of Faith, of Justice, of Rebirth, of Paradise in front of us. It reminds us that we should search for what is Good, even if—and especially because—the path will be difficult. It teaches us Fortitude and Patience. It develops our Strength and teaches us Compassion.

When we search for our own personal Grail, it serves us by removing our Suffering as we accomplish what we were destined to be. It serves everyone as we use our acquired skills in the service of others and we have learned to treat all with Compassion.

We serve the Grail by building a better world through the lessons it shares with us.

Whom Does the Grail Serve?

By now you have a good grasp on what your Grail is and how achieving it will help heal your personal sufferings. Contemplate whom your Grail serves besides yourself. How can your accomplishment spread out to help many? See how widespread your vision can be.

Parsifal healing King Amfortas
by Franz Stassen
(1869–1949)
Illustration, 1903

The New Grail Family

Gump will complete his family when Jenny brings little Forrest to him. Roy Hobbs will retire to a farm with Iris and his son. Will Hunting will find Skylar in San Francisco. Siddhartha will learn of his son with Kamala, and have a bittersweet learning experience of fatherhood. Just as the Fisher King has become whole, Parzival himself will become whole by uniting with his wife and sons. He will need Condwiramors with him for the New Grail procession, because they are to rule together. This will be a celebration of their own Sacred Marriage.

His sons are twins and they will carry on into the future the promise of the Grail. Loherangrin will be the future Grail King and Kardeiz will win fame as a king of many lands. They will continue the work of ruling in the Spiritual and Physical World.

Twins in myth signify complementary opposites, the Yin and Yang of the world. Sometimes they refer to two kings who rule one throne. Popular mythical Twins were Romulus and Remus, Apollo and Artemis, Mazda and Ahriman, Freyr and Freya, Dylan and Lleu, and Castor and Pollux as the Gemini twins who appear in the constellations.

The Twins represent the future creativity of your life. You have achieved one Grail, and there are others yet to be discovered and obtained. These children are a summation of all you have learned and which will infuse your adventures of the future.

Ancient Future-Family / Knights of Endurance by Leo and Diane Dillon

Photo: Courtesy of Leo and Diane Dillon ©2002

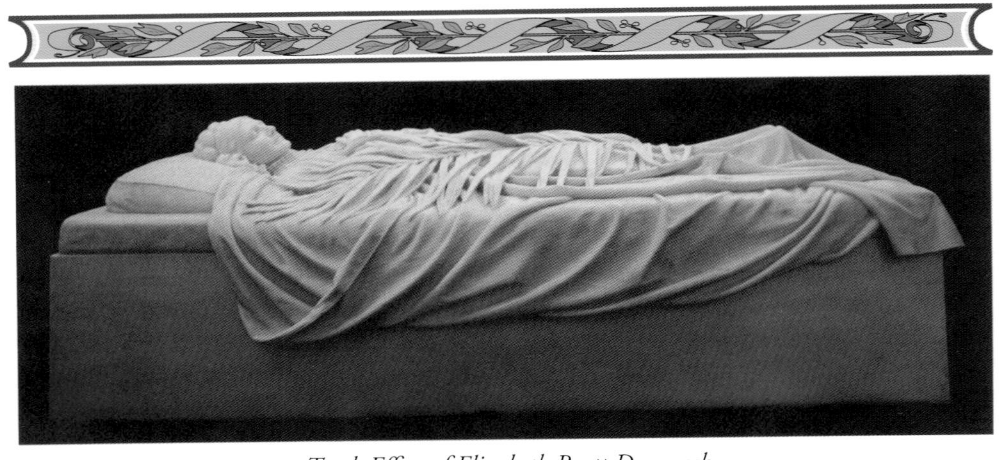

Tomb Effigy of Elizabeth Boott Duveneck
by Frank Duveneck (1848–1919) and Clement J. Barnhorn (1857–1935)
Courtesy Museum of Fine Arts Boston, Gift of Frank Duveneck. (12.62)
Marble, 1891–94. 28 x 86 x 39 ½ in.

The Death of Sigune

In most of the Grail legends, once the Maimed King is healed, he dies. This would mean that the wounds of the old life must be healed before being put aside for the new life to come. However, in the *Parzival* story, Anfortas will be healed and have more adventures.

It will be the death of Sigune, the Maimed Queen, which will serve as the starting point of the new life. While the Maimed Fisher King is a man alive, he has the pallor of one who is dead. Sigune's love, Schianatulander, is dead, yet he has the freshness of a young, vibrant man. Her release of energy that takes her to death is commensurate with the revitalizing of the Fisher King.

There is another self-sacrificing woman in Arthurian myth—Dindrane, Perceval's sister. She is the one who weaves the scabbard for Galahad's sword from her hair. Like Sigune, she is a virgin, and living a platonic love with Galahad. While Dindrane, Galahad, Bors, and Perceval travel on the Grail Quest, they come to a castle whose queen is ill. Only the blood of a virgin will help heal the queen, so Dindrane is told to give her blood. The men would prefer to fight, but Dindrane willingly submits. The queen is healed, but Dindrane has given too much blood and dies. Before her death, she tells Perceval to put her corpse on a boat, which will take her to Sarras. She says that they will meet up with her body there, where she can be buried in holy ground. Eventually, Galahad and Perceval will also be buried there. Dindrane's sacrifice here enables the men to continue on their Grail Quest. Otherwise, they may have met death in fighting the queen's men. Dindrane's death correlates with the healing of the Grail King by the men she has empowered, just as Sigune's death is timed with the Fisher King's Healing.

In *Apocalypse Now,* there are two books of myth analysis that Francis Ford Coppola points to by showing them as part of Kurtz' library—*The Golden Bough* by James

Frazier and *From Ritual to Romance* by Jessie Weston. Though both books have suffered the criticism of modern scholarship, the work surrounding the Sacrificial King is mythically valuable. Basically, when the old king has lost his vitality and fertility, he must be replaced by the young, healthy king. For Frazier, this meant a ritual killing of the king, and that is what we see played out in *Apocalypse Now.* Obi-Wan "Ben" Kenobi's self-sacrifice to Darth Vader in *Star Wars* also demonstrates this theme. In the Peredur legend, Peredur kills his teacher, the Witch of Gloucester, as it had been foretold. The young Obi-Wan knows he has to pick up the sword of his mentor, Qui-Gon Jinn, so that the next generation can also continue.

Forrest Gump will lose his Jenny, but she leaves him with a future Grail King. Siddhartha also loses his Kamala, but she also leaves a son. Behind the deaths of these women are the hopes of the future.

Sigune has served a vital role in directing Parzival along his trail, reminding him of the Suffering about him. Though she knows she is lost, she continues to keep him searching for the Grail Castle, ready to heal others. She shows Parzival what it is to sacrifice your life to the past, and that he should choose a path of Life and Healing. Her efforts are rewarded, and she now passes on in peace.

Sacred Landscapes

Inner Truth

Hexagram 61

Zhōng Fú

Inner Truth comes from Perseverance along the Right Path. It is time to cross the River.

The New Grail Procession does not begin until Parzival makes a circle, gathering those he needs to acknowledge, and physically touching the Sacred Sites that enabled his journey. These sites serve as Touchstones and reminders for the essential invigoration of what lies inside him.

He first goes to the Cave of Trevrizent, where the final clues of the Grail were revealed to him. To enter the Cave is to enter the womb of Mother Earth. From the caves painted with animal spirits in Lascaux to the *kivas* of the Hopis, from the Newgrange burial mounds to those of the Pharoahs, the descent into the earth is the return to the womb of the first mother. In this landscape, we feel a sense of enclosure, safety, and peace. It is a place of waiting for rebirth.

Parzival next goes to the meadow of Plimizoel, where he had his vision of Condwiramors. It is no longer covered with ice and snow. In this place of flowers and grasses, he meets his wife, no longer a vision, but alive and bringing the best evidence of their love—their sons. Whether we are gazing at the Serpent Mound of Ohio, the heathers of Scotland, or immense expanses of the Gobi Desert, we are experiencing the wonder of openness and expansion. We feel a sense of unfolding and release as we enter these landscapes.

Next, he goes to Sigune's hermitage in a forest with a running brook flowing through it. Broceliande still exists. And we have the Amazonian rain forest, Yellowstone National Park, and the Black Forest. We have the Mississippi, the Rhine River, and the Yellow River. Forests and waters give us a perception of renewal and growth.

The White Knight by Walter Crane (1845–1915)
Private Collection.
Watercolor, 1870. 18 x 24 in.

Finally, he returns to Munsalvaesche. Our mountains are Kilimanjaro, Denali, the Eiger, Annapurna, and never to be outdone, Everest. From here we understand what it is to see the whole, and to know accomplishment.

Forrest Gump traversed the country for his inner healing. When Jenny says she wished she could have been him, he assured her that she was. As he meditated on his love, he experienced all the magic the land had to offer.

The pilgrims whom Parzival met on the road understood that there is a time when you simply must go out and walk and be a part of all nature, which is sacred. For ourselves, we must integrate nature into our beings by allowing it to replenish us. In return, we take the responsibility for its caretaking. For us, this is symbiosis at the highest level. This is understanding Spirit as it relates to the phenomenal world about us.

Sacred Landscapes

1. Look for landscapes in your area which give you a sense of what Parzival felt on his last circle of visitations. Look for places of enclosure, openness, sustenance, and high views. When your Spirit needs any particular source of healing, you know where to go.

2. Think of ways you can take care of the land, whether it is in the form of gardening, recycling, or membership in organizations that support gardens and parks. Even small deeds multiply on a large scale.

The Lessons of Second Chance

- We learn that we can create our own Second Chances. The primary lesson here is not to give up, even when obstacles make the Grail seem impossible.
- We should ask of ourselves, "Whom Does the Grail Serve?" This will help us understand how we fit in the big picture. It reminds us of our greater responsibilities.
- In achieving our Grail, we also give birth to our future possibilities. These talents and skills serve in both the Spiritual and Physical World.
- Once we have healed the issues of the past, lay them to rest. Let that suffering end so the new life can begin.
- We must search out Sacred Landscapes in our lives as Touchstones to the spirituality of Nature. We'll exchange energies with Sacred Landscapes by taking measures to care for them.

Now that the Healing has been achieved, a new realm must be announced.

Chapter 20 – A New Grail Procession

The Divine Mother revealed to me in the Kali temple that it was She who had become everything. She showed me that everything was full of Consciousness. The Image was Consciousness, the altar was Consciousness, the water-vessels were Consciousness, the door-sill was Consciousness, the marble floor was Consciousness — all was Consciousness.

— from *The Gospel of Sri Ramakrishna*
trans. Swami Nikhilananda

Parzival will now live in the presence of the Grail as its new King. His brother, Feirefiz, will have his first experience with the Grail, which will reveal its other truths.

The Damsel of the Sanct Grael
by Dante Gabriel Rossetti (1828–1882)

Tate Gallery, London
Watercolor, 1857. 13 ¾ x 4 ⅝ in.
Photo: Tate Gallery, London / Art Resource, N.Y.

New Grail Kingdom

When Parzival and his family return to Munsalvaesche, Feirefiz greets them, but Loherangrin is afraid to kiss Feirefiz. Anfortas is there, as well as Repanse de Schoye. There is now the Grail Procession for Parzival and Condwiramors. However, Feirefiz cannot see the Grail, only its bearer, Repanse de Schoye. Titurel says the reason Feirefiz cannot see the Grail is because he is not baptized. Feirefiz will only be baptized if it will help him love Repanse. The next day he is baptized. On the Grail is written that any Templar over a foreign people shall not be asked his name or race to receive help.

Twelve days later, Feirefiz and Repanse leave, with Cundrie being an advance messenger. News comes that Secundille has died. Years later, Repanse gives birth to Prester John in India. Loherangrin is married to the Princess of Brabant. He goes to her lands in a boat pulled by a swan. She was not to ask who he was, which she later did, and he was forced to return to the Grail. Wolfram finishes the book saying he wrote this poem for a woman.

— Summary of *Parzival*, Book XVI, ¶ 805–827

The Grail Procession

With joy, the Grail is now presented: their worries completely slain.

— from *Parzival,* Book XVI, ¶ 807

The Grail is a source of Life and of Joy. Before, the Grail was brought forth for consolation during a time of pain. Now it is brought out for celebration. It hearkens a return of the Court of Joy. Wookiees, Droids, Gungans, Ewoks, and humans celebrate each stage of victory of the *Star Wars* series. Roy Hobbs saves the team for Pop Fisher with his final home run, and he has proven to himself his ability and destiny. The scoreboard explodes in celebration. The patients of Parry's hospital now sing along with him and Jack. The curse of the Wasteland is lifted. They are mended and given hope.

In the prior Grail procession, the purpose was to keep the ailing king alive and to test a potential healer. The atmosphere was one of mourning. Now it is brought out to celebrate Parzival and Condwiramors as the King and Queen of the Grail, and the surroundings are festive. Feirefiz escorts Condwiramors in, and takes his place sharing a seat with Parzival and Anfortas. This Queen of Sovereignty sits with Three Kings, a motif found in other myths. Ganieda shares a glass palace with Merlin, Taliesin, and Maeldinus.

As Condwiramors takes her place for the procession, she recognizes Anfortas, a King who has a Healed Spirit and Body, fully rejuvenated from past ills. She will see an unusual and wealthy King, Feirefiz, ready to ride out into the world, extending his influence with his child and wife. She will gaze with love on her husband, the Reigning Grail King, who has proved himself strong and compassionate, prepared to guide his kingdom through the future with values and clear vision.

When we have finally achieved our own personal Grail, we will have honored our own Sovereignty. We too will have a Healed Spirit, an Active Spirit, and a strong Reigning Spirit. With such royalty within us, it truly is a time for celebration.

When you have made significant progress with your Grail, share that happiness with others. Celebrate by offering appreciation to all of those who stood by and encouraged you in your struggles. Anfortas was supported by his court, almost beyond the point he really desired, and now the Grail is brought out to commemorate their kindness and concern. We should do the same for our family and friends.

> *Court of Joy*
>
> *Plan that party for family and friends who have patiently stood by as you worked your way towards your Grail. Show how much you cherish each one, and personally thank them. This is part of the wonder and joy of the Grail. Create a Court of Joy.*

The Invisible Grail

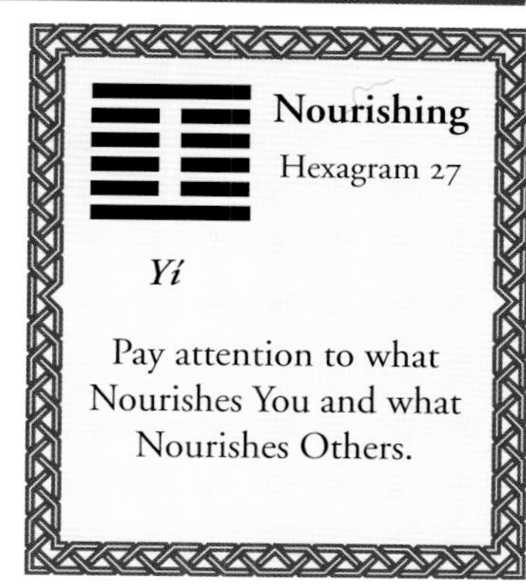

O Marvel! a garden amidst the flames
My heart has become capable of every form:
It is a pasture for gazelles
And a convent for Christian monks,
And a temple for idols,
And the pilgrim's Kaa`ba,
And the tables of the Torah,
And the Book of the Quran.
I follow the religion of Love:
Whatever way Love's camels take,
That is my religion, and my faith.
— from *Tarjumán Al-Ashwáq* by Muḥyi'ddín Al-'Arabí

Feirefiz continues to be the strange one. Even his trusting nephew is unsure of his unconventional uncle. And while everyone is marveling at the splendor of the Grail and how it provides food, Feirefiz is sitting there like a dope, falling in love. Feirefiz is blind to the Grail.

We can look at this marvel from several standpoints. The most obvious one is provided in the story. Titurel says Feirefiz cannot see the Grail because he is still a heathen, and he must be baptized to view the wonders. For those who choose their Grail to be one of faith, this is a steppingstone on their spiritual discovery. So this is a very plausible explanation.

Another way of viewing this phenomenon is the sheer power of falling in Love. No matter what else is happening, nothing else matters in the world. Feirefiz has met his Soul-Mate and that is all he can see. This love is so great that he will renounce anything and embrace anything which will allow him to love this woman. Sacrifice is nothing to him, as long as it guarantees a place in her heart. This is the stuff movies are made of. This is what we dream life is made of.

Let's step back and look at the idea that Feirefiz is seeing the Woman, not the Object. The Grail is only representative of the Spirit behind it. Let everyone else drink from the Grail—Feirefiz will take the Power behind that Grail. This is pure ecstatic vision that recognizes the Source of Power. Feirefiz understands that he is to love the work and the process of the Grail. He is able to see the Spirit of the Grail. Any rituals demanded of him are mundane and inconsequential. Ask anything of him, he is Ready. This is the same healing that Jack Lucas was able to perform, as the Grail was only a thank you trophy for work done for a school. It was the caring and the love behind the Grail that mattered, not the object.

There is yet another view of recognizing that Parzival's Grail is not Feirefiz' Grail. Parzival can bring Feirefiz into his fold to share this Grail, but it does not belong to Feirefiz. In Malory's tale, Lancelot does not renounce his relationship with Gwenevere, so he is not able to bear the presence of the Grail. This, of course, points out a certain morality that the sinful are not able to enjoy the blessings of the Grail. I have always preferred to interpret it as Lancelot has already found his Grail in the form of Guenevere. He has no need of the Grail. We must remember this as we share our Grail with others. They may not need it because they already have their own.

The Baptism has its own magic. The baptismal fount fills up with Holy Water on its own accord as it is tipped towards the Grail. This again shows a restoration of the Wasteland, as the Grail now provides the Water of Life.

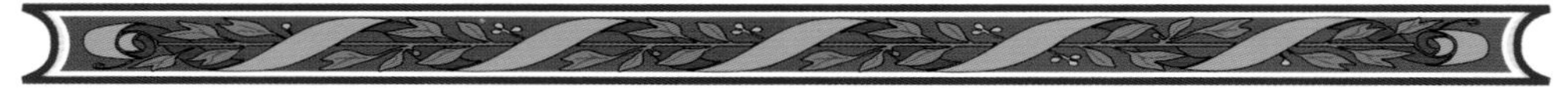

Amnesty International, Medieval Style

After Feirefiz' baptism, mysterious writings appear on the Grail. It states that any Templar sent to rule over others in a foreign land must help them in their rights, unless those people ask the Templars what their race or name is. This enigmatic statement must be examined in two parts, because its ideas come from two different sources. The secret name part is discussed next under the Lohengrin section, while here we look at Wolfram's remarkable declaration of liberties.

The most inspiring part of the final writing on the Grail is that foreigners are to be helped in obtaining their rights. This is an amazing viewpoint since it took until the twentieth century for us to even envision a concept of international civil rights. People of different races, different religions and different cultures could count on the Knights of the Grail to protect their own individual rights. It was a valiant call to the end of racism, a struggle we still face. The Healing from the Grail Castle specifically extended to other lands.

The Rights of Foreigners

Many of us will not visit other foreign countries as tourists, much less as defenders of human rights. So how do we extend our healing out to others?

1. The first step is basic. Treat those around us with respect and care, no matter how different they are from us. Rely on that wondrous web of the Tao and universe to deliver that kindness. Voice your own feelings about others' rights, even when they are unable to do so. Recognize that those of different faiths and races may need compassion and help.

2. Send a contribution to organizations working in the world sending supplies and manpower to others. Even $10 can help. As you find success through the work with your Grail, then your contributions can increase. But just starting to help reaches more than you can imagine.

Lohengrin

Will and Sean watch the swans.
(Will-Matt Damon, Sean-Robin Williams)

Will Hunting and Sean Maguire sit at the Boston Commons facing the lake view, where swans float peaceably by them. In an attempt to avoid real issues they have to discuss, Will sarcastically asks Sean if he has an interest in swans. Those swans play a bigger part of our story than you would imagine.

The part of the Grail inscription of people not asking the Templars their names or race was a literary ploy to hook the Lohengrin legend to the Parzival legend. The story says because it took so long for Parzival to ask his question, people were fed up with questioning. Don't believe it. The diminished literary finesse in this chapter sometimes leads me to think that Wolfram's writing had several editors working over his shoulder, but that is an another issue. Not revealing your name is the same custom we saw earlier of the power of one's name. There are many fairy tales where a being from the OtherWorld has to keep his name secret. Otherwise the OtherWorld would call him back. Sometimes that being changed his shape, and the spell would be broken. The legend of Lohengrin (Loherangrin in *Parzival*) is the story of the Knight of the Swan. It relates to the Germanic and Scandinavian myths of the Swan Maidens, and I believe, all the way back to the Greek stories of Leda coupling with a swan. Her two sons, Castor and Polydeuces (Pollux), are the Gemini Twins in the heavens. Ludwig II's Bavarian castle is called *Neuschwanstein,* meaning "New Swan Stone." Inside, many decorative items honor the Swan Knight legend, including murals, door knobs, fabrics, and utensils. Wagner wrote an opera about Lohengrin—not surprising, since Ludwig II was Wagner's biggest patron.

Swan Maidens were beautiful women who could don their *aptar-hamir,* swan dresses, and fly through the air as swans. Some of these maidens were the legendary Valkyries, who oversaw the heroes of battles. There are tales of men stealing the maidens' swan dresses to blackmail the maidens into marrying them. Later, when the women regain their dresses, they put them on and fly away. In some stories, these women have sons who could also shape-change into swans, as long as they wore a magic necklace. If a necklace was lost or destroyed, the man would take on the swan shape. For Loherangrin, the taking of his name and past was enough to call him back to the Grail Castle, this time in a boat pulled by a Swan.

In one legend, the Duchess of Bouillon needed a hero to defend herself against charges made by the Saxon Duke Renier. A mysterious man appears on a swan boat and defends her. He marries her daughter, Beatris, on the promise that she would not ask about his name and lineage. They have a daughter Ida (Ide D'Ardennes, Saint Ida). After seven years, Beatris asks the taboo questions, so he leaves. Ida later marries Count Eustache II and one of their sons is the famed Godfrey of Bouillon, who went on to lead the first Crusades. (Going way back on Godfrey's family tree on his father's side is Dagobert II. *Star Wars'* fans will recognize a similarity between that name and the "Dagobah System," where Yoda lives. A coincidence?) To this day, there are people claiming they are of the Grail family, with their assertions going even further, saying the Grail lineage is one of Christ's.

Now for Leda. At some time, you may have seen a painting of a nude woman with a swan between her legs. That is Leda, wife of King Tyndareus, being "seduced" by Zeus in the form of a swan. From this encounter, she gave birth to an egg (Cosmic Egg) from which came Castor and Polydeuces, Helen of Troy, and Clytemnestra. Various legends split the paternity between the offspring, though all were born from a swan egg. Both Clytemnestra and Helen of Troy were central figures of Abduction Myths, with Helen's being the start of the Trojan War. In various stories the Twin brothers aide their sisters. Castor and Polydeuces were also part of the Argonauts who went on the Quest for the Golden Fleece. They participated in the games following the death of Pelias, who believed he would be resurrected as a young man from Medea's Cauldron. (Note that Pelles is the name of the Fisher King in several Grail myths.) And to really stretch the point, the two brothers were sometimes called the Oebalides, which can be translated to mean "sons of the temple threshold" or "of the *speckled* sheep-skin." Maybe Parzival and Feirefiz just split that definition in half. Nevertheless, Leda is sometimes thought of as the goddess Nemesis, who ruled over a Peloponnesian swan cult. Nemesis is the goddess who carries an apple-bough in one hand, and a wheel in the other. That wheel is the Wheel of Fortune, which she will turn upside down when someone gets too uppity.

Just as the Goose was considered a master of the land, sea, and air, so too, was the Swan. The Swan moves through the different realms even more elegantly than the Goose, which is a loving, deserving legacy Parzival would pass on to his children.

So, there is a lot more to think about mythically when we see that little addendum to Parzival's story with a son who rides a boat pulled by a swan.

Prester John

Will your grace command me any service to the world's end? I will go on the slightest errand now to the Antipodes that you can devise to send me on; I will fetch you a toothpicker now from the furthest inch of Asia, bring you the length of Prester John's foot, fetch you a hair off the great Cham's beard, do you any embassage to the Pigmies, rather than hold three words' conference with this harpy. You have no employment for me?

—from *Much Ado About Nothing* by William Shakespeare

Very few people today are familiar with the character of Prester John, but in the mid twelfth century, he was a very famous man. Priest (Presbyter) John was supposedly a Christian king who ruled in India, and by some accounts, Ethiopia. This fits in, of course, with Feirefiz, whose roots were in Africa and who was a hero in India. Now that Feirefiz was baptized a Christian, what better achievement than to have his son known as the most famous person of that century?

It is possible that there was a historical impetus to the character built on the visit of one John, the Patriarch of the Indians, to Pope Calixtus II in 1122. In the "Letter of Prester John," which is believed to have been doctored throughout the years, he tells of ruling seventy-two countries which contain many magical entities. These include a sea without water, salamanders who live in fire and weave silk for clothes that are washed by fire, and a cave that fills with healing waters. Marco Polo supposedly found his kingdom by the Gobi desert and that Chingis-khan (Ghenghis Khan) was one of his servants. When Prester John refused marriage of his daughter to Chingis, there was a battle, and Prester John was killed. John Mandeville wrote of horned men in Prester John's kingdom, who grunted like pigs instead of speaking. His thrones and beds are made of precious stones, and his banners in battle were three large gold crosses set with jewels.

The myths of Prester John stayed alive for several centuries, until people realized that there was no place as magical as described in all of the fables, so the interest died down. Yet every time we go off to look for Paradise, we are searching for a land that Prester John ruled.

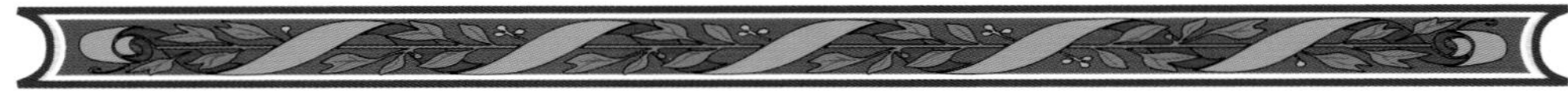

The Death of Secundille

Wolfram had to kill off Queen Secundille so Feirefiz and Repanse can have a guilt free marriage. I chose to also find another lesson in her death. Since Sophia was known to send her soul in the form of the dove, and the Shakti was known to incarnate as an earthly wife, I chose to think of Secundille's spirit blessing the union of Feirefiz and Repanse. Feirefiz had known Three Queens before his marriage to Repanse. For me, this was the unifying of the Triplicate Goddess into One.

Too often in our marriages, we fragment our partners by only viewing them through one role. Whether it is the Virgin, Mother, Crone model of the female, or the male counterparts, we relegate them to only one position. We daydream of the young, virile man of past years (Consort), we demand the most of the current Father, and we almost dread the "dirty Old Man." We are unfair to our loved ones if we only appreciate one aspect of them. We must learn to love the whole Individual, not just particular aspects of our partner that we choose to focus on.

Loving the Whole

If you have been viewing your partner in only one role, look at the whole person. Let your loved one know how much you love those other parts of him/her. If the children have been draining your wife of energy, let her know that you still find her beautiful as when you were first together. If you have been relating to your husband only as the prime provider, reexperience some carefree activities you had enjoyed in earlier years. And as you both start spouting off idiosyncratic notions that come during old age, love and embrace those also.

The Lessons of A New Grail Procession

ꕤ When we are able to achieve our Grail, it is a time to celebrate with all of those people whom we love and who encouraged us. We can create our own Court of Joy.

ꕤ More important than the object of the Grail are the people and the Spirit behind the Grail. This is where real Power lies.

ꕤ Our Grail is not someone else's Grail, but we can still embrace and bring in others to the Joy of the Grail.

ꕤ We have a spiritual duty to help those who are different from us, even if we can only do it in small ways. Changing our own hearts and actions is the beginning of building a New World of Harmony.

ꕤ We must embrace the Whole of our Loved Ones. We must stop fragmenting those we love into roles which are convenient for ourselves.

The story of Parzival has ended, but we must look into the future about what it means to be the Healed King and what our obligations are to our Brighter Sons and Daughters.

Where Do We Come From? What Are We? Where Are We Going? by Paul Gauguin (1848–1903)

Courtesy: Museum of Fine Arts, Boston, Tompkins Collection. (36.270)
Oil on Canvas, 1897. 54 ¾ x 147 ½ in.

Chapter 21 - The Healthy King

Illuminated with tropical romanticism, Paul Gauguin asks questions of the Soul—

> *Where Do We Come From? What Are We? Where Are We Going?*

These are questions that we can now ponder with more substance and proper response. We now have a better understanding of ourselves and how we want to fit into the world about us. It is time that we evaluate exactly what it means to be *The Healthy King.*

Where Do We Come From?

I felt so sure they could not possibly know the things I knew.
— Marlow in *Heart of Darkness* by Joseph Conrad

When people asked them why they were living thus, they would reply:
'Go where we went, and you will know why.'
— from *Perlesvaus* trans. by Nigel Bryant

One day, after reaching success with your Grail, you will run into people whom you haven't seen for awhile. They will correctly notice that something has changed in you, because anyone who ventures into the OtherWorld emerges a changed person—you cannot work so hard, with such focus, confronting grievous pain and responding with compassion, without being changed. Your awareness and your perceptions of your purpose in life have crystallized, and living the old life will no longer be possible.

This learning experience will have the positive and negative results of any inquiry into knowledge. You will have healed old wounds, and picked up a few new ones. You will have gained new friends, and have alienated some old.

It is time to reflect on the whole process you have been through. What goodness have you accomplished? What could you have done differently? Despite the trials you have gone through, have you achieved a sense of peace?

Look over your journey and note the milestones—

Whom have you met has taught and influenced you? Whom did you reach out to give direction and help?

What were the most significant events that marked your learning process and achievements? Were these initially negative or positive?

While the World's history changed, how did this affect your path? How did your contribution change the World?

How have you changed physically? Does your face show worry lines, aging lines, or lines of experience?

How have you changed at an emotional level? How has your character changed?

What Spiritual changes have come about in your life?

Introspection on your changes will give you a foundation for your future endeavors. It will give you confidence to face a new set of challenges, and help you formulate a fresh perspective on the values you wish to enhance and carry forward. When asked about the changes in your life and where you have been, you will have ready answers built on wisdom and experience.

What Are We?

God Speed by Edmund Blair Leighton (1853–1922)
Painted 1900

Anfortas has been healed and now will go out into the world as a representative of the Grail Castle. He represents those wounds we thought would devastate us, but instead have given us more wisdom and strength for the future. The New Grail King is where he is because of the tests he has survived, and his willingness to choose compassion when the sword didn't work.

Joseph Campbell lists the various transformations that a hero goes through once he leaves behind his childhood. They are Warrior, Lover, Emperor, World Redeemer, and Saint. Parzival is the New Grail King because he has succeeded at all of these roles. His Warrior skills are undeniable, and his loyalty and need of his wife confirms his role as a Lover. He Redeemed the World by restoring the Wasteland by Healing the Fisher King. He ruled as the King of Pelrapeire and now as King of Munsalvaesche. One of Campbell's definition of Saint is also Ascetic or World-Renouncer. Parzival successfully renounced the world as he searched his own path, until he had the ability to return and heal the world.

How do you fare against this list? Have you honed your skills as a Warrior, ready to utilize all that you have learned in the pursuit of your dreams? Do you do so responsibly? Do you freely show Love to the important people in your life, making sure that you make time and memories with them? When it is necessary to remove yourself from the world to finish the necessary steps to achieve your Grail, can you do it? Do you encourage Healing in the land by showing acts of Compassion? Are you ready to act as Emperor of your own domain?

Where Are We Going?

For us to determine where WE are going, you must ask yourself where are YOU going? We know that the actions of the Individual influences the Community as well as directly influencing one's Spiritual life. So you must ask yourself how you will improve the connections between all three Kingdoms.

In your life as King of the Individual, you must ask yourself—

What other Grails reside within you? What other accomplishments do you envision and what purpose will sustain you as you work?

What can you do in the work environment so that everyone can work in a nurturing, purposeful environment that benefits all?

What more can you do to enhance your relationships with your family and friends? How do you empower them to achieve their Grails?

In your life as King of the Community, you must ask yourself—

What can you do at the local level to enhance the Community?

How can this produce a ripple effect that extends beyond the immediate neighborhood?

What can you do to produce or improve the lives of people at the national and world level?

And when the time comes, how do the actions of today affect the worlds beyond this one?

In your life as King of the Spirit, you must ask yourself—

What rituals can I create that keep me in touch with my Spirit? Do I have places of sanctuary to go to when I must make difficult decisions and where I can refresh my Spiritual life?

Am I content with the values I use to direct my life, or can I improve my decision-making processes by incorporating higher standards?

Have I found peace with my relationship with a higher deity or spirit? If not, what must I resolve to find spiritual sereneness and power?

As each of us evaluates our lives, and determines paths which give positive results, we can answer the question "Where Are We Going?" with optimism. By placing trust in our individual visions which recognize our impact on the world, we create a world greater, and with more hope, than we can possibly dream of.

How Do We Rule as a Healthy King?

After all of this, settling down to be a King seems easy. Pages fetch things for you, damsels in the wings play harpsichord music, and your own stable of knights takes care of the nasty business.

Remember Arthur? He set up the golden age of knighthood, and then his kingdom suffered severe stagnation. Being King now means you are strong and organized enough to prepare yourself for the next stage of challenges and adventures. The *I Ching* Hexagram of Contentment tells us that this is the time we gather resources and prepare. We don't sit back smiling like contented Cheshire cats.

> *Thus the balance of his scale weights down, increasing his own fame, while causing the fame of his opponents to fall.*
>
> — from *Parzival,* Book IX, ¶ 434

Wolfram liked the idea that the more solid you become, the lower your side of the scale drops, yet your fame rises. This is a lot like the Tai Chi practice of Pushing Hands, where you concentrate on making your root (base) more solid, so that it is easier to push off your own opponent. Do this many times and your own fame increases. So the Healthy King remembers to work on his root, continually building his strength. Don't forget that Lady Fortuna shows up at the most inopportune times.

Remember that this Healthy King is now the Grail King. Keep your Grail in focus. By honoring the learning and benefits you have received from achieving your Grail, you can continue to be uplifted by its presence. As Grail King, you have the authority to share what you have discovered, and inspire others. There is much power in this sharing.

> *However numberless sentient beings are, I vow to save them.*
> *However inexhaustible the hindrances are, I vow to end them.*
> *However immeasurable the gates of learning are, I vow to master them.*
> *However unattainable enlightenment is, I vow to attain it.*
>
> — Bodhisattva vows

Despite Parzival's abilities and test survivals, he became king by showing compassion. Remember to give people a chance and treat them with kindness. If they abuse it, you may then turn away, but many people turn away before even acknowledging that a living, sentient being stands before them. We need to proliferate kind hearts and make many Grail Kings.

Christ and Buddha by Paul Ranson (1861–1909)

Private Collection
Oil on Canvas, ca. 1890–92. 28 5/8 x 20 1/4 in.

Chapter 22 – Brighter Son

The Infant Moses
by Gustave Moreau (1826–1898)
Courtesy: Fogg Art Museum, Harvard University Art Museums, Bequest of Greenville L. Winthrop. Oil on Canvas, 1878. 72 x 52 ½ in. Photo: Rick Stafford.

Those sons of Parzival represent the seeds of creativity and the future. They are to be nurtured and cared for, challenged and sent into the world.

Those sons also represent the real children, adolescents, and young adults of our world. Though everyone's future is clouded, and there are no certainties, we can make efforts to give the next generation a real chance at being the best they can be.

Teach Your Children Well

First, for adults: Teachers in school are not the only ones educating children. We are all teachers. Young people feel our anger and love, see our successes and failures, and learn values by not only what we say, but by what we do. We must speak to them honestly and without hypocrisy. They must understand our own motivations for what we do so they will be able to make reasonable choices on their own. They must be allowed the freedom to be creative and adventurous, yet they must understand that every action has a direct and indirect outcome. We must make time to answer their questions. We must not hold back on truth, even if it is ugly. They will learn it anyway, and in a harsher, more destructive environment. If you have made mistakes in life, be honest about them so they can learn from you. The hard lessons they learn from your mistakes may help their futures. They are not only our sons and daughters, they are our Brighter Sons and Daughters. We must present them with the ability to pursue their own dreams, without burdening them with our lost ones. We cannot shackle them with our own fears and agendas. We have a duty to help them recognize what is best in them, whether it is athletics, language, music, art, or the ability to deal with people. Holding them back will not strengthen our futures. Only unconditional support and a presentation of our own wisdom will help them.

Being Your Own Mentor

Carnation, Lily, Lily, Rose by John Singer Sargent (1856–1925)
Tate Gallery, London
Oil on Canvas, 1885–86. 68 ½ x 60 ½ in.
Photo: Tate Gallery, London / Art Resource, N.Y.

This section is addressed to our Brighter Sons and Daughters.

I saw the John Singer Sargent painting *Carnation, Lily, Lily, Rose* in London, at a museum called The Barbican. A barbican is a fortressed place, so you can imagine a large, cold, gray fortress of a museum. Inside was a wonderful exhibition of Impressionism in Britain. When I entered the doorway and saw this painting, I felt the contrast of this glowing work of art against the looming, dark museum. Immediately, I equated the bright lanterns as the children's hopes, still ignorant of the gray gloom surrounding them. How do you keep the light burning in the lantern — alive and warming? How do you not succumb to the gray? You do so by recognizing that you are responsible for your own future, and you must keep your own possibilities alive.

Look at the adults around you whom you admire, and figure out why you admire them. Is it because they have achieved financial success? Is it because of athletic ability or literary achievements? Is it because they are truly nice, fun people, and you simply enjoy being with them? You will know people who represent all of the above. Make them mentors for your own development. When you have questions about any of those areas you are interested in, ask the best person you know. Too often, as you are growing up, you are told to be silent, but it is time that you learn to ask the Question. Even if you are shy, speak up and learn. If someone has made a million dollars, ask him how he did it, and be prepared for a long discourse. If someone has written books that you like, ask her about her writing process. There is a wealth of personal information out there not found in books. So gather what you can, and think about what you can put into your life to get similar results.

Now for the down side. There will be times when adults will fail you. Sometimes they will do so intentionally. Other times it will be from their own inability to understand or handle a situation. It may come from their own ignorance and fears, or from a condescending attitude that you are "only kids." If there are no people around you who can serve as mentors, learn to be your own. Learn to ask the important questions of yourself, and learn how to find the answers. Learn to be your own Master and your own Prodigy.

Search out the knowledge that is lacking around you. Use books, internet, television, or magazines. You may have to research colleges or training that specialize in your desired subject, and you may have to leave home to get that knowledge.

Create your own self discipline by imagining the Master telling you what to do. If you want to be a marathon runner, get a book to see how other marathoners have trained. Then have the Master inside you be relentless in telling you what you need to do. Anyone who is successful has developed self discipline to achieve what she wants to achieve. Sometimes a personality you see on television may appear frivolous, or easy going, or outrageous, but everyone you see there is a relentless risk taker. If that person doesn't have self-discipline, someone who is guiding her does. Don't let a wild persona trap you into believing that you don't have to work hard to achieve something.

Even when others around you discount your abilities, ignore the nay-sayers and keep working on your dreams. Their put-downs cover up their own fears. Develop yourself and focus on what you want out of life. If you can work on your dreams now, do so. Many adults have been forced down the "safe path" that did not charge their souls. They suffer because of that.

Understand this—you can be successful in anything. Some things bring more financial success than others, but success has to be determined by the whole package. Love for what you do, enough money to live the life you desire, and enough time to spend with friends and those you love is great success. No matter what someone does, we always appreciate excellence, so whatever your dreams are, find a way to work on them, and be the best you can. The earlier you start on the path to your Grail, the sooner you will benefit from its lessons and rewards.

Final Thoughts

When Fortuna spins you downward, go out to a movie and get more out of life.
— from *A Confederacy of Dunces* by John Kennedy Toole

Yes, movies can give us a little more of life, because we can see how others live and interact, even in worlds which do not exist. The old myths are taught to us in movies, and we don't even know what we are learning. But after the movies, we have to find our own Quests. There are Grails and Arks and Golden Fleeces. There are also Obsessions about Whales with White Foreheads. The difference between a Quest and an Obsession is what will come at the end of the Road. The difference is in choosing a path which yield positive results for yourself, your family, your friends, your loved ones, your community, and the world. If the Tao is going to give us choices that are both Good and Bad, let's choose the Good. Let's develop Clear Thinking and Good Intention. Everything we do has a consequence, so let's choose what enhances and not what destroys. When in doubt of what to do, choose words and actions of Compassion.

Though we have goals and roads in front of us, we need to travel them with a sense of Balance. We need to appreciate every day given to us as a new chance at Adventure, a new chance at our Grail. We need to take time to pause and Listen Intently—to the voices around us and those within us.

Let's start living today with what is in our Hearts. This is the path of the Grail.

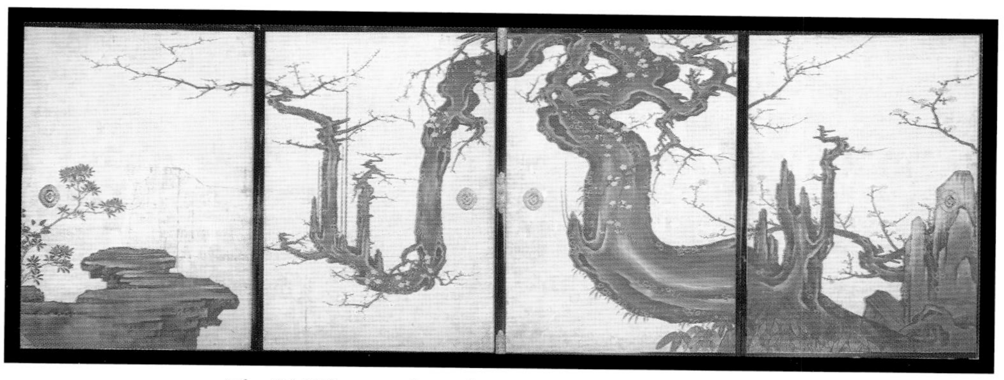

The Old Plum attributed to Kano Sansetsu (1590–1651)

Courtesy: The Metropolitan Museum of Art, New York, The Harry G. C. Packard Collection of Asian Art, Gift of Harry G. C. Packard, and Purchase, Fletcher, Rogers, Harris Brisbane Dick, and Louis V. Bell Funds, Joseph Pulitzer Bequest, and The Annenberg Fund Inc. Gift, 1975. Sliding Door Panels, Colors and Gold Leaf on Paper, 1647. 68 ¾ x 191 ⅛ in. Photo: ©1977 The Metropolitan Museum of Art

Dark young pine, at the center of the earth originating,
I have made your sacrifice.
Whiteshell, turquoise, abalone beautiful,
Jet beautiful, fool's gold beautiful, blue pollen beautiful,
reed pollen, pollen beautiful, your sacrifice I have made.
This day your child I have become, I say.

Watch over me.
Hold your hand before me in protection.
Stand guard for me, speak in defense of me.
As I speak for you, so do ye.
As you speak for me, thus I shall do.
May it be beautiful before me.
May it be beautiful behind me.
May it be beautiful below me.
May it be beautiful above me.
May it be beautiful all around me.

I am restored in beauty.
I am restored in beauty.
I am restored in beauty.
I am restored in beauty.

— Traditional Navaho Prayer

Backstory - Appendix

Selected Bibliography

This is a list of some of the books which inspired and aided me in writing this book. The levels of scholarship are varied, so use a questioning mind, but all lay a foundation for a discussion of personal myth making. Also check out readings listed in the "First Billing - Acknowledgment" section at the front of this book. Enjoy, think deeply, feel deeply, and expand the list.

Literature

Bromwich, Rachel, trans. *Trioedd Ynys Prydein: The Welsh Triads.* Cardiff: University of Wales Press, 1961

Bryant, Nigel, trans. *The High Book of the Grail: A translation of the thirteenth-century romance Perlesvaus.* 1978. Cambridge: D. S. Brewer, 1996

Bryant, Nigel, trans. *Merlin and the Grail: Joseph of Arimathea, Merlin, Perceval: The trilogy of prose romances attributed to Robert de Boron.* Cambridge: D. S. Brewer, 2001

Cable, James, trans. *The Death of Arthur.* Harmondsworth, U. K.: Penguin Books, 1971

Chrétien de Troyes. *Arthurian Romances.* Translated by William W. Kibler and Carleton W. Carroll. Harmondsworth, U. K.: Penguin Books, 1991

Chrétien de Troyes. *Perceval: The Story of the Grail.* Translated by Nigel Bryant. Woodbridge, U. K.: D. S. Brewer, 1982

Conrad, Joseph. *Heart of Darkness and The Secret Sharer.* 1902. New York: Bantam Doubleday Dell Publishing Group, Bantam Books, 1981

Corley, Corin, trans. *Lancelot of the Lake.* Oxford: Oxford University Press, 1989

Dawood, N. J., trans. *The Koran.* 5th ed. Harmondsworth, U. K.: Penguin Books, 1997

Ford, Patrick K., trans. *The Mabinogi and Other Medieval Welsh Tales.* Berkeley: University of California Press, 1977

Gantz, Jeffrey, trans. *The Mabinogion.* Harmondsworth, U. K.: Penguin Books, 1976

Geoffrey of Monmouth. *The History of the Kings of Britain.* Translated by Lewis Thorpe. Harmondsworth, U. K.: Penguin Books, 1966

Geoffrey of Monmouth. *Life of Merlin: Vita Merlini.* Translated by Basil Clarke. Cardiff: University of Wales Press, 1973

Heinrich von dem Türlin. *The Crown: A Tale of Sir Gawein and King Arthur's Court.* Translated by J. W. Thomas. Lincoln: University of Nebraska Press, 1989

Hesiod. *Theogony; Work and Days; Shield.* Translated by Apostolos N. Athanassakis. Baltimore, Md.: John Hopkins University Press, 1983

The Holy Bible. Philadelphia: A. J. Holman, 1876

Jewish Publication Society. *Tanakh: A New Translation of the Holy Scriptures According to the Traditional Hebrew Text.* Philadelphia: Jewish Publication Society, 1985

Kühn, Dieter. *Der Parzival des Wolfram von Eschenbach.* Frankfurt am Main, Ger.: Fischer Taschenbuch Verlag, 1997

Lacy, Norris J., ed. *Lancelot-Grail: The Old French Arthurian Vulgate and Post-Vulgate in Translation.* 5 vol. New York: Garland Publishing, 1993

Malory, Sir Thomas. *Le Morte D'Arthur.* New York: Gramercy Books, 1995

Matarasso, P. M., trans. *The Quest of the Holy Grail.* Harmondsworth, U. K.: Penguin Books, 1969
Roach, William. *The Continuations of the Old French Perceval of Chrétien de Troyes.* 6 vol. Philadelphia: American Philosophical Society, 1965
Skeels, Dell, trans. *The Romance of Perceval in Prose: A Translation of the E Manuscript of the Didot Perceval.* Seattle: University of Washington Press, 1961
Stone, Brian, trans. *King Arthur's Death: Alliterative Morte Arthure and Stanzaic Le Morte Arthur.* Harmondsworth, U. K.: Penguin Books, 1988
Stone, Brian, trans. *Sir Gawain and the Green Knight.* 2nd ed. Harmondworth, U. K.: Penguin Books, 1974
Tennyson, Alfred, Lord. *Idylls of the King.* Edited by J. M. Gray. Harmondsworth, U. K.: Penguin Books, 1983
Thompson, Albert Wilder. *The Elucidation: A Prologue to the Conte Del Graal.* New York: Institute of French Studies, 1931
Wolfram von Eschenbach. *Parzival.* Translated by A. T. Hatto. Harmondsworth, U. K.: Penguin Books, 1980
Wolfram von Eschenbach. *Parzival.* Edited by André Lefevere. New York: Continuum, 1991
Wolfram von Eschenbach. *Parzival: A Knightly Epic by Wolfram von Eschenbach.* Translated by Jessie. L. Weston. London: David Nutt in the Strand, 1894
Wolfram von Eschenbach. *Parzival: A Romance of the Middle Ages.* Translated by Helen M. Mustard and Charles E. Passage. New York: Random House, Vintage Books, 1961
Wolfram von Eschenbach. *The Parzival of Wolfram von Eschenbach.* Translated by Edwin H. Zeydel with Bayard Quincy Morgan. Chapel Hill, N. C.: Univ. of North Carolina, 1951
Wolframs von Eschenbach. *Parzival und Titurel.* 3 vol. Edited by Karl Bartsch. Leipzig, Ger.: F. A. Brockhaus, 1937

Further Readings

Ashe, Geoffrey. *King Arthur: The Dream of a Golden Age.* London: Thames & Hudson, 1990
Bakhtiar, Laleh. *Sufi: Expressions of the Mystic Quest.* London: Thames & Hudson, 1976
Bancroft, Anne. *Zen: Direct Pointing to Reality.* New York: Crossroad Publishing, 1979
Biedermann, Hans. *Dictionary of Symbolism: Cultural Icons and the Meanings Behind Them.* Translated by James Hulbert. Harmondsworth, U. K.: Penguin Books, Meridien, 1994
Blofield, John. *Gateway to Wisdom.* London: George Allen & Unwin, 1980
Blofield, John. *Taoism: The Road to Immortality.* Boulder, Co.: Shambala, 1978
Bly, Robert and Marion Woodman. *The Maiden King.* New York: Henry Holt, 1998
Burrows, David J., Frederick R. Lapides, and John T. Shawcross, ed. *Myths and Motifs in Literature.* New York: Free Press, 1973
Campbell, Joseph. *The Hero with a Thousand Faces.* 2nd ed. Princeton, N. J.: Princeton University Press, Bolingen Series, 1972
Campbell, Joseph. *The Masks of God: Creative Mythology.* Harmondsworth, U. K.:Penguin Books, 1968
Campbell, Joseph. *The Mythic Image.* 2nd ed. Princteon, N.J.:Princeton University Press, Bollingen Series, 1981

Campbell, Joseph. *Myths to Live By.*
New York: Bantam Doubleday Dell Publishing, Bantam Books, 1972
Campbell, Joseph with Bill Moyers. *The Power of Myth.*
New York: Bantam Doubleday Dell Publishing Group, Doubleday, 1988
Campbell, Joseph. *Transfornations of Myth Through Time.*
New York: Harper & Row, Perrenial Library, 1990
Cleary, Thomas, trans. *The Essential Koran: The Heart of Islam.*
San Francisco: HarperCollins Publisher, HarperSanFrancisco, 1994
Coghlan, Ronan. *The Illustrated Encyclopedia of Arthurian Legends.*
New York: Barnes & Noble Books, 1995
Crosley-Holland, Kevin. *The Norse Myths.* New York: Random House, Pantheon Books, 1980
Das, Lama Surya. *Awakening the Buddha Within: Eight Steps to Enlightenment: Tibetan Wisdom for the Western World.* New York: Bantam Doubleday Dell Publishing Group, Broadway Books, 1997
Davidson, H. R. Ellis. *Gods and Myths of Northern Europe.*
Harmondsworth, U. K.: Penguin Books, 1981
Eliade, Mercea. *A History of Religious Ideas: Volume 1: From the Stone Age to the Eleusinian Mysteries.* Translated by Willard R. Trask. Chicago: University of Chicago Press, 1981
Eliot, Alexander. Joseph Campbell and Mircea Eliade, cont. *The Universal Myths: Heroes, Gods, Tricksters and Others.* New York: Penguin Books, Meridien Books, 1990
Estés, Clarissa Pinkola. *Women Who Run With the Wolves: Myths and Stories of the Wild Woman Archetype.* New York: Random House, Ballantine Books, 1992
Fenster, Thelma S. *Arthurian Women: A Casebook.* New York: Garland Publishing, 1996
Frazier, Sir James George. *The New Golden Bough: A New Abridgment of the Classic Work.* Edited by Dr. Theodore H. Gaster. New York: New American Library, Mentor Book, 1964
Getty, Adele. *Goddess: Mother of Living Nature.* London: Thames & Hudson, 1990
Godolphin, F. R. B. *Great Classical Myths.* New York: Random House, Modern Library, 1964
Godwin, Malcolm. *The Holy Grail: Its Origins, Secrets & Meanings.*
Harmondsworth, U. K.: Penguin Books, Viking Studio Books, 1994
Goodrich, Peter, ed. *The Romance of Merlin: An Anthology.*
New York: Garland Publishing, 1990
Graves, Robert. *The Greek Myths.* Combined Edition.
Harmondsworth, U. K.: Penguin Books, 1992
Graves, Robert. *The White Goddess: A historical grammar of poetic myth.* am. and enl.
New York: Farrar, Straus & Giroux, Noonday Press, 1966
Gray, Louis Herbert, ed. *The Mythology of All Races.* 13 vol.
Boston: Marshall Jones Company, 1916
Grimal, Pierre. *Larousse World Mythology.*
New York: W. H. Smith Publishers, Gallery Books, 1989
Halevi, Z'ev ben Shimon. *Kabbalah: Tradition of Hidden Knowledge.*
London: Thames & Hudson, 1997
Hamilton, Edith. *Mythology.* New York: New American Library, Mentor Book, 1942
Henderson, Joseph L. and Maud Oakes. *The Wisdom of the Serpent: The Myths of Death, Rebirth, and Resurrection.* 2nd ed. Princton, N. J.: Princeton University Press, Mythos Series, 1990

Jackson, Kenneth Hurlstone. *A Celtic Miscellany: Translations from the Celtic Literatures.* Harmondsworth, U. K.: Penguin Group, 1971
Jagannathan, Shakunthala. *Hinduism: An Introduction.* Bombay: Vakils, Feffer & Simons, 1984
Jung, Carl G., ed. *Man and His Symbols.* New York: Dell Publishing, Laurel Edition, 1968
Jung, Carl G. and Carl Kerényi. *Essays on a Science of Mythology: The Myth of the Divine Child and the Mysteries of Eleusis.* Translated by R. F. C. Hull. Princeton, N. J.: Princeton University Press, Bolingen / Mythos Series, 1969
Jung, Emma and Marie-Louise von Franz. *The Grail Legend.* Translated by Andrea Dykes 2nd ed. Boston: Sigo Press, 1980
Kerényi, Carl. *Eleusis: Archetypal Image of Mother and Daughter.* Translated by Ralph Manheim. Princeton, N. J.: Princeton University Press, Bolingen / Mythos Series, 1967
Klossowski de Rola, Stanislas. *Alchemy: The Secret Art.* 1973. London: Thames & Hudson, 1997
Kwok Man Ho and Joanne O'Brien, trans. *The Eight Immortals of Taoism: Legends and Fables of Popular Taoism.* Harmondsworth, U. K.: Penguin Group, Meridien, 1991
Lacy, Norris J., ed. *The New Arthurian Encyclopedia.* 1986 New York: Garland Publishing, 1996
Lamy, Lucie. *Egyptian Mysteries: New Light on Ancient Knowledge.* London: Thames & Hudson, 1997
Larsen, Stephen. *The Mythic Imagination: The Quest for Meaning Through Personal Mythology.* Rochester, Vt.: Inner Traditions, 1996
Lash, John. *The Hero: Manhood and Power.* London: Thames & Hudson, 1995
Layton, Bentley, trans. *The Gnostic Scriptures.* New York: Bantam Doubleday Dell Publishing Group, Anchor Bible Reference Library, 1995
Littleton, C. Scott and Linda A. Malcor. *From Scythia to Camelot: A Radical Reassessment of the Legends of King Arthur, the Knights of the Round Table, and the Holy Grail.* New York: Garland Publishing, 1994
Loomis, Roger Sherman. *Celtic Myth and Arthurian Romance.* Chicago: Academy Chicago Publishers, 1997
Loomis, Roger Sherman. *The Grail: From Celtic Myth to Christian Symbol.* Princeton, N. J.: Princeton University Press, Mythos Series, 1991
MacNulty, W. Kirk. *Freemasonry: A Journey through Ritual and Symbol.* London: Thames & Hudson, 1991
Mahoney, Dhira B. *The Grail: A Casebook.* New York: Taylor & Francis Group, Garland Publishing, 2000
Markale, Jean. *Merlin: Priest of Nature.* Translated by Belle N. Burke. Rochester, Vt.: Inner Traditions, 1995
Matthews, Caitlín. *Arthur and the Sovereignty of Britain: King and Goddess in the Mabinogion.* Harmondsworth, U. K.: Penguin Books, Arkana, 1989
Matthews, Caitlín. *Sophia: Goddess of Wisdom: The Divine Feminine from Black Goddess to World-Soul.* London: HarperCollins Publishers, Aquarian Press, 1992
Matthews, Caitlín and John. *Ladies of the Lake.* London: HarperCollins, Aquarian Press, 1992
Matthews, John. *Gawain: Knight of the Goddess:Restoring an Archetype.* London: HarperCollins, Aquarian Press, 1990
Matthews, John. *The Grail: Quest for the Eternal.* London: Thames & Hudson, 1981

Neumann, Erich. *The Great Mother.* 2nd ed. Translated by Ralph Manheim. Princeton, N. J.: Princeton University Press, Bolingen Series, 1972

Parulski, George, Jr. *A Path to Oriental Wisdom: Introductory Studies in Eastern Philosophy.* Burbank, Ca.: Ohara Publications, 1976

Perry, Whitehall N., comp. *A Treasury of Traditional Wisdom.* Louisville, Kentucky: Fons Vitae, 2000

Rawson, Philip and Laszlo Legeza. *Tao: The Chinese Philosophy of Time and Change.* London: Thames & Hudson, 1979

Rowland, Beryl. *Birds with Human Souls.* Knoxville: University of Tennessee Press, 1978

Sharkey, John. *Celtic Mysteries: The Ancient Religion.* London: Thames & Hudson, 1992

Shearer, Alistair. *Buddha: The Intelligent Heart.* London: Thames & Hudson, 1992

Stewart, R. J. and John Matthews, ed. *Merlin Through the Ages: A Chronological Anthology and Source Book.* London: Cassell, Blandford, 1995

Walker, Barbara G. *The Woman's Dictionary of Symbols & Sacred Objects.* San Francisco: HarperCollins Publishers, HarperSanFrancisco, 1988

Walker, Barbara G. *The Woman's Encyclopedia of Myths and Secrets.* San Francisco: Harper & Row Publishers, 1983

Weston, Jessie L. *From Ritual to Romance.* Princeton, N. J.: Princeton University Press, Mythos Series, 1993

Wilhelm, James J., ed. *The Romance of Arthur: An Anthology of Medieval Texts in Translation* exp. ed. New York: Garland Publishing, 1994

Wilhelm, Richard, trans. (Chinese to German) *The I Ching or Book of Changes.* Translated by Cary F. Baynes (German to English). Foreward by C. G. Jung. Princeton, N. J.: Princeton University Press, Bolingen Series, 1997

Yeats, William Butler, ed. Book 1, and Lady Isabella Augusta Gregory, trans. Book 2. *A Treasury of Irish Myth, Legend, and Folklore: Fairy and Folk Tales of the Irish Peasantry (Book 1) and Cuchulain of Muirthemne: The Story of the Men of the Red Branch of Ulster (Book 2).* New York: Gramercy Books, 1986

Arthuriana and International Arthurian Society: http://dc.smu.edu/Arthuriana

Camelot Project – University of Rochester: http://www.lib.rochester.edu/camelot/cphome.stm

Art

Ash, Russell. *Sir Edward Burne-Jones.* New York: Harry N. Abrams, 1993

Bacou, Roseline. *Odilon Redon: Pastels.* New York: George Braziller, 1987

Becks-Malorny. *Wassily Kandinsky, 1866–1944: The Journey to Abstraction.* Cologne, Ger.: Benedikt Taschen, 1994

Chadwick, Whitney. *Women, Art, and Society.* London: Thames and Hudson, 1990

Donnell, Courtney Graham, comp. *Ivan Albright.* New York: Hudson Hills Press, 1997

Fong, Wen C. and James C. Y. Watt. *Possessing the Past: Treasures from the National Palace Museum, Taipei.* New York: Metropolitan Museum of Art; Taipei: National Palace Museum, Taipei, 1996

Forty, Sandra. *The Pre-Raphaelites.* New York: Barnes & Noble Books, 1997

Gibson, Michael. *Symbolism.* Cologne, Ger.: Benedikt Taschen, 1995

Hobson, Anthony. *J W Waterhouse.* London: Phaidon Press Limited, 1989
Huckel, Oliver. *Parsifal: A Mystical Drama by Richard Wagner Retold in the Spirit of the Bayreuth Interpretation by Oliver Huckel.* New York: Thomas Y. Crowell, 1903
Hudson, Wade and Cheryl Willis Hudson, comp. *In Praise of Our Fathers and Our Mothers: A Black Family Treasury by Outstanding Authors and Artists.* East Orange, N. J.: Just Us Books, 1997
Jaffe, Irma B. *Joseph Stella's Symbolism.* San Francisco: Pomegranate Artbooks, 1994
Johnson, Meredith. *Lovers in Art.* New York: Portland House, 1991
Kaplan, Janet. *Unexpected Journeys: The Art and Life of Remedios Varo.* New York: Abbeville Press, 1988
Kemplay, John. *The Paintings of John Duncan: A Scottish Symbolist.* San Francisco: Pomegranate Artbooks, 1994
Lee, Sherman E. *A History of Far Eastern Art.* Englewood Cliffs, New York: Prentice-Hall and Harry N. Abrams, 1973
Mathieu, Pierre-Louis. *Gustave Moreau.* New York: Flammarion, 1995
McConkey, Kenneth. *Impressionism in Britain.* London: Barbican Art Gallery, 1995
Metropolitan Museum of Art (New York, N.Y.). *The Metropolitan Museum of Art: Modern Europe.* New York: Metropolitan Museum of Art, 1987
Metropolitan Museum of Art (New York, N.Y.). *The Metropolitan Museum of Art: The United States of America.* New York: Metropolitan Museum of Art, 1987
Michler, Ralf and Lutz W. Löpsinger. *Salvador Dali: Catalogue Raisonné of Etchings and Mixed-Media Prints 1924–1980.* Munich, Ger.:Prestel-Verlag, 1994
Montreal Museum of Fine Arts. *Lost Paradise: Symbolist Europe.* Montreal: Montreal Museum of Fine Arts, 1995
Museum of Fine Arts, Boston. *Masterpiece Paintings from the Museum of Fine Arts, Boston.* New York: Harry N. Abrams, 1986
Peltre, Christine. *Orientalism in Art.* New York: Abbeville Press, 1998
Poulson, Christine. *The Quest for the Grail: Arthurian Legend in British Art, 1840–1920.* Manchester: Manchester University Press, 1999
Roberts, Brady M., and others. *Grant Wood: An American Master Revealed.* San Francisco: Pomegranate Artbooks in association with Davenport Museum of Art, 1995
Sala, Charles. *Caspar David Friedrich: The Spirit of Romantic Painting.* Paris:Terrail, 1994
Stebbins, Theodore E., Jr. *The Lure of Italy: American Artists and The Italian Experience, 1760–1914.* New York: Harry N. Abrams in association with Museum of Fine Arts, Boston, 1992
Sullivan, Charles, ed. *American Beauties: Women in Art and Literature.* New York: Harry N. Abrams, 1993
Thornton, Lynne. *The Orientalists: Painter-Travellers.* Paris: ACR PocheCouleur, 1994
Walker, John. *National Gallery of Art, Washington.* New York: Harry N. Abrams, 1975
Whitaker, Muriel. *The Legends of King Arthur in Art.* Cambridge: D.S. Brewer, 1990
Wilmerding, John. *American Masterpieces from the National Gallery of Art.* New York: Hudson Hills Press, 1980
Wood, Christopher. *The Pre-Raphaelites.* New York: Crescent Books, 1994

ArtMagick: www.artmagick.com
Art Renewal Center: www.artrenewal.com

Synopses and Filmography

Synopses are provided for film versions of the works used for examples in this book, except for *Siddhartha* and *Heart of Darkness,* which are based on the novels.

Apocalypse Now (1979)

Production Studio: Zoetrope Studios. Written by John Milius and Francis Ford Coppola. Directed and Produced by Francis Ford Coppola. Original Music by Carmine Coppola, Francis Ford Coppola, and Mickey Hart. Cast: Marlon Brando, Robert Duvall, Martin Sheen, Frederic Forrest, Albert Hall, Sam Bottoms, Laurence Fishburne, Dennis Hopper, G. D. Spradlin, Harrison Ford.

Benjamin Willard languishes in a Saigon hotel until he receives orders to go after a renegade officer, Colonel Kurtz. He is sent out on a boat with Chief Philips, Chef Hicks, Tyrone Miller (Mr. Clean), and Lance Johnson.

They go to the camp of Captain Kilgore, who bombs a village to clear a way for surfing and helicoptering Willard's boat to the river. Down the river, Chef wants mangoes, so he and Willard get off the boat. They are confronted by a tiger, but get back to the boat safely. As Willard reads Kurtz' dossier, he becomes more impressed with the man. The men come to a camp where they can restock. There is a Playmate show being staged, but the men in the crowd become too rowdy, and the entertainers have to be taken away. Willard's crew leaves the next morning.

The crew stops to investigate a sampan. When a girl runs towards a basket, Tyrone fires, and the others follow. The girl was only going for a dog, which Lance adopts. The girl is still alive, and Chief wants to take her to a hospital, but Willard shoots her, saying they are moving on.

They come to the last outpost, Do Long Bridge, where there is mayhem. Down the river they are attacked, with Tyrone being shot. Continuing on, they are harassed by natives shooting arrows. Chief is speared and tries to choke Willard as he dies. Further down the river, they enter Kurtz' territory, being greeted by the native people. The Freelance Photographer beckons him in and gives Willard advice on approaching Kurtz. Chef stays on the boat while Willard and Lance go to Kurtz. If they don't return in twenty-two hours, Chef is to call an air strike.

Willard is taken to Kurtz, who is dying of malaria. Kurtz speaks philosophically to Willard, then cages Willard. The Photographer tells Willard that he must help Kurtz, not kill him. Later, Kurtz puts Chef's head in Willard's lap.

Willard is freed and fed. Kurtz tells Willard he must make friends with horror to be successful. Kurtz is worried that his son will only hear lies about him and tells Willard to tell the truth when he returns stateside.

Lance dances with the native people as they prepare a cow for slaughter. Willard hears the radio saying the attack is on standby, but he knows he is no longer part of the status quo military. He knows Kurtz wants to go out like a soldier. He kills Kurtz with a machete at the same time the cow is being killed. He takes Kurtz' notes and leaves with Lance. As the boat pulls away, the radio is still trying to make contact and helicopters are appearing.

The Fisher King (1991)

Production Studio: Columbia Pictures Corporation. Written by Richard LaGravenese. Directed by Terry Gilliam. Produced by Debra Hill and Stacey Sher. Original Music by George Fenton. Cast: Jeff Bridges, Adam Bryant, Robin Williams, Mercedes Ruehl, Paul J. Lombardi, Amanda Plummer, David Hyde Pierce.

Jack Lucas is a successful shock talk radio host whose caustic words inflame a listener to kill diners at a New York restaurant. Jack is blamed for the event and loses his girlfriend, his job, his wealth, and his self-respect. He ends up working at a video store owned by Anne Napolitano, who also becomes his girlfriend. One night Jack is drinking and decides to end his life. While readying himself to jump in a river, two thugs mistake him for a homeless man. They beat him and douse him with gasoline, ready to light him. He is saved by Parry and a group of homeless people. Parry takes Jack to his home, and tells Jack that he is destined to help Parry retrieve the Grail. Jack later learns that Parry was a professor who taught Medieval literature and whose real name was Henry Sagan. Parry's life changed when his wife was killed at the diner that the deranged listener attacked.

Later, Jack returns offering Parry money. Parry is following the woman he loves, Lydia Sinclair. Afterwards, Parry shows Jack the home of Lanny Carmichael, whom Parry believes keeps the Grail. While outside the home, a vision of the Red Knight appears to Parry, terrifying him. Jack's presence drives the Red Knight away. They then hear a cry for help, and rescue the Homeless Cabaret Singer, who has been buried in mud. They take the man to an asylum and see the suffering of the patients there.

Jack and a nude Parry are lying on the ground in Central Park trying to "bust clouds." Parry relates the story of the Fisher King as one where a fool shows compassion to a dying king. Parry is momentarily disturbed when he sees the Red Knight again. He also tells Jack how a man must earn a woman's love.

With the help of Anne and the Cabaret Singer. Jack orchestrates a dinner between Lydia and Parry. After Parry walks Lydia home, he is attacked, and has to be hospitalized. He is in a coma, and there is no indication of improvement. Lydia visits and comforts him regularly, but Jack doesn't feel he can do anything more for him. Anne and Jack break up, as Anne is ready to move forward in the relationship, but Jack isn't ready.

Jack's life improves and he is about to be offered a television show. While entering the building where he has an appointment for the show, he sees the Cabaret Singer, but ignores him. The show he is offered is a comedy about homeless people. The concept upsets Jack.

Deciding to help Parry, Jack breaks into the home of Carmichael to retrieve the Grail, which is only a trophy. Jack steals the "Grail," but also finds that Carmichael has overdosed on medications. Jack sets off an alarm and Carmichael is rescued.

Jack brings the Grail to Parry, who awakens from his coma. Lydia comes to visit and finds Parry leading patients in a song. Jack goes to Anne, and tells her that he loves her. At the end of the film, both Jack and Parry lie nude in Central Park "cloud busting" and the city skyline lights with fireworks.

Forrest Gump (1994)

Production Studio: Paramount Pictures. Written by Winston Groom (novel) and Eric Roth (screenplay). Directed by Robert Zemeckis. Produced by Wendy Fineman, Steve Starkey, and Steve Tisch. Original Music by Alan Silvestri. Cast: Tom Hanks, Robin Wright, Gary Sinise, Hanna R. Hall, Mykelti Williamson, Sally Field, Rebecca Williams, Michael Conner Humphreys.

Forrest Gump waits on a bus bench. He picks up a white feather, placing it in his book, *Curious George.* He relates the story of his life to various people who come to sit next to him. He tells the first woman about the braces on his legs, about General Forrest starting the KKK, and how his mom seduced the principal of his school so he could stay at the school. His mother rented rooms to travelers—one being Elvis Presley. Forrest dances for Elvis, influencing Elvis' dance style.

On the school bus, Forrest meets Jenny Curran. They become best friends. One day, three bullies throw rocks at Forrest and Jenny tells him to run. While he runs, the braces fall apart, and from that day forward Forrest runs everywhere. One time, Forrest runs to Jenny's house. Her father sexually abuses her and her sisters. This time Jenny hides in the cornfield with Forrest when her father looks for her. Later, the police come and takes her father away and Jenny goes to live with her grandmother. At times, Jenny comes and sleeps with Forrest because she is afraid.

Jenny and Gump are walking home from high school. Forrest is chased by three boys, and when he runs away this time, he runs into the middle of a football game. His running skills enable him to play on Bear Bryant's college football team. When George Wallace comes to the college to prevent black students from entering, Forrest picks up a dropped book of one of the black students. Some of the coaches do not like Forrest being involved.

Forrest continues his story of his days in college when he visited Jenny at her girls college. Forrest sees Jenny kiss a man in a car, and when the man tries more, Forrest rescues her. Jenny is upset with him, but invites him inside to her dorm room. Confirming he is a virgin, Jenny tries seducing him, but Forrest becomes overly excited, and there is no consummation.

Gump's college football successes allow him to meet President Kennedy. After graduation, Forrest joins the army, where he becomes friends with Bubba Blue at boot camp. Bubba teaches him everything about the shrimping business. During that time, Jenny is thrown out of college for posing nude for Playboy, and ends up singing at a Memphis theater. Forrest goes to a performance, where she plays nude, and is harassed by the male audience. Again, Forrest comes to her defense, but she is angry and tells him to stop trying to help her. He tells her that he is going to Viet Nam, and she tells him not to be brave, but run when in trouble. She then hitches a ride from a passerby. Gump visits his mother who tells him to come home safe.

Bubba and Gump are to serve under Lt. Dan in Viet Nam. They trudge the countryside in rain for four months. Finally the rain stops, and they are ambushed. Forrest saves many men in his platoon, even though he is wounded by a bullet to the buttocks. However, Bubba dies, and Lt. Dan wants to die. At the hospital, Forrest becomes a ping-pong champion. Lt. Dan has lost both of his legs and blames Forrest for not letting him die. When Forrest receives notice he is to get the Medal of Honor, he tries to find Lt. Dan to share the news, but the Lieutenant has already left.

Back in the U. S., Forrest receives the medal from President Johnson, and is not shy in showing the president where he got shot. There is an anti-war protest at the Washington D.C. Mall, and Forrest is unwittingly put on the podium. His speech is thwarted when speaker wires are pulled, but Jenny is in the crowd and the two are reunited. Jenny takes him to a Black Panther's meeting place. Before Jenny leaves, she is slapped by her boyfriend, Wes. Forrest tries to convince her to be his girlfriend. She says she'll always be his girl, and he gives her his medal. She gives Forrest a hug, but goes off to San Francisco with Wes.

Forrest becomes famous by fighting communism with his ping-pong—notably playing the Chinese team. He shares an interview spot with John Lennon on the Dick Cavett show. Lt. Dan is waiting outside the Cavett show and makes snide comments about Gump's Medal of Honor. Lt. Dan's wheelchair slips on the ice, but Forrest saves him. They go to Dan's apartment to celebrate the holidays. On New Year's Eve, Forrest thinks of Jenny, who at that time is leaving her apartment in San Francisco with a black eye. Forrest and Lt. Dan bring two prostitutes to the apartment, but one is nasty when Gump doesn't want to sleep with her. They insult Gump as being stupid and Dan as being a cripple.

Forrest meets President Nixon when the ping-pong team visits the president. Later that night, Forrest sees flashlights at the Watergate complex, and complains about the lights keeping him awake. Nixon resigns and Forrest is discharged. When Forrest goes home, his mother informs him that many people want him to endorse their ping-pong equipment, and one had left a check for $25,000.

Gump goes to Bubba's family and buys a shrimping boat. He doesn't catch anything, then is told he needs to name the boat for good luck. He names it Jenny. She is shown doing cocaine and considering suicide. One day, Lt. Dan shows up to see Forrest, prompted by a letter Gump sent him. He works on the boat and they have discussions about God. A storm comes along, and Dan defies God, but they and the boat survive. As they are the only boat left after the storm, they are able to take in all of the shrimp, and become successful. Lt. Dan thanks Forrest for saving his life and swims away.

During the time that President Ford is shot, Forrest's mother is dying, so he returns home. They have a discussion of destiny before she passes away. Gump stays in town and gets a job cutting grass. But Lt. Dan has invested their money and he becomes wealthier. One day, Jenny returns home and they resume their friendship. Jenny gives him running shoes. Gump proposes to Jenny, but she refuses. She comes to his bed one night, but leaves the next morning before he awakes. She has left his medal behind.

Gump starts running cross-country thinking about those he loves, but mostly about Jenny. He becomes a celebrity and attracts followers. One day, he decides it is time to go home, leaving his followers bewildered. Back at home, Gump watches TV and sees President Reagan shot. He receives a letter from Jenny asking him to come visit her in Savannah. Forrest has been sitting on the bus bench waiting for the bus to take him to Jenny. The woman next to him informs Forrest he can walk to Jenny's home.

At Jenny's apartment, Forrest is introduced to his son, Little Forrest. Jenny tells him she is sick from a virus and Forrest again asks her to marry him. This time she agrees and they are married at his home. Lt. Dan comes to the wedding with his oriental fiancée. Forrest is happy with his family life, and takes care of Jenny until she passes away. Forrest raises his son with love and finally the day comes when Little Forrest must board the school bus. He is carrying Forrest's book, *Curious George.* The feather falls out and lands at Forrest's feet.

Good Will Hunting (1997)

Production Studio: Miramax Films, Larence Bender Productions, and Be Gentlemen Limited Partnership. Written by Matt Damon and Ben Affleck. Directed by Gus Van Sant. Produced by Su Armstrong, Jonathan Gordon, Bob Weinstein, and Harvey Weinstein. Original Music by Danny Elfman. Cast: Robin Williams, Matt Damon, Ben Affleck, Stellan Skarsgård, Minnie Driver, Casey Affleck, Cole Hauser, John Mighton.

Professor Gerald Lambeau presents a difficult math problem to his class. Will Hunting is a janitor who solves the problem, but doesn't take credit. Will and his friends get into a fight and Will is arrested. Lambeau puts up a new problem. Will gets out of jail. and solves this problem also. The professor sees Will writing the solution, but Will leaves before Lambeau can stop him.

Will is in a Harvard bar with his friends. His friend Chuckie flirts with Skylar. When some Harvard men harass Chuckie, Will comes to the rescue. Skylar gives Will her phone number.

Professor Lambeau tracks Will down and shows up at Will's arraignment. Lambeau gets Will released to his supervision, on the condition Will will work on math and receive counseling. Will intimidates all of the therapists, so the professor involves his old roommate, Sean Maguire. At the first meeting, Will tries pushing all of Sean's buttons, finally finding the most sensitive one, Sean's dead wife. Still, Sean tells Lambeau he will take Will on as a patient.

Skylar and Will run into each other at a game shop and go out for burgers, but Will does not follow up on the date. During a session, Sean takes Will to the park and tells Will that he doesn't know anything, since his learning is from books, and not about experiencing life. After some time, Will goes to Skylar's dorm asking her for a date. He helps her with her homework and they go out. When they talk about their pasts, Will, an orphan, lies about his twelve brothers. In therapy, Sean talks about how he gave up World Series tickets to be with the woman he would eventually marry. Sean had told his friends he had to go "see about a girl."

Lambeau wants Sean to direct Will to accept a prestigious job. Sean says he won't manipulate Will. Will's friend, Chuckie, takes Will's place at one of the interviews. Skylar wants Will to come with her to California. Will starts a fight with her to push a break up. While working math problems, Will insults Lambeau, with the professor retorting that this is too easy for Will and he is throwing his life away. When interviewing with the NSA, Will points out how the work can negatively affect people. In therapy he defends the common life to Sean. When Sean asks Will what he really wants to do with his life, and Will doesn't answer, Sean throws him out. Will won't leave.

Will calls Skylar before she leaves for California, but he doesn't show up at the airport. When he meets with Chuckie later, Chuckie tells him that it is an insult that Will doesn't make an effort to get out of their lower class way of life. He hopes to call on Will one day, and Will won't be there. Lambeau accuses Sean of undermining him, and are arguing when Will shows up for a session. In this session, Sean is finally able to get Will to confront his abandonment issues.

Will seriously interviews now and takes a job. He tells Sean about the job, and Sean announces that he is going to be doing some traveling. They exchange phone numbers to keep in touch. Sean tells Will to do what is in his heart, and he'll be fine.

Will is together with his friends on his twenty-first birthday. They give him an old car to get back and forth to his new job in Cambridge. The professor and Sean reconcile. Will's friends come to Will's house to pick him up, but he isn't there. Will leaves a message for Sean that if his job calls asking about him, tell them he had to see about a girl. Will drives off.

Heart of Darkness by Joseph Conrad (1903)

Note: A television movie of this novel was produced by Turner Pictures in 1994, starring Tim Roth and John Malkovich. It closely follows the plot of the novel.

Charlie Marlow is relating his adventures of meeting Kurtz in the Congo to members of the Company. He did this as a boat captain on the Company's African trade route.

A French Steamer takes Marlow to the Company outpost, which is a place of slavery. He meets the Company's Accountant who talks about how Kurtz sends the Company as much ivory as all of the other men put together.

Marlow begins the two hundred mile trek to his boat with sixty men. There were deserters along the way, but they arrive at the Central Station along the river. Marlow discovers that his boat has been sunk. The Manager comes to tell Marlow that there is a possibility that Kurtz is ill. Marlow is determined to make his trip and for the next several months, works on restoring the boat. During that time, a store-house goes up in flames, and it is hinted that Kurtz is behind it. The Manager is nervous that Kurtz could stand in the way of Company promotions. During that time, the Manager's uncle came with his Eldorado Exploring Expedition company. The manager and his uncle complains that the quality and amount of Kurtz' ivory was unfair competition. Reports come back of the expedition's donkeys died on the routes.

Marlow finally leaves on his boat with a crew that included cannibals. Along the river they are harassed by natives. At a hut on the river, they find a note indicating that wood had been stacked for them to use in their boiler, and a book on seamanship was also left for them. When they are about a mile and a half from Kurtz' place, they are attacked by arrows, with the helmsman being killed by a spear. Marlow throws the body overboard, to the dismay of the cannibals. At the Station, they are met by a man in scruffy clothes who tells them it is OK to land. He is the man who had left the wood and book for them. The man says the natives attacked Marlow's crew, because the natives don't want Kurtz to leave. The man says he should take Kurtz away quickly.

Kurtz is brought to the steamer on a stretcher. He is pleased with the letters Marlow has brought. A black woman appears on shore, then leaves. The man in ragged clothes says he would have shot her if she tried to come on board, as she had been causing trouble between him and Kurtz. Kurtz argues with the Manager that he is there to save the ivory, not Kurtz. The Manager claims Kurtz methods are unsound. Marlow confirms to the scruffy man that the men there have it in for Kurtz.

Marlow awakens to find Kurtz not on the boat. He finds Kurtz with a sorcerer. Kurtz tells Marlow that he should go on without him, but Marlow takes Kurtz back to the boat.

They leave the next morning and are followed by a mob led by the dark woman. Marlow scares them with a screech from the boat whistle and they all leave, except for the woman. Kurtz has hallucinations and is dying. Their boat breaks down by an island and they stop. Kurtz gives his papers and belongings to Marlow, as he doesn't trust anybody else. Kurtz dies with the words "the horror, the horror" on his lips. Marlow knows he has a loyalty to Kurtz.

Marlow returns home, but acts strangely. A man comes for Kurtz' documents and Marlow hands over the treatise of "Suppressing of Savage Customs," but does not hand over personal letters. More people show up to reminisce about Kurtz.

A year after Kurtz' death, Marlow goes to Kurtz' fiancée to return a portrait and letters. She is still mourning. She asks of Kurtz' last words, and he tells her they were her name. She is relieved. The book finishes with Marlow surrounded by darkness, sitting in a position of the Buddha.

The Natural (1984)

Production Studio: TriStar Pictures and Delphi II. Written by Bernard Malamud (novel), and Roger Towne, Phil Dusenberry (screenplay). Directed by Barry Levinson. Produced by Philip M. Breen and Roger Towne. Original Music by Randy Newman. Cast: Robert Redford, Robert Duvall, Glenn Close, Kim Basinger, Wilford Brimley, Barbara Hershey, Robert Prosky, Richard Farnsworth, Joe Don Baker.

Roy Hobbs is a young boy playing baseball with his father, who tells him that being gifted is not enough. He is watched by a young Iris. Later, Roy's father dies under an oak tree, which is later splintered by a lightning strike. From the wood remnants, Roy carves a bat and names it "Wonderboy." In his teens, Roy is picked to try out for the Chicago Cubs. He tells Iris that he loves her and will send for her.

Roy travels with his agent, Sam Simpson, on a train to Chicago. They meet Max Mercy, a noted sports-writer, and the Whammer, the best baseball player of that time. They are rude to Sam and Roy. Also traveling on the train is Harriet Bird, and Whammer wastes no time in trying to impress her. The train makes a stop, and during the break, bets are placed as to whether Roy can strike out the Whammer in three pitches, which Roy does. Later on the train, Harriet Bird approaches Roy and questions him as to how good he really is. Roy brags he is the best.

At the hotel in Chicago, Harriet calls Roy to her room. When he enters, she shoots him.

Sixteen years later, Roy shows up to play for the Knights baseball team. The team is coached by Pop Fisher, who reluctantly takes Roy on. In the locker room, he meets the star of the team, Bump Baily, who will be Roy's nemesis. Max Mercy is there, but doesn't remember Roy.

At the hotel, Roy meets Memo Paris, Bump's girlfriend and Pop's niece, and is attracted to her. At a dinner with the team manager, Red, Roy is evasive about his past, and learns that winning the pennant is the most important thing to Pop Fisher. An investor, the Judge, will take the team from Pop if he loses again.

The Knights are going through a losing streak, but Pop won't play Roy. Finally, when Bump is not playing well, Roy is given a chance. He destroys the ball with his homerun hit, and soon everyone including an investor of the team, the Judge, wants to know where he came from. Max Mercy approaches Roy, saying Roy looks familiar to him, but Roy says he doesn't know Max.

At a baseball game, Bump runs into a wall, and dies from the injury. Roy now takes leadership of the team, making it a winning team. Back in Chicago, Iris learns of Roy's accomplishments.

The Judge attempts to bribe Roy to throw the games, but Roy says he won't let Judge take the team. Max remembers something of Roy's past and invites him to a dinner with Gus and Memo. Gus talks about how he bets against Roy. Memo and Roy dance together, then go to a lake, where Memo talks about love, Bump, and Gus. When they return to the hotel, Pop sees Roy and warns him about Memo being bad luck. Roy strikes out the next day, the beginning of the Knight's losing streak. Memo and Roy begin a relationship.

The Knights travel to Chicago, and Iris comes to the game. Roy finally hits a home run. Iris sends a note to him, and they meet at a diner. After another winning game in Chicago, they meet again and Roy tells her the story of what happened to him years earlier. He learns that she has a son.

The Knights continue winning, to the consternation of the Judge and his group. Pop Fisher has warned the team not to jinx the team with partying, but the team attends a victory party at Memo's. The pitcher of the team, Al Fowler, dances with Memo. At the party, Roy collapses.

Roy is taken to a maternity hospital The attending doctor finds the old bullet that has been affecting Roy's stomach, and tells Roy he shouldn't play baseball. Memo visits Roy and tries to convince him to go away with her, rather than play. The Judge offers him a "bonus" and shows pictures of Roy shot and Harriet Bird dead on the street. The Judge tells Roy he has someone else on the team. Iris is more encouraging, saying she will bring her son to the game tomorrow.

Gus and Memo are at Judge's office when Roy returns the money. Memo threatens to shoot Roy, but he takes the gun from her. After he leaves, Gus says his insider will do the job.

Roy is having a difficult time playing and strikes out his first time at bat. He sees Fowler looking at Judge's box, and realizes that Fowler is the traitor. Roy tries to talk Fowler out of it. Roy strikes out again, then Iris sends a note to Roy telling him his son is in the stands. The next time up, Roy breaks his "Wonderboy" bat, but the bat boy gives Roy a bat he has made. Roy smashes the ball with a grand slam, and the Knights win. Everyone celebrates, except for those in the Judge's box. In the last scene, Roy is playing baseball with his son while Iris watches.

Siddhartha by Hermann Hesse (1922)

Siddhartha grows up in idyllic circumstances with his friend, Govinda. He is destined to be a Brahmin and studies hard. But Siddhartha is not satisfied—he believes there are things he has not been taught about the world. One day, Siddhartha meets three *Samanas* (ascetics) and decides he is going to join them. His father reluctantly allows him to go, but tells Siddhartha to come back and teach them of enlightenment. Govinda follows Siddhartha.

Siddhartha learns about suffering and corruption, but still is not satisfied with his learning, noting that his teachers are old, but still have not achieved Nirvana. One day, Govinda speaks of a friend who had met Gotama Buddha, and hoped that one day they could do the same. They leave the *Samanas*.

Gotama Buddha is at a grove of a wealthy merchant and they go there. Siddhartha immediately recognizes which beggar is Gotama, and is impressed. They listen to his talks of peace, suffering, and Buddhism. Govinda formally asks to be taken into the community, but Siddhartha does not. Siddhartha meets Gotama and tells him that he does not doubt that Gotama is Buddha, but still Gotama does not talk of the secret of his experience. Siddhartha knows he must go discover his own experience.

Siddhartha stays at a ferryman's hut. The next morning the ferryman, Vasudeva, takes Siddhartha across the river. Siddhartha has no money, so the ferryman says when Siddhartha comes back, he can give something at that time. At a village, a girl tries to seduce Siddhartha, but he turns her down.

In a town, Siddhartha sees the beautiful courtesan Kamala. He no longer wants to be an ascetic. He finds a barber's assistant to groom him and the next day he asks her to be his teacher. She teases him that her students usually have fine clothes and money. He says that she is already teaching him, as he has cleaned himself up. He bargains a kiss for a poem, and she learns he can read and write. She has a visitor, so he is given a white robe before he leaves.

The next day he returns to Kamala, who tells him to go to Kamaswami, the richest merchant in town. Siddhartha is to act as an equal, not a servant. His goal was to learn from the most beautiful woman, and that goal has now set up ripples in the water, which some consider magic.

Kamaswami tells Siddhartha that he understands Siddhartha is a Brahmin in need. Siddhartha points out his poverty and fasting were a choice. Kawaswami tests Siddhartha's reading and writing skills, then invites Siddhartha to stay. Siddhartha is well taken care of, but views everything as a game. Everyday

Siddhartha goes to Kamala to learn the arts of love, and learns of giving, receiving, and appreciation. Kamaswami teaches him to be a merchant, but Siddhartha is more interested in people than goods. But Siddhartha is beginning to think real life is passing by and decides to leave. Kamala closes her doors to others, as she is now pregnant with Siddhartha's child.

Siddhartha wanders the forest, thinking there is no purpose in life. He comes to the river, and is about to jump in, until he hears OM inside of him. He meditates, then falls asleep. He awakens refreshed, to see a monk keeping safe watch over him. The monk is Govinda, and both are happy to see each other. Siddhartha says he is on pilgrimage, and when Govinda mentions the rich clothing, Siddhartha says he is no longer a *Samana,* though he is still a pilgrim. Govinda is doubtful, but bows to Siddhartha as he leaves. Siddhartha decides to go to the ferryman to learn of the river and life.

Siddhartha offers his rich clothes as payment for his previous trip. He asks to be Vasudeva's apprentice. Travelers soon regard the two as brothers. Rumors spread that they are wise men or magicians, but upon visiting, would only find two old happy men.

One day a group of Gotama's followers came to cross the river, as Gotama was ill and dying. Siddhartha thought fondly of Gotama. Other pilgrims came by, including Kamala. She is traveling with her son, who had been cantankerous along the way. Stopping by the river, she is bit by a black snake. Her scream summons Vasudeva, who takes her and the boy to his hut. Siddhartha recognizes Kamala, and is told the boy is his son. She dies in Siddhartha's arms. Siddhartha had been rich, but now he is richer with a son. The next morning, Siddhartha and Vasudeva build a funeral pyre while the boy slept.

The boy is in shock. He is spoiled, and though Siddhartha tries to win his love, the boy's actions bring sorrow. Vasudeva says the boy should be taken to his mother's home or a teacher. Siddhartha is afraid that the boy will have the same pitfalls as him, and Vasudeva finds this amusing. Finally, the boy rebels—stealing money, taking the boat, and running away. Siddhartha goes in search of his son. At one point he realizes the search is useless, and sits in meditation. Vasudeva finds him and they return to the hut, never to speak of the boy again.

The pain in Siddhartha's heart does not ebb. He decides again to look for his son, but when he looks in the river, he sees the face of his own father, who died without ever seeing his son again. Siddhartha goes back, still hurting, but wiser.

Vasudeva is too old to work, so weaves baskets. Siddhartha finally speaks of the wound in his heart and Vasudeva works as a confessor, taking the pain of the wound. He takes Siddhartha to the river where Siddhartha hears the voices of all he has known blend into OM. Now that Siddhartha is serene, it is time for Vasudeva to leave.

In Kamala's grove, Govinda has heard of a sage ferryman and searches wisdom from the man. Siddhartha says many seekers see the goal but do not see what is under their noses, and Govinda realizes the ferryman is Siddhartha. Govinda stays with him and asks of Siddhartha's doctrines. Siddhartha talks of knowledge, wisdom, illusion and love. Govinda finds Siddhartha to be strange, yet holy. He sees that Siddhartha's smile is Gotama's smile. Govinda does not know of time. Govinda cries, seeing all that he has loved in the smile of his friend.

Star Wars (1977)

Production Studio: Lucasfilm Ltd. Written, Directed, and Produced by George Lucas. Original Music by John Williams. Cast: Mark Hamill, Harrison Ford, Carrie Fisher, Peter Cushing, Alec Guinness, Anthony Daniels, Kenny Baker, Peter Mayhew, David Prowse, Phil Brown, James Earl Jones.

Princess Leia's ship is detained by Darth Vader. Before being captured, she places a card in her droid, R2-D2, who leaves the ship on a shuttle with C-3PO. The shuttle lands on an arid planet, and soon the droids are picked up by a transport. Darth Vader's men discover the shuttle. C-3PO and R2-D2 are purchased by Luke Skywalker's aunt and uncle to work on their farm. As Luke cleans the droids, he hits a switch on R2-D2 which plays a message from Leia to Obi-Wan "Ben" Kenobi. Luke wonders if this is Old Ben Kenobi. He mentions the message to his uncle, who says to erase the message as Obi-Wan died the same time as Luke's father. Luke wants to go to the university if the droids work out. That night R2-D2 takes off.

In the morning, Luke and C-3PO find R2-D2, but they have to fight sand people. Obi-Wan shows up and the sand people take off. Obi tells Luke that he and Luke's father were best friends, and it was Darth Vader who killed his father. He gives Luke his father's light saber. The message on R2-D2 is Leia requesting Obi-Wan to come to Alderaan to help her father. Obi-Wan wants to train Luke to be a knight, but Luke says that is not possible. Obi-Wan says that is Luke's uncle talking.

They find the transport destroyed by Storm Troopers looking for the droids. Luke is worried about his family and hurries home. When he gets there, he finds everyone dead. Now Luke is ready to go with Obi-Wan.

They go to a bar, where they meet Han Solo and Chewbacca. Obi-Wan makes a deal for Han to fly them to Alderaan. Han is harassed for money he owes Jabba the Hutt. When all meet at the ship, Storm Troopers fight them, but Han is able to get the ship off the ground and zip them into hyperspace.

In the meantime, Darth Vader has been questioning Princess Leia on where the rebel base is. She won't reveal it, so he destroys Alderaan. He also orders her execution.

In the ship, Obi-Wan has a headache when Alderaan is destroyed. He talks of the Force and starts training Luke. When they come out of hyperspace to where Alderaan is suppose to be, they are in a meteor shower—the remnants of Alderaan. Their ship gets caught in a tractor beam and they are pulled into Darth Vader's ship. Luke and the crew hide, until they are able to overpower the Vader's men. R2-D2 plugs into the spaceship's computer. Obi-Wan says he will destroy what he needs to so they can leave. R2-D2 finds out that Leia is to be executed. Solo says Leia is rich, so they should rescue her for the reward. They dress as Storm Troopers with Chewbacca as prisoner so they can walk the halls. They go to the prisoner area, and rescue Leia.

Darth Vader feels Obi-Wan Kenobi's Force close by. Leia's escape is noted. In the hallway, Vader's men fight Luke, Leia, Chewbacca, and Han. They fall into a trash compactor, where a one-eyed creature lives. As the walls close in, Luke calls C-3PO, and R2-D2 is able to plug into the computer to stop the walls. Obi-Wan turns off the tractor beam. Luke and his group move to their ship. Darth Vader encounters Obi-Wan and they fight. When Luke appears, Obi-Wan allows himself to be cut down by Darth Vader. There is more fighting, then Obi-Wan's voice tells Luke to get on the ship. They are able to take off, but there is still more fighting. Leia knows they are being tracked, and says the rebel plans are in R2-D2. Both Han and Luke like Leia.

They land at the rebel base and plan the attack on the Death Star. They will use fighter planes to explode the reactor system, which will set off a chain reaction of destruction. Han Solo leaves to pay his debts, saying the plan to attack the Death Star is impossible. Everyone else prepares for battle.

Darth's men are defeating the rebels, until Obi-Wan's voice tells Luke to feel the Force so he can drop the bombs perfectly. The Death Star is destroyed. At the end, Princess Leia gives awards to the heroes.

Star Wars: Episode V - The Empire Strikes Back (1980)

Production Studio: Lucasfilm Ltd. Written by George Lucas (story) and Leigh Brackett, Lawrence Kasdan. Directed by Irvin Kershner. Produced by George Lucas. Original Music by John Williams. Cast: Mark Hamill, Harrison Ford, Carrie Fisher, Billy Dee Williams, Anthony Daniels, David Prowse, Peter Mayhew, Kenny Baker, Frank Oz, Alec Guinness.

Luke Skywalker and the Rebel Forces are stationed on the ice planet Hoth as they are pursued by Darth Vader's forces. A pod falls onto the planet. While Luke is scouting, he is captured by a snow monster.

Back in the Rebel Forces' main hangar, Han prepares to leave, since Jabba the Hutt is after him. Han and Leia flirt, but they won't admit they like each other. Before Han leaves, he hears Luke is missing and goes after him. Back in the snow creature's cave, Luke is able to use the Force to retrieve his sword and fight the monster. Luke is out in a snowstorm when he sees a vision of Obi-Wan "Ben" Kenobi telling him to go to Yoda's in the Dagobah system. Soon after, the creature he is riding falls over dead. Luke hides inside the creature to keep warm. Han finds Luke and brings him back to the main camp. Everyone is happy that Luke is fine. Leia kisses him.

The rebel station picks up the signal of the pod and knows it to be an Imperial Probe Droid which has revealed their presence. The rebel forces know it is time to evacuate. Darth Vader sends Imperial Walkers with forces to attack. Luke fights the Walkers so the Rebels can evacuate. Han is able to help Leia escape. Afterwards, R2-D2 and Luke leave for Dagobah.

Han is pursued by Vader's men. They hide in a cave on an asteroid. While Han is repairing some ship damage, he and Leia finally kiss. They discover they are in a giant serpent and must take off immediately. They are pursued again, and this time take refuge at Lando Calrissian's Cloud City.

Luke lands on Dagobah and is offered hospitality by Yoda. He is unsure about training the impatient Luke, but finally does so. One time, Luke sees a vision of Darth Vader. He cuts off Vader's head, but Luke's head replaces it. Luke senses that Han and Leia are in trouble and feels he must leave. Yoda and Obi-Wan's spirit try to prevent him from leaving, but Luke goes anyway. Yoda says there is another hope if Luke fails.

Lando welcomes Han and his passengers. As they walk away, C-3PO lags behind and is taken. Chewbacca finds C-3PO and rescues him from being melted down. When Leia and Han are invited by Lando for refreshments, he hands them over to Darth Vader. Lando apologizes, saying he has remained neutral, to keep him exempt from the Empire. Lando says that they are bait to get Luke. Han is taken to be carbonized. Han and Leia finally show feelings of love before Han is carbonized. Lando says Han is still alive, but in hibernation. Han is given to a bounty hunter to be taken to Jabba the Hutt. Leia and Chewbacca are taken to Darth Vader's ship.

Luke and R2-D2 land in Cloud City and see Solo in carbonite. Leia sees Luke and tells him it is a trap. He meets up with Darth Vader, who confirms Luke has the Force with him, but is not yet a Jedi Knight. They fight. Meanwhile, Lando's men rescue Leia and Chewbacca. Lando convinces them that they can still save Han. Lando orders evacuation of the city and they leave.

Luke and Darth Vader fight, with Luke almost being carbonized. Darth Vader cuts off Luke's sword hand, and admits he is Luke's father. Darth wants Luke to rule with him, but Luke jumps into a chute. He is catapulted outside the city and must hang on. Leia senses Luke's plight, and makes Lando turn back to rescue Luke. Darth Vader still tries to telepathically influence Luke, while Luke asks Obi-Wan why he didn't tell him Darth was his father. Lando and Chewbacca will go look for Solo at Jabba's. Luke gets an artificial hand. Leia, Luke, R2-D2, and C-3PO watch as the Lando and Chewbacca leave.

Star Wars: Episode VI – Return of the Jedi (1983)

Production Studio: Lucasfilm Ltd. Written by George Lucas (story) and Lawrence Kasdan, George Lucas. Directed by Richard Marquand. Produced by George Lucas. Original Music by Jerry Hey, John Williams, and Joseph Williams. Cast: Mark Hamill, Harrison Ford, Carrie Fisher, Billy Dee Williams, Anthony Daniels, Peter Mayhew, Sebastian Shaw, Ian McDiarmid, Frank Oz, James Earl Jones, David Prowse, Alec Guinness, Kenny Baker.

Luke Skywalker goes to Tatooine to rescue Han Solo from Jabba the Hutt. R2-D2 and C-3PO first delivers Luke's message that he wants to negotiate for Han, but Jabba is not interested. C-3PO is kept as a translator and R2-D2 is sent to a sail barge. A bounty hunter has made a deal with Jabba for Chewbacca. Lando Calrissian is hiding in the crowd in Jabba's enclave. Princess Leia releases Han Solo from the carbonite, but he is blind and sick. Jabba has been watching her the whole time. Han is thrown in prison with Chewbacca, and Leia is brought to Jabba. Luke gets into Jabba's place, and tries to force Jabba to release his friends. A pit door opens, dropping Luke into the lair of a creature. Luke escapes the creature, but is recaptured. Lando also makes his move, but is captured. All of the them will be sent to be fed to a desert creature.

Jabba is partying on a large ship in the desert. Luke is on a plank, ready to be forced to jump into a hole in the ground, when a small ship pulls up with Luke's friends. Luke gives Jabba one last chance, but then the whole group attacks. The main ship is destroyed and Luke's crew escapes on the small ship. Luke heads back to the Dagobah system.

Darth Vader tells the Emperor that the new Death Star is almost completed. The Emperor says Luke will seek Vader out, and that Luke should be brought to the Emperor. They will try to turn Luke to the Dark Side.

Luke is back with Yoda, who is dying. Yoda confirms Darth Vader is Luke's father and that Luke's training was not complete before, so he could not defeat Vader. He must learn that anger and fear belong to the Dark Side. Yoda dies. Back on the ship, Luke is losing confidence, but Obi-Wan puts the past in perspective. Obi-Wan says Luke had a twin sister, and Luke realizes Leia is his sister.

Han, Leia Lando, Luke, and Chewbacca are on a starship by Endor. They are told that the Emperor is on the Death Star to oversee its completion. They make a plan to destroy the shield on Endor which is protecting the Death Star. They can then destroy the Death Star. Lando will lead a strike on the Death Star, and Han will lead the assault on Endor. On the Death Star, Darth Vader is aware of Luke's presence.

On Endor, the crew battles Storm Troopers. Leia falls off her rover and is lost, so Luke goes to look for her. Leia has been saved by an Ewok. R2-D2 and C-3PO are taken by the Ewoks, but C-3PO is believed to be a king. When the rest of the crew are caught, the Ewoks want to cook Han and serve him to C-3PO. Luke convinces them that C-3PO will be angry and uses the Force to make C-3PO fly. Everyone is freed and made part of the tribe. After telling the Ewoks the story of the Death Star, they agree to lead the group to the shield's generator.

Luke and Leia go off together to talk. He tells her that they are brother and sister, and she confirms that she has similar powers to his. She advises Luke to go away, but Luke says he senses there is good in Darth Vader. Han sees them together and is jealous.

Luke surrenders to Darth Vader. He tells Vader that he still believes the goodness of Anakin Skywalker is still within Vader, but Vader tells Luke he does not know the Dark Side.

The group on Endor is planning to take over the shield station. But the emperor has known about the plans, and has laid a trap. When the group breaks into the station, Storm Troopers follow them. Lando's planes in space are jammed, so they pull back from their attack. While Luke watches the battle with Vader and the Emperor, the Emperor tries to convince Luke to use hate to strike the Emperor down. The Ewoks come to help the group at the station. The Death Star starts attacking, and Lando fights back to enable more time to bring down the shield. The Emperor still works to anger Luke, and when Luke does attack the Emperor, Darth Vader protects the Emperor. Luke and Vader fight, with Luke deciding he will not kill Vader, only using his sword to defend himself. The group on Endor finally enter the shield station and plant charges. Darth Vader tries to convince Luke to come to the Dark Side, saying he knows that Leia is Luke's sister, and maybe she will come over. Luke then attacks. The shield station is blown up, and attacks commence against the Death Star. The Emperor attacks Luke, and Luke calls to Darth, who finally steps in to save Luke and kills the Emperor. Darth is seriously wounded. Lando has enters the Death Star and bombs the center. Vader asks Luke to remove his helmet, so he may look at Luke. Luke wants to save him, and Vader says he already has. Darth Vader dies. Lando and Luke barely make it off of the Death Star before it is destroyed. Luke cremates Vader. Back on Endor, there is celebration. Luke sees the spirits of Obi-Wan, Yoda, and Darth Vader (Anakin Skywalker).

Star Wars: Episode I – The Phantom Menace (1999)

Production Studio: Lucasfilm Ltd. Written, Directed, and Produced by George Lucas. Original Music by John Williams. Cast: Liam Neeson, Ewan McGregor, Natalie Portman, Jake Lloyd, Ian McDiarmid, Pernilla August, Oliver Ford Davies, Hugh Quarshie, Ahmed Best, Anthony Daniels, Kenny Baker, Ray Park, Frank Oz, Terence Stamp

Queen Amidala's kingdom of Naboo has been blocked by the greedy Trade Federation being manipulated by Darth Sidious. Two Jedi Knights, Qui-Gon Jinn and Obi-Wan Kenobi, have been set to negotiate the conflict. Qui-Gon and Obi-Wan enter the Federation's ship, but are discovered. They battle and escape, ending up on Naboo. They are chased by the Federation, and run into a Gungan, Jar Jar Binks. He takes them to his underwater world of Otoh Gunga. There they are given transport which will take them through the core of Naboo to reach the palace of Queen Amidala.

When Qui-Gon, Obi-Wan, and Jar Jar arrive, they see Amidala's decoy with her court, including Padmé Naberrie (the real Queen Amidala), who have been captured by the Federation. The Jedis rescue the queen and they escape on a spaceship, intending to take Amidala to the Senate in Coruscant. They are chased, but their shields are hit. R2-D2 is able to fix the shield, and they make way to the planet Tatooine, hoping to find safety and parts to repair the damaged spaceship.

On Tatooine, they make friends with Anakin Skywalker, a slave, who races pods. Qui-Gon recognizes that Anakin has Jedi tendencies. Anakin wins a pod race to get parts to fit the spaceship, and also his freedom. Just before leaving Tatooine, Qui-Gon fights Darth Maul, apprentice to Darth Sidious.

At Coruscant, Naboo's case is presented to the Senate, but because of corruption, immediate help is not given to Amidala. She had been instructed by Senator Palpatine to call for a vote of no confidence, and he is chosen as the new Supreme Chancellor. Amidala wants to return to Naboo. At the same time, Qui-Gon tries to convince the Jedi council that Anakin is the Chosen One, and he wants to apprentice Anakin. Yoda can not see Anakin's future clearly, so the council is against it.

They go back to Naboo, and Amidala wants to approach the Gungan leaders to help her, as she learned from Jar Jar that they have an army. The real Queen Amidala humbles herself to the Gungans and they become partners. The plan is to have a diversionary battle of the Gungans against the Federation's Droid Army. A group of them will go back to the palace, capture the Federation's Viceroy, and fighter pilots will destroy the ship which controls the droids.

The battle begins. The Jedis and Amidala with her people enter the palace. Anakin is told to find a safe place, which ends up being a fighter plane. As they fight their way in, Darth Maul challenges them. Qui-Gon and Obi-Wan fight Darth Maul. Amidala is able to capture the Viceroy. Anakin shoots droids from the fighter plane, but it is on auto-pilot and takes him to the control ship. The Gungans lose to the droids, but when Anakin's plane is hit, his plane enters the control ship. He attacks droids there, and accidentally shoots into the reactor room. This sets off a chain reaction, destroying the control ship. The droids have no power and the Gungans are released. Darth Maul kills Qui-Gon, but Obi-Wan kills Darth Maul. Qui-Gon's dying request of Obi-Wan is to take Anakin has his apprentice.

Obi-Wan tells Yoda he will train Anakin, and Yoda reluctantly approves it. Qui-Gon is given a funeral. There is celebration on Naboo with Amidala's people, the Gungans, the Jedi council, and Palpatine.

Index

A

Abbey, Edwin Austin 312
Abduction myth 84, 330
Abel 282
Abraham 286
Accolon 189
Accountant (*Heart of Darkness*) 87
Adam 32, 61, 197, 277, 314
Adam Walsh Foundation 267
Adam-Kadmon 314
Adonis 277
Agni 304
Ahriman 319
Al-'Arabi', Muhyi'ddin 327
Alan 37
Albright, Ivan 235, 218
Alchemy 61, 99, 138, 210, 261
Allah 188
All-Seeing Eye 44, 48, 174, 308
Alma-Tadema, Lawrence 29
Amadan Mor 42
Amalthea 58
Amangons, King 33
Amidala, Queen
  angel 83
  Buddhism 100
  challenge 114
  colors 207–208
  Goddess of Sovereignty 54
  Wasteland 87
  See also Portman, Natalie
Ampflise, Queen 70–71, 208
Ancient Future-Family / Knights of Endurance (Dillon) 319
Andrew 37
Anfortas, King
  Dolorous Blow 32
  family 69, 72, 254, 267
  Fisher King 169
  Grail King 21
  Grail Procession 325–326
  Healing 261, 313–315, 320, 336
  Malcreatiure 271
  Orgeluse 32, 264, 271, 273, 275
  Parzival 170–171
  Secundille 271
  Spear 62, 177
Anfortas, King *(cont.)*
  Sword 181
  Wounded King 21, 39, 186, 255
Angels
  Jinn 172
  myth 77
  Neutral 61, 262, 315
  Parzival 82–83
Angels of Night (Degouve de Nuncques) 80, 83
Angevin 303
Annwvyn 234
Antanor 117, 125–126, 201
Antikonie, Queen
  chess 248
  Gawan 232, 240, 245–247
  Mother 246–247
  Vergulaht 249
Aoife 150
Aphrodite 78, 85, 99–100
Apocalypse Now
  bridge 284
  film 17
  music 31
  myth 320–321
  quotes 120
  story 24
  Triplicate Goddess 207
  Wasteland 73
  See also Coppola, Francis Ford; Freelance Photographer; Hicks, "Chef" Jay; Johnson, Lance B.; Kilgore, Lt. Col.; Kurtz, Col. Walter E.; Philips, Chief; Willard, Capt. Benjamin L.
Apocrypha 307
Apollo 286, 319
Apple
  Avalon 243
  Bible 32, 174
  Core 279
  myth 99
  Nemesis 330
Arabian myth 172
Ares 277
Argante 243
Argonauts 330
Argus 174
Ariadne (Waterhouse) 101
Arnive, Queen 219, 226, 273, 290, 293–294
Art of War (Sun Tzu) 108–109
Artemis 286, 319
Arthur, King
  Avalon 243, 261
  bear 138
  birds 77
  challenge 60, 107, 113–114, 129, 139
  chess 248
  Community 212, 300
  court 24, 33, 81, 97, 113, 117, 132, 140, 157, 163, 203–204, 215, 274, 338
  Cundrie the Sorceress 219, 221, 226
  dragon 210
  Excaliber 62, 86, 189, 243
  family 40, 68, 89–90, 226
  Feirefiz 303, 305
  Gawan 212, 273, 290, 296
  generosity 120–122
  Ginover 209
  Grail 178
  Grail Quest 227
  Gwenevere 19
  Iseult 240
  kiss 214
  Lambeau, Gerald 23
  Logres 275
  mantle 181
  Mordred 286, 298
  Morgause 286
  Orilus 193
  Parzival 81, 124, 134, 201–203, 213, 300
  Ragnall 237–238
  reconciliation 293–294
  Round Table 60
  ship 298
  sisters 208
  Star Wars 23
  story 18, 21
  Surrendering 298
  Tristan 240
  Twrch Trwyth 277

Arthur, King *(cont.)*
Wasteland 87
water 91
Wounded King 39
Arthurian Romances (Chrétien)
Blancheflor 100
Elucidation 33
Escavalon 243
Gawain 212
Knight of the Cart (Lancelot) 284
Knight with the Lion (Yvain) 85
Perceval 93, 101, 212, 223
Story of the Grail 33
unfinished book 211
Ascalun 219, 232, 243
Astarte 78
Atalante 277
Attainment: The Vision of the Holy Grail to Sir Galahad, Sir Bors, and Sir Percival (Burne-Jones and Morris) 316
August, Pernilla 92
See also Skywalker, Shmi
Avallach, King 243
Avalon 174, 243–244, 261
Awakening Conscience (Hunt) 192
Axis Mundi 174–176, 287

B

Bailey, Bump 205
Balin 176
Banshee 64
Barnhorn, Clement J. 320
Baruch of Baghdad 69, 72
Bathsheba 132
Bean Sidhe 57, 64, 91
Bearosche 231
Beatris 330
Beaucurs 219
Bed. *See* Carbonite Bed, Wonder Bed
Belacane, Queen 69–73, 163, 208, 219
Belobraydich, Don 99
Bene 272–273, 293–294, 297
Benjamin-Constant 222
Bible 99, 286
quotes 99, 108, 287
Bikaner School 247
Bilibin, Ivan 65, 299
Bird, Harriet
birds 78
colors 208
Goddess of Sovereignty 54
hubris 263
quotes 263
shooting 24, 75, 132, 246
Triplicate Goddess 243
Birds
crane 245
dove 60, 78, 260, 308, 332
duck 187, 207
eagle 245
falcon 77, 201, 203–204, 245, 273
goose 185, 187, 201, 204, 209, 275, 330
hawk 207, 212
heron 245
magpie 48, 72, 77
Merlin 77
myth 77
nightingale 78
ostrich 245
owl 77
Parzival 69
peacock 174
pelican 261
Perceval 91
Phoenix 260–261
raven 77, 207
rooster 98
sparrow-hawk 245
stork 77
swan 77, 325, 329–330
Yvain 85
Birth of Venus (Stella) 86
Black Beauty 91
Black Bran 248
Black Elk 311
Blancheflor 100, 306
Blodeuwedd 99
Blood
Christ 244, 261, 317
Dindrane 320
pelican 261
tree 282
Blow, Red 138
Blowin' In The Wind (Dylan) 114, 217
Blue Whipper (Mitchell) 123
Blue, Benjamin "Bubba" Bufford 22, 146, 302
See also Williamson, Mykelti
Boann 38
Boar 271, 277
Bodhisattva vows 338
Bors 246, 298, 320
Bouillon, Duchess of 330
Bouillon, Godfrey of 330
Boyne River 38
Brabant, Princess of 325
Bradley, Marion Zimmer 243
Brahma 174, 209
Bran 37, 59, 177
Brandelidelin, King 294
Brando, Marlon 30
See also Kurtz, Col. Walter E.
Brandubh 248
Branwen 280
Branwen Daughter of Llyr. *See Mabinogion*
Braveheart 214
Bride and Groom of the Eiffel Tower (Chagall) 156
Bridge 284
Bridges, Jeff 22, 194
See also Lucas, Jack
Brihad-Aranyaka Upanishad 234
Brimley, Wilford 30
See also Fisher, Pop
Brizljan 97–98
Broceliande 98, 322
Bron 37, 177
Brooch 97, 107, 112–113
Brumbane, Lake 37, 177, 255
Bryant, Bear 138, 144
Bryant, Nigel 335
Buckingham Palace 106
Buddha 25, 34, 174
See also Gotama Buddha
Buddhism
Bodhisattva vows 338
Eightfold Path 88, 104, 109, 134, 182, 194, 204, 233, 239
Four Noble Truths 31, 109, 135
Lotus 100
suffering 186

Buddhism *(cont.)*
Ten Perfections 134, 161, 206, 220, 223, 233, 236, 265, 267, 296
tradition 268
Zen 36
Burgh, Chris de 278
Burne-Jones, Edward 264, 316
Burton, William Shakespeare 106

C

C-3PO 31, 83, 186, 233, 248
Cabaret Singer (*Fisher King*) 218
Cailleach 220
Caliburn 243
Calixtus II, Pope 331
Camelot (film) 18, 77, 206
Cameron, Julia Margaret 195
Campbell, Joseph 18, 147, 336
Candi 159
Canterbury Tales 238
Capitol 287
Capote, Truman 184
Carbonite Bed 270, 282
Carmichael, Lanny 22, 316
Carnation, Lily, Lily, Rose (Sargent) 342
Carrington, Leonora 234–235
Casket 193, 254
Castle of Dinas Bran 176
Castle of Maidens 86, 226, 284
Castle of Marvels 226
Castle of Montségur 176
Castle of Wonders
Arthur's court 219, 226, 274
Clinschor 293
Gawan 272–273, 288
horse 281
Secundille 307–308
water 86
Wonder Bed 282
Castor 319, 329–330
Catching Fish (Ni Tuan) 38
Cathars 48
Catherine of Aragon 106
Catholic tradition 268
Catlin, George 128
Cauldron
basin 85
Branwen 280
Cauldron *(cont.)*
Cerridwen 58, 277
Cup 60
Dyrnwch 58
Four Hallows 62
Grail 57–58
Medea 330
Rebirth 58, 177
Spoils of Annwfn 243
womb 38
Celtic myth
Avalon 174
birds 77
Bran 59, 177
Cerridwen 277
cup 113
female warrior 150
fish 37
fool 42
Four Hallows 57
Lleu Skilful Hand 108
Cerberus 279
Cerridwen 58, 277
Chagall, Marc 156
Chakras 176
Chalice Well 244
Chaplin, Charlie 45
Chapterhouse: Dune (Herbert) 179
Charon 279
Chart of Virtues 175
Chaucer, Geoffrey 238
Chess 232, 248
Chess Players (Wagrez) 248
Chessboard of Gwenddolau 248
Chewbacca 78, 235, 248
Chi 173
Chi Kung 33, 173, 176
Children of Dune (Herbert) 212
Chinese myth 261
Chinese tradition 138, 177
Chingis-khan 331
Chomo-Lung-Ma 175
Chosen One 38, 119, 171–172, 234
Chrétien de Troyes. *See Arthurian Romances*
Christ
bird 174
blood 244, 261, 317
chalice 60
Cross 174
Cup 63, 220
Christ *(cont.)*
Eucharist 59
fish 37
Grail 63, 330
marriage 282
pelican 261
Resurrection 177
ritual 268
Second Coming 314
Spear 176
suffering 34
Christ and Buddha (Ranson) 339
Christ Purging the Temple (Giotto) 125
Christian
feminine principle 225
fish motifs 37
Merlin 172
myth 174
philosophy 211
ritual 99
story 59–60, 132, 209
Wasteland 32
Chuckie 23, 144, 230
Churchill, Winston 138
Cidegast, Duke 273, 290, 298
Cirque du Soleil 116
Clamide, King 157, 161, 219
Clarke, Grant 137
Clauditte, Queen 303
Cleopatra 286
Clias the Greek 219
Clinschor, Duke 39, 272–273, 281–282, 293
Cloak 56, 169, 180–181, 214
Close, Glenn 52
See also Gaines/Lemon, Iris
Clytemnestra 330
Colors
black 48, 72, 99, 207
green 138, 214, 254, 274
red 49, 99, 138, 201, 207, 210, 214, 231, 234
Taoist 261
white 48, 72, 99–100, 138, 201, 207, 210, 231, 234
yellow 202
Combat de cavaliers (Knightly Combat) (Dali) 304

Company Doctor (*Heart of Darkness*) quotes 260
Condwiramors, Queen
- Curran, Jenny 22
- foreshadowing 160
- Goddess of Sovereignty 159
- Grail Procession 325–326
- Healing 313
- inspiration 294, 303, 306
- kiss 202, 214
- marriage 163, 319
- name 159
- Parzival 21, 100, 157–158, 161, 164–165, 209, 240, 273
- trance 201–202, 204, 321
- Triplicate Goddess 208

Confederacy of Dunces (Toole) 50, 87, 179, 186, 344
Conference of the Birds (Farid) 77
Conrad, Joseph 17, 90, 217, 260, 335
Consort 332
Continuations 211–212, 317
Coppola, Francis Ford 24, 207, 320
Core (Kore) 279
Cornucopia 58
Coruscant 87
Cosmic Egg 330
Countess of the Fountain 86, 98
Court of Joy 326
Coyote 123
Crab Fishing (Homer) 168
Crane, Walter 322
Creation of the Birds (Varo) 78
Crone 138, 208, 220, 275–276, 332
Crown. See Diu Crône
Crusades 34, 60, 330
Cu Chulain 150
Culhwch 123
Cunda 307
Cundrie (Gawan's sister) 159, 219, 226, 273, 294
Cundrie the Sorceress
- Arthur's court 219, 221–222, 226, 274
- Bird, Harriet 24
- Boar 277
- description 218
- Feirefiz 303
- Gawan 273, 285
- Goddess of Sovereignty 54
- Grail Procession 325
- Healing 313
- Malcreatiure 271
- name 159
- Parzival 21, 221, 308
- Secundille 271, 303, 307–308
- Sigune 254, 256

Cunneware, Duchess
- avenged 201–202, 213–214
- beating 117, 125, 129, 140
- Clamide 219
- dragon 210
- Kingrun 157
- laugh 97, 126
- name 159
- Orilus 193, 198
- Parzival 214

Cup
- Christ 34, 60, 63
- Four Hallows 62, 91
- Ginover 113, 129, 140
- Grail 179
- Hallows 57
- Kingship 60, 140
- Redemption 60

Curious George (Rey & Rey) 48, 68
Curran, Jenny
- birds 78
- challenge 114
- childhood 68
- death 25, 321
- family 68, 319
- flowers 100
- gifts 112
- Goddess of Sovereignty 52, 54
- Grail 256
- Gump, Forrest 158, 162, 165, 243, 275, 282
- love 22
- marriage 163, 292
- quotes 217
- ship 298
- suffering 187
- synchronicity 83
- Taoism 48
- teacher 144, 150
- trance 204
- tree 188
- Triplicate Goddess 208
- water 39
- *See also* Wright, Robin

Custodian (*Fisher King*) 164, 190
Cyrano de Bergerac (Rostand) 18

D

Daddy (Plath) 93
Daedalus 264
Dagda 188
Dagobah System 330
Dagobert II 330
Dali, Salvador 304
Damon, Matt 23, 162, 329
- *See also* Hunting, Will

Damsel of the Sanct Grael (Rosetti) 324
Dark Goddess 159
Dark Woman 220
David, King 62, 132, 282
Death of Abel (Doré) 135
Degouve de Nuncques, William 80, 83
Delville, Jean 16
Demeter 234, 240, 277, 279–281
Dickenson, Emily 284
Didot-Perceval 64, 91, 220
Dillon, Leo and Diane 319
Dindrane 282, 298, 320
Disc 57, 59–60, 62, 64
Disney, Walt 59, 99, 159
Diu Crône (The Crown) 139, 212, 286
Divine Beauty 209
Divine Majesty 209
Dodinel 195
Dog 44, 234
Dolorous Blow 32–33, 35, 281
Don't Pay the Ferryman (Burgh) 278
Doors 31
Doré, Gustave 42, 135
Down the Long Beam Stole the Holy Grail (Kirk) 63
Dracula 200, 210
Dragon 193, 200, 210
Dreaming Fool (Sandburg) 42
Drepung Gomang Monks 36

Driver, Minnie 52, 159, 162
  See also Skylar
Droit Du Seigneur 214
Druids 188
Duchess of Bouillon 330
Duino Elegies (Rilke) 46
Dukkha 31, 109, 135
Duncan, John McKirdy 57
Dune (Herbert) 85
Durgā 159, 208, 247
Duveneck, Frank 320
Dwarfs 126, 210
Dylan 319
Dylan, Bob 114, 217

E

Earth Serpent 210
Eckuba 219
Eden 61, 174
Egyptian myth 174, 261
Ehcunat 232, 271
Eight Immortals 45, 175
Eightfold Path
  Right Action 109, 134
  Right Concentration 109, 204
  Right Effort 109, 194
  Right Intention 104, 109
  Right Livelihood 109, 233
  Right Mindfulness 109, 182
  Right Speech 109, 239
  Right View 88, 109
Elaine 208
Elen 248
Eleusinian Mysteries 279–282, 285
Eliot, T.S. 17, 31, 120, 168
Elizabeth II, Queen 64
Elucidation 33, 85
Empire Strikes Back 23
Empress of Constantinople 60
Empress of the Chessboard Castle 248
End (Doors) 31
Episode 1, The Phantom Menace 23
Epona 234
Escavalon 243
Ethnise 255
Eucharist 59, 63
European myth 261
Eustache II, Count 330
Eve 32, 99, 197, 282, 314
Evelake, King 243
Everest, Mount 175
Excaliber 62, 86, 91, 189, 243
Eye. *See* All-Seeing Eye

F

Fabry, Émile 227
Family of Saltimbanques (Picasso) 45–46
Famorgan 243
Fan Niu 49
Far Field (Roethke) 283
Farid ud-Din Attar 77
Father 60, 332
Feirefiz
  Gahmuret 307
  Grail Procession 324, 326
  Healing 313
  Oebalides 330
  Parzival 219, 222, 302–305, 308
  Prester John 331
  quotes 304, 307
  Repanse de Schoye 325, 327–328, 332
  Secundille 277, 306–307, 332
Feng Shui 210, 287
Feng-Huang 261
Ferrer, Jose 18
Ferryman 55, 272–273, 278–281, 289
Fifth Elegy (Rilke) 46
Finding of Moses (Alma-Tadema) 29
Finn the Seer 38
Fire 304–305
First Knight 84
Fish 37–39, 244, 281
Fisher King
  Anfortas 21, 39, 169
  Bron 37, 177
  character 19, 26, 30
  Continuations 211
  Dan, Lt. 22
  Darth Vader 23
  fertility 174
  fishing 37–39, 85
  Gotama 25
  Grail King 34
  Greedy Fisherman 112
Fisher King *(cont.)*
  hat 174
  Healing 39–40, 190, 219, 304–305
  Kurtz 24
  Maguire, Sean 23
  Parry 22
  Parzival 31, 170
  Pelles 330
  Peredur 189, 211
  Question 36, 64, 182, 185, 316
  Rich 37
  Spear 62
  story 179
  Wasteland 17
  Wounded King 33, 35, 37, 246, 320
Fisher King (film)
  film 17
  Fisher King 37
  story 22
  Wasteland 31, 73, 87
  See also Cabaret Singer; Carmichael, Lanny; Custodian; Lucas, Jack; Napolitano, Anne; Parry; Red Knight (*Fisher King*); Sinclair, Lydia
Fisher, Carrie 52, 84
  See also Leia, Princess (Organa)
Fisher, Pop
  Dolorous Blow 33
  Fisher King 24, 30
  Healing 326
  Hobbs, Roy 275
  Judge 223
  Paris, Memo 275
  quotes 31, 275
  Wasteland 31
  water 85
  See also Brimley, Wilford
Fisherman (Greedy). *See* Greedy Fisherman
Fisherman (*Shield of Herakles*) 281
Flegetanis 254
Florant of Itolac 219, 273, 293–294, 303
Flower Bride 24, 99, 113, 275
Flower Maiden 54

Flowers
- lotus 99–100
- OtherWorld 98
- Parzival 97
- Red Knight 129, 131
- rose 44–45, 99, 138
- White 100

Following the Example of the Gods (Siemiradzki) 306
Fontane la Salvatsche 254
Fool
- clothes 180
- Great 18–19, 26, 42–43, 45–46
- Gump, Forrest 83
- Oriental 45
- Parzival 81, 89, 103, 137, 194, 204
- Prince of 314
- Tarot 44, 48, 99
- Trickster 123

Force 173
Forcing the Buffalo (Fan Niu) 49
Ford, Gerald 33
Ford, Harrison 230
- *See also* Solo, Han

Forrest Gump (film) 17–18, 73
- *See also* Blue, Benjamin "Bubba" Bufford; Curran, Jenny; Forrest, General Nathan Bedford; Gump, Forrest; Mrs. Gump; Prostitutes; Taylor, Lt. Daniel

Forrest Gump (Groom) 42
Forrest, General Nathan Bedford 73
Fortuna 78
Fountain 33, 85–87, 98
Four Hallows 57, 64, 91, 176
Four Noble Truths 31, 109, 135
Fowler, Al 78
Frazier, James 321
Freelance Photographer 50, 179, 278
- *See also* Hopper, Dennis

Freemason 287
Fresleven 177
Freya 277, 319
Freyr 209, 319
Friedman, Milton 154
Friedrich, Caspar David 166
Frimutel 254–255
From Ritual to Romance (Weston) 321
Fromentin, Eugène 245
Fuji, Mount 175

G

Gahmuret
- Belacane 72
- casket 254
- death 186, 307
- family 69
- Feirefiz 219
- knight 75
- marriage 70–71, 163
- Parzival 255, 303
- Templars 73
- Triplicate Goddess 208

Gaia 100
Gaines/Lemon, Iris
- family 319
- flowers 100
- Goddess of Sovereignty 52, 54
- Hobbs, Roy 75, 154, 165
- love 24
- trance 204
- Triplicate Goddess 243
- water 91
- *See also* Close, Glenn

Galahad
- Christ 314
- Dindrane 320
- Evelake 243
- Grail Quest 243
- King Solomon 282
- ship 282, 298
- Spear 62
- sword 282
- virgin 246

Galahad and the Dying Amfortas (Abbey) 312
Gambenis, Prince 254, 258, 322
Ganesha 220–221
Ganieda 195, 240, 286, 326
Gasozein 139
Gatekeeper 185, 187, 279
Gaudi, Antonio 288
Gauguin, Paul 334
Gawain 237–238, 284, 317
Gawan
- Antikonie 232, 240, 245–247
- Arthur 273, 290, 293
- Arthur's court 119
- Ascalun 243–244
- Beaucurs 219
- birds 245
- boar 277
- Castle of Wonders 279–281, 285
- character 123
- chess 248
- Chuckie 230
- Clamide 157
- Courage 236
- Crone 275–276
- Cundrie (sister) 159
- Cundrie the Sorceress 285
- Duty 233, 239
- family 226, 273, 286
- Feirefiz 305
- final battle 308
- Florant 273
- Ginover 293
- God 224
- Goddess of Sovreignty 275
- goose 209, 275
- Govinda 25
- Grail Quest 62, 232, 271, 285
- Gramoflanz 273, 290, 293–295, 297, 300
- honor 249
- horse 49
- Kingrimursel 219
- Kingrisin 249
- lion 272, 282
- Mother 246–247
- Obilot 231–232, 242, 247
- Orgeluse 209, 270–273, 275–276, 286, 288, 295
- Parzival 21, 212–213, 217, 222, 230–231, 240–241, 293–294
- pillar 287, 307
- Plippalinot 272
- Quest 228
- quotes 236, 240
- reconciliation 293–294, 296
- Secundille 308
- Solo, Han 23
- Surrendering 298
- Sword 62, 274

Gawan *(cont.)*
- Trader 272
- trance 202
- Tree of Life 289, 297
- Triplicate Goddess 208
- Urians 271, 277–278
- Vergulaht 232, 271
- Virgin 242
- water 86
- Wonder Bed 272, 282

Gemini 319, 329
Geoffrey of Monmouth
- *Vita Merlini* 195, 243

George, Saint 210
Géricault, Théodore 94
Germanic myth 174, 188, 329
Ghenghis Khan 331
Gimbel, Norman 53
Ginover, Queen
- Arthur 209
- challenge 117, 125
- Cup 60, 107, 113, 129
- Goddess of Sovreignty 296
- Iwanet 129
- kiss 202, 214
- Parzival 201–203
- reconciliation 293–294
- Red Knight (Ither) 129, 139

Giotto di Bondono 125
Girdle 214
Girl from Ipanema (Gimbel) 53
Girl I Left Behind Me (Johnson) 66
Giveaways 120
Glastonbury 60, 243
Gnostic story 60, 314
God
- angels 262, 315
- David 132
- dualism 48
- Father 209
- Holy Ghost 209
- Moses 175
- Parzival 69, 81, 97, 224–225, 231, 242, 254, 258
- Son 209

God Speed (Leighton, E. B.) 336
Goddess Durgā Fights Buffalo Demon (Bikaner School) 247
Goddess of Love 159
Goddess of Sovereignty
- abduction 84, 86
- Arthur's court 226
- challenge 114
- character 19, 26, 53–54
- Condwiramors 326
- Cup 60, 113
- film characters 52
- Flower Bride 24, 99
- gifts 56, 91
- Ginover 296
- Jeschute 101
- Liaze 151
- OtherWorld 55
- Parzival 53, 275
- Sacred Marriage 60
- Skywalker, Anakin 23

Godfrey of Bouillon 330
Goethe, Johann Wolfgang von 302
Golden Bough (Frazier) 320
Goliath 132
Good Knight 17, 33
Good Will Hunting
- film 17
- story 23
- Wasteland 73
- *See also* Chuckie; Hunting, Will; Lambeau, Gerald; Maguire, Sean; Skylar

Gorre 284
Gospel of Sri Ramakrishna (Nikhilananda) 324
Gotama Buddha 25, 170, 257
- quotes 257

Gourd 45
Govinda 25, 145
Graham, Bill 207
Graham, Katherine 184
Grail
- Alchemy 260–261
- Anfortas 313
- Christ 330
- Christ's blood 244
- Compassion 179
- court 314
- Feirefiz 327–328
- food source 37, 58, 169
- gift 56
- Hallows 57, 62
- head 211

Grail *(cont.)*
- Heart's Desire 34–35, 56, 288
- Holy 63
- Parzival 240
- platter 61
- Procession 56, 178, 319, 321, 325–326
- protector 260
- Quest 170, 178, 227
- Second Chance 314–315
- service 316–318
- ship 298
- Siege Perilous 64
- source 56
- Spear 265
- Stone 61
- story 254
- Table 60
- Templars 328
- trance 204
- writings 255, 328–329

Grail Castle
- Anfortas 32, 39
- *Axis Mundi* 174
- Balin 176
- court 267, 280
- Herzeloyde 78
- horse 231, 254–255, 259
- Parzival 169

Grail King
- Anfortas 21
- Dolorous Blow 33
- gifts 281
- Healing 262
- marriage 264
- Parzival 180
- Pellam 176

Grail Knights 203, 254, 259, 264, 328
Grail Maiden 19, 56, 78, 180, 280
Grail Quest
- Dindrane 320
- Galahad 243
- Gawan 62, 232, 240, 271, 285
- Secundille 308
- Vergulaht 232, 240, 271

Grail Table 169
Gramoflanz, King
- Castle of Wonders 295
- Cidegast 290

Gramoflanz, King *(cont.)*
- Gawan 273, 290, 293–294, 300
- Itonje 273
- Orgeluse 290, 295
- Parzival 294, 300
- reconciliation 297
- Round Table 303
- Surrendering 298

Graves, Robert 53, 55, 188
Great Goddess 225
Great Tower 174–175, 273, 287
Greedy Fisherman 107, 112, 179
Greek myth
- Adonis 277
- Ares 277
- Argus 174
- Atalante 277
- Daedalus & Icarus 264
- Demeter 240, 277, 279–281
- Gaia 100
- Gorgons 208
- Hades 240, 279–281
- Hebe 208
- Hecate 208
- Hera 208
- Hercules 281
- Nine Graces 243
- Persephone 240, 279–281
- Rhea 280
- Zeus 279–280

Gringuljete 231, 234, 271–273, 277, 289
Groom, Winston 42
Guenevere. *See* Gwenevere, Queen
Guinness, Alec 145
- *See also* Kenobi, Obi-Wan "Ben"

Gump, Forrest
- birds 78
- challenge 114
- clothes 118
- Curran, Jenny 54, 158, 162, 165, 275, 282, 321
- Direct Experience 256
- Dolorous Blow 33
- family 22, 68, 73, 319
- Fool 42
- foreshadowing 160
- generosity 120
- gifts 112

Gump, Forrest *(cont.)*
- God 224
- Healing 317
- Karma 103
- marriage 100, 163, 292
- mother 215
- name 108
- natural abilities 74–75, 130
- number nine 243
- Parzival 19, 22
- prostitutes 152, 220
- Quest 228
- quotes 42
- red 138
- rules 90, 146
- Sacred Landscapes 322
- ship 298
- synchronicity 83
- Taoism 48
- teacher 144–145, 150
- trance 204
- tree 188
- twins 302
- Wasteland 31
- water 39, 85
- *See also* Hanks, Tom

Gungans 114, 221
Gunslinger: The Dark Tower I (King) 70
Gurnemanz
- family 143, 151, 157
- Liaze 151
- Parzival 151, 153
- quotes 144
- rules 145–149, 160, 180, 219
- teacher 143, 145

Gwalchmai 212
Gwelljus, Lischois 271–273, 293–294, 303
Gwenevere, Queen
- abduction 84
- Arthur 139
- *Camelot* (film) 206
- Flower Bride 99–100, 113
- Ginover 107
- Goddess of Sovereignty 54
- Lancelot 19, 139, 328
- Meleagant 284
- Redgrave, Vanessa 18
- Round Table 60
- water 91

Gwion 58
Gwyddbwyll 248

H

Hades 240, 279–281
Hallow. *See* Four Hallows
Hamill, Mark 23, 145, 252
- *See also* Skywalker, Luke

Hampton Court 106
Hanks, Tom 19, 22, 302
- *See also* Gump, Forrest

Hathor 174
Head, Cult of the 59, 62, 177, 317
Heart of Darkness 170
Heart of Darkness (Conrad)
- novel 17
- quotes 90, 217, 260, 335
- story 24
- Wasteland 33, 73
- *See also* Accountant; Company Doctor; Kurtz; Man at Central Station; Marlow, Charlie

Heart of Darkness (film)
- courage 236
- Direct Experience 256
- Fool 42
- ford 91
- Grail 34
- head 211, 256
- painting 276

Hebe 208
Hecate 208
Heinlein, Robert 154
Helen of Troy 99, 330
Henry VIII, King 106
Henwen 277
Hephaestus 126
Hera 99, 174, 197, 208, 286
Herbert, Frank 85, 179, 212
Hercules 188, 281, 287
Hero with a Thousand Faces (Campbell) 18
Heron Hunt (Fromentin) 245
Herzeloyde, Queen
- birds 77–78
- clothes 129, 137
- death 81, 93, 103, 204, 255
- family 69, 117, 254, 267
- Gahmuret 186

Herzeloyde, Queen *(cont.)*
- God 224
- marriage 70, 163
- name 109
- Parzival 23, 75, 92, 151, 157, 164
- rules 75, 81, 90–91, 98, 101, 124, 143, 145
- sabotage 89
- Triplicate Goddess 208

Hesiod 281
Hesperides 99
Hesse, Hermann 17, 151, 252, 257, 278
Hexagram
- 1: Creative Power 340
- 2: The Passive 245
- 3: Difficult Beginnings 179
- 4: Immaturity 96
- 5: Waiting 162
- 6: Conflict 270
- 7: Multitude 260
- 8: Unity 292
- 9: Small Tamed 184
- 10: Treading 133
- 11: Peace 296
- 12: Stagnation 113
- 13: Fellowship 226
- 14: Great Harvest 326
- 15: Modesty 263
- 16: Contentment 338
- 17: Following 298
- 18: Healing Decay 311
- 19: Approaching 116
- 20: Contemplation 200
- 21: Punishment 211
- 22: Adorning 214
- 23: Destruction 128
- 24: Return 259
- 25: Innocence 67
- 26: Taming Power of the Great 205
- 27: Nourishing 327
- 28: Excess 106
- 29: The Abyss 283
- 30: Flaming Brightness 80
- 31: Attraction 156
- 32: Perseverance 253
- 33: Retreat 68
- 34: Great Power 334
- 35: Advancing Forward 230

Hexagram *(cont.)*
- 36: Darkening of the Light 197
- 37: The Family 319
- 38: Diversity 302
- 39: Stumbling 258
- 40: Deliverance 312
- 41: Decreasing 265
- 42: Increasing 314
- 43: Resolution 223
- 44: Temptation 246
- 45: Assembling 290
- 46: Growing Upward 274
- 47: Exhausting 217
- 48: The Well 85
- 49: Changing 192
- 50: Cauldron 168
- 51: Thunderbolts 218
- 52: Still As A Mountain 206
- 53: Developing 142
- 54: Marriageable Maiden 151
- 55: Abundance 120
- 56: Wanderer 167
- 57: Willing Submission 233
- 58: Joy 324
- 59: Dispersing 308
- 60: Restraining 75
- 61: Inner Truth 321
- 62: Small Gets By 130
- 63: Ferrying Complete 279
- 64: Not Yet Across 289

Hicks, "Chef" Jay 59, 211
Hicks, Edward 292
Hildegard of Bingen 188
Hinduism 159, 209, 221
History of the Holy Grail. *See* Vulgate Cycle
Hobbs, Roy
- bat, Wonderboy 188, 304
- Bird, Harriet 54
- birds 78
- challenge 205
- clothes 118
- Court of Joy 326
- destiny 50
- determination 223
- family 24, 68, 319
- father 131
- Fisher, Pop 275
- flowers 100

Hobbs, Roy *(cont.)*
- Gaines/Lemon, Iris 54, 75, 154, 165
- hubris 263
- Judge 284
- Karma 103
- name 108
- natural abilities 74–75, 130
- number nine 243
- Paris, Memo 54, 214, 246, 275, 282
- Parzival 19, 24
- quotes 74, 263
- red 138
- rules 90
- Second Chance 314
- shooting 132, 246
- synchronicity 82
- trance 204
- water 39, 85, 91
- *See also* Redford, Robert

Hockney, David 175
Hollow Men (Eliot) 120
Holofernes 59
Holy Spirit 61, 78
Homer, Winslow 168
Honey and Salt (Sandburg) 158
Hong Bao 138
Hope in the Prison of Despair (Morgan) 118
Hopper, Dennis 278
- *See also* Freelance Photographer

Horn of Plenty 58, 63
Horse
- Castle of Wonders 281
- Cult of 234
- Demeter 281
- Gawan 49
- Grail Castle 231, 254–255, 259
- Ingliart 231, 240
- Parzival 49
- red 49–50, 55, 158
- *See also* Gringuljete

Hounds of Annwvyn 234
How at the Castle of Corbin a Maiden Bare in the Sangreal and Foretold the Achievements of Galahad (Rackham) 1

Howell, Chris 133
See also Red Knight (Fisher King)
Hsieh 261
Huang Ti, Emperor 261
Huang Wei Lun 131
Hunt, William Holman 192
Hunting, Will
challenge 114, 128
Chief 102
Chuckie 230
clothes 118, 137
destiny 50
Direct Experience 256
family 68, 319
Fool 42–43
Good Knight 33
Healing 316
Lambeau, Gerald 203
Maguire, Sean 154, 156, 168, 170
marriage 163
name 108
natural abilities 74, 132, 144
Parzival 19, 23
Question 179
red 138
response 133
Skylar 54, 158–159, 161–162, 282
swans 329
Taoism 48
Wasteland 31
water 39
See also Damon, Matt

I

I Ching 27
See also Hexagram
I Have Had to Learn to Live with My Face (Wakoski) 170
I, Claudius (Graves) 188
Ibert, King 293
Iblis, Queen 293
Icarus 264
Ida (Ide D'Ardennes, Saint Ida) 330
Idunn 99
If Ever I Would Leave You (Lerner and Loewe) 18
Imane of the Beafontane 81, 84–85, 231
Indian story 208, 277
Indian tradition 110, 138
Indra 174
Infant Moses (Moreau) 340
Ingliart 231, 240
Initiator 19, 55, 159, 279–281
Inner Army 240
Inner Station 87, 170
Innocents Abroad (Twain) 67
International Arthurian Society 20
Into the World There Came a Soul Called Ida (Albright) 218
Irish myth 91, 111, 126, 150, 208
Irot, King 273, 293, 297–298
Iseult 240, 248, 298
Ishwara 209
Isis 85, 286
Islamic tradition 61, 174, 268
Isle of Glass 243
Isolation (Khnopff) 197
Ither von Gaheviez.
See Red Knight (Ither)
Itonje 219, 226, 273, 293–294, 297
Iwanet 117, 129, 140

J

Jabba the Hutt 282
Jacob's Pillar-Stone 64
Jalāl 209
Jamāl 209
Jamor 240
Janfuse 219
Jedi Knights 83, 114, 138, 145, 172
Jehovah 188
Jeschute, Duchess
Brooch 113
Goddess of Sovereignty 101
Orilus 102, 197
Parzival 97, 103
reconciliation 193–194, 254, 259
Triplicate Goddess 208
Jewish tradition 32, 59, 108, 132, 268
Jinn 172
Jinn, Qui-Gon
death 321
name 172–173
Skywalker, Luke 161
synchronicity 82
teacher 144, 253
John the Baptist 59, 62, 274
John, the Patriarch of the Indians 331
Johnson, Eastman 66
Johnson, Lance B. 179, 196
Joplin, Janis 237
Jormungand 210
Joseph D'Arimathie (Robert) 60, 63
Joseph of Arimathea 37, 60, 62, 220, 243
Judge (*Natural*) 103, 187, 223, 284
See also Prosky, Robert
Judith 59
Jung, Carl G. 39, 82, 305
Jupiter 188

K

Ka'bba 61
Kabbalah 174, 307
Kachina 123
Kali 208, 304
Kamala 25, 100, 204, 319, 321
Kandinsky, Wassily 258
Kano Sansetsu 345
Kardeiz 303, 313, 319, 340
Karidoel 201
Karma 103, 211, 277
Karnahkarnaz, Count 81
Karnant 185
Kay 123
Keats, John 53
Keie
beating 117, 126, 140, 157, 193
challenge 201–202, 211
Trickster 123
Keisai Eisen 152
Kennedy, Bobby 33
Kennedy, John 33
Kenobi, Obi-Wan "Ben"
death 321
name 63
Skywalker, Luke 298
teacher 23, 142, 145, 253

Kenobi, Obi-Wan "Ben" *(cont.)*
Vader 253
See also Guinness, Alec
Kerouac, Jack 54
Khnopff, Fernand 197
Kilgore, Lt. Col. 133, 179
King of Gors 231
King of Suffering 58
King of the Land 60
King, Stephen 70
King's Road 106
Kingdom of the Community
Arthur 40, 163, 296, 300, 305
Feirefiz 305
Gawan 296
Parzival 163
reconciliation 308
triad 295
Kingdom of the Individual
Clinschor 39
Feirefiz 305
Gawan 222, 289, 295, 297, 305
Orgeluse 289
reconciliation 308
sword 274
triad 295
Kingdom of the Spirit 39, 181, 222, 295
Kingrimursel 219, 232, 249
Kingrisin, King 243, 249, 271
Kingrun 157, 161, 193
Kirk, M. L. (Maria Louise) 63
Kiss 97, 101, 214
Klimt, Gustav 242
Knight of the Cart (Lancelot). *See Arthurian Romances*
Knight of the Swan 329
Knight with the Lion (Yvain). *See Arthurian Romances*
Knights (*Natural*) 24, 75, 205, 214
Knives 177
Koans 36
Koran 34, 103, 279
Kristofferson, Kris 237
Kun Lun Mountains 175, 261
Kunda 159
Kundalini 176, 307
Kung Fu 131, 173
Kung Fu Calligraphy (Huang) 131
Kupka, Frantisek 71
Kurtz
Courage 236
Direct Experience 256
fiancée 24, 276
Fisher King 24
head 59, 211
Heart's Desire 34
Inner Station 170
OtherWorld 55
Kurtz, Col. Walter E.
Ferryman 278
Fisher King 24, 30
flowers 100
Karma 103
OtherWorld 196
Question 179
response 133
synchronicity 82
Willard, Benjamin 170–171
See also Brando, Marlon
Kushner, Harold 277
Kwan, General 138
Kyot 254

L

La Belle Dame Sans Merci (Keats) 53
La Japonaise (Camille Monet in Japanese Costume) (Monet) 138
Lady and the Unicorn: To my one desire 96
Lady Fortuna 263, 275, 277
Lady in White 100
Lady of the Chessboard Castle 248
Lady of the Lake 62, 86, 91, 181, 243
Lailoken 126
Lakshmi 100
Lambeau, Gerald
Arthur 23
challenge 114, 128
foreshadowing 160
Healing 316
Hunting, Will 203
name 108
red 138
response 133
Lancelot
Camelot (film) 206
chess 248
Lancelot *(cont.)*
Grail 59
Gwenevere 19, 139, 328
name 108, 177
Perilous Bridge 284
ship 298
Wild Man 195
Land of Maidens 39
Land of Salvation 21, 190
Land of Wonders
Clinschor 39
Gawan 272, 289, 295
Orgeluse 264
queens 296
See also Castle of Wonders
Lao Tzu 47, 51
Lapsit Exillis 61, 255
Last Supper Table 60
Laudine 98
Le Destin (Mowbray) 208
Le Morte D'Arthur (Malory)
Evelake 243
Galahad 62, 246, 282
Gawan 212
Grail Quest 178
Lancelot 59, 328
mantle 181
Perceval 246
quotes 74, 227
ship 298
Spear 62, 176
Sword 62, 189
Wasteland 33
Leda 329–330
Leeke, Ferdinand v
Legends of the Fall 240
Lehelin 81, 107, 231, 255
Leia, Princess (Organa)
abduction 84
Goddess of Sovereignty 52, 54
Quest 228
Skywalker, Luke 23, 161, 286
Solo, Han 270
trance 204
See also Fisher, Carrie
Leighton, Edmund Blair 241, 336
Leighton, Frederic 280
Lennon, John 33
Leopold, King 55, 87
Lerner and Loewe 18
Li Tieh-kuai 45

Liaze
- Goddess of Sovereignty 151, 159
- Parzival 143, 153, 157, 158
- Triplicate Goddess 208

Liddamus 232
Lindholm Høje 298
Lion 235, 272, 282
Lippaut, Prince 231–232
Lleu (Skilful Hand) 108, 319
Lloyd, Jake 92
- *See also* Skywalker, Anakin

Loathly Lady
- character 26
- Cundrie the Sorceress 226, 308
- Goddess of Sovereignty 54
- Initiator 124, 217
- Orgeluse 275
- Truth 220

Logres 275
Logrois 271, 275
Lohengrin 329
Loherangrin
- Feirefiz 325
- Grail Castle 313
- Lohengrin 329
- Parzival 303, 340
- Princess of Brabant 325
- twins 319

Loki 123, 210
Longinus 62, 176, 317
Lord's Right 214
Lost Bridge 284
Lot 286
Lot, King 273, 297
Lucas, Jack
- atonement 192, 194, 266
- clothes 44
- Court of Joy 326
- Custodian 190
- Fisher King 179
- Fool 43
- foreshadowing 160
- girlfriend 152
- Healing 33, 316, 327
- hubris 264
- Karma 103
- marriage 163
- Napolitano, Anne 54, 153, 156, 165, 282

Lucas, Jack *(cont.)*
- Parry 100, 153, 164, 171, 306
- Parzival 22
- pig 277
- rebuke 218
- Red Knight 130
- scream 64
- Wasteland 87
- water 39
- *See also* Bridges, Jeff

Lucifer 262, 315
Ludwig II 159, 329
Luned (Lunette) 91
Lybbeals 255
Lyr (Lir) 37
Lyrisches (Lyrical) (Kandinsky) 258

M

Mabinogion
- Arthur 277
- *Branwen Daughter of Llyr* 58
- Cauldron 58
- *How Culhwch Won Olwen* 123
- Owein 86
- Peredur 126, 150, 177
- *Peredur Son of Evrawg* 58, 113
- *Pwyll Lord of Dyved* 234
- Twrch Trwyth 277
- Witch of Gloucester 150

Macbeth 208
MacCumhail, Finn 38
Mackintosh, Charles Rennie 182
Mäda Primavesi (Klimt) 242
Madame X (Madame Pierre Gautreau) (Sargent) 276
MADD (Mothers Against Drunk Drivers) 267
Maeldinus 326
Magic Circle (Waterhouse) 58
Maguire, Sean
- Direct Experience 256
- Fisher King 23, 30
- fortune 144
- Healing 316
- Hunting, Will 102, 156, 168, 170
- Question 179
- red 138
- sabotage 89
- swans 329

Maguire, Sean *(cont.)*
- wife 54, 154
- *See also* Williams, Robin

Maidens (*Parzival*)
- quotes 182

Maidens of the Fountain 33
Maimed Queen 110, 320
- *See also* Sigune

Malamud, Bernard 31, 74, 187, 205, 263, 275
Malcreatiure 271, 277, 307
Malory, Sir Thomas.
- *See Le Morte D'Arthur*

Man at Central Station (*Heart of Darkness*) 90
Man Contemplating His Destiny (Fabry) 227
Manannan (Manawydan) 37
Mandeville, John 331
Mark, King 240
Marlow, Charlie
- Courage 236
- destiny 50
- Direct Experience 256
- Fool 42
- head 211
- Heart's Desire 34
- Inner Station 170
- natural abilities 74
- OtherWorld 55
- Parzival 19, 24
- quotes 260, 335
- ship 298
- synchronicity 82
- Wasteland 87
- water 39, 91

Masonic Memorial 287
MatriPadma 100
Matsya 39
Matters of Britain 18
May 201, 203, 212
Mayan myth 174
Mazda 319
Me and Bobby McGee (Kristofferson) 237
Mecca 61, 268
Medea 330
Meditation 206
Meldred, King 126
Meleagant 84, 284
Meljacanz 81, 84, 86, 231

Meljanz, King 231–232, 240–241
Mercy, Max 130, 160, 284
Merlin
  Arthur 120–121
  Balin 176
  birds 77
  Broceliande 98
  childhood 172–173
  family 68
  Ganieda 195, 286, 326
  laugh 126
  Pellam 176
  Round Table 60
  Thirteen Treasures 58
  tree 174
  Vortigern 210
  Wild Man 195, 240
Merlin (Rhead) 172
Merlin Continuation.
  See Vulgate Cycle
Meru, Mount 175
Mfumu 177, 236
Middle Way 245, 262, 264
  See also Eightfold Path
Midi-chlorian 172
Midnight Ride of Paul Revere (Wood) 142
Mies van der Rohe, Ludwig 265
Millennium Falcon 50, 78
Miller's Wife (Peredur) 60
Mimir 59
Minnesingers 159
Minos, King 264
Mists of Avalon (Bradley) 243
Mitchell, L. 123
Mitochondria 172–173
Modron 243
Monet, Claude 138
Monty Python and the Holy Grail 211, 298
Moon Is A Harsh Mistress
  (Heinlein) 154
Mordaf the Generous 120
Mordrains 243
Mordred 84, 286, 298
Moreau, Gustave 340
Morfrans 58
Morfudd 90
Morgan, Evelyn de 118
Morgan, Morgaine Le Fay
  Accolon 189
  Arthur 90, 189
  children 90
  mantle 181
  name 243
  Triplicate Goddess 208, 243
  Uriens 90
Morgause 208, 286
Morrighan 91
Morris, William 316
Moses 68, 85, 175, 286, 307
Mother
  Antikonie 246–247
  colors 138
  Dark 304
  Earth 53, 100, 240, 321
  Gawan 246–247
  Great 53, 224
  Lotus 100
  Trinity 60
  Triplicate Goddess 208,
   246–247, 332
Mountain of Salvation.
  See Munsalvaesche
Mounted Officer of the Carabineers (Géricault) 94
Mouse, Mickey and Minnie 159
Mowbray, H. Siddons 208
Mrs. Gump 68, 75, 163, 215
Mt. Fuji and Flowers
 (Hockney) 175
Much Ado About Nothing
  (Shakespeare) 331
Mule 220, 254, 256
Mummers 45
Munch, Edvard 216
Munsalvaesche
  Anfortas 39, 201
  Axis Mundi 174
  court 255
  Gawan 285
  Healing 311, 313
  Parzival 176, 303, 305, 312,
   322, 325
  Sigune 185
  Sword 189
  Templars 254
  Terre de Salvaesche 190
  See also Grail Castle
My life closed twice before its close (Dickenson) 284
Mystical Knight (Redon) 59

N

Naberrie, Padmé.
  See Amidala, Queen
Naboo 114, 130
Name 108
Nantes 107, 113, 117
Napolitano, Anne
  atonement 194
  Goddess of Sovereignty 52, 54
  Karma 103
  love 22
  Lucas, Jack 154, 156, 165, 282
  red 138
  See also Ruehl, Mercedes
Nascien 189
National Center for Missing and Exploited Children 267
Native American
  fool 45
  Medicine Wheel 27, 138
  myth 123
  stone 61
  tradition 120
Natural (film) 17, 207
Natural (Malamud)
  birds 78
  Karma 103
  quotes 31, 74, 187, 205,
   263, 275
  story 24
  Wasteland 73, 87
  See also Bailey, Bump; Bird, Harriet; Blow, Red; Fisher, Pop; Fowler, Al; Gaines/ Lemon, Iris; Hobbs, Roy; Judge; Knights (*Natural*); Mercy, Max; Paris, Memo; Sands, Gus; Simpson, Sam; Tower Maternity ; Whammer
Navaho Prayer 345
Nemesis 330
Neuschwanstein 159, 270, 329
Ni Tuan 38
Nikhilananda, Swami 324
Nimue 196

Nine Graces (Muses) 243
Nine Witches of Gloucester. *See* Witches of Gloucester
Ninefold Goddess 243
Nirvana 109
Nirvana, the Death of the Buddha 104
Noah 39
Norgals 313
Norns 59, 208
Norse myth
- dwarfs 126
- Frey 209
- Freya 277
- Idunn 99
- Jormungand 210
- Loki 123, 210
- Mimir 59
- Norns 208
- Odin 177, 209
- Tyr 209
- Yggdrasil 59, 174

Notre Dame (Our Lady) 225
Nuada, King 111
Nudd the Generous 120

O

Obie 231–232, 237, 240–241
- quotes 237

Obilot 231–232, 239, 241–242, 247
- quotes 239

Odin 177, 209, 260
Odysseus 100
Oebalides 330
Oedipus 68
Old Man 332
Old Man Seated in an Armchair (Rembrandt) 91
Old Plum (Kano Sansetsu) 345
Olimpia, Queen 303
Olwen 123
Olympus, Mount 175
On the Road (Kerouac) 54
Once and Future King 261
Once and Future King (White) 18, 77
One-Eyed Herdsman 44, 279
Orb 57, 64, 91
Order of the Dragon 210
Order of the Poor Knights of Christ and the Temple of Solomon. *See* Templars
Orgeluse, Queen
- Anfortas 32, 264, 271, 273, 275
- Cidegast 273
- Crone 275–276
- Gawan 209, 270–273, 286, 288, 293–294
- Gramoflanz 273, 290, 295, 297
- Malcreatiure 271
- Parzival 273
- quotes 275
- reconciliation 296
- Surrendering 298
- Tree of Life 289
- Urians 278

Orilus, Duke
- Cunneware 198
- dragon 210
- horse 231
- Jeschute 97, 102, 197
- reconciliation 193–194, 254, 259
- Schianatulander 107, 111

Ormond, Julia 240
Osiris 85, 174, 286
OtherWorld
- Avalon 243
- bridge 284
- Broceliande 98
- challenge 131
- Ferryman 279
- flowers 24
- Fool 44
- Ginover 139
- Goddess of Sovereignty 55
- Grail Castle 78, 170
- Henry VIII 106
- horse 49
- magic 69
- name 329
- portal 44, 62
- Red Knight (Ither) 139
- time 150
- women 91, 163

Ouroborus 210
Outer Army 240
Owain 90
- *See also* Owein

Owein 86, 91, 235, 248
Ox 49

P

P'ang Te-kung 38
Palpatine, Senator 87
Paris 99
Paris, Memo
- Fisher, Pop 275
- Goddess of Sovereignty 54
- Hobbs, Roy 214, 246, 275, 282, 284
- Triplicate Goddess 243

Parry
- atonement 192, 194
- Blancheflor 306
- challenge 114
- Court of Joy 326
- Custodian 190
- Dolorous Blow 33
- dwarfs 126
- family 68
- Fisher King 22, 179
- flowers 100
- Healing 33
- Lucas, Jack 164, 171
- marriage 163
- Red Knight 130, 133
- scream 64
- Sinclair, Lydia 54, 75, 153–154, 156, 158, 218
- trance 204
- wife 316
- *See also* Williams, Robin

Parsifal 133, 159
Parsifal (Delville) 16
Parsifal healing King Amfortas (Stassen) 318
Parsifal in Quest of the Holy Grail (Leeke) v
Parsifal in Quest of the Holy Grail (Stassen) ii
Partinial 211
Parvati 208
Parzival
- Adam 314
- Anfortas 170–171

Parzival *(cont.)*
- angels 82
- Arthur 122, 203, 213
- Arthur's court 117, 163
- as Red Knight 138, 143, 157, 201, 214, 293
- atonement 198, 266
- Avalon 243
- birds 77
- challenge 205
- childhood 167
- Chosen One 119
- Christ 314
- Cloak 181
- clothes 118, 129, 137, 143, 180
- Compassion 239
- Condwiramors 100, 156–159, 161, 164–165, 209, 240, 246, 273, 294, 306
- Cunneware 140, 213–214
- Cup 60, 140
- determination 223
- Direct Experience 256–257
- dragon 210
- Duty 233
- family 21, 70–72, 89, 97, 110, 222, 306, 319, 340
- Feirefiz 302–305, 307
- final battle 308
- Fisher King 31, 37, 39, 168
- Fool 18, 26, 43, 116
- foreshadowing 160
- Gawan 212, 217, 222, 230–231, 240–241, 293–294
- gifts 112
- God 224–225, 254, 258
- Goddess of Sovreignty 275
- goose 187, 209, 275
- Grail Castle 169, 176, 178, 182, 217
- Grail King 324, 336, 338
- Grail Knight 259
- Grail Procession 325–326
- Grail Quest 248
- Gramoflanz 294, 297, 300
- Gump, Forrest 22
- Gurnemanz 143, 145–146, 153
- Healing 313–315
- Herzeloyde 23, 92–93, 164
- horse 49
- Jeschute 97, 101, 193–194

Parzival *(cont.)*
- Karma 103
- Keie 126
- kiss 202, 214
- knights 81–82, 84, 231
- Liaze 151, 153, 157–159
- Lucas, Jack 22
- Marlow 24
- marriage 163
- Munsalvaesche 312
- name 48, 69, 107, 109
- natural abilities 74–75
- Oebalides 330
- Orgeluse 273
- Orilus 111, 193
- pilgrims 254, 258
- Plippalinot 272
- Question 36, 180, 262, 329
- quotes 144, 223, 240
- rebuke 185, 190, 219, 221, 226, 274
- Red Horse 143
- Red Knight (Ither) 62, 107, 113, 125, 129–130, 132, 177
- response 133–135, 148
- rules 90–91, 98
- Sacred Landscapes 321–322
- Secundille 308
- Siddhartha 25
- Sigune 107, 187, 254, 321
- Spear 62, 177, 195–196
- story 19, 21
- suffering 186
- Sword 62, 180–181, 185, 189, 304
- synchronicity 82, 84
- Taoism 50
- teacher 144, 253
- trance 200–202, 204
- Tree of Life 297
- Trevrizent 177, 253–255, 259, 261, 268
- Triplicate Goddess 208
- vengeance 211
- Vergulaht 232
- Wasteland 87, 99
- water 86
- Wild Man 214
- youth 69

Parzival (Wolfram)
- courtly love 224
- Goddess of Sovereignty 53
- Grail 58
- name 108
- poem 19
- quotes 31, 47, 56, 110, 139, 144, 153, 182, 197, 223, 236–237, 239–240, 253, 256, 260, 263, 274–275, 304, 307, 326, 338
- racism 72
- Stone 61
- story 17–18, 21–24, 26, 38
- Taoism 47–49
- times 48
- Wagner, Richard 159
- Wounded King 39

Passover 138

Paul 314

Peaceable Kingdom (Hicks) 292

Peaches of Immortality 174

Pelias, King 330

Pellam, King 176

Pelles, King 189, 330

Pelrapeire 157, 202, 303

Pendragon, Uther, King 60, 68–69, 107, 210

Pentecost 201

Perceval
- birds 91
- chess 248
- Dindrane 282, 320
- Escavalon 243
- Gawain 212
- *Good Will Hunting* 160
- Grail Quest 223
- head 211
- lion 235
- Loathly Lady 220
- mother 93
- Pryderi 234
- ship 298
- Siege Perilous 64
- story 18
- tent 101
- virgin 246
- Wild Man 195

Peredur
- challenge 113
- chess 248

Peredur *(cont.)*
  Cup 60
  dwarfs 126
  gifts 91
  head 59, 211, 317
  King of Suffering 58
  name 177
  Spear 177
  story 19
  Sword 62, 189, 304
  teacher 150
  tent 101
  trance 207
  Witch of Gloucester 321
Peredur Son of Evrawg.
  See Mabinogion
Perilous Bridge 284
Perilous Ford 91
Perlesvaus
  Arthur 139
  Gawan 62, 212, 274
  mule 220
  quotes 335
  Spear 317
  story 19
Persephone 240, 279–281
Persida 293
Peter 37
Phillips, Chief 177
Philosopher's Stone 61
Picasso, Pablo 45–46
Pilate 60
Pilgrims. *See* Gambenis, Prince
Pillar of Marvels 273, 287, 307–308
Pisces 244
Pitt, Brad 240
Plate 57
Plath, Sylvia 93
Plato 36
Plimizoel 193, 313, 321
Plippalinot 272–273, 281
Plummer, Amanda 52, 194
  See also Sinclair, Lydia
Pollux. *See* Polydeuces (Pollux)
Polo, Marco 331
Polydeuces (Pollux) 319, 329–330
Portman, Natalie 100, 207
  See also Amidala, Queen
Potter, Harry 61, 181, 248
Presley, Elvis 103
Prester John 325, 331
Primordial Man 314
Prince of Light & Prince of Darkness 48
Princess of Brabant 325
Principle of Life (Kupka) 71
Progress of the Soul (Traquair) 26–28
Prophetic Laugh 126, 140
Prosky, Robert 284
  See also Judge (*Natural*)
Prostitutes (*Forrest Gump*) 220, 314
Prowse, David 30
  See also Vader, Darth
Ptolemy 286
Punturtois 254
Pushing Hands 148, 338
Pwyll Lord of Dyved.
  See Mabinogion
Pyle, Howard 295
Pyramids 175

Q

Queen's Ford 91
Quest 228, 330
Question
  Gawain 317
  Grail 316–317
  Healing 36, 180, 255, 262
  knowledge 342
  Parzival 62, 186, 329
  Sigune 185
  Sword 181
  West 147

R

R2-D2 31, 83, 142, 204
Rackham, Arthur i, 250
Ragnall, Dame 237–238
Ranson, Paul 339
Rash Boon 122–123
Reagan, Ronald 33
Red Horse 143–144
Red Knight (*Fisher King*) 130, 133, 316
  See also Howell, Chris
Red Knight (Ither)
  armor 117, 135, 180
  challenge 107, 113–114, 117, 140
  Clamide 157
  death 62, 129, 202, 211, 214, 266
  OtherWorld 139
  Parzival 107, 124, 130, 132–134, 177, 255
  red 138
Red Knight (Parzival).
  See Parzival: as Red Knight
Redford, Robert 19, 24, 130
  See also Hobbs, Roy
Redgrave, Vanessa 18
Redon, Odilon 59
Reilly, Ignatius 50
Rembrandt Harmenszoon van Rijn 91
Remus 319
Renier, Duke 330
Repanse de Schoye
  cloak 180–181
  family 267
  Feirefiz 325, 332
  Grail Maiden 169, 255
Return of Persephone (Leighton, F.) 280
Return of the Jedi 23
Rhea 280
Rhead, Louis 62, 172, 228
Rhiannon 234
Rich Fisherman 37
Ride of the Valkyries (Wagner) 133
Riders of the Sidhe (Duncan) 57
Rider-Waite 44
Rilke, Rainer Maria 46
Ring
  Fisherman's 37
  gifts 56, 81, 91
  Jeschute 97, 101
  Liaze 151
  Perceval 101
  Peredur 101
  Pope's 37
Ring des Nibelungen (Wagner) 133
Robert de Boron 60, 63
Roethke, Theodore 283
Roman Church 48
Romulus 319

Rosicrucians 99
Rossetti, Dante Gabriel 324
Rostand, Edmond 18
Round Table 60, 64, 97, 201, 303
Rousseau, Henri 188
Ruehl, Mercedes 52, 194
  See also Napolitano, Anne
Rydderch the Generous 120

S

Sabins 273, 293
Sacred Central Mountain 174–175, 261
Sacred Geometry 287
Sacred Marriage 60, 280, 282, 319
Sacrificial King 321
Sagrada Familia Church 288
Sagremors 201, 211
Salmon of Wisdom 38
Salome 59
Samanas 82–83, 145
Samson 287
Sandburg, Carl 42, 158
Sands, Gus 284
Sangive, Queen 219, 226, 273, 294
Saracen Reclining on a Divan (Benjamin-Constant) 222
Sarasvati 174
Sargent, John Singer 276
Sarmatians 210
Sarras 320
Satan 48, 82
Satyavrata 39
Saul 132
Scandinavian myth 329
Scathach 150
Schanpfanzun 219, 232
Scherules 231
Schianatulander 107, 110, 254, 313, 320
Schoysiane 255
Scream (Munch) 216
Scythian myth 188, 210
Second Coming 314
Second Hand Rose (Clarke) 137
Secret of the Golden Flower 100
Secundille, Queen
  Cundrie the Sorceress 271, 277
  death 325, 332
Secundille, Queen *(cont.)*
  Feirefiz 303
  Malcreatiure 271, 277
  Pillar 273
  Sophia 307–308
Self Portrait (Carrington) 234–235
September 11 32–33, 267
Seven Arrows (Storm) 61
Shakespeare, William 59, 331
Shakti 307, 332
Sheath 282
Sheen, Martin 24, 278
  See also Willard, Capt. Benjamin L.
Shekina 307
Shield of Herakles (Hesiod) 281
Ship 246, 282, 298
Shiva 209
Siddhartha
  Direct Experience 257
  family 25, 319
  flowers 100
  Fool 43
  Gotama 170
  Kamala 321
  name 57
  Parzival 19, 25
  quotes 257
  rules 90
  synchronicity 82–83
  teacher 145
  temptation 152
  trance 204
  Vasudeva 278
Siddhartha (Hesse)
  novel 17
  quotes 151, 252, 257, 278
  story 25
  Wasteland 73
  See also Gotama Buddha; Govinda; Kamala; Siddhartha; Vasudeva
Sidhe. See Bean Sidhe
Sidious, Darth 100, 114
Siege Perilous (Perilous Seat) 64, 234
Siemiradzki, Henryk 306
Sigune
  Cundrie the Sorceress 254
  death 313, 320–321
  Direct Experience 256
Sigune *(cont.)*
  hermitage 322
  Maimed Queen 110
  name 107, 109
  Orilus 111
  Parzival 254
  quotes 31, 110
  rebuke 185, 190
  Schianatulander 254
  Schoysiane 255
  suffering 187
  Sword 189
  teacher 124
  tree 188
Simpson, Sam 82, 90, 130
Sinai, Mount 175
Sinclair, Lydia
  atonement 194
  fear 75
  Goddess of Sovereignty 52, 54
  Karma 103
  love 22
  Parry 153–154, 156, 158, 162, 218
  trance 204
  See also Plummer, Amanda
Sinise, Gary 30, 302
  See also Taylor, Lt. Daniel
Sir Gawaine finds the beautiful Lady (Pyle) 295
Sisyphus 315
Skylar
  challenge 114
  family 68, 319
  Fool 42
  Goddess of Sovereignty 52, 54
  Hunting, Will 158–159, 161–162, 282
  love 23
  marriage 163
  See also Driver, Minnie
Skywalker, Anakin
  Amidala 54
  birth 172–173
  challenge 114
  clothes 118
  destiny 23
  Jinn, Qui-Gon 161
  mother (Shmi) 92
  natural abilities 74, 130
  synchronicity 83

Skywalker, Anakin *(cont.)*
teacher 144, 253
water 85
See also Lloyd, Jake
Skywalker, Luke
clothes 118
destiny 50
family 68
gifts 112
Healing 317
Karma 103
Kenobi 63, 253, 298
Leia 54, 84, 161, 286
name 108
natural abilities 74–75
OtherWorld 55
Parzival 19, 23
red 138
Solo, Han 230
synchronicity 82–83
Tao 142
teacher 144–145, 253
Vader, Darth 161
Yoda 111, 223, 252–253
See also Hamill, Mark
Skywalker, Shmi 92
See also August, Pernilla
Snow White 99
Solo, Han
Chewbacca 235
destiny 50
Gawan 23, 230
Leia 54, 270
Millennium Falcon 78
name 108
Quest 228
Wonder Bed 282
See also Ford, Harrison
Solomon, King 99–100, 282
Solomon's Wife 62, 282
Sophia 287, 307–308, 332
Sophocles 280, 282
Sovereignty. *See* Goddess of Sovereignty
Sow 277, 279
Spear
Bleeding 169, 177, 316–317
Dolorous Blow 33
Elizabeth II 64
Four Hallows 57, 62
Grail 265
Spear *(cont.)*
Ither 129
Longinus 62, 176, 317
medicine 63
Taurian 193, 195, 254
Wild Man 201, 205, 220
Wounds & Heals 62, 176, 255
Sphinx 59
Spoils of Annwfn 243
Staff 62, 91, 243
Stag 62
Star Wars
Court of Joy 326
film 17
story 23
Sword 62
Wasteland 73
See also Amidala, Queen; C-3PO; Carbonite Bed; Chewbacca; Coruscant; Dagobah System; Gungans; Jinn, Qui-Gon; Jabba the Hutt; Kenobi, Obi-Wan "Ben"; Leia, Princess (Organa); *Millennium Falcon;* Palpatine, Senator; R2-D2; Naboo; Skywalker, Anakin / Luke / Shmi; Solo, Han; Vader, Darth; Yoda, Jedi Master
Stassen, Franz ii, 318
Stella, Joseph 86
Sting 82
Stone
chessboard 248
Hallows 57
Jacob 64
Lia Fail 64
Native American 61
of Destiny 64
Yvain 85
Storm, Hyemeyosts 61
Story of Merlin. See Vulgate Cycle
Story of the Grail. See Arthurian Romances
Styx 279–281
Sufi 175, 209
Summer (Rousseau) 188
Summer Maid 240, 279
Sun Tzu 109
Sunlight on Mountain (Willumsen) 310
Susannah 240
Suttee 110
Swan Maidens 329
Sword
Anfortas 169, 181, 185, 189
David 282
Dolorous 33
Elizabeth II 64
Excaliber 243
Four Hallows 57, 62, 91
Galahad 282
Gawan 274
gift 56
Grail 271
in Stone 123
Ither 129
of David 62
of Kingship 123
Parzival 180, 304
Red Knight 169, 185
Solomon 189, 282
Trebuchet 185
Sword Bridge 284
Synchonicity I (Sting) 82
Synchronicity 82

T

Table 60
Tabronit 303
Tai Chi 67, 134, 148, 338
Taliesin 58, 277, 326
Tanakh 99
quotes 108, 287
Tandereis 246
TANSTAAFL 154
Tao Te Ching (Lao Tzu) 47, 51
Taoist
art 138
Five Elements 261
myth 261
philosophy 47–48, 67, 109, 209, 224, 240, 259
practice 134, 282
text 100, 108
Way 210
Taoist Immortal, Li Tieh-kuai (Yen Hui) 45
Tara 64

Tarjumán Al-Ashwáq (Al-'Arabi') 327
Tarot 44, 48, 99
Taurian 193, 195, 254
Taylor, Lt. Daniel
  Dolorous Blow 33
  fiancee 292
  Fisher King 22, 30
  God 224
  Healing 39, 317
  prostitutes 220
  rules 146
  twins 302
  See also Sinise, Gary
Tegau Gold Breast 181
Templars 48, 73, 254, 325, 328
  See also Grail Knights
Temple of Solomon 287
Ten Perfections
  Courage 236
  Duty 233
  Giving 161, 164
  Insight 206
  Loving Kindness 267
  Patience 134
  Renunciation 265
  Resolution 223
  Serenity 296
  Truth 220
Tennyson, Alfred Lord 98
Terre de Salvaesche 190
That Which I Should Have Done I Did Not Do (The Door) (Albright) 35
Thirteen Treasures of Britain 58, 248
Thor 188
Three Damsels of the Fountain 208
Three Fates 208
Three Gorgons 208
Three Norns. *See* Norns
Three Witches 208
Titurel 169, 254–255, 267, 325, 327
Tlaloc, Mount 175
Tomb Effigy of Elizabeth Boott Duveneck (Duveneck and Barnhorn) 320
Tonight Show with Johnny Carson 218
Toole, John Kennedy 50, 87, 179, 186, 344
Tower Maternity 284
Tower of Babel 176
Trader (Castle of Wonders) 272, 279, 281
Transylvania 200, 210
Traquair, Phoebe 26–28
Tree
  apple 99
  Bodhi 174
  Clinschor 273
  Cross 174
  erica 174
  Eve 282
  linden 185, 188, 271
  oak 174, 188
  of Knowledge of Good & Evil 99, 174, 297
  of Life 174, 177, 289, 297
  Solomon's Wife 282
  sycamore 174
  yaxché 174
  Yggdrasil 59, 174, 177, 261, 289
  Yvain 85
Trevrizent
  angels 262
  cave 193, 195, 321
  Direct Experience 256–257
  family 72, 267
  Grail 313
  hubris 264
  Parzival 254–255, 259, 261–262, 266, 268
  poverty 265
  quotes 256, 260, 263
  Second Chance 314
  teacher 177, 253
Trickster 123–124
Trinity 60
Triple Morrighan 208
Triplicate God 209, 326, 332
Triplicate Goddess
  Antikonie 246
  Castle of Wonders 296
  colors 99, 138, 207
  Gawan 246
  Mother 246
  myth 58
Triplicate Goddess *(cont.)*
  Ninefold Goddess 243
  Secundille 332
Tristan 195, 240, 248, 298
Tristan and Isolde (Leighton, E. B.) 241
Trojan War 99, 330
Twain, Mark 67
Twins 159, 319, 329
Twrch Trwyth 277
Tyndareus, King 330
Tyr 209

U

Underwater Bridge 284
UnderWorld 234, 240, 279–280
Unicorn 62
Universal Medicine 61
Upanishads 234
Uriah 132
Urians 277–278
Uriens 90
Utepandragon, Uther Pendragon.
  See Pendragon, Uther, King

V

Vader, Darth
  abduction 84, 161
  cloak 180
  Dolorous Blow 33
  Fisher King 23, 30
  Healing 317
  Kenobi 253, 321
  Skywalker, Anakin 172
  Skywalker, Luke 103, 111
  See also Prowse, David
Valkyries 329
Varaha 277
Varo, Remedios
  Creation of the Birds 78
Vasudeva 278
Venus. *See* Aphrodite
Vergulaht, King
  Antikonie 249
  birds 245
  Gawan 219, 232, 271
  Grail Quest 232, 240, 271
  Parzival 232, 243

Very Honorable Courtesan in Springtime (Keisai Eisen) 152
Virgin 138, 208, 320, 332
Virgin Mary 99, 225
Vishnu 39, 209, 277
Vita Merlini (Geoffrey) 195, 243
Viviane and Merlin (Cameron) 195
Vivienne 98, 195, 196
Vortigern, King 68, 172, 210
Vulgate Cycle
    Alan 37
    Bron 37
    Evelake 243
    History of the Holy Grail 37
    Joseph of Arimathea 37
    Lost Bridge 284
    Merlin Continuation (Post-Vulgate) 91
    Story of Merlin 120
    Table 60

W

Wagner, Richard 133, 159, 329
Wagrez, Jacques Clément 248
Wakoski, Diane 170
Waleis 313
Wallace, George 33
Walsh, John and Reve 267
Wanderer Above the Sea of Fog (Friedrich) 166
Washington D. C. 287
Washington Monument 287
Washington, George 287
Wassail (Mackintosh) 182
Waste Land (Eliot) 17, 31, 78, 168
Wasteland
    Adam 314
    Healing 40, 326
    Hidden Disease 87
    Parzival 21
    stories 31
Water 85–86, 90–91, 328
Waterhouse, John William 58, 101
Well Maidens 85
Well of Destiny 59
Welsh myth
    Blodeuwedd 99
    Cerridwen 58
    Club 62
    dragon 210
Welsh myth *(cont.)*
    Gwalchmai 212
    Gwion 58
    Morfrans 58
    Taliesin 58
    See also Peredur
Welsh Triads 58, 90, 120, 181, 277
Weston, Jessie L. 321
Whammer 108, 130, 263
Wheel of Fortune 44, 78, 263, 330
Wheel of Fortune (Burne-Jones) 264
Where Do We Come From? What Are We? Where Are We Going? (Gauguin) 334
White Cloud, Head Chief of the Iowas (Catlin) 128
White Goddess (Graves) 53, 55, 188
White Knight (Crane) 322
White, T. H. 18, 77
Wife of Bath's Tale (Chaucer) 238
Wild Man 193, 195, 214, 220, 240
Willard, Capt. Benjamin L.
    bridge 284
    destiny 50
    Ferryman 278
    flowers 100
    Fool 43
    Freelance Photographer 179
    head 59, 211
    Kurtz 170–171
    OtherWorld 55
    Parzival 19, 24
    Question 179
    response 133
    ship 298
    synchronicity 82
    Wasteland 31
    water 39
    Wild Man 196
    See also Sheen, Martin
Williams, Robin 30, 194, 329
    See also Maguire, Sean *and* Parry
Williamson, Mykelti 302
    See also Blue, Benjamin "Bubba" Bufford
Willumsen, Jens Ferdinand 310
Winter King 240
Witch 220
Witches of Gloucester 150, 211, 321
Wolfram von Eschenbach 73, 325
Wolsey, Cardinal 106
Woman of the Mound 91
Womb 38
Wonder Bed 270, 272, 282, 293
Wood, Grant 142
Wounded Cavalier (Burton) 106
Wright, Robin 52
    See also Curran, Jenny
Wu Chi 67
Wyeth, N. C. 15, 300

X

Xi Wang-Mu 175

Y

Yellow Emperor 261
Yen Hui 45
Yggdrasil. *See* Tree
Yin/Yang
    balance 286
    duality 47, 125
    Grail 62
    medicine 177
    Parzival 69
    twins 319
Ynys Witrin 243
Yoda, Jedi Master 23, 111, 223, 252–253, 330
Yvain 98
    See also Owein

Z

Zazamanc 70, 72
Zen 49
Zeus
    Amalthea 58
    Argus 174
    Demeter 279–280
    Hades 279–280
    Hera 174, 197, 286
    Leda 330
    oak 188
    Persephone 279–280
Ziggurats 175
Zipporah 85

List of Meditations - Journal Reflections

Grail and the Dolorous Blow 36
Kingdoms of Your Life 41
Playing the Fool 47
Riding That Red Horse 51
Gifts of Your Life 56
Standing on the Shoulders of Your Ancestors ...70
Thinking of Destiny 72
Taking Stock of Your Natural Abilities 74
False Paradigms 76
Angels and Synchronicity 83
Looking for the Hidden Disease 88
Friends Like These ... .89
Permission to Move On 92
Preparing for the New Life 94
Missed Chances 98
Loving Our Spirit 101
Misunderstandings 102
Karma 103
Right Intention 104
The Maimed Queen 110
Preparing for Your Grail 111
The Gifts You Have 112
Laziness of the Spirit 114
Making Us Handsome 119
Hollow Words 121
The Trickster 124
Greed 125
Easy Victories 131
Proper Response 134
Unclenching the Fist 136
Getting Rid of the Old Clothes 137
Appreciation for Those Who Believe in Us 140
Opportunities Around Us 144
Gurnemanz' Code of Conduct 149
Teachers and Students 150
Wrong Face 152
Saying No 153
Worthy of Love 154
Raising Your Voice 160
Silence is Golden 161
First Perfection of Giving 161
Messages to the Outer World 164
Spear That Wounds and Heals 178
First Encounter With Your Grail 178
Gift of the Sword 181
Source of Suffering 186
Mending the Sword 189
Continuing the Wasteland 190
Righting Our Wrongs 194
Wild Man 196
Moving Into the Trance 207
Moving Out of the Trance 207
Balanced Trinity 209
Completing the Task 213
Broken Spear 214
Loathly Lady 221
Determination 223
Face of God 225
Path of the Individual 228
Right Livelihood 233
Fifth Perfection-Courage 236
Sovereignty in Marriage 238
Creating Avalon 244
Letting Go 246
Right Question 263
Less Is More 266
Spiritual Ritual 268
Picking Up the Sword 274
Ferryman 281
Being Reborn 285
Path to Peace 296
Love and Hate 297
Surrendering 299
Shadow Side 305
In the Name of Love 306
Final Tests 309
Impossible Dream 315
Whom Does the Grail Serve? 318
Sacred Landscapes 322
Court of Joy 326
Rights of Foreigners 328
Loving the Whole 332